One cannot understand Montreal and its destiny without reference to its geographic situation on the North American continent. Nor can its growth be understood without reference to its site, an island adorned with a hill and steep terraces, natural characteristics which helped determine the urban landscape. In this particular setting other forces responsible for the physical development of Montreal have intervened: techno-economic, social, and cultural forces. *Montreal in Evolution*, first published in French in 1974, relates the history of Montreal's architecture and environmental development, from the first fort of Ville-Marie to the skyscrapers of today's metropolis. It also analyses the many forces which shaped Montreal during the three centuries of its evolution.

The abundantly illustrated work is divided into four parts: Where the Old World and the New World Meet; The Frontier Town (1642–1840); Victorian Montreal (1840–1914); and Montreal in the Twentieth Century, which discusses Place Ville-Marie and other large downtown projects, the metro, and Man and His World. The epilogue, written especially for this edition, considers the projects of the 1970s and the future of the city. *Montreal in Evolution* reveals the richness and complexity of the city's development and points the way to a future that would be worthy of its remarkable past.

Jean-Claude Marsan received a B.Arch. degree from the Université de Montréal and his M.Sc. and Ph.D. in urban design and regional planning from the University of Edinburgh. Director of the School of Architecture at the Université de Montréal from 1975 to 1979, he is currently connected with the Institut québécois de recherche sur la culture and is vice-president of the Montreal Museum of Fine Arts. Through his writings and his support of citizens' groups, he actively participates in the battle that Montrealers are waging for the protection and improvement of their environment.

*Historical Analysis of the
Development of Montreal's Architecture
and Urban Environment*

Montreal

MONTREAL
IN EVOLUTION

JEAN-CLAUDE MARSAN

McGILL–QUEEN'S UNIVERSITY PRESS

© McGill–Queen's University Press 1981
ISBN 0-7735-0339-0
Legal deposit first quarter 1981
Bibliothèque Nationale du Québec

Printed and bound in Canada by
T. H. Best Printing Company Limited, Don Mills, Ontario

Design by Naoto Kondo

Originally published as *Montréal en évolution*
© Editions Fides 1974

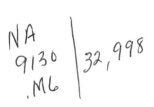

*To all Montrealers
at heart and in spirit*

CONTENTS

ILLUSTRATIONS

FIGURES

PREFACE *to the English Edition*

Montréal en Evolution was published in May 1974 by Editions Fides. A second edition, with only minor corrections and changes, was printed in April 1976. The work was well received by the critics and by the general public. Some were even kind enough to call it a classic in its field.

Two factors may explain the interest that this book created. To begin with, it is the first synthesis undertaken on the development of architecture and the Montreal environment. Addressed to the general public, it seems to have answered certain expectations of the readers. Secondly, the book was published at a time when Montrealers were showing renewed interest in their surroundings as well as concern about the unstructured development of their city during the last two decades.

We would be the last to say that the work is perfect; it contains some good points as well as certain gaps in its approach. If it has succeeded in depicting a fairly well structured and complete image of the transition of our city up to the twentieth century, it is less effective, perhaps through lack of perspective, in setting forth and interpreting the complexities of recent developments.

Another potential weakness is inherent in the continually evolving subject, the city itself. Thus, since this book was printed, various studies were started or finished, some of which have added supplemental data, different or more detailed interpretations, and even revised facts or dates. Furthermore, some buildings mentioned in the first edition have now been demolished.

Despite these qualifications, it seems proper to present an English translation based exactly on the French version. An epilogue has been added, however, in order to focus on the major projects implemented since 1974, and also to offer a new interpretation that has arisen from the recent evolution of the metropolis.

It is our profound hope and our humble belief that the reader will derive from *Montreal in Evolution* an interest and a stimulus toward the reflection necessary to a true renaissance of Montreal.

ACKNOWLEDGEMENTS

I wish to express my gratitude to the following persons who have generously contributed to the completion of this work. I am deeply indebted, for their competent and devoted services, to Marie Baboyant of the Municipal Library of Montreal, Richard Lescarbeau of the Municipal Archives of Montreal, and Edward H. Dahl of the Public Archives of Canada. The aid from Denys Marchand and Clément Demers, architects and then staff members of the City Planning Department of Montreal, was indeed very much appreciated. Many photographs and graphs which enhance this study have been courteously supplied by the City Planning Department.

At the Faculté de l'Aménagement of the Université de Montréal, the kind assistance and collaboration of my colleagues were constant. I wish to express my thanks especially to Jacqueline Pelletier, Chief Librarian, to Serge Carreau, then director of the School of Architecture, to Roger Thibault, photographer, to Laszlo Demeter and Peter Jacobs. I am deeply indebted to my friend Claude Provencher who has designed, with art and great accuracy, most of the graphs for this study. Furthermore, I must acknowledge that many ideas developed in this study took shape during conversations and exchanges with my colleagues and students at the Faculty. I wish to extend my gratitude to all of them and to apologize for not being able to list their names here.

At the University of Edinburgh where I spent marvellous years completing my postgraduate studies, my debt to Professor Percy Johnson-Marshall and Dr. F. R. Stevenson is considerable. Professor Johnson-Marshall, Head of the Department of Urban Design and Regional Planning, inspired me by his concern and love for the city and aroused this interest in me. I wish also to express my deep appreciation to Dr. Stevenson for his understanding and his concern for this project, and for his numerous constructive criticisms which are reflected in many pages of this work.

I would like to extend my gratitude to Arnaud de Varent, who translated the text from my native French into English, and to Marcelle Roberge, who with patience and application typed the whole text. I hope that this study will have justified the confidence vested in me by the Central Mortgage and Housing Corporation of Canada and by the Canada Council of Arts which financed in part the postgraduate studies that led to this book.

Finally, I wish to thank my wife Hélène for her understanding and encouragement over the many years during which the preparation of this work was carried on.

INTRODUCTION

This study deals with the development of architecture and the evolution of the urban environment in Montreal. The description of the city as a physical entity, with its structures and streets, its parks and monuments, its dwellings, its places of work and of worship, is an attempt to circumscribe its evolution as an economic, social, and cultural organism, inasmuch as this evolution manifests itself in visible and tangible ways. Our aim is to trace a broad picture of the development of Montreal, from the time of the first visits of the Sieur de Champlain at Place Royale to today's metropolis.

We do not intend to limit our study, however, to the description of the evolution of construction or to the characteristic traits of the environment and architecture of certain periods. We shall attempt to isolate and analyse the forces and influences, many and varied in significance, which generated changes in the configuration of the urban environment as well as in its architecture, although we could not identify all of them. However, for the purpose of this study, we may divide these forces and influences into two categories: those dictated by the physical environment and those emanating from the activities of men, acting individually and collectively within this environment, according to their needs, technologies, and ideologies.

Geography is the most significant among the forces and influences of the first category. Montreal and its destiny cannot be separated from its geographical situation on the North American continent, and the growth of the city is intimately linked with its location on an island crowned with a hill and steep terraces: such natural characteristics tend to mark the development of the townscape. A knowledge of the geology of the site is basic to an understanding of the total picture. Thus, before the transportation revolution of modern times, Montreal, like other cities, extracted the necessary materials for construction from the strata of its soil. But the influence of such geological characteristics extends beyond the physical field. As we shall see later, the fact that the Montreal Plain and soil lent themselves to agriculture was of great significance to the industrial development and the social composition of the city in the second half of the nineteenth century and the first half of the twentieth century. Finally, we shall consider the climate. Montrealers are very aware of their weather, whether they are enjoying periods of mildness or fighting its rigours. How climate has influenced our past and present way of life, as well as our architecture, is not very well known.

In contrast with these forces and influences, which remained fairly constant throughout the course of history, stands a second category that includes technology, economics, demography, politics, social structure, culture, and other factors which seem to be in a state of constant flux, forever changing, with frequent rapid and radical mutations. Hence the need to place all these forces in their overall context and in their chronological appearance in the development of the city. To this end, the study has been divided into four parts.

The first part deals with the location and the geography of Montreal, the characteristics of its soil, substratum, and climate. A brief account of the way in which Europeans, who came from a variety of backgrounds, reacted to the environment of New France completes the first part. We shall follow them through their early settlement of the land in and around the island of Montreal. This first establishment is of the greatest significance, for, as we shall see in the course of this study, it will indelibly mark the future structures and landscape of the city.

The remaining three parts reflect the evolution of technological and economic forces. Historical periods are easily identifiable by such landmarks as the steam engine, industrial production, electronics, and the transportation revolution, all of which will be used as background for our study. Indeed, the steam engine and electronics seem to have had a greater influence on the urban environment than did political and historical changes such as the conquest.

The second part, covering the pre-industrial period, deals with the evolution of both architecture and the urban environment of the city from its foundation as a small community until about 1840. Relevant social and cultural characteristics of successive colonies that settled on the St. Lawrence will be analysed to determine their influence on the architecture and framework of urban life. This analysis will include both French colonial architecture—what remains of it—and the architecture of the first century of British domination. The comments of contemporary observers and visitors on the qualities and deficiencies of the urban environment of a preindustrial frontier town conclude the second part.

Part III deals with the industrial revolution on the continent and its effects on economics, society, and culture, and hence on the urban environment. This was undoubtedly a crucial period in the brief history of our city because it signalled the onset of the kind of urban development which was to uproot the traditional urban landscape. Montreal's identity was deeply marked during that period, which remains one of the least known or documented segments of the city's history. Nevertheless, an attempt will be made to discover the interacting forces and their effects on the growth, structures, and shaping of the city, on public and religious architecture, on the rather remarkable commercial architecture, and on the lesser-known domestic architecture. Evaluations of our heritage from the Victorian era complete Part III of this study.

Part IV deals with twentieth-century Montreal. It depicts a growing metropolis in the process of undergoing changes as deep and drastic as those of the industrial period in the nineteenth century. On the one hand, the "telephone-and-traffic" city is spilling over its traditional boundaries and invading the rural plains; on the other hand, increasing concentration in the core drives its skyscrapers upwards. In the present active state of the city's development, it is difficult to judge Montreal as a whole. However, before concluding this account of the evolution of the city, we look at the most significant developments of our era to complete the picture. Indeed, Place Ville-Marie, Place Victoria, and Place Bonaventure stand out as the heart of the emerging city.

To sum up, this study covers the history of Montreal's architecture within the context of the Montreal environment. However, dates, matters of aesthetics, and classifications according to schools of art are of lesser concern here than are the forces and contingencies which determined the birth and development of successive kinds of environments and architectures.

The story of the emergence of these forces from the social, economic, and cultural structure is as compelling as the study of their expression in topographical landmarks and artistic manifestations. This is, to our knowledge, the first investigation of its kind on this Canadian metropolis. We shall therefore briefly describe the sources of this research to enable the reader to understand the spirit in which the work was written as well as the field it covers.

Our study is a synthesis and as such demands a large amount of information in various fields relating to cities and architecture in general. Such printed references have been grouped in the bibliography under the heading "General Sources." *Technics and Civilization, The Culture of Cities,* and *The City in History,* by Lewis Mumford, are basic works on the evolution of the city in general. Other books treat the same topic from a different point of view: *Towns and Cities* by Emrys Jones, *Towns and Buildings Described in Drawings and Words* by Steen Eiler Rasmussen, and *The Geography of Towns* by Arthur E. Smailes. Other studies deal with a particular period in the history of the city: *Victorian Cities* by Asa Briggs and *The Modern Metropolis* by Hans Blumenfeld.

The following books deal with the history of western architecture, to which Canada and Montreal contributed to a certain extent: *An Outline of European Architecture* by Nikolaus Pevsner, *Space, Time and Architecture* by Sigfried Giedion, and *Architecture: Nineteenth and Twentieth Centuries* by Henry-Russell Hitchcock. Supplementary readings on more particular aspects include *Victorian Architecture* by Robert Furneaux Jordan and *An Introduction to Modern Architecture* by James Maude Richards. Because Montreal has undergone in turn specific influences from France, England, and the United States (the latter is predominant today), the following books have been consulted: from France, *L'architecture française* and *Les villes françaises* by Pierre Lavedan; from England, *A History of English Architecture* by Peter Kidson, Peter Murray, and Paul Thompson, *British Townscapes* by Ewart Johns, and the masterpiece by Rasmussen, *London the Unique City;* from the United States, *The Making of Urban America* by John William Reps, a reference containing a wealth of information. Another important source, *American Skyline* by Christopher Tunnard and Henry Hope Reed, is essential to an understanding of American architecture. Together with *London the Unique City,* it inspired the author of the present study to undertake his research. Mumford has also written short studies on American urban architecture and civilization. Two of these greatly assisted us in the present project: *Sticks and Stones* and *The Brown Decades.* Specialized journals, like *Architectural Forum,* are the best sources of information on the manifestation of contemporary architecture and city planning in the United States.

In Canada, and particularly in Quebec, three names stand out in the field of the history of architecture: Traquair, Morisset, and Gowans. Ramsay Traquair, leader of the McGill school, has written several authoritative articles, a number of which have been collected in his book *The Old Architecture of Quebec.* On the French side, Gérard Morisset was the pioneer responsible for the Inventaire des oeuvres d'art de la province de Québec and was the author of *L'architecture en Nouvelle-France* and *Coup d'oeil sur les arts en Nouvelle-France*. His works have inspired others like Michel Lessard and Huguette Marquis, authors of the *Encyclopédie de la maison québécoise*, which is not a very rigorous study but a good popular book. Alan Gowans's important contribution in this field includes several solid articles, to which we often refer. He also wrote *Church Architecture in New France*, the best monograph to date on the subject, and *Looking at Architecture in Canada*, which has been revised and incorporated into *Building Canada: An Architectural History of Canadian Life*. To follow the development of contemporary architecture in Canada, one must rely on specialized publications such as the *Journal of the Royal Architectural Institute of Canada* and *The Canadian Architect*.

Our knowledge of the architecture and environment of Montreal has been enriched by the writings of Mgr. Olivier Maurault and of E.-Z. Massicotte. Maurault was rector of the Université de Montréal and, besides several articles, he published an important monograph, *La Paroisse*, concerning the present Notre-Dame Church on Place d'Armes. His *Marges d'histoires* was published in three volumes, the second of which includes several essays on the city's history and architecture. Massicotte, a hard-working researcher, left us a large number of articles published in the *Bulletin des recherches historiques* and *Les cahiers des Dix*. His famous "collection," now in the National Library of Quebec (Fauteux Annex), includes a large number of old prints, photographs, newspaper clippings, and other interesting documents about our city.

One must look at the architecture and environment of Montreal in the light of the social, economic, and cultural development of the metropolis. Several books on the history of Montreal cover these various subjects. William Henry Atherton's *Montreal, 1535–1914* (3 vols.) contains a wealth of information on various subjects. John Irwin Cooper's *Montreal: A Brief History* is a very informative book. Other works are of a more narrative nature: *Histoire de Montréal* by Robert Rumilly (5 vols.) and Kathleen Jenkins's *Montreal: Island City of the St. Lawrence*.

Apart from studies by Raoul Blanchard on Montreal's geography (particularly *L'Ouest du Canada français*), few reports cover fully the economic, social, and cultural aspects of the city's development. Among the attempts to deal with these topics, *Montréal économique* is a collection of essays published on the occasion of the city's three hundredth anniversary. The *Géographie humaine de Montréal* was written by Raymond Tanghe, and to our knowledge he was the only researcher who dealt with the question of housing in the more populous quarters. Norbert Lacoste's *Les caractéristiques sociales de la population du grand Montréal* is a valuable study on urban sociology in postwar Montreal. Finally, *Montréal: Field Guide*, a collection of articles on the most important aspects of Montreal's geography, was prepared for the 22nd International Geographical Congress convened in Montreal in August 1972. This source contains a great deal more information than the ordinary excursion guide. Let us also mention the numerous issues of the *Bulletin technique* and the *Cahiers d'urbanisme* published by the City Planning Department of the City of Montreal; they constitute the basis for a data bank on our physical and human environment.

Montreal has always played a key role in the history and development of Quebec and of Canada, and one must not neglect this aspect of its history. However, Quebec francophones, preoccupied by cultural survival, do not perceive Canadian history in the same manner as English-speaking Canadians or a foreigner impressed by the country's potential. It is therefore preferable to make parallel studies of works like the *Histoire du Canada français* (2 vols.) by Lionel Groulx and *The French Canadians, 1760–1967* (2 vols.) by Mason Wade; the *Histoire du Canada* by the Parisian Robert Lacour-Gayet and the famous *Dominion of the North* by Donald Creighton. One must also read *Canadians in the Making*, a unique and outstanding social commentary by Arthur R. M. Lower. Similar investigations concerning the province of Quebec include several short studies assembled in *Essais sur le Québec contemporain* and in *French-Canadian Society*, a collection prepared under the direction of Marcel Rioux and Yves Martin. Finally, in the field of economics, there is a selection of good essays by W. T. Easterbrook and M. H. Watkins in *Approaches to Canadian Economic History*.

All the previously cited works, as well as several books and articles indicated in the bibliography of each chapter, constitute secondary sources. Whenever possible, we have attempted to draw on primary sources. Hence, for the purpose of this study, the most important primary reference was Montreal itself, with its streets, its parks, its monuments, its dwellings, its places of work. During the course of this research, we have attempted as often as possible to refer to the existing, visible, tangible reality. At times, we had no other choice: for example, there are hardly any writings on the commercial or the domestic architecture of the Victorian era. However, Montreal, like any other city, is an organism in perpetual mutation and many of its streets, parks, and buildings have disappeared over the years or been transformed. The only way to retrace the past and assess such changes would be to reconstruct the evolution of the city with historical maps, drawings, sketches, illustrations, and other relevant documents.

Massicotte left us an exhaustive list of maps and plans of Montreal and of the island (refer to the *Bulletin des recherches historiques* 20, nos. 2 and 3, February and March 1914). These documents are kept in the Archives of the City of Montreal and in the National Archives of Canada in Ottawa. For Montreal, during the French regime, we already possess two worthwhile reconstructions: one by H. Beaugrand and P. L. Morin, *Le Vieux Montréal, 1611–1803,* and the very scholarly *Images et figures de Montréal sous la France* by Gustave Lanctôt. The historian Marcel Trudel has collected in his *Atlas of New France* a set of historical maps on the French occupation of the American continent.

The iconography of the buildings of our past may be found in municipal, provincial, and national archives, as well as in such newspapers and magazines of the past century as the *Illustrated London News,* the *Canadian Illustrated News,* and *L'opinion publique.* A selection of pictures, engravings, and illustrations has been published in *Montreal: A Pictorial Record* (2 vols.) by Charles P. de Volpi and P. S. Winkworth. For *Les vieilles églises de la province de Québec, 1647–1800* and *Vieux manoirs, vieilles maisons,* Pierre-Georges Roy has collected a substantial number of photographs of old buildings in the province of Quebec and in the Montreal region. Some of these buildings still exist today. William Notman, a pioneer in the art of photography, has left us a collection of photographs, now at the McCord Museum of McGill University; some of his best pictures may be found in *Portrait of a Period: A Collection of Notman Photographs, 1856–1915.* Finally, anybody interested in the evolution of architecture and urban landscapes in Montreal ought to consult the "Massicotte collection" to which we have referred earlier.

This study is above all a synthesis. Therefore we did not attempt to consult all the original manuscripts and documents relating to our subject matter. At any rate, it would have been an impossible task, given the scope of our topic and the large number of documents—not all of them classified—piled up in the various archives. Manuscripts have been consulted occasionally to clarify certain points, like the characteristics of the Montreal "côte" or the role played by the ruling colonial French class in the control of construction and organization of the physical environment. Luckily, a large number of documents pertaining to such matters have already been collected, classified, and published, some in the *Rapport de l'archiviste de la Province de Québec,* published annually for over half a century. Others appear in various catalogues like the *Inventaire des ordonnances des intendants de la Nouvelle-France conservées aux archives provinciales de Québec* (4 vols.); *Edits, ordonnances royaux, déclarations et arrêts du Conseil d'Etat du roi concernant le Canada* (3 vols.); and *Répertoire des arrêts, édits, mandements, ordonnances et règlements conservés dans les archives du Palais de Justice de Montréal, 1640–1760,* the last-named having been prepared by Massicotte.

The memoirs, descriptions, and accounts of journeys left to us by men stationed here, as well as by observers and travellers of different eras, constitute another primary source. As witnesses of their times, works like the famous *Jesuit Relations,* the reports by Gédéon de Catalogne and by Chaussegros de Léry, as well as the very detailed *Topographical Description of the Province of Lower Canada* by Joseph Bouchette in the nineteenth century, enable us to follow the evolution of the settlement of Montreal. We have also relied on the reports by Jacques Cartier, Samuel de Champlain, Father de Charlevoix, the Swede Peter Kalm, and the American Benjamin Silliman. As steamboats made navigation across the ocean less perilous, such accounts became more numerous. The eyewitness testimonies of John M. Duncan, Théodore Pavie, Edward Allen Talbot, Henri de Lamothe, and others are irreplaceable and enable us to follow the topographic and architectural evolution of Montreal.

These are the works consulted in the preparation of this study. The author does not claim to have completely assimilated all the information and opinions contained in them. He is particularly aware of the numerous shortcomings and lack of thoroughness in forming some of the opinions expressed in this study. Nevertheless, he hopes that such a synthesis will be found useful, if it were only to acquaint the reader with a fascinating city—Montreal.

Part I

WHERE THE OLD WORLD AND THE NEW
WORLD MEET

*La situation de la ville est fort agréable. Du costé
du sud, et [du] sudoüest est une très belle plaine qui
se termine à la Rivière St-Pierre et coste St-Paul, où
les terres sont très fertiles en toutes sortes de grains
et [de] légumes. Du costé de l'oüest les terres se lè-
vent en amphithéâtre jusques au pied de la montagne distante de la ville de trois quarts de lieue.
. . . Derrière et autour de la d[ite] montagne sont les
costes Ste-Catherine, Nostre Dame des Neiges, de
Liesse et des Vertues, nouvellement establies. Les
terres y sont très belles et de bonne qualité pour les
arbres fruitiers et pour produire toutes sortes de
grains et [de] légumes. Du costé du nordoüest et du
nord de la ville, il y a aussy de belles plaines, en-
trecoupées de petits costeaux qui se terminent à St-
Laurent, St-Michel et la Visitation, costes aussy
nouvellement establies et où les terres sont très
belles tant pour les arbres fruitiers que pour rappor-
ter toutes sortes de grains et [de] légumes. Du costé
du nordest de la ville sont les costes de Ste-Marie,
St-Martin et St-François qui se terminent à la
Longue Pointe où finit la paroisse.*

*"Mémoire sur les plans des seigneuries et habita-
tions des gouvernements de Québec, les Trois-
Rivières, et de Montréal," by* GÉDÉON DE CATA-
LOGNE, *engineer, 7 November 1712* [1]

1

The Key to the West

*It will some day be a place most suitable for the
site of a large and wealthy city.*
Jérôme Lalemant, Jesuit Relations, *year 1663*[2]

At the Crossroads

A glance at the map of North America clearly shows the St. Lawrence River as the most deeply penetrating route into the continent.
Running between the mountain masses of the Canadian Shield and
the Appalachians, it reaches to the "Mediterranean" of North America (the Great Lakes) and the vast interior plains.

The river's deep penetration played a key role in the history of European exploration of the New World and accounts for the importance explorers attached to the waterway. At the beginning, they did
not grasp the extent of the network as we know it today, but the
river itself kept hopes alive: they believed it might lead them to
countries rich in gold. Indeed, not even the plentiful catches of fish
in the bays of the Atlantic coast could help them forget that gold.

Jacques Cartier, Canada's discoverer, received the order from
Francis I "to discover certain islands and lands where it is said that a
great quantity of gold, and other precious things, are to be found."[3]
Even if he were never to discover the Klondike, the search for the
northern passage to China remained an attractive proposition. It
was not Canada that Cartier and his peers were hoping to discover,
but gold or the route to Cathay. From the account of his first voyage
to Canada in 1534, it is clear that he searched in vain for the passage
to the Orient.[4]

The following year, during his second voyage, he thought he had good luck when the Indians showed him "the way to the mouth of the great river of Hochelaga and the route towards Canada."[5] Cartier was convinced that this was the famous passage, and, in his report to the king on his second voyage, he insisted that this river of some eight hundred leagues could lead to Asia.[6]

Thus, in the fall of 1535, Cartier sailed up the St. Lawrence and on 2 October reached Hochelaga, a small fortified Huron town at the foot of a mountain which he named Mont-Royal. The fast rapids rendered all navigation impossible and he was unable to sail any farther. Unwittingly, Cartier was actually the first European to set foot on Montreal Island and to behold the site of the future Canadian metropolis. It is interesting to note that these rapids (the Lachine Rapids), although robbing him at the time of all hopes of reaching Asia, were to contribute to the prosperity of Montreal.

Jacques Cartier discovered not only Canada, but also one of the largest rivers in the world, for the St. Lawrence commands a wide territory. Its vast drainage basin comprises a region of the greatest geographic and economic importance. Its network of waterways is far-reaching and stretches from the vast continental plain to the many riches of the Canadian Shield, of which it drains most of the south side. Some 2000 kilometres inside the continent, it opens into a "sea" of fresh water: the Great Lakes. The latter lead into the Mississippi Basin, to the Hudson Basin through the Mohawk River, and to the Mackenzie. This hinterland has grown into today's industrial heartland of America and on the shores, as well as in the immediate vicinity of the Great Lakes, cities like Kingston, Hamilton, Toronto, Rochester, Buffalo, Cleveland, Windsor, Milwaukee, Detroit, and Chicago testify to the geographical and economic importance of this continental network.[7]

The French founded their American empire on the great river axis, on this "vital route which would carry eager explorers towards Hudson Bay, towards the mysterious horizon of the western sea, and towards the Mississippi," to quote the historian Trudel.[8] Even better than Cartier, the great figures of French colonization, Champlain, Frontenac, and Talon, grasped the geographic and economic significance of the deep thrust of the St. Lawrence into the American continent. It was obviously not the passage to the Orient—although it seems Champlain still believed it was—nor was it the road to the lands of gold. The river did, however, offer important economic possibilities and, for the time being, a ready access to regions rich in fur. On this particular topic, Intendant Talon, in one of his enthusiastic letters to the court of France, refers to this vast country "drained by the St. Lawrence River as well as beautiful rivers flowing into it on all sides, and through the same rivers, reaching several native nations rich in furs."[9]

From a geographical as well as from an economic viewpoint, the location of Montreal Island is exceptional: about 1600 kilometres inland, at the confluence of three important waterways. The latter formed natural corridors into the land, along which roads were eventually built. The island is in the St. Lawrence River, which reaches out to the Atlantic Ocean and Europe through its lower stretches and to the Great Lakes, Ohio, and Mississippi regions by its upper corridor. Sixty-five kilometres downstream, the Richelieu River traces a route southward through the Adirondack Mountains to the Hudson River. The latter, which cuts another channel into the continent, flows into the Atlantic Ocean alongside New York City. Above Montreal Island, the Ottawa River, somewhat neglected today, played an important part at the beginning of colonization. Trappers used it in their search for the rich furs of the western region.

The significance of Montreal's location at one of North America's most important crossroads was not lost on Father Barthélémy Vimont, editor of the *Relation de la Nouvelle-France* in 1642: "From the entrance of the great river and Gulf of Saint Lawrence to that Island, they count nearly two hundred leagues; and the whole of that great stretch of water is navigable,—in part by great Ships, and in part by Barks [and the island] gives access and an admirable approach to all the Nations of this vast country; for, on the North and South, on the East and West, there are rivers which fall into the river Saint Lawrence and the Rivière-des-Prairies that surround the Island."[10] Further, Father Paul Ragueneau, editor of the *Relation* of 1651, pertinently concluded that "it is a very advantageous place for all the upper Nations who wish to trade with us."[11]

Not only was Montreal Island at the crossroads of navigable waterways, but also the surrounding geographical features insured its position as the heart of the network. The Hochelaga archipelago, made up mainly of the islands of Montreal and Jésus, divides the St. Lawrence River into three streams, each of which flows through rapids which are difficult to cross, especially the more turbulent Saint-Louis Rapids. Hence the name Tiotiake which the natives had given the island of Montreal, meaning "the Island amidst Rapids."[12]

The Saint-Louis Rapids, later renamed the Lachine Rapids, prevented any further navigation. They stopped Jacques Cartier in 1535, and Champlain and others later on. Below this obstacle nature had created an excellent natural harbour several metres deep. One could disembark there and, through portages, attempt to reach the navigable upper part of the St. Lawrence River. Thus Montreal became a bridgehead, a transit point between sea and inland navigation, an indispensable trade and storage centre. Montreal was therefore the key to the lower and upper St. Lawrence, and the Ottawa valley route, to the Atlantic, and to the West, to the Old World and to the New World.[13] (See figure 1.)

The whole destiny of the future metropolis rests on its role as a communication link. The economic and technical revolutions of the nineteenth and twentieth centuries would further enhance its favourable geographical location on this vast continent where transportation was to play such an important part. Natural obstacles on rivers were to be progressively eliminated or circumvented, steamboats would replace sailboats, and railroads would use the corridors cleared beside the waterways. With the colonization of the West, Montreal, located at the crossroads of continental traffic, was to grow rich as a trade, production, and distribution centre. Such a unique destiny would leave its mark on the very character of our city. In her novel *The Tin Flute* (1947), Gabrielle Roy expressed this feeling in her description of a humble house on the shores of the Lachine Canal: "But the house lay not only in the path of the freight boats. It was also on the railway line, at the crossroads, so to speak, of the East-West railroads and the shipping lanes of the city. It was on the road to the ocean, the Great Lakes and the prairies."[14]

With the trade of goods came the exchange of ideas. Montreal was to become a privileged centre where ideas would merge or sometimes clash. In Montreal the Old World and the New World met. Both its architecture and the character of its town planning were to be deeply affected by this encounter.

An Exceptional Location

The exceptional geographical location of the island of Montreal could not by itself account for the city's prosperity from the second half of the seventeenth century onwards. In those days, urban development was closely tied to the productivity of surrounding land and to the limited ability to transport surplus production to the city in exchange for equipment and services. The soil of the Montreal Basin was undoubtedly suitable for farming. The fact that the Montreal Plain was highly desirable for human occupation has been established by the geographer Blanchard. There are several navigable waterways, the soil of the plain is the most fertile in the province, and the configuration of the land does not present any obstacle to settle-

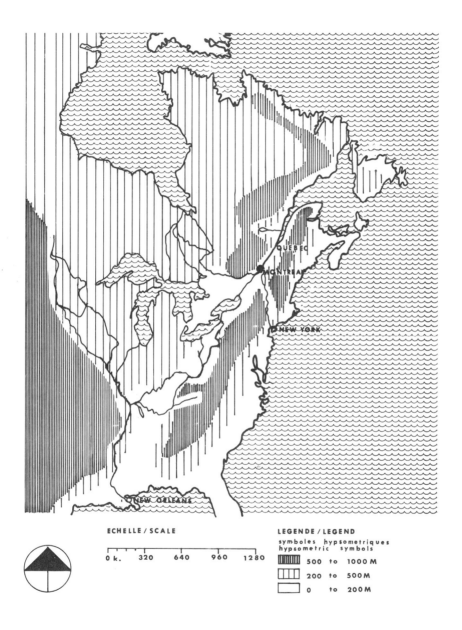

ECHELLE / SCALE

0 k.   320   640   960   1280

LEGENDE / LEGEND

symboles hypsometriques
hypsometric symbols

500 to 1000 M

200 to 500 M

0 to 200 M

Fig. I   *Geographic situation of the island of Montreal*

ment or transportation anywhere. The climate constituted the only hindrance, in the form of periodic freezing of the waterways, but this was to be a drawback only until the advent of mechanized means of land transportation.[15]

On 3 October 1535, Jacques Cartier and his companions realized that the site was suitable for settlement:

> On reaching the summit [of Mount Royal] we had a view of the land for more than thirty leagues round about. Towards the north there is a range of mountains, running east and west, and another range to the south. Between these ranges lies the finest land it is possible to see, being arable, level and flat. And in the midst of this flat region one saw the river.[16]

This was Cartier's description of the plain of Montreal, which is part of the vast plain of the St. Lawrence Basin. Lying between the mountain ranges of the Canadian Shield and of the Appalachians, the St. Lawrence Basin stretches westward from a point east of Quebec City to the Great Lakes and the huge continental plains.

The geological formation accounts for the evenness and richness of the Montreal Plain. It was flooded by the ocean at the very beginning of the Palaeozoic era. Sediments settling in thick layers were the source of the plain's calciferous substrata. It then underwent erosion during the Secondary and Tertiary eras, a period of 250 million years. The Laurentian Plain was to acquire the characteristics with which we are familiar today as a result of the four consecutive glaciations of the Quaternary. Hard rock formations that became Mount Royal, and other hills in the region, were the only ones to have withstood the long periods of erosion as well as the pressure of glaciers, some of which were 900 metres thick. Collapsing under the weight of such a mass, the eastern continental crust was again flooded by the ocean, named the Champlain Sea, which left rich alluvial deposits and masked some of the disparities in elevation. This shows clearly on a map of isohyptic lines of the plain (figure 2), representing an area equivalent to that described by a 50-kilometre-long radius having its point of origin at the centre of Montreal Island. Except for the rather small hills of Oka, Rigaud, and Montreal, one rarely encounters grades of more than 5 percent, and most of the land lies less than 60 metres above the mean sea level.[17]

This land is not only the most even and the richest in Quebec but it also benefits from climatic conditions that are mild and the most suited for human settlement. There are more than 140 successive frost-free days, more than anywhere else in the province. Snow

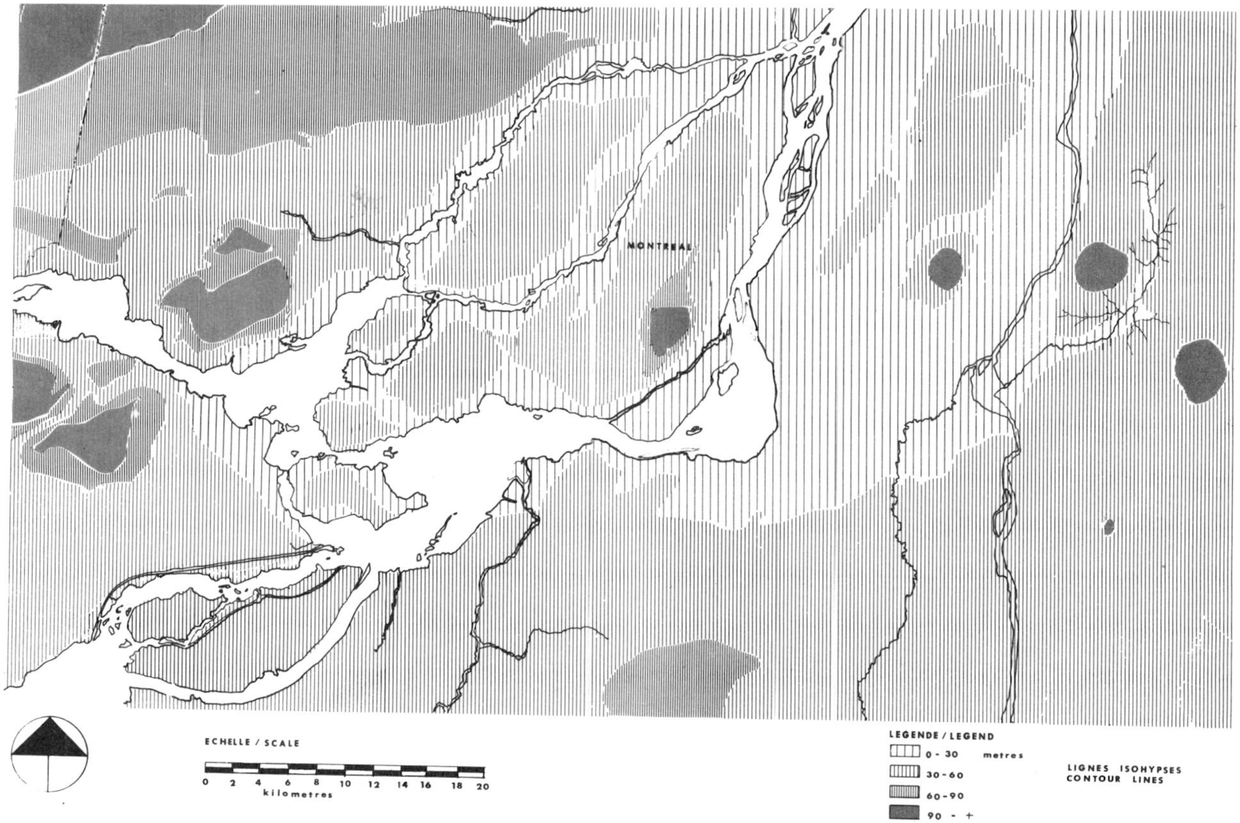

Fig. 2
Natural
topography of
the plain of
Montreal

MONTREAL

LEGENDE / LEGEND
0 - 30 metres
30-60
60-90
90 - +

LIGNES ISOHYPSES
CONTOUR LINES

ECHELLE / SCALE
0 2 4 6 8 10 12 14 16 18 20
kilometres

covers the ground for only about twelve to fifteen weeks, twice as
short a period as in some other inhabited regions of Quebec. Following the configuration of the Laurentian Valley, winds blow predominantly from the southwest, the west, and the northeast, carrying
moisture from the Gulf of Mexico, the Great Lakes, and the Atlantic Ocean and regularly releasing more than 100 centimetres of rain
annually. Except for a somewhat dryer month of April, the average
monthly precipitation is over 7 centimetres but below 10 centimetres. The summer is hot: the June, July, and August temperatures average 18°C with sunshine for more than 50 percent of the
days. Such climatic conditions are highly suited for growing vegetables during the sunny season.

Montreal is located at latitude 45°30', as are Milan and Venice,
but it lies somewhat further north than Bordeaux. Its climate is continental: hot summers followed by long, cold winters. In December,
January, and February, the average temperature is around −9°C. The
percentage of sunny days in January is 25 percent and in February 40
percent. The rate of snow accumulation is more dramatic: an average of 3 metres falls annually in the plain. Such a thick layer has the
advantage of protecting the soil against the rigorous cold.[18] Nowadays the climate is much less an inconvenience, but in the days
when colonization depended directly on the European metropolis
the development of Montreal and of the colony came to a temporary
standstill when the waterways used for communications and supplies were frozen for four months of the year. French vessels were
able to sail to Quebec but once a year, compared with twice or three
times a year to the Caribbean. In that respect, the British colonies
on the Atlantic coast had a definite advantage. Montreal would have
to wait until it was linked by rail in 1853 to an ice-free Atlantic port
before prospering at a faster pace.

The richness of the soil of the great Montreal Plain as well as
favourable climatic conditions during the sunny season encouraged
farmers to settle on the land and stimulated exchanges between
food producers and suppliers of goods and services. Such interactions are essential to the life of a city. As early as 1684, Baron de
Lahontan confirms this in the account of his voyage when he notes:
"their Seignories or Cantons that lye on the South-side of the Island,
produce a considerable Revenue; for the Plantations are good, and
the Inhabitants are rich in Corn, Cattle, Fowl, and a thousand other
Commodities, for which they find a Mercat in the City."[19]

During its first centuries, Montreal Island with its area of some
46,540 hectares[20] was to become the base of this agricultural community. Judging from the testimony of the first European who visited the island, the natives were aware of the qualities of its soil:

We marched on, and about half a league thence, found that the land began to be cultivated. It was fine land with large fields covered with the corn of the country, which resembles Brazil millet, and is about as large or larger than a pea. They live on this as we do on wheat. And in the middle of these fields is situated and stands the village of Hochelaga, near and adjacent to a mountain, the slopes of which are fertile and cultivated.[21]

Testimonies abound also in the *Jesuit Relations* on the splendour and fertility of the island. Here is the testimony of one Jérôme Lalemant (1663):

This spot even exceeds all the others in beauty; for the islands met with at the junction of these two streams are so many large and beautiful prairies, some oblong and others round, or so many gardens designed for pleasure, both because of the various fruits found there, and because of the shape of the gardens themselves and the artifice wherewith nature has prepared them with all the charms possible for Painters to depict in their landscapes.[22]

Finally, nearly two centuries later, Joseph Bouchette wrote in his *Topographical Dictionary of the Province of Lower Canada*: "Montreal is the most considerable island in the province and its superior fertility has acquired for it the distinguished appellation of the Garden of Canada."[23]

It is with a precise reason in mind that we have lingered on the very hospitable character of the plain as well as of the island of Montreal: the rural settlement which such conditions favoured would have many significant repercussions on our urban environment. For, as we shall see in the next chapter, the structures as well as the orientation of the urban landscapes of the metropolis grew with scarcely any alterations from the initial pattern of rural settlement. Moreover, from the second half of the nineteenth century onward, this populous agricultural community was to supply the budding industry with such a source of manpower that to this day Montreal owes the success of its industrial expansion to this abundant source of inexpensive labour.[24] Today, the rich land of the plain is still a matter of concern but for other reasons. Indeed, as the process of development accelerates to the point of becoming uncontrollable, the best terrain for urban settlement unfortunately remains the best for agricultural exploitation: a tragic dilemma.

From the point of view of architecture, the geological formation of the Montreal soil has yielded a vast choice of materials used in the construction of buildings in the city. There was an abundance of timber, both on the island and in the neighbouring countryside. Gédéon de Catalogne, a French engineer, was undoubtedly the best-informed man on the physical resources of the colony. He confirms that in 1684 the Parish of Montreal "was almost nothing but a forest of all kinds of very big trees, in particular, pines, maples, elms, basswood, beech, yellow birch, and cedars."[25] At the time, the parish included an important part of the island, stretching from Verdun to Long Point; besides half of Côte Saint-Pierre and Côte Saint-Paul, it included the following "côtes": Notre-Dame-des-Neiges, de Liesse, des Vertus, Saint-Laurent, Sainte-Catherine, Saint-Michel, and de la Visitation.

Rocky outcrops in about fifteen locations on the island, in Rosemont, Côte Saint-Michel, Bordeaux, and Cartierville, as well as in some districts of Ile Jésus (Saint-Martin, Saint-Vincent de Paul, and Saint-François de Sales), were turned into quarries which supplied almost all the stone required for construction in Montreal. Most of it is limestone from the Trenton and Chazy formations and comes in three varieties: grey semi-crystalline building stones of average roughness, hard and dark fine-grained stones, and a third type combining characteristics of the previous two. Two important quarries, those of Martineau and Villeray, were still cutting stone from these formations in the first decades of the twentieth century. They have now been filled and changed into neighbourhood parks. The rather dark and cheerless colour of these limestones tainted the old streets of Montreal with a particular local flavour, a fact which was not lost on visitors, as we shall see in chapter 6.

The detritic mantle, covering about 90 percent of the island area, as well as a large part of the great plain, is partly composed of marine sedimentary clay, called Leda clay, which is particularly well suited for the manufacture of bricks. Samuel de Champlain, a great geographer, had already noticed this characteristic of the Montreal soil during his voyage in 1611: "There are also many level stretches of very good rich potter's clay suitable for brickmaking and building, which is a great convenience."[26] The marine clay on the island lies mainly in wide strips stretching from Verdun to Pointe-aux-Trembles between the river and the Sherbrooke Terrace. Bricks were made from the clay, and with their characteristic red they became the most commonly used covering material for domestic construction. This red is now the dominant colour of whole neighbourhoods. Such bricks were manufactured chiefly by two brickyards located in the east end of the city, one on Iberville Street and the other on Davidson Street, off Sherbrooke Street.

The layer of clay stretching between the Sherbrooke Terrace and the river varies in depth from a few metres to over 45 metres. It is therefore a poor site for construction. Yet, it was on this very band of soft clay that the heart of the town as well as the industrial centre of the metropolis was built for reasons dictated by the geography of the site. Engineering techniques made up for the inherent weaknesses of the ground, but at ever-increasing costs and with mounting difficulties. Luckily the rest of the island is covered with a clay which is more resistant to compression and is thus more suitable for foundations. This is particularly true in a wide zone, roughly delineated by Côte-des-Neiges Road, Metropolitan Boulevard, Pie IX Boulevard, and Mont-Royal Avenue, where solid rock lies less than 3 metres below the surface.[27]

Leaving aside for the moment the influence of climate on architecture, a topic to be treated with reference to specific situations, let us look into some particular aspects of the island's natural topography which dictated the choice of site for the first settlement and would determine its future orientation.

Mount Royal stands almost at the centre of the island. It is a massive and rolling hill, created by volcanic intrusions which penetrated through the sedimentary crust. The mountain, as it is familiarly known, rises 235 metres above sea level, then slopes down towards the extremities of the island. There remains, however, an area surrounding the mountain at about 60 metres above sea level, falling off to a height of 1 to several metres at the shores. The contour lines which incline gently downwards along the length of the island dip more abruptly across its breadth, especially on the east side of the mountain where they reach the river in successive terraces. There is a drop of 23 metres in the short distance between Lafontaine Park and Sainte-Catherine Street. Certain geographers maintain that these terraces correspond to the old beaches of the Champlain Sea. According to Blanchard, however, they conform to underwater ridges caused by cumulative deposits on the east side of Mount Royal in an age when the mountain stood in the way of the currents of the Champlain Sea.[28] (See figure 3.)

Two main terraces border the southern side. The first, about 45 metres in altitude and extending roughly from Maisonneuve Park to the municipality of Montreal West, is referred to as the Sherbrooke Terrace, for this street follows the escarpment for several kilometres. Immediately below, at an average altitude of 25 metres, lies a low terrace extending to the river between McGill Street and the Canadian Pacific marshalling yard at Hochelaga. At the time of Montreal's foundation, a network of valleys with small rivers ran through the lower terrace. A muddy creek, the Saint-Martin River,

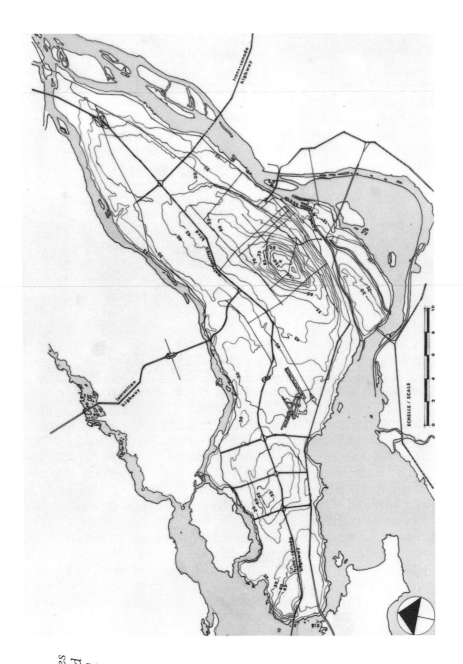

Fig. 3
Map of the
contour lines
of the island
of Montreal

flowed along the very path of today's Saint-Antoine Street to the site of today's Chaboillez Square, where it emptied into the Saint-Pierre River. The latter ran from the southwest into the St. Lawrence near the site of today's Place d'Youville. The development of Montreal during its first centuries was deeply influenced by the topography of the lower terrace (figure 4).

The First Settlement

Samuel de Champlain should be given credit for the choice of the site of the future City of Montreal, for he was undoubtedly qualified for the task. He was a great explorer, an excellent cartographer and geographer; he won fame as an ethnographer and as the founder of several cities and of an empire. Champlain, who was born around 1570 in Brouage, near La Rochelle, was truly a man of the Renaissance. He combined the energetic temperament of a man of action with that of a patient and methodical observer, stimulated by an intense curiosity. He was the author of a treatise on Indian ethnography, among other learned works, and of a superb geographical inventory of Acadia, the St. Lawrence, and the Great Lakes region.

Champlain had been hired by a group of businessmen from Rouen who had obtained monopolies in the fur trade from Henry IV. At first, he sought to install trading posts on the Atlantic coast. In 1604 he established a settlement on Ile Sainte-Croix (now known as Dochet Island on the coast of Maine), although he abandoned it in the following year in order to found Port Royal on the north shore of the Annapolis Basin in Nova Scotia.[29] But he quickly realized that the Acadian posts were difficult to defend and that the Appalachian Range constituted an obstacle to trade with the native people of the interior of the country. He therefore advised his patrons "to settle along the St. Lawrence River where trade and commerce could better be undertaken than in Acadia."[30]

With surprising perspicacity, Champlain had grasped the geographic and economic significance of the deep penetration of the river into the interior of the continent. Being a geographer and an astute soldier, he established a settlement in 1608 at Quebec, precisely at the narrowest part of the river, so as to guard the entrance to the future French empire in America.[31] He quickly realized that the fur trade would greatly benefit from a trading post on Montreal Island, which was at the crossroads of the river network. Thus, on 28 May 1611, he surveyed the approaches to Grand Saut Island "in order to find a suitable place for the site of a settlement, and also to prepare the ground for building."[32]

What precise place did Champlain choose? In his own words, "but

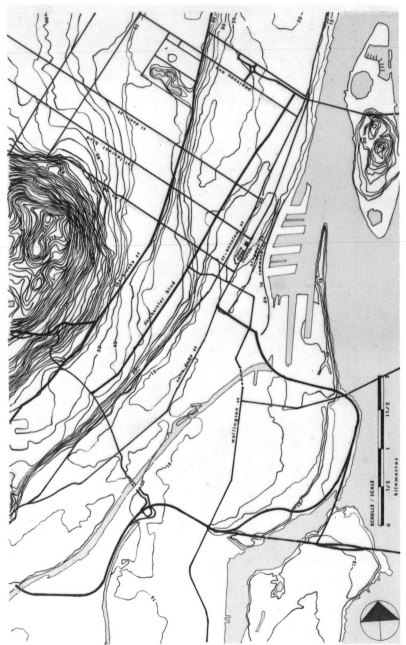

Fig.4   Map of the contour lines of the island of Montreal: the terraces

after looking everywhere [I] found no spot more suitable than a little place to which pinnaces and shallops can ascend." Champlain therefore chose a site at the very limits of navigable waters, at the foot of the Lachine Rapids, and named it Place Royale:

> And near this Place Royale there is a small river, which leads some distance into the interior, alongside which are more than sixty arpents of land, which have been cleared and are now like meadows, where one might sow grain and do gardening. . . . So having examined very carefully and found this spot to be one of the finest on this river, I ordered the trees of the Place Royale to be cut down and cleared off, in order to level the ground and make it ready for building.[33]

This Place Royale, which was chosen, named, and cleared by Champlain, today corresponds to Pointe-à-Callières: the triangle bounded by de la Commune Street and Place d'Youville, with the monument to John Young at one of its apexes. In those days, as mentioned earlier, the small Saint-Pierre River flowed through the site of the present Place d'Youville. This provided the area with a means of protection that was not lost on Champlain: "Water can be made to encircle the place very easily, and a little island formed of it, on which to erect such an establishment as one may wish."[34] The penetration of the Saint-Pierre River also presented other advantages. As it was navigable for a great part of its course, it shortened the portages required to go around the Lachine Rapids; moreover, its mouth offered a small harbour sheltered from the strong currents which prevailed in that section of the St. Lawrence River.

Unfortunately, and for reasons that were to remain obscure, the projects that Champlain nurtured for his Place Royale would not be carried out during his lifetime. The site undoubtedly was not forgotten and the natives, trappers, and merchants probably used it at some time or another as a meeting place. However, another thirty years would pass before a permanent settlement would be established on Place Royale, which Champlain had left "ready for construction."

Finally, in the summer of 1642, about forty colonists settled permanently at Place Royale under the governorship of the Sieur Chomedey de Maisonneuve who will be remembered by history as the founder of Montreal. One is tempted to believe that this group of pioneers had been attracted by the economic prospects of the site, but it was not so. The founding of Montreal is unparalleled in the history of European colonization. In fact, it was sponsored by a society of devout people,[35] most of whom owned considerable fortunes and some of whom were titled and had been received at the court of France. It was the avowed purpose of this foundation "to assemble a nation composed of French and Natives, the latter to be converted so as to render them sedentary. They would be taught to cultivate the land, would be united under the same discipline, and practice the Christian way of life."[36] With that purpose in mind, the society had acquired the island of Montreal precisely because it was "for eighty barbaric nations, a centre likely to attract them, because rivers lead to it from all directions."[37]

The project of the Société Notre-Dame quickly proved utopic, and Montreal's first settlement became a prosperous trading post rather than a centre of religious proselytism. The fort of Ville-Marie, erected by Maisonneuve and his companions, was not very different from the quarters erected by Champlain at Sainte-Croix in 1604. There still exists a plan of this fort, which was located near the present-day Alexandra Pier, somewhere between de Callières and du Port Streets. It is a rather rough drawing made in 1647 by Jean Bourdon and is the very first plan in our possession on the origins of the city of Montreal. Although the buildings were probably very rustic in character, their location on the plan denotes a classical layout. The living quarters of the civil and religious authorities, the public buildings, the store, the kitchen, and the bake-house are grouped with a certain symmetry around a small central square. The settlers' dwellings are also symmetrically located on either side of an axis leading from the main gate to the governor's house. We do not know whether Bourdon's drawing accurately depicts the exact location of the buildings, nor do we know whether the plan Champlain left us of his settlement at Sainte-Croix conforms to reality. We know one thing for certain: both plans are so much alike in spirit that we are compelled to accept the fact that, in those days, a certain classical conception inspired either the layout of colonial settlements or at least their graphic representation, or perhaps a bit of both.[38] (See plate 1.)

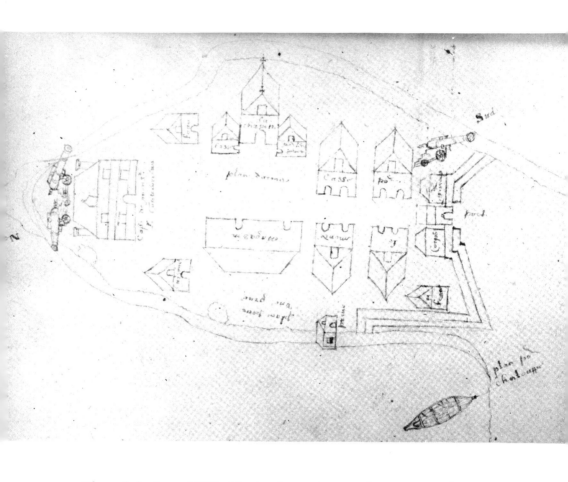

1. Plan of the fort of Ville-Marie, drawn in 1647 by Jean Bourdon

2

The Island Colony

> *Modern towns which have arisen little by little can only be understood by the study of their history.*
> STEEN EILER RASMUSSEN [1]

Dispute over an Empire

Professor John Summerson, in his excellent book on Georgian London, devised a way of presenting a broad picture of the development of London in the seventeenth and eighteenth centuries. He suggested that the reader imagine himself suspended a mile above the city for a period equal to two centuries, with the years going by at the rate of one per second.[2] If we follow the same procedure to study the progression of human occupation on Montreal Island during the same period, two facts come to light. First, the fort of Ville-Marie is the hub of a centrifugal topographical growth expanding somewhat like the surface rings caused by a pebble thrown in the water. This is hardly surprising for, according to Summerson, a city is like a plant or an ant-hill: it is the product of a collective, unconscious will with few preconceived intentions.[3] A second fact becomes evident from our imaginary observatory: as Ville-Marie expands, other settlements appear simultaneously at various points on the island and in the neighbouring plain, and all seem to mesh into an overall preconceived plan. What did happen?

A study of the particular set of contingencies leading to the colonization of the Montreal Basin will clarify the matter. At a time when the fur trade became one of the most important economic resources of the continent, Montreal's geographical location made it a natural controlling centre for the trade. It became the rival of other European colonies competing for the monopoly. Moreover, its command over the river network opened the way for the colonization of America's interior by the French. The great explorations by Jolliet, Marquette, Cavelier de La Salle, and others were stimulated by the necessity to discover new fur territories. They tended to centre the French empire on the St. Lawrence and the Mississippi and deny the other European colonies on the Atlantic coast the right to expand beyond the Appalachians.

The first to react were the Dutch settlers of New Amsterdam and Fort Orange. They would later be dislodged from these towns by the British, who would then rename the towns New York and Albany. One of the forts was located at the mouth of the Hudson River and the other at the confluence of the Hudson and Mohawk Rivers. They controlled the Hudson–Champlain waterway that penetrated the continent, cutting into the St. Lawrence Basin and separating Montreal from its natural hinterland. This was a very real menace, for the economy of the Atlantic colonies was more diversified than that of the French settlements, although their inland network of natural communications did not extend so deeply as did that of the St. Lawrence.[4] Moreover, rival colonies used to form alliances with the various Indian nations to carry on the fur trade.

Indians were indispensable allies in the fur trade. As natives, and familiar with the New World environment, they knew the habits and habitats of the animals; and they knew how to catch them and how to transport the pelts in their frail boats over turbulent rivers. Besides, they were not demanding; they gave a great deal in exchange for very little. Yet, to the Indians, this kind of trade with the white man was more than a paying proposition: it was vital.

First, the fur trade required but few agents; this maintained the hunting grounds intact and fostered a respect for the integrity of the vital environment of the natives. Second, the latter acquired metal tools and weapons in exchange for the pelts. Indeed, the North American Indians had not yet reached the Iron Age. They made implements out of wood, bone, stone, and sometimes copper. Iron was a revelation, a revolution in their way of life. Europeans became "The Men of Iron": their arrival with cauldrons, knives, and muskets made of iron upset the primitive culture. With the trading of metal implements for pelts, life for the Indians changed radically. Weapons and tools made of metal increased their strength and natural skills. Relationships between the various Indian nations were particularly affected, depending upon which had metal weapons and

tools. It soon became a matter of survival: the Hurons were extermi-
nated because the French had not supplied them with guns, whereas
their enemy, the Iroquois, had received weapons from the British
and the Dutch.[5]

Thus, two European colonies had settled in two different regions
and the economic territory of one colony became an obstacle for the
other's expansion. Both formed alliances with different Indian nations to secure for themselves the monopoly of the fur trade. The
French were associated with the Hurons and the Algonquins of the
Great Lakes region, the traditional enemies of the Iroquois. The latter were grouped into a league of five nations spread over the fertile
land stretching from Lake Champlain to Lake Ontario, and their domain extended from the English and Dutch settlements to the fur
territories. They became the natural allies of these colonies and
were granted better exchange rates, including brandy and muskets.
They were politically organized and more advanced socially than
their opponents; they were sedentary and cultivated the soil and
lived in fortified villages. They were fierce warriors and started an
economic war to secure the fur trade monopoly for the whites of Orange and New Amsterdam.[6]

Their main objective for more than half a century, from 1641 to
1701, was to destroy the land of the Hurons, thus depriving the
French of helpers and forcing them to evacuate their trading posts
on the St. Lawrence. They wanted to clear Montreal Island of all settlers, eliminating control by this centre over the fur trade. It is
within this very context of resistance to Iroquois invasion that the
land was settled and Montreal Island colonized.[7] These important
contingencies were to influence the first settlement in a significant
manner.

The Highway of the Colony
New France was populated under the impetus of the seigneurial system. Entrepreneurs, called seigneurs or lords, were granted portions
of land with the express obligation of establishing colonists or vas-
sals on their land. This system, administered since 1663 under the
common law of Paris, had inherited the rights, the vocabulary, and a
little of the spirit of feudalism, but resembled the latter only out-
wardly. In New France it was essentially an economic system for the
development of the land through which the government maintained
a vigilant eye on the rights and duties of all parties concerned.[8]

This system would scarcely have worked under the rule of the
trading companies; they were more interested in a colony of traders.
Yet, when war broke out against the aborigines, the underpopulated

colony took a loss. For the economic life of the colony was entirely dependent on the fur trade which was only possible if the waterways to the interior of the continent were sufficiently protected to ensure the freedom of traffic.[9]

Confronted with this failure, Colbert reorganized the colony in 1663 and placed it under the direct control and authority of the king. New France thus became an ordinary French province, governed by royal functionaries, among whom the governor, the intendant, and the bishop became the main figures. Furthermore, in order to pacify the natives, Louis XIV dispatched to the colony the Carignan-Salières Regiment, composed of a thousand hardy soldiers who had previously won fame in the battlefields of Europe. This army immediately set out to block the invasion road of the Iroquois and erected fortified posts on the Richelieu River, which was part of a network leading from New Amsterdam to Montreal via the Hudson River and Lake Champlain. In 1665 they built three forts on the Richelieu: Fort Richelieu at the mouth of the river, Fort Saint-Louis at the foot of the Richelieu Rapids (today's Chambly), and Fort Sainte-Thérèse, three leagues upstream from Fort Saint-Louis.[10]

At the same time the first government intendant, Jean-Baptiste Talon (1625?–94), inaugurated his administration. His activity in New France would be of the utmost importance. As a career administrator who had proved himself as intendant of Hainaut in Flanders, he was the first to establish the colony on a solid economic foundation. He devised a quasi-military plan for settling the land in order to protect the exposed regions of the country against the invasions of natives or foreigners. This is of particular relevance to our subject matter.

With this purpose in mind, Talon advised the king to keep the soldiers of the Carignan-Salières Regiment in the colony by granting them land:

> This manner of distributing a recently conquered country is in keeping with the old Roman usage which consisted in distributing to the soldiers the fields of the conquered provinces which they called *praedia militaria*. In my opinion, this practice by countries which were as able in politics as they were fierce at war could justifiably be introduced in a country separated from its ruler by 1000 leagues. This separation might force such a country to rely entirely on its own forces.[11]

In his assessment of the location of the settlements, Talon correctly judged that the most vulnerable region of the colony was the Montreal area and in particular the access provided by the Richelieu Valley.

Some twenty-five officers of the Carignan-Salières Regiment, mostly captains and lieutenants, agreed to stay in New France and were granted seigneuries along the shores of the Richelieu and St. Lawrence Rivers, from Montreal to Lake Saint-Pierre. The new seigneurs attracted to their land some of the discharged soldiers whom they had previously commanded. The number of the latter who became colonists on such military concessions is estimated at four to five hundred.[12]

Thus, for instance, Talon granted to Monsieur de Sorel, captain of the Carignan Regiment, Fort Richelieu, located at the mouth of the Richelieu River, together with an estate two and a half leagues wide by two leagues deep. According to the king's engineer, Gédéon de Catalogne, who, in 1712, wrote the remarkable "Mémoire sur les plans des seigneuries et habitations des gouvernements de Québec, les Trois-Rivières, et de Montréal," the location of this seigneury was "very attractive and most suitable and had the only store house between Montreal, Three-Rivers and Chambly."[13] In time, the city of Sorel was to develop on this well-located estate. To better control the mouth of the Richelieu River, Monsieur de Berthier, captain of a company of foot soldiers, was granted an estate two leagues wide by two leagues deep on the other side of the river from Monsieur de Sorel's estate; this is now Berthierville. The plans for the defence of the Richelieu River included another strategic outpost, Fort Saint-Louis; Talon granted this fort, with land on either side of the river, one league deep and six leagues running alongside the river, to Monsieur de Chambly, captain of the troops. The town of Chambly originated on this estate.

Much land had already been granted on the left bank of the St. Lawrence River, between Montreal Island and Lake Saint-Pierre, including the Seigneuries of Lachenaie, Repentigny, and Saint-Sulpice. Talon reinforced the settlements on this shore by granting to the Sieur de la Valtrie, a company lieutenant, an estate with one and a half leagues of frontage and with the same depth. This seigneury adjoined that of Saint-Sulpice and was but a few leagues upstream from Monsieur de Berthier's estate. Today, towns and villages located on these estates perpetuate the names of the legatees.

Familiar names may also be found among the towns and villages on the right bank, all dating back to Talon's early distribution of seigneuries. The Sieur de Contrecoeur, a captain from the Carignan Regiment, received an estate two leagues wide by two leagues deep; his ensign, the Sieur de Verchères, was granted an estate one league wide and of equal depth. Monsieur de Varennes, a retired lieutenant from a company of the king's troops, received an estate on the riverfront twenty-eight arpents wide and one and a half leagues deep. Pierre Boucher, from whom the name Boucherville comes, received a plot on the riverfront, fourteen arpents wide and two leagues deep. Engineer de Catalogne remarked about this domain that the "estate, with all its dependences, is among the most beautiful and most even in Canada; its inhabitants are amongst the most affluent in the system."[14] Charles Le Moyne's numerous services to the colony earned him all the land not yet granted along the right bank of the river from the previous seigneury to that of the Jesuits (Laprairie de la Magdeleine, granted in 1647). He named his domain Longueuil, a name he borrowed from his native Normandy. The following year (1673) he was granted another important estate, on Lake Saint-Louis, and he named it Chateauguay. Finally, Monsieur Perrot, then governor of Ville-Marie, received the island which still bears his name, and the Sieur de Berthelot was granted Ile Jésus.[15]

Both shores of the St. Lawrence, from Montreal to Lake Saint-Pierre, and those of the Richelieu were distributed into fiefs which Intendant Talon granted during October and November 1672 to soldiers "with the obligation to settle there themselves, to cultivate the land, and attract colonists, especially discharged soldiers whom they had previously had under their command."[16] There is little doubt as to the intention of the systematic occupation of the land and to quote Faillon: "fortifying the land against the Iroquois was one of the king's aims in granting land; the fiefs which he granted his officers were therefore almost all located near the island of Montreal and on the shores of the rivers used by the barbarians: the Richelieu River and the St. Lawrence River, from Lake Saint-Pierre onwards." Faillon adds that "they settled with a number of their soldiers who became farmers and they [the officers] formed the nucleus from which various towns grew, which, with Ville-Marie, became the highway of the French colony."[17]

This policy of national defence through occupation of the land is of great importance. It marked the onset of the structuration of the great Montreal Plain and was to determine the orientation of its future development.

Redoubts and fortifications were being built on the seigneuries and offered safe refuge against attack by the natives; during troubled times their proximity encouraged settlement by the colonists. They were often erected near the seigneurial domains. The first chapels and churches, and sometimes town mills, were built near the fortifications. Boucherville erected its first wooden redoubt in 1668 and its first church in 1670. A wooden fort was constructed near Laprairie in 1670 and a chapel around 1687. Varenne's first church was built in 1692 and a wooden fort in the next year. In Contrecoeur the seigneurial house itself was used as a chapel until 1711; in Sorel the Richelieu fort of 1665 became a refuge, and the first church was built in 1708. In Chambly the chapel was incorporated into the fort when it was rebuilt in 1710.[18] Longueuil provides a most interesting example; from 1685 to 1690 Charles Le Moyne, the second seigneur and first baron of Longueuil, had a remarkable stone fort built for himself and for the protection of his numerous settlers. The castle with its built-in church was located near the southwest corner of today's Saint Charles Street and Chambly Road. It was two storeys high, with four turrets, and was at least 210 feet (French measure) wide by 170 feet deep. It burned down in 1792 and was demolished in 1810. The Sieur Le Moyne also had a flour mill and a brewery built near his fort, both of good stonework.[19]

The fort or the redoubt, the seigneurial manoir, the church, and the mills constituted the first nucleus of community life in the seigneuries. In time, and despite the difficulties of colonization and the lack of interest shown by the settlers for clustered dwellings, several of these centres grew into larger settlements. Towards the end of French rule, Laprairie, Boucherville, and Verchères, as if predestined by their very location, grew into villages with several hundred inhabitants and served as parishes and trading centres for goods and services. The census of 1723 lists for Boucherville five bakeries, one general store, one wheat store, four grain storehouses, and one smith shop.[20] Around the same period (1760), Longueuil and Chambly, whose sites had also been chosen by the seigneurs for development as villages, were only hamlets with fewer dwellings and inhabitants and offering fewer services than the villages. This was not the end of the story, however. Indeed, in the early 1830s, according to Joseph Bouchette's *Topographical Dictionary of the Province of Lower Canada*, Longueuil and Chambly became larger villages: Longueuil with sixty-five houses, two schools, and a splendid church; Chambly with almost one hundred houses and a "collège" with some seventh-five students.[21] With its magnificent fort, built between 1709 and 1711 by the chief engineer of New France, Josué Boisberthelot de Beaucourt, Chambly was among the villages which best exemplified the genesis of such a centre. According to Bouchette, other groupings such as Berthier grew, or were still growing, into villages.

Roads soon linked the seigneuries, villages, and hamlets. At the beginning, the location of routes was dictated by military objectives; as early as 1665, a road was built by the soldiers between Fort Sainte-Thérèse and Fort Saint-Louis (Chambly) and later another one was built between the latter and Montreal. The following year, on the Richelieu River, the army built the fort of Saint-Jean (today's town of Saint-Jean), which would eventually be linked to Montreal. The purpose of such land communications was evident and the engineer de Catalogne confirms this fact when he regrets that the Baron de Longueuil failed to complete a road four and a half leagues long between his seigneuries and Chambly, "in spite of the necessity to complete it in order to be able to come quickly to the rescue of Chambly in case of attack, whereas presently help must come after thirty-six leagues of voyage on water."[22] Soon, however, military objectives yielded to considerations of trade and convenience. Sorel and Laprairie were linked by a road joining the intermediate settlements all along the St. Lawrence River. Sorel and Chambly were joined by a route on the left bank of the Richelieu River, with a side-road going to Contrecoeur. Chambly furthermore was located on the main route between Montreal and the United States, a fact which "occasions a good deal of activity," to quote Joseph Bouchette.[23] On the left bank of the St. Lawrence River, Berthier, located between Montreal and Trois-Rivières, enjoyed the same privileged position as Chambly: indeed the stagecoach run passed through the town.[24] From 1735 onwards the road between Montreal and Quebec was fit for carriages; Voyer Lanouiller boasted that he travelled the distance in four days by coach.[25]

"Linear villages" progressively appeared along the roadways and especially along the river. Buildings were close to each other but not adjacent, and settlements dotted the road for several miles, sometimes reaching beyond the limits of their respective seigneuries. Thus, for instance, before the end of French rule, the Seigneuries of L'Assomption and Saint-Sulpice and of Terrebonne and Lachenaie were already linked by a ribbon of buildings; today, they still typify the landscape along the shores of the St. Lawrence River.

Names like Sorel, Berthier, Chambly, Contrecoeur, Lavaltrie, Repentigny, Verchères, Varennes, Boucherville, Longueuil, Laprairie, Châteauguay are still familiar today. They are villages, municipalities, and towns that dot the Montreal Plain, and through their participation in the economic life of the metropolis they constitute its zone of regional influence. These settlements, as well as others such as Saint-Jean, Iberville, Beloeil, Beauharnois, Valleyfield, Sainte-Thérèse, Saint-Jérôme which grew from later concessions, have become urban satellites of the large city. Thus, from the early cores of social organization and community life in the seigneuries, urban centres grew with two, five, ten, twenty, or thirty thousand inhabitants. They were linked by a road network laid out like a spider web, the material result of complex trade patterns originating in Montreal.

One may well wonder about the character of the Montreal Plain today had the seigneurial system not existed and the need to defend the country not arisen. Some urban centres like Sorel, Chambly, and Longueuil probably would have developed on, or almost on, the same location. Indeed, the seigneurial system was not a political institution but a purely economic system, able to fulfil its role inasmuch as it rested on sound geographical reality. The policy of Intendant Talon consisted in populating the nerve centres of the great natural routes of communication. It was therefore normal that the more important agglomerations should grow from some of these concessions; such urban centres probably would have appeared one way or another.

The significance of Talon's "military" plan for the development of the territorial system of Montreal lies in the fact that it shaped this formation from the start and presided over the settlement of the plain. During the French regime, colonists who were attracted by land concessions settled first along the natural routes of communication on both shores of the St. Lawrence, on part of the shores of the Ottawa River, and in the Richelieu Valley. Later on, the settlements expanded and gained in strength, while at the same time British and Loyalist immigration boosted the populations taking root on the plain between the rivers.[26]

Today's rural and urban landscapes are the permanent heritage of the regime of territorial organization and land distribution. For reasons of defence as well as of communication via the rivers, the seigneuries were on the whole narrow and deep, laid out perpendicular to the rivers. Along the St. Lawrence and Richelieu (up to Saint-Jean d'Iberville), the seigneuries were trapezoidal and oriented from the northwest to the southeast. Inside the seigneuries, land was leased to the colonists. In most, the concessions resembled long narrow rectangles, running parallel to the lateral limits of the seigneury, with measurements forming a ratio of 1 : 10. This pattern is not an exclusive feature of the seigneurial system of the St. Lawrence River. It is also found in the French settlements of Illinois and Louisiana and even in some localities of New England. Its origin probably dates back to the European Middle Ages, and, according to Professor Max Derruau, the pattern which the settlers of New France followed may be traced to the medieval system of clearing the land into "streets": the region of France known as "Le Perche" displays such patterns.[27] Whatever its origin, subdividing the land into long, narrow strips perpendicular to the rivers was particularly suitable for the St. Lawrence and Richelieu Valleys. As the St. Lawrence River was the most important communications route of the colony, this mode of distribution allowed for the spacing out of several farms along the river and its affluents. When the shores were fully settled, the same method of subdivision prevailed when parcels of land were granted along the roads. They formed units of population and basic agricultural structures called "rangs" or strip farms. Such long strips of land allowed the farmers to enjoy privacy on their land while they remained close to their neighbours, an important feature in a vast, sparsely populated country with a rigorous climate. Thus, for instance, in order to keep the roads open during the long winter months a farmer had only to keep his section of the road clear of snow over a distance equal to the width of his land.[28]

The rural landscape of the Montreal Plain has retained the same appearance to this day, with hundreds of narrow parallel strips of land. Their boundaries are often marked by hedges, parallel rows of trees, and thickets; the repetition of this strict geometry is typical and of some interest. In time, this mode of subdivision would result in the development of linear villages, still characteristic of the plain; it was also to constitute the framework within which the massive development of housing would take place during urban growth in the twentieth century. The features of urban development on Montreal Island attest to this fact, as we turn our attention to the first settlement of the island.

The Villages on the Island

Montreal Island was the key to the waterways and could not be left out of the overall plan for the defence of the colony. Granted as a seigneury in 1663 to the Gentlemen of Saint-Sulpice Seminary in Paris, the island was one of the largest (some 58 kilometres long and 11 kilometres wide) as well as one of the most beautiful concessions in New France. Fort Ville-Marie had been built on the shore of the island where the Saint-Pierre River flowed into the St. Lawrence River. It was the first European establishment and the embryo of to-day's metropolis.

To protect this advanced post of European civilization in America against attacks by the natives, the seigneurs of the island decided in 1671 to create noble fiefs in certain parts of their huge domain. These remote plots were like small seigneuries within the larger one, and the owners were under obligation to build fortified residences, to live there, and to attract colonists. The immediate goal was obviously to occupy vulnerable and strategic spots on the island in order to defend it.[29]

One such vulnerable spot was the lower island, at the confluence of the St. Lawrence and the Rivière-des-Prairies. The Sieur Picoté de Belestre was granted the concession on 28 July. A wooden fort was built at Pointe-aux-Trembles as early as 1675,[30] a windmill followed in 1677,[31] and in 1678 a church opened its doors: the first outside Montreal itself.[32] To better fortify the tip of the island on the side of Rivière-des-Prairies and to block the entrance to the Assomption River, two adjacent fiefs were created on 7 December 1671 by Dollier de Casson, who, as director of the Seminary of Saint-Sulpice of Montreal, was then seigneur of the island. These domains measured two hundred arpents each and were granted to Carion du Fresnoy and Paul de Morel, both military men. Early in 1672 other smaller concessions were granted to reinforce the two fiefs. A wooden redoubt and a windmill were built in 1688 on territory now known as Rivière-des-Prairies, and parish registers appeared around the same date.[33] In 1671 Monsieur Zacharie du Puy, then major of Montreal Island, had been granted a noble fief of some 320 arpents near Sault Saint-Louis; it was called Verdun, a name which remains with the municipality to this day. A wooden fort appears to have been built there in 1662.[34]

The creation of these fiefs, including that of Lachine, which had existed since 1667, enabled the eastern tip of the island as well as the approaches to Sault Saint-Louis to take care of its own defence. The other end of the island, Bout-de-l'Isle, projecting into Lake Saint-Louis and into the Lake of Two Mountains, was still to be protected.

Demand for land on Bout-de-l'Isle was strong, as it was the landing place for the natives who came down the Ottawa River to trade furs. Dollier de Casson took advantage of this trend and created four noble fiefs on Bout-de-l'Isle. The first measured 200 arpents and was located on the shores of the Lake of Two Mountains and was granted to the Sieur de Boisbriant, a captain in the Carignan Regiment. Later on, as it changed hands, this fief was called Senneville, a name which has been retained to this day. A stone fort was built there in 1692. An adjacent parcel was granted on 12 April 1672 to Charles d'Ailleboust des Musseaux. On 30 July of the same year, Dollier granted a plot of 400 arpents in the same neighbourhood to the two de Bertet brothers. They called it Belle-Vue; a wooden redoubt was built in 1683 and a chapel in 1686. Finally, Claude Robutel de Saint-André inherited the fourth fief of about two hundred arpents, adjacent to the previous one. The historian Faillon confirmed that "by creating these fiefs and by handing them over to the military, the seigneurs of Montreal did their best to protect the colonists and to enable the island to defend itself."[35]

1671 and 1672 are important years in the genesis of the structure of today's metropolis. The establishment of noble fiefs along the left bank of the St. Lawrence, from Pointe-aux-Trembles to Bout-de-l'Isle, did not by itself determine the growth of human agglomerations along this axis, the shores of the large waterway being a natural location for settlement. Nevertheless, it did make such developments possible by creating a system of defence and refuge for the local inhabitants. A good indication of the evolution of settlements is the creation of parishes, which depended on the community to support the expenses of the services. The first parishes established on the island, besides the town's own (1642), were L'Enfant-Jésus in Pointe-aux-Trembles (1674), Les Saints-Anges in Lachine (1676), Saint-Joseph in Rivières-des-Prairies (1687), and Sainte-Anne at Bout-de-l'Isle (1703). Others would appear later; Saint-Joachim in Pointe-Claire in 1713, Saint-Laurent in 1720, Saint-François d'Assise in Longue-Pointe in 1722, La Visitation in Sault-au-Récollet in 1736, and finally Sainte-Geneviève in 1741[36] (plate 2).

There seems to be a direct link between the foundation of the first parishes on the island and the settlement of the land which the fiefs and forts made possible. With the exception of the parish of Saint-Laurent, the first chapels and churches were built close to the fortifications. Pointe-aux-Trembles is typical, as one may gather from reading the census of 1731 on the seigneury of Montreal Island: "above the church and adjacent to it, the fort is built on a lot measuring one hundred fathoms by ninety fathoms. It stands at Pointe-aux-Trembles, enclosed with stakes, flanked, and bastioned, and contains the church of l'Enfant Jésus, built of stonework."[37]

Villages grew on the island from the smaller embryonic communities just as they had formed elsewhere on the Montreal Plain. Thus for instance, according to the "Aveu et dénombrement" of 1731, part of the land of the fort of Pointe-aux-Trembles was subdivided "into lots distributed into streets in the form of a town"; at Rivière-des-Prairies, "a village had been built, measuring one arpent and belonging to the said seigneurs."[38] At the end of the French regime, the territory of Pointe-aux-Trembles did in fact contain a compact village, with the same name, which served as a parish and administrative centre for the inhabitants of that end of the island.[39] Gédéon de Catalogne adds that the inhabitants were very industrious and well-off.[40] At the opposite end, Pointe-Claire was a hamlet and not so large as the aforementioned settlement, but the parish nevertheless served 800 worshippers (1765).[41] Other settlements on the island would probably have reached the status of village or hamlet had they not been destroyed or their development not been hampered by natives. Indeed, with reference to the Parish of Lachine. Catalogne points out in his "Mémoire sur les plans des seigneuries et habitations des gouvernements de Québec, les Trois-Rivières, et de Montréal" that "the inhabitants used to grow rich from their trade with the natives who disembarked there when they came to Montreal. But since the destruction wreaked there in 1689, by the Iroquois, who burned the houses and took most of the inhabitants as prisoners, the parish has regressed in every manner."[42] And about the Parish of Rivière-des-Prairies, he writes: "because the Iroquois killed most of the inhabitants, the growth of the settlement was retarded."[43]

However, better days were ahead. Joseph Bouchette in 1815 tells us that "La Chine is a place of greater importance than any other village on the island, being the centre of all the commerce between the upper and lower provinces, and the north-west country also." He states that the village of Pointe-Claire "contains from ninety to one hundred houses, built with regularity, and forming small streets that cross the main road at right angles."[44] In his *Topographical Dictionary*, published sixteen years later, Bouchette described Saint-Laurent, Sainte-Geneviève, Sault-au-Récollet, and Rivière-des-Prairies as well established and organized parishes and villages.[45]

The creation of fortified fiefs gave rise to the construction of the island's first road network. To make the various fortifications of the defence system as quickly accessible as possible, they were linked to one another all along the shores by a network of trails and paths starting at Fort Senneville and going through Sainte-Anne, Pointe-Claire, Roland, Saint-Rémi, Lachine, Ville-Marie, Longue-Pointe, and Pointe-aux-Trembles to the redoubts of Rivière-des-Prairies. Thus originated the route around the island. This continuous road probably became the "chemin du roy" for the riparian "côtes" such as Saint-Martin, Saint-François, Sainte-Anne, and Saint-Jean stretching from Ville-Marie to Pointe-aux-Trembles.

In time, this first road network would be reinforced and extended as some of the fortifications evolved into villages and parish centres. An analysis of historical maps and of Beaugrand and Morin's reconstitutions[46] tends to reveal that, before the end of the French regime, the rimroad was completed on the side of Rivière-des-Prairies, and that the town of Montreal was directly connected to Lachine, Saint-Laurent, and Sault-au-Récollet. The latter roads subsequently be-

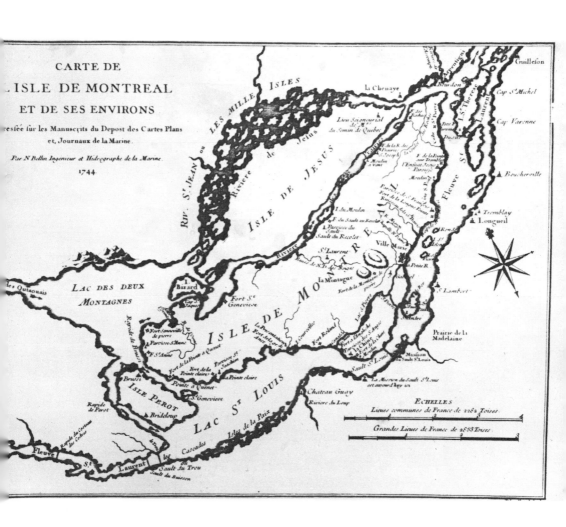

2. *Map of the island of Montreal and surrounding region, by N. Bellin, 1744*

came St. James Street, Saint-Joseph Boulevard (Montreal–Lachine), Guy Street, and Côte-des-Neiges Road (Montreal–Saint-Laurent), and probably St. Lawrence Boulevard (Montreal–Sault-au-Récollet). Likewise, paths or roads crossed the island from Pointe-Claire to Sainte-Geneviève, and from Pointe-aux-Trembles to Saint-Joseph of Rivière-des-Prairies.

Thus, from the outset, both on the island and in the great plain of Montreal, a particular set of contingencies during colonization determined the manner in which the island was to be settled and presided over the territory's first configuration. Such frameworks would have long-range effects on urban development, but for the time being we will briefly turn our attention to the study of the "côtes" of the island.

The "Côtes" of the Island

The "côte" played an important part in the development of the urban environment and the townscape of Montreal, as well as in the genesis of the orthogonal grid of streets. Few researchers have been interested in this reality, and the original significance of the "côte" seems almost lost today. It is all too often connected to paths or roads; Côte-des-Neiges and Côte Sainte-Catherine Roads are noticeable for their steep gradients and the word "côte" is presumed to be synonymous with "slope": this is confirmed by both the Larousse dictionary and the Robert dictionary. Yet the "côte" in Montreal and in Quebec has nothing to do with gradients. Indeed, regions as flat and even as Côte-de-Liesse and Côte-Vertu were originally called "côte" as were Côte Sainte-Catherine and Côte-des-Neiges. The "côte" is essentially a definite organic unit of territory and is perhaps synonymous with "neighbourhood," to quote Arthur Lower.[47]

On the island of Montreal as well as elsewhere in New France, the côte designated the rows of farmland drawn perpendicularly, or almost so, to the river shores. When the banks were settled, a second row, or côte, was created and was linked with the first one by a road called a "montée." A third, a fourth, a fifth row of farmland followed in the same manner. In time, the word côte was replaced by the word "rang," or range. The côte, or range, is thus an alignment of farmland settled by colonists living side by side on narrow but long individual strips, facing a road or a river, or both. The côte, or range, constituted in fact the basic territorial unit responsible for social cohesion. Its spatial delineation tended to arouse the colonist's feeling of identification with a definite territory and of belonging to a specific human community.[48]

On the island of Montreal these characteristics seemed even more remarkable than elsewhere. In other seigneuries, côtes were created according to a continuous process of land occupation, starting at the river and progressing inward. In the huge seigneury of Montreal, several côtes were first created here and there as autonomous entities to improve the most appropriate regions. The côte was best suited for this purpose. Indeed, its predetermined area allowed for accidents of natural topography, such as in sectors adjacent to Mount Royal. Moreover, it fostered the social cohesion required for the improvement and defence of an individually and collectively identifiable heritage.

A splendid "terrier" (land register) dated 15 October 1702 is, according to Trudel,[49] the only cartographical document yielding statistics on the population of the seigneuries on the island of Montreal at the beginning of the eighteenth century. It bears the lovely title of *Description générale de l'isle de Montréal Divisée par costes où sont Exactement marquées toutes les distances de place en place, les noms de chaque habitant, la quantité de terre qu'ils possèdent tant de front que de profondeur, les forts, Eglises et Moulins, le tout de suitte avec le Meilleur Ordre que l'on a peu*, and gives us a good idea of the spirit which presided over the creation of the côtes on the island, and describes their features. The first ones were located on the shores of the St. Lawrence River and the Rivière-des-Prairies, where concessions were divided into long, narrow strips perpendicular to the river. The same holds true for those located between Ville-Marie and Pointe-aux-Trembles: Côte Saint-Martin, Côte Saint-François, Côte Sainte-Anne, Côte Saint-Jean, as well as Côte Saint-Dominique on the Rivière-des-Prairies side. The concept of côte did not apply solely to the banks of the river: from the map of 1702, we learn that several types were created inside the seigneuries, the first being very much like those on the shore. Côte Saint-Pierre and Côte Saint-Paul were located on either side of Lake Saint-Pierre (where the Lachine canal was to be built), whereas the strips of land of Côte Saint-Joseph and Côte Sainte-Catherine were located perpendicularly to a road (plate 3).

The second kind and most typical côte in the Montreal area is the "côte double," consisting of two rows of farmland located on either side of a central common. The common was shared by the community of colonists, normally for cattle grazing, and a public road, usually called "chemin du roy" (king's way), ran through it. This kind of côte is indicated in a very descriptive manner on the 1702 map. Côte Notre-Dame-des-Neiges, Côte Notre-Dame-des-Vertus, Côte Saint-Laurent, and Côte Saint-Michel were of that type. The "Aveu et dénombrement" of 1731 gives an almost identical description for each

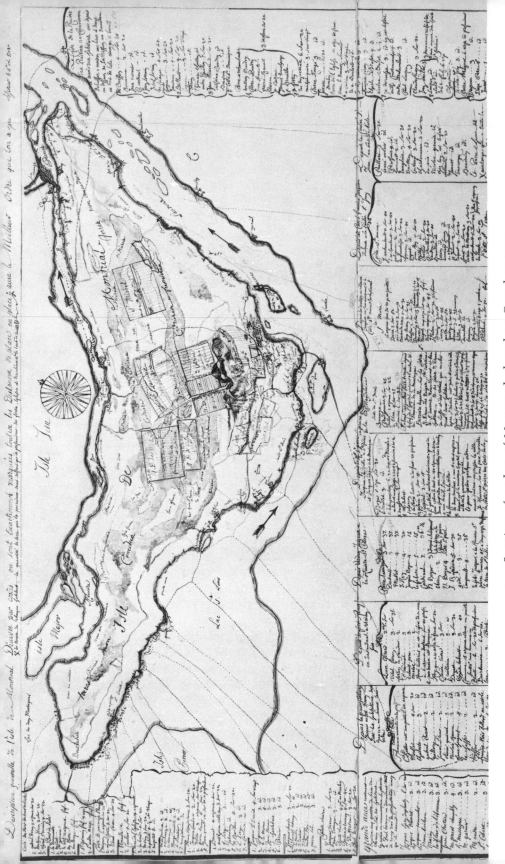

3. *Section of a plan of Montreal, dated 15 October 1702*

of these "côtes doubles." The following, for example, is a description of Côte Saint-Michel: "That in the area of the said Côte Saint-Michel, divided into two ranges of inhabitants by a common two arpents wide, in the middle of which there is a king's way, running from the northeast to southwest."[50]

Côte Notre-Dame-des-Neiges, Côte Notre-Dame-des-Vertus, Côte Saint-Laurent, and Côte Saint-Michel were at that time homogeneous, autonomous territorial areas which were not contiguous. Thus, for instance, Côte Saint-Laurent and Côte Saint-Michel were separated by wide strips of land which had not yet been granted, tending to confirm that the côte constituted a self-sufficient predetermined territorial unit and seemed to have been an important element within the island's defence system. Indeed, this "terrier" dates back to about one year after signing (in 1701) the great peace pact with the natives, implying that most of the côtes depicted on the register must have been created before the end of the hostilities.

The côte thus appeared as the most elementary and most homogeneous unit of the territorial system of Montreal; it constituted the basis of territorial organization of the human community, whereas the parish, which usually encompassed several côtes, formed the basic unit of civil and social organization, as is obvious from Gédéon de Catalogne's "Mémoire" (1712). He reports that the seigneury of Montreal "is subdivided into six parishes: Montreal, Lachine, Haut de l'Isle, the Pointe au Tremble, the Rivière des Prairies and the Mission du Sault au Récollet."[51] In his description of the Parish of Montreal, he noted that to the latter "belong the inhabitants of the côtes from Verdun to Longue-Pointe, as well as from half of Côtes St-Pierre and St-Paul, the Côtes de Notre-Dame-des-Neiges, de Liesse, des Vertues, St-Laurent, Ste-Catherine and St Michel and la Visitation."[52] He also mentioned the "parish of Pointe au Tremble to which côte St-Lionnard belongs."[53]

It would take too long to retrace the genesis of each one of the côtes which eventually covered the whole of the island, as may be gathered from a map drawn in 1834 by Jobin.[54] (See plate 4.) The example of Côte Notre-Dame-des-Neiges, located in the heart of the island, is a good illustration of a strong neighbourhood unit and an inland "côte double." It is also one of the oldest on the island.

We owe the creation of Côte Notre-Dame-des-Neiges to Dollier de Casson. He played an important part in the early development of the island, and in the course of the following chapters we shall have more opportunity to learn about the man and his work. The site chosen for the establishment of this côte was a succession of beautiful terraces on the northwest side of Mount Royal amidst which a creek flowed from its source in the mountain to the Rivière-des-Prairies. The site was beautiful and rich in resources. The soil was ideal for growing vegetables and the ground yielded good building stones. The fast waters of the creek could be used to activate saw-mills and flourmills. Various kinds of trees grew in abundance in the area among which cedar and ash in particular could provide small industries with raw materials.

In the spring of 1698 Catalogne, the king's engineer, was asked by de Casson to subdivide this area into concessions for the colonists. Catalogne chose the creek as the dividing line for the "côte double," created a common on this axis, and drew the outline for a byway. The "Aveu et dénombrement" of 1731 informs us that the common was two arpents wide and that the king's way ran in the middle of it from southeast to northwest.[55] He then subdivided the land into strips perpendicular to the creek and the common (see figure 5); the plots had an area of forty arpents, with two arpents of frontage on the common and a depth of twenty arpents. The same 1 : 10 ratio, alluded to before, prevailed here as in other concessions and with the same advantages: shared use of the equipment and a close community life. Thus, Côte Notre-Dame-des-Neiges was established as a definite territorial unit of thirty-seven separate strips of land with predetermined boundaries. The colonist who was granted such a plot of land undertook to build a permanent dwelling on it as soon as possible, to maintain the stretch of the common road fronting on his lot, and to have his wheat ground at the common mill.[56]

Côte Notre-Dame-des-Neiges is an apt example, for it shows how the côte constituted an organic unit, capable of adaptation to the natural contours of topography, while remaining both homogeneous and autonomous. The concessions on Montreal Island usually lay from the southeast to the northwest, as they were located either on the shores or perpendicular to roads running roughly parallel to the rivers.[57] On Côte Notre-Dame-des-Neiges, however, the concessions ran in the opposite direction, or southwest to northeast, this alignment being determined by the creek which irrigated the terraces of that territory. Another fact that comes to light from an analysis of Côte Notre-Dame-des-Neiges reveals the social cohesion among residents who belonged to an identifiable territory (see figure 5). For over one hundred years a large number of its inhabitants had been tanners and curriers, and leather dressing was the côte's main industry. Until the end of the nineteenth century, Côte Notre-Dame-des-Neiges was often called "le village des tanneurs." According to Jacques Godbout, in spite of a complete change of its function in today's society, "Côte-des-Neiges is one of Montreal's few districts still retaining a life of its own, which is easily identifiable."[58]

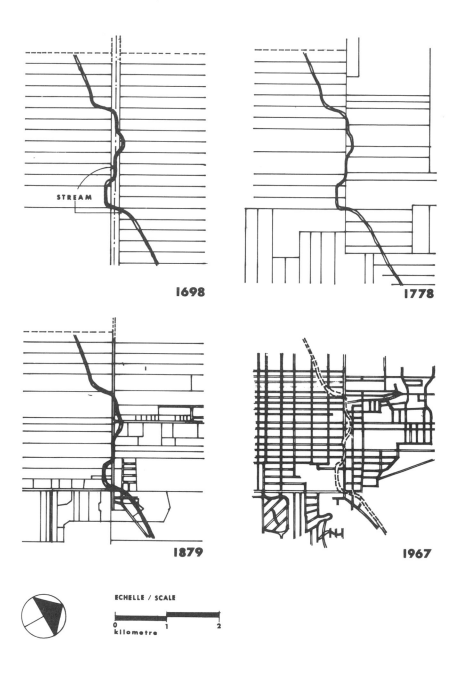

1698

1778

1879

1967

ECHELLE / SCALE

0   1   2
kilometre

Fig. 5   Evolution of Côte Notre-Dame-des-Neiges

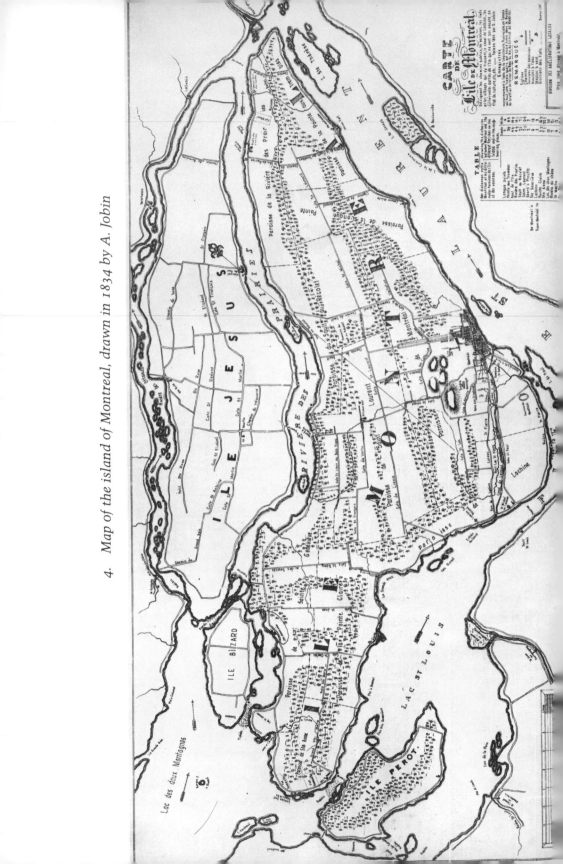

4. *Map of the island of Montreal, drawn in 1834 by A. Jobin*

The Influence of Rural Structures

From what we have established thus far, the territorial organization of the seigneury of Montreal Island, from the very beginning, seems to have fostered the establishment of two basic types of habitats: clustered dwellings and scattered dwellings. The clustered habitat originated with Ville-Marie and with the embryos of social organization springing up around the fortifications and parish churches. In time, most of these cores would develop into more compact settlements and become the main villages on the island: Longue-Pointe, Pointe-aux-Trembles, Rivière-des-Prairies, Sault-au-Récollet, Sainte-Geneviève, Pointe-Claire, Lachine, and Saint-Laurent. On the other hand, the côte constituted the sole basic model for scattered dwellings in the organization of the rural territory of the island.

As we have seen earlier, land communications were soon established between the villages, trading posts, and parishes and constituted the island's first road network. Towards the end of the eighteenth century, a secondary road system was linking the king's ways with the primary network. The two were well integrated and constituted a balanced and well-organized system of land communications, as may be gathered from an analysis of Jobin's map of 1834 (plate 4). Moreover, today's roads are still largely patterned after this original network.

Thus, the outline of the belt road around the island had changed little since earlier days. Between Pointe-aux-Trembles and Décarie Boulevard, the Metropolitan Boulevard, the first expressway of the metropolis, is superimposed on the old king's way of the interior côtes Saint-Léonard, Saint-Michel, and Saint-Laurent. Between Boulevard Décarie and Bout-de-l'Isle, the Trans-Canada Highway (an extension of the Metropolitan Expressway) steers away from the old byways of Côte Notre-Dame-de-Vertu and Saint-François, but further west it veers closer to the old king's way of Petite and Grande Côte Sainte-Marie. As for the Côte de Liesse Expressway, it follows exactly the path of the old king's way of the côte.

The origin of several arteries crossing the island could be traced in this manner. They date back to the old king's ways of specific côtes or to connecting roads or montées linking the various côtes together or to the rimroads. A few examples should suffice: Côte-des-Neiges Road is one, and Côte Vertu is another. In the east end, the Rivière-des-Prairies Boulevard and Broadway Avenue were built on top of two old roads that linked Côte Saint-Léonard to the villages of Rivière-des-Prairies and Pointe-aux-Trembles. Likewise, the origin of Boulevard Saint-Michel dates back to a connecting road between Côte de la Visitation (today's Rosemont section) and Côte Saint-

Michel, which also joined these territories to the belt road somewhere near Sault-au-Récollet. On the west side of the island there
are three successive montées: des Sources, Saint-Jean, and Saint-
Charles. These roads run across the island and correspond exactly
to three distinct côtes: Côtes des Sources, Saint-Jean, and Saint-
Charles. Together with Côte Notre-Dame-des-Neiges, these were
the only côtes on the island whose concessions were oriented in a
direction opposite to that of the other terrains of the seigneury, probably because of some features of local topography. This explains the
orientation of the present montées.

The balance between clustered and scattered dwellings on the island seems to reflect the remarkable organization of the system; the
côte constituted the basic unit of territorial organization, the parish
represented the core of social and civil structure, and both operated
within the seigneurial framework.[59] Yet, this human ecosystem was
to prove vulnerable to the economic and technological revolution of
the nineteenth century. The advent of telegraph, steam navigation,
and railways would polarize economic activities in Montreal and determine the pace of the city's industrialization; it heralded the onset
of the modern process of migration to the city: the ancient equilibrium soon broke down. Indeed, from the second half of the nineteenth century onward the city of Montreal no longer appeared as a
relatively stable urban entity linked with others and standing out
against a background of rural scenery, but projected the image of a
dense agglomeration of people in search of employment in budding
industries, a city at the centre of frenzied, unplanned development.

Today the old villages on the island, originally created as autonomous and identifiable entities, with residents who enjoyed the feeling of belonging to distinctive human communities, are slowly
being swallowed by the urban tide. Lachine, Longue-Pointe, and
Pointe-aux-Trembles were located on the very axis of a growing
heavy industry and were quickly absorbed. In other villages, such as
Saint-Laurent, Sault-au-Récollet, and Pointe-Claire, remnants of
some older structures and of a somewhat tighter pattern of habitation are reminiscent of their origin. Thus far, only Rivière-des-
Prairies, Sainte-Geneviève, and Sainte-Anne have managed, to some
extent, to escape the levelling action of the metropolitan magma
and to retain a certain character.

When they were created, the côtes gave their inhabitants a feeling
of belonging to a distinct community and territorial unit. Yet, they
were to suffer a comparable demise, with important consequences
for the city. Indeed, this rural configuration of the territory is at the
origin of our orthogonal grid of streets. At a time of rapid and uncon-

trolled urban growth, vested interests unavoidably perpetuated the old subdivision of land in the street patterns. Demographic as well as economic pressures forced the partition of the individual parcels of land of the côtes into building lots; to preserve acquired rights, streets were laid out to follow rigorously the original boundaries between the strips of land. A simple superimposition of a contemporary map of Montreal on one of the island dating back to 1830 or 1850, and showing the côtes with their individual parcels, would prove this assertion. The typical street patterns of Greater Montreal follow closely the grids of subdivision of the land into concessions from the original côtes, except for certain specifically planned urban developments, such as the Town of Mount Royal, Cité de Saint-Léonard, and Hampstead.

It is important to realize that the simple geometrical lines of a côte, based on straight lines and right angles, were well suited for urban structures. To quote the urbanist Hans Blumenfield: "The right angle and the straight line, convenient for the division of land, are equally convenient for the erection of buildings, for the laying of pipes and rail, and for the regulation of traffic lights . . . simple geometric forms have justified themselves as a permanent framework for varying functions." [60] Thus the côte, which used to have a stabilizing influence on the rural landscape, was to become a powerful factor of uniformity in urban development. The old populous districts of Montreal owe their strong gregarious and egalitarian character to the perpetuation of the structures of the côte. Its influence would even be felt in the shaping and spacing of green spaces. Except for Mount Royal and de Maisonneuve Parks, there are no large public parks in Montreal, but there is a proliferation of smaller green spaces, most of them square or rectangular in shape and traced over the same typical street pattern. Originally, most of Montreal's territory had been subdivided into individual parcels of similar shape, and occasionally some of these concessions have been handed down to us as undeveloped green spaces.

Another heritage from the rural côte to the urban domain is the "block": an identifiable urban area, it is a definite homogeneous and monolithic mass. Blocks are typical of Montreal and usually correspond to the territories or parts thereof from the old côtes. Thus, for instance, Côte-des-Neiges constitutes an identifiable block if only because the orientation of its streets does not follow the general orientation of the orthogonal pattern of the metropolis, but rather the alignment dictated by the old subdivision of the côte. Finally, to the rural côte, despite its geometrical rigour, we owe the few irregularly traced arteries of today. Such winding roads usually correspond to the old king's ways of individual côtes, routes which followed the contours of natural topography. Good examples are Côte Sainte-Catherine Road and rue des Carrières; the latter corresponds in part to the byway of the old Côte-de-la-Visitation. This pattern is also shown by Côte Saint-Antoine and Côte Saint-Luc Roads, and by St. James Street which leads to Lachine and which traces its origin to the king's way of the very ancient Côte Saint-Pierre. From this brief analysis, it appears that both the regularity and irregularity of the typical grid of streets which developed from the second half of the nineteenth century onward find their origin in the perpetuation of the old structures of the island's rural côtes. (See plates 5 and 6.)

Thus, the claim that Montreal is a typically American city because of the regularity and uniformity of the orthogonal grid of streets is both correct and incorrect. The claim is incorrect if by American-type grid of street is meant a rigorously geometrical pattern like the one imposed in New York City by the city commissioners in 1811, or in San Francisco, or in several other cities. Indeed, in Montreal the development of the grid was never the result of an imposed will or conscious planning. It was brought about by the power of vested interests and the speed of urban development. The claim is correct if one acknowledges that the grid issued directly from the rural structures of the côte and that the latter constituted an organic element which was perfectly suited to the conditions of settlement in what was a "new" environment for the settlers of the St. Lawrence Valley and Montreal Island. How this grid of streets, inherited from the structures of the rural world, fulfilled its role as a framework for urban development will be analysed in the chapter on Victorian Montreal. We now return to Place Royale, in Fort Ville-Marie, to witness the progress and development of the city during the first centuries.

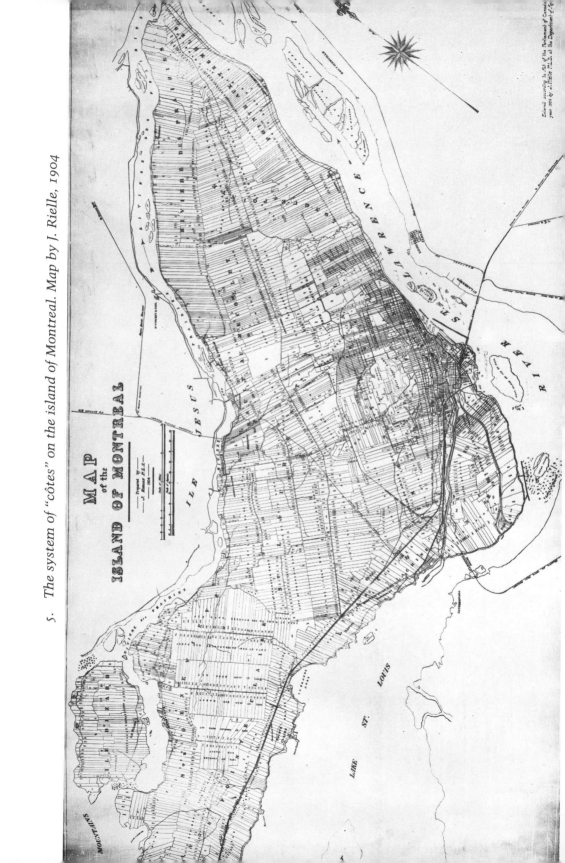

5. The system of "côtes" on the island of Montreal. Map by J. Rielle, 1904

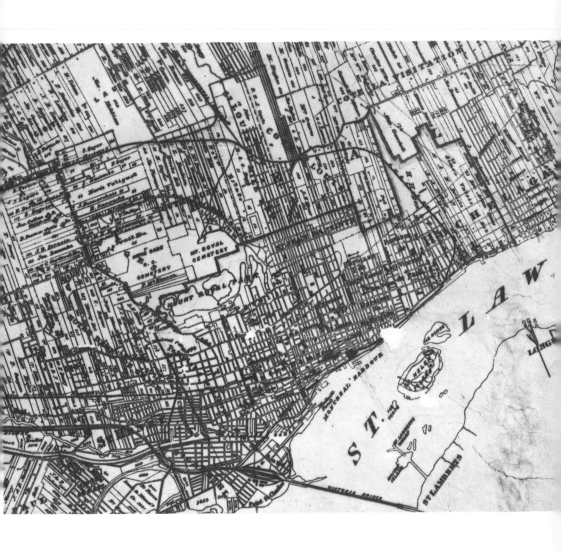

6.   *Relationship between the system of "côtes" and the orthogonal grid of streets of Montreal. Map by J. Rielle, 1890*

Part II

THE FRONTIER TOWN: 1642–1840

La Ville de Montréal a un aspect fort riant; elle est bien située, bien percée, & bien bâtie. L'agrément de ses environs & de ses vûës inspirent une certaine gayeté, dont tout le Monde se ressent. . . .

Montréal est un quarré long, situé sur le bord du Fleuve, lequel s'élevant insensiblement, partage la Ville dans sa longueur en Haute & Basse; mais à peine s'aperçoit-on que l'on monte de l'une à l'autre. L'Hôtel-Dieu, les Magasins du Roi & la Place d'Armes, sont dans la Basse Ville; c'est aussi le Quartier de presque tous les Marchands. Le Séminaire & la Paroisse, les Récollets, les Jésuites, les Filles de la Congrégation, le Gouverneur & la plûpart des Officiers sont dans la Haute. Au-delà d'un petit Ruisseau, qui vient du Nord-Ouest, & borne la Ville de ce côté-là, on trouve quelques Maisons, & l'Hôpital Général; & en prenant sur la droite au-delà des Récollets, dont le Couvent est à l'extrémité de la Ville du même côté, il commence à se former une espèce de Faux-bourg, qui avec le tems fera un très-beau Quartier.

PÈRE DE CHARLEVOIX, *à Montréal, ce vintiéme de Mars, 1721*[1]

3

Society During the Old Regime

*Old Quebec is at its best in the cottage, the
manor and the parish church. These were the
work of the people, unassisted by academic architects, and passed entirely unnoticed at the
time of their creation.*
RAMSAY TRAQUAIR[2]

Popular Traditions

From 1667 onward, thanks to its geographic location, Montreal became the main centre of fur trade in the colony, outdistancing Trois-
Rivières and Québec. Every summer a fair was held on the common,
where natives came to trade their furs for European goods. Many
"Montréalistes" found it financially rewarding to act as go-between
for the natives and the king's agents. The small community benefited from this trade and prospered: from 625 inhabitants in 1665,
the population grew to 1,468 in 1698, and to 2,025 in 1706.[3] The old
Fort Ville-Marie was no longer large enough to shelter such a large
number of people. It was not destined to be enlarged, either, for the
low and damp area of Pointe-à-Callières was subjected to seasonal
floods and was too uncomfortable. Besides, times had changed. As
the danger of attacks by natives decreased, and as trade grew in importance, the desire to make good the economic promises of the environment replaced the proselytism of the heroic years. Numerous
colonists had already settled on the Saint-Louis hillside on the other
side of the Saint-Pierre River. One of the locations they chose was

the path leading to the Hôtel-Dieu of Jeanne Mance and to Notre-Dame-de-Bonsecours Chapel, a route that would later become Saint-Paul Street.[4] Thus, some ninety-four dwellings were built between 1650 and 1672 on the high ground of the hillside.[5]

In fact, the Saint-Louis hillside was much better suited for colonization than Pointe-à-Callières. It had steep ridges with a crest 13 to 15 metres above the river, was bounded by the St. Lawrence River and the Saint-Martin River, and was thus naturally protected. It could easily be fenced and fortified, a task which was soon accomplished. A sector of about 40 hectares was free for development, and in those days such an area was considered sufficient for a small town. To make the best of such advantages and to give some direction to the development of the land which had thus far gone uncontrolled, Dollier de Casson, superior of the Seminary of Saint-Sulpice and Seigneur of Montreal Island, traced the first streets of the town on 12 March 1672.[6] This was Montreal's first plan and one of the earliest town-planning documents in the history of Canada; it left a deep imprint on the Montreal of today. Before looking into this plan and to get a clear picture of the first manifestation of architecture which would soon result from it, we should delve more deeply into some of the demographic, social, and cultural characteristics of the colonial society which had settled in New France in the seventeenth century and the beginning of the eighteenth century.

At the end of the French regime, the population of New France was very small, about sixty-five thousand inhabitants.[7] At the same time, the English colonies on the Atlantic coast numbered almost 1.5 million inhabitants. In 1760 there were about 5,000 citizens in the town of Montreal; the population of the entire island was a mere 8,300.[8] It seems like a relatively high density when compared with the whole colony, but it remains a small population. Boston for instance, with but 300 to 400 inhabitants in 1630, numbered 16,000 in 1742;[9] in the same year, Philadelphia, founded in 1682 (some forty years after Montreal), numbered 13,000 residents.[10] There are several possible reasons for Montreal's small population, but their analysis is outside the scope of this study. Let us note, however, that the colonization of America never aroused any national effort on the part of France and more money seems to have been lavished on the king's recreation than on New France.[11]

The following figures speak for themselves: of the 65,000 inhabitants in the colony in 1760, scarcely 10,000 were originally from France, particularly from Normandy and neighbouring provinces, including the Paris region. Not counting the years 1740–60, with a rather high immigration rate (3,565 immigrants from France) reflecting the arrival of His Majesty's soldiers to defend the colony during the fatal Seven Years' War, the slow immigration from France reached a peak during the vigorous administration of Intendant Talon (1665–72). Indeed, from 1640 to 1700, 4,598 French colonists settled in North America; from 1700 to 1740, the number dwindled to 1,667. One may assume that during the period of peace and relative prosperity which followed the Treaty of Utrecht in 1713—an important period for the social and cultural formation of the small colonial society—the population of New France was largely autonomous and increased by natural demographic process. In 1760, almost five-sixths of the population must surely have been native born;[12] this fact constitutes an important element which would be reflected in colonial architecture. In our opinion, the remarkable adaptation of the traditional Quebec house to the local climatic conditions stems from this very fact. More on this topic later.

For the time being, let us briefly survey the social and cultural background of the 10,000 French immigrants who settled in New France. Considering the little interest aroused by Voltaire's "quelques arpents de neige" infested with inhospitable natives, what kind of immigrants thought of settling in Canada? Society in France was then divided into clearly defined social classes, and no privileged noble or wealthy bourgeois or any other rich man would be interested in crossing the ocean. At the time, France was in the midst of industrial organization and specialized labour easily found work and good wages within the kingdom.[13] Those who were tempted to come to America made sure they safeguarded their right to return to France at the end of their contract. That left only the peasant, the poor, and the disfavoured who could at least hope to acquire property or master a trade in New France. There were also adventurers, the unstable, and people in search of freedom, tired of the constraints of old Europe, or people attracted by fast profits in the fur trade.[14] Huguenots would have come if Richelieu had not barred them in 1628 from emigrating to New France.

This is the picture of French immigration to America in the seventeenth and eighteenth centuries: of the 10,000-odd colonists who settled in New France, 3,500 were discharged soldiers, 1,100 were "filles du roi" (king's brides), 1,000 were convicts, about 3,900 were hired under contract, and some 500 were individuals who came at their own expense.[15] From this group, only those who were hired were likely to have a trade; most, according to Jean Hamelin, had no special skills.[16]

This is confirmed by the Swede Peter Kalm who visited Canada in 1749:

Mechanics, such as architecture, cabinet-work, turning, and the like, were not yet so forward here as they ought to be; and the English, in that particular, outdo the French. The chief cause of this is, that scarce any other people than dismissed soldiers come to settle here, who have not had any opportunity of learning a mechanical trade, but have some times accidentally, and through necessity been obliged to it.[17]

This sounds like an objective testimony. Kalm was a well-known scientist who visited America as a member of a scientific expedition and who must have been well disposed towards the French at that time when Sweden's relations with France were very friendly.

Yet, Kalm must have judged "the mechanical arts" according to criteria set by an educated class, that is, as a university scholar aware of new techniques and fashionable tastes. With the British colonies' wider spectrum of social classes, ranging from peasants to servants, from skilled workers to professionals, from bourgeois merchants to aristocrats, it is small wonder that Kalm was more impressed by the achievements of craftsmen from these colonies.

In New France, however, most immigrants came from the peasant and lower classes of the poor western provinces, isolated from the activities and splendours of Versailles. Such a society was not likely to bring to the New World any of the more advanced philosophical thoughts, or any of the more recent arts and techniques of building and town planning. This does not mean that the French colonists were simple, insignificant people. On the contrary, they had inherited a very old ancestral culture, with deep roots in the Middle Ages, rich in customs and habits entrenched in the realities of life, and rich in solutions for the organization of their habitat and their environment. Alan Gowans recounts:

> Though the Middle Ages proper were long since gone, the people who settled early New France had remained essentially medieval in their basic attitudes and outlook on life, and therefore medieval principles of building still seemed self-evidently right to them. The folk architecture of New France not merely looked medieval, it was an integral expression of the medieval tradition in Western architecture.[18]

The medieval character of our traditional popular architecture has been noticed by several commentators, and Gérard Morisset insisted on "the spirit of Romanesque style on the bare walls superficially resembling the architecture of our earlier past."[19] Some structures still existing on Montreal Island and in the neighbouring region attest to this character, such as the windmills of Pointe-aux-Trembles and Ile Perrot (Pointe-du-Moulin), the two austere turrets at the entrance of the Grand Séminaire on Sherbrooke Street West, or the Maison de la Ferme Saint-Gabriel in Pointe-Saint-Charles.

The same spirit prevailed at the level of organization of the physical environment. Thus, for instance, Talon saw in the star-shaped villages (Charlesbourg, Bourg-Royal, and Petite-Auvergne), of a very classical conception, prototypes for the colonization of the land.[20] Yet, the people preferred the côte, a simple and appropriate model as we have seen, dating back to the very colonization of Europe.

This popular tradition was the heritage of the first immigrants and it would have an enormous influence on the development of Quebec's native building style, inasmuch as one is willing to consider the popular, anonymous buildings, created outside the framework of academic architecture, as true manifestations of it. Academic architecture existed in New France from the very beginning. We now turn our attention to its influence.

The Academic Tradition
New France was not solely populated by a class of poor colonists. Following the social pattern in the metropolis, French society in America had its hierarchy based on privileges and on the political or social usefulness of various groups. Thus the class of small landowners was surrounded by a class of seigneurs, both lay and ecclesiastic; at the top was a ruling class, composed mostly of people from the metropolis, which enforced the absolute will of the king.[21]

This class of royal functionaries differed from the other two because its members were recruited among France's high-ranking aristocrats; it included the governor (responsible for politics and for the army), the intendant (head of administration, justice, and the police force), and other important dignitaries. These officials enjoyed extensive powers in all fields of activities in the colony; the plans of any public building in New France had to be approved by the intendant or the governor. They were thus in a position to significantly prevail upon architecture and the planning of the physical environment. This influence would be markedly different from that of the peasant and lower middle class to which most of the French immigrants belonged.

A portrait of one of the noble representatives of the king should illustrate the gap that separated the ruler and his subjects. One of the more colourful administrators was Louis de Buade, Comte de Frontenac et de Palluau, who was governor general of New France from 1672 to 1682 and again from 1689 until his death in 1698. The Buades belonged to a very old family of military aristocracy, one which undoubtedly enjoyed the king's favour since Louis XIII himself was godfather to young Louis de Buade. As could be expected, Louis chose a military career, took part in several campaigns during the Thirty Years' War, and earned himself as many promotions as he suffered wounds. When not in the army, Frontenac spent his time at the king's court with his wife, Anne de la Grange, who was famous for her beauty. There he lived in luxury in a manner which suited his vanity more than it did his purse. His debts seem to have motivated his departure for the colony. Indeed, for a ruined aristocrat, the fur trade often provided the means to replenish his purse.[22]

Frontenac frequented the upper circles of France's highest aristocracy and was even interested in architecture; he had supervised the improvements of his château on Ile Savary.[23] There is no doubt that people like him did in fact transmit to the colony some of the academic tastes as well as some of the French genius on which European civilization thrived in those days. It is small wonder, then, that upon his arrival in the town of Quebec Frontenac began criticizing the poor layout as well as the lack of order and symmetry of buildings in the budding capital. Here is what he wrote to Colbert, the minister, on 2 November 1672: "I think it was a grievous mistake to have allowed private citizens to build houses to suit themselves, without any order." His solution: "to mark the roads and squares to be built, so that later on when private citizens wish to build they may be able to do so with symmetry and in such a manner as may enhance the decoration and ornamentation of the city."[24] Thus, for the governor, symmetry was a vital element for the beauty of urban development. This is a purely "classical" concept of town planning, implying mastery over nature and control over the forces of development. When he wrote these lines Frontenac probably had in mind some French towns, like Vitry-le-François (1634) or Charleville (1656), which had recently been planned according to the most rigorous canons of seventeenth-century classicism. Linking beauty in a development to the symmetry of its constituent parts is an attitude totally foreign to the medieval tradition. The humble colonists of Quebec (or Montreal) looked upon organic development dictated by daily needs as the sole possible mode of growth, a concept which Frontenac equated with fantasy. Which medieval town or ancestral village (aside from the "bastides") ever developed otherwise? Lower may be exaggerating when he refers to Frontenac as Canada's first town planner,[25] but in the colony individuals from Frontenac's social class were persons of culture and held posts of authority. Their position enabled them to counterbalance popular tradition, still steeped in medievalism, and to influence architecture and the development of the physical environment in New France.

This should become evident from a consideration of the achievements of the ruling class in that particular field. First and foremost there is Louisbourg; it had been planned since 1712 according to the theory and principles of the famous military engineer Sébastien Vauban. Louisbourg was located on the eastern shores of Cape Breton Island and was designed to protect the Gulf of St. Lawrence, the gateway to New France. It took over twenty years to build and cost some thirty million francs, much to the king's despair, and all to no avail since it fell both times when besieged (1745 and 1758) by the British who razed it after the second siege. This does not in any way diminish the quality and contemporary nature of its design. With its elaborate fortifications, its rigorously orthogonal grid of streets, and its parade ground, it could compete favourably with the best towns ever created or remodelled in Europe by Vauban.[26] The recent reconstruction of the king's bastion, and of the Château Saint-Louis which served as a residence for the governor and the officers, tells us much about the character and quality of this colonial project. Because of its mass and the harmony of its architectonic rhythms, the Château Saint-Louis imparts a sense of serenity and discreet grandeur so characteristic of French classicism (plate 7).

The same holds true for another Château Saint-Louis, in Quebec City, which was the residence of the governor of New France. It was built around 1724 and the drawings of Chaussegros de Léry, the king's engineer, are still extant. Its turrets and pavilions were placed symmetrically with respect to the central axis of a main door with a classical pediment; it was an imposing building in spite of its austere but harmonious bareness. The intendant's palace probably looked more monumental and more ornate. It was completed in 1718 by Chaussegros de Léry himself and, like Château Saint-Louis, it no longer exists. This palace featured a curb roof obviously inspired by the models of architect Mansart, a fact which clearly indicated where official architecture had its source.

Philippe de Rigaud, Marquis de Vaudreuil, scion of one of the most illustrious—though not the richest—families in the south of France, came to New France to seek his fortune and indeed followed a brilliant career: he was governor of Montreal (1699–1703) and governor general of the colony (1705–25). In Montreal, between 1723 and 1726, he built himself a château which bore his name.[27] Located on Saint-Paul Street, at the foot of today's Place Jacques-Cartier, this château became the official residence of the governors in Montreal during the French regime. In 1773 it became the College of Montreal and unfortunately was completely destroyed by fire in 1803.[28]

PLAN DE LA
VILLE DE LOUISBOURG
dans l'Isle Royale

A. Porte Dauphine et Corps de Garde
B. Porte de la Reine
C. Porte de Maurepas
D. Bastion Dauphin et Magasin a Poudre
E. Bastion du Roy, Cazernes, Logement du
    Gouverneur et des Officiers
F. Bastion de la Reine
G. Bastion de la Princasse
H. Bastion Broüilla
J. Bastion de Maurepas
K. Magasins des vivres &.ᵃ
L. Logement de l'ordonnateur &.ᵃ
M. Hopital du Roy
N. La Paroisse et les Recolets
O. Les Sœurs de Notre Dame.

Echelle de Deux Cent Toises.

7.   Plan of the city of Louisbourg on Isle Royale, by N. Bellin, 1764

Reputedly the most beautiful building in Montreal during the old regime, the little Château de Vaudreuil was a perfect example of the French classical tradition, with formal inner and outer layouts and a formal façade and a small French garden. Gowans refers to it as the Canadian equivalent of the great Baroque palaces of French nobility in the seventeenth century.[29] To say that the Château de Vaudreuil possessed the same refined forms as the French palaces would be carrying a generous comparison too far, but it certainly was built in the same spirit. The same may be said of the Châteaux Saint-Louis in Quebec and in Louisbourg or of the intendant's palace. The high-ranking Marquis de Vaudreuil was definitely aware of the architecture of his time. Chaussegros de Léry, who had been Vaudreuil's architect, was the king's engineer and the son of a well-known engineer from Toulon; he had been a pupil and protégé of the great Vauban, and had certainly studied the most fashionable architectural techniques and concepts of his days.[30] (See plate 8.)

What has been said about the effect of the ruling class on town planning and civic architecture in the colony holds true, with slight nuances, for the influence of church authorities on religious architecture. Missionary orders such as the Jesuits, the Sulpicians, and the Récollets came to settle in New France. Like the class of royal functionaries, they depended heavily on the metropolis and competed for substantial financial contributions as well as for talents. In the beginning at least, these communities used to recruit members almost exclusively in the mother country, a practice that contributed to the import of some of the tastes and fashions of the Old World into the New World. Some of these orders had their own architectural style: the Society of Jesus adopted a model of their famous Gesù, a trade mark which they imposed on their missions to identify their achievements. Thus the College of the Jesuits built in 1648 and the Jesuit Church built in 1666, both in Quebec City, showed many similarities to the college and chapel of the Jesuits at La Flèche in France, a complex of buildings completed a few decades earlier with the participation of an excellent architect named Etienne Martellange. In Montreal the Jesuits started erecting an establishment on Notre-Dame Street in 1692, but it has since disappeared. Like those of Quebec City, these buildings were very European in character and would not have been out of place in a small French provincial town. The same may be said of the monastery and church of the Récollets in Montreal, then located between the following streets: Notre-Dame and des Récollets, Sainte-Hélène and Saint-Pierre. The buildings were demolished in 1867. A similar comment could be made about the first Notre-Dame Church and the old Seminary of Saint-Sulpice to which we shall return in chapter 5.

The bishop of Quebec would also have a pro-academic effect on the religious architecture of the colony. In his sphere of influence he enjoyed the same absolute authority as the governor and, to quote the historian Frégault, both "look like brothers . . . they are in fact brothers. They come from the same social class and sometimes even from the same families. They hold similar views on public life, on authority, and on the precedence and prestige attaching to their functions."[31] Thus François de Laval, the first bishop of New France, came from the old family of Montmorency, so ancient that Vachon de Belmont said about them "that their origin is unknown, like that of the Nile."[32] The same is true of Laval's successor who was as noble as his name sounded aristocratic: Jean-Baptiste de La Croix de Chevrières de Saint-Vallier. Laval and Saint-Vallier, like Frontenac and Vaudreuil, belonged to a privileged elite for whom the study of the concepts and styles of contemporary architecture was an indispensable asset for a well-educated mind. Their personal experience complemented this knowledge: Frontenac had himself undertaken the improvements of his own château, and Saint-Vallier, an ordinary chaplain at the court of Louis XIV, witnessed the birth of the splendours at Versailles.

In fact, the cathedral and the episcopal palace of Quebec reflected very academic tastes. The former, reconstructed in 1744 by Chaussegros de Léry and now completely disfigured, was built in a severe but powerful Jesuit style very much in fashion in France during that period. The latter was unfortunately altered in 1831 to the point of being unrecognizable. With its front court it followed the typical plan of the French château of the seventeenth century and, according to Gowans, constituted the most elaborate construction of the century in New France.[33]

The influence of a Laval or a Saint-Vallier affected buildings mainly of an official nature but, like the authority of great religious communities, it was reflected in all the religious architecture of Quebec for a long time after the end of French domination in America. How did this come about? A likely explanation is that the bishops and religious orders, with their great prestige and authority, had handed down to the rather orthodox and conformist population a stereotyped "image" of the church as a place of worship. This image was perpetuated for two centuries and transmitted from one generation to another through the system of apprenticeship: from the master to the journeyman and from the journeyman to the apprentice, according to the traditions of artisans.

Just as the governor or the intendant had to approve the plans for

8. *Château de Vaudreuil, drawing by James Duncan. Gaspard
Chaussegros de Léry, architect, 1723*

public buildings, the bishop of Quebec was required to do the same for all churches built in the colony. As a faithful disciple of the Jesuits, Monseigneur Laval favoured centralization and found it to his advantage to impose an identical model, drawn from his academic background, for places of worship. This much he did: the churches constructed during his reign on the seigneuries of the Côte Beaupré and Ile d'Orléans had almost the same features, one of which was their shape in the form of a Latin cross ending in a semicircular apse.[34] To ensure consistency in the quality of work, Laval founded in 1675, at Saint-Joachim near Quebec, a school of arts and crafts for the teaching of carpentry, sculpture, painting, church decoration, masonry, and joinery. French masters such as Frère Luc (1614–85), who had worked in Paris and Rome with the best-known craftsmen of his times, and Jacques le Blond dit Latour (1670–1715), architect, sculptor, and painter from Bordeaux, helped transmit to the artisans of New France the architectural and artistic concepts that prevailed in France. This arts and crafts school lasted until the end of the French regime and contributed to the formation of many important Quebec artists, of whom Jean Baillargé was the first in a long line of architects and master sculptors in Quebec.[35]

Laval and his successors proposed models and saw to it that the knowledge and skills required for their completion would be taught. This is as far as they were able to go, for they lacked the material and human resources required to build each parish church in the country. Moreover, they depended to a large extent on local manpower and finances.

This explains why old parish churches in Quebec look like the result of a unique and original blend of architectural elements belonging to two different traditions. The popular usage, on the one hand, perpetuated the medieval culture through local craftsmen and builders; on the other hand, the Baroque classical traditions represented the legacy of the cultural and religious authorities. Thus, churches with classical layouts were built with steep roofs and with massive walls made of rough stones. Carefully cut protruding corner stones decorating the walls, arched windows and dormers, openings with regular arches, symmetrically placed niches, and a bell tower with the soaring spire of a Gothic church but the contours of a classical lantern complete this architectural picture.

Inside the churches, where the effects of the rigorous climate were not quite so noticeable, the Baroque classical tradition was more freely expressed with well-proportioned masses, basket vaults, and, most of all, gilded wooden sculptures in Louis XIV, Louis XV, and even Rococo styles. The original freshness of these sculptured interiors makes up for their doubtful academic genuineness, and Ramsay Traquair refers to them as one of North America's most remarkable artistic achievements.[36] The sculptures were the work of master artisans who had studied Vignole, the Grand and the Petit Blondel, craftsmen like Levasseur and Baillargé in Quebec or Louis-Amable Quévillon (1749–1823), one of Montreal's best-known sculptors, whose name was linked with the decoration of more than twenty-five churches in the Montreal region. Unfortunately, most of these places of worship have disappeared, often razed by fires, as for example the magnificent Church of l'Enfant-Jésus in Pointe-aux-Trembles, built from 1705 onwards and destroyed by a fire on 21 February 1937.[37]

In the Montreal region there are still a few churches to remind us of this happy blend of the academic and popular traditions and also to give us a good idea of the degree of excellence attained in the field of wood sculpture. The small Church of Sainte-Jeanne-Françoise-de-Chantal, on Ile Perrot, was completed in 1786, although most of its interior decoration dates back only to the early nineteenth century; with its cruciform layout, it is typical of the village churches of Old Quebec. The ugly front that was added to it in 1901 must not be allowed to detract from the vigour and individuality of its sculptured interior decoration, or from the three remarkable altars, attributed to Quévillon.[38] The Church of Saint-Michel-de-Vaudreuil is another example, in spite of the alterations to its front. Built in 1773–75, it contains many sculptures, most of them by two competing masters, Liébert and Quévillon.[39] But, in our opinion, the most important church remains the Church of the Visitation, located at Sault-au-Récollet, on Gouin Boulevard, west of Papineau Street. It is the only church in Montreal for which most of the building dates back to the French regime. Indeed the main part was started in 1749, and work had sufficiently progressed in 1751 to allow mass to be celebrated; Charles Guilbaut, born in that parish, was the "contracting mason." The main building was an example of good peasant masonry, with classical arched windows, but several additions were made to it later on. A new front was added in the early 1850s, and was designed in a severe English neo-Baroque style by the prolific Montreal architect John Ostell. (His work will be dealt with in later chapters.) Inside the church the spectacle is unique: master sculptors of great talent succeeded one another in the task. The tabernacle of the main altar is the work of Liébert (1792); the altars are by Quévillon (1802–6); Fleury David did the vault and the major part of the present interior, completed between 1816 and 1831; the pulpit is the work of Chartrand (1836).[40] (See plates 9 and 10.)

9.   *Church of Sault-au-Récollet, exterior*

Enduring Attitudes

From the very beginning, management of the environment as well as architecture in New France showed signs of a strong dichotomy, which had its origin in two distinct traditions that were almost impervious to one another and that brought their own ideology and cultural heritage to French America. The popular classes were very homogeneous and came almost exclusively from the same social stratum, the lower middle class. They were people without great resources or much specialization in their trades and without much self-awareness. Yet, their legacy to the New World was a precious heritage of popular artisan traditions, in the fields of architecture and management of the environment, that were deeply anchored in their mentality and dated back to the earliest Middle Ages when dwellings, villages, and towns were recovering from the ashes left by Norman destruction.

When transplanted to North American soil, the immigrant population multiplied naturally and rapidly became indigenous, adapting to the new harsh and uncultivated environment. This was especially true in the Montreal region which, until the arrival of the Loyalists in 1775, remained the most remote colonization centre on the North American continent. It was therefore natural for the indigenous population to adapt the cultural and artisan heritage of their parents to living conditions on the continent. This process of adaptation is apparent in their bare unpretentious buildings. The traditional Quebec house in the Montreal region, which was inspired by identifiable models from France, and more accurately from Brittany, underwent transformations dictated by the climate and the way of life that made it unique. Its foundations rose above the ground as a safeguard against snow accumulations, the gallery projected intermediate between the ground and the house or as a summer extension of the latter. The roof was widened and the eaves were extended beyond the vertical plane of the walls, covering the gallery and protecting it against heat and bad weather. The summer kitchen was developed as a result of activities during the warm season.[41] These give just a few examples.

The ruling class, or even better, caste, constituted the other founding group, which was very homogeneous: the church and the state were working hand in hand. The members of this ruling class transplanted to New France a paternalistic, absolutist regime which was at its zenith during the reign of King Louis XIV (1661–1715). They were recruited from the highest aristocracy and were thus aware of the latest ideas in the fields of architecture and town planning. Moreover, unlike the lower class, they enjoyed an excess of resources, both financially and in talent, and their architecture thus underwent few changes from one continent to another. Of course, their achievements did not reach the same heights or the same degree of refinement as their great French models, and the magnitude of a project was always related to the interest the king took in the colony. Nevertheless, they remained true to the spirit and character of French architecture. Both in America and in Europe, whether or not through a conscious process, aristocrats and rulers were identified with their architecture: it was a symbol of their social role, of their pretensions, and of their privileges.

Parish church architecture was the only architecture to have blended both traditions in a relatively homogeneous manner. The close relationship imposed on both classes within the religious context probably accounts for this fusion. The lower class and lower clergy were dependent for pastoral guidance on the ecclesiastical hierarchy, and the latter relied on local resources and manpower for the construction of places of worship.

The discovery of this dichotomy of traditions, one artisan and one academic, which was to shape Quebec's architecture from the very beginning, is not recent: Gowans, Morisset, and Traquair have all raised the matter in one manner or another. One aspect that has not yet been thoroughly investigated is that of the mentality, attitudes, and activities of each class in regard to management of the environment, and their perpetuation beyond the French colonial period.

The scope of such a study is too vast and complex to be treated fully here; besides, for lack of relevant research, it would be incomplete. For example, it would be interesting to know the exact origin of the French colonists who settled in the small town of Montreal and in the neighbouring côtes. Did they come from towns and villages or from the countryside? Were their traditions and attitudes rural or urban?

All we know is that, at the time of colonization of the North American continent, France already had an urban tradition dating far back into the past. Such a heritage must have played a part in the founding of towns like Quebec, Trois-Rivières, and Montreal which, towards the end of French rule, harboured close to 20 percent of the population of New France.[42] On the other hand, the fact remains that, for various reasons mentioned in the previous chapter, compact villages did not find much favour with the people, who preferred the côte, or range, as a model of human community and found its structure fulfilled a particular need. Although each individual settler owned his own lot, he nevertheless depended greatly on the community of neighbours because of his isolation and the harshness of the climate. This remarkably simple and orderly organization, in a land inhabited by an increasingly homogeneous population, pro-

10.   *Church of Sault-au-Récollet, interior*

duced an egalitarian attitude which is still prevalent today in the rural countryside.

The old rural structures and the côte in particular were at the origin of the orthogonal grid which is typical of the older districts of Montreal. These sectors were inhabited mainly by people who had emigrated from the côtes and rural ranges. Hence, one would expect the spirit of rural organization, both territorial and social, to have penetrated the urban environment. It would be pointless to make a definitive statement without adequate study, but it may be suggested that the cohesion, uniformity, and gregariousness which characterize the old francophone neighbourhoods of Montreal, with their uninterrupted rows of anonymous houses and clusters of individual dwellings, originated in the perpetuation of certain traditions and attitudes.

One fact which stands out during the French regime is the total absence of participation by the people in public and, particularly, municipal administration. Gustave Lanctôt studied this phenomenon and expressed a categorical opinion on this point. In the administration of New France, all the powers were centralized in the hands of two men: the governor, who was the king's personal representative, and the intendant, the administrator who "ruled in fact and totally" by ordinances. "What part does the population take in such an administrative system?" asks Lanctôt. "None whatsoever."[43] The same situation prevailed in municipal government. To quote Lanctôt:

> from this survey of municipal government in the days of New France, one may conclude that towns were administered by authorities devoid of any popular representation. . . . To sum up, according to the concept and the methods of the time, the administration, which was both benevolent and paternalistic, established a moral and a material order which encompassed the following facets of life: proper behaviour, security, hygiene, road maintenance, fire protection, nourishment, and even the cost of living. This order left no room for personal initiative or collective cooperation which would have enabled these small towns to progress and to grow and allowed the citizens to develop their intellectual capacities, to improve the quality of their work, and to foster their ambitions. All such lanes of endeavours were closed to the city dwellers of Canada, even though they were open to those of metropolitan France.[44]

No more need be said.

The evolution of Montreal under the French regime will be studied in the next chapters, together with the character and significance of the influence exerted by the ruling class on the organization of the urban environment. The effect of the lower class was minimal and was limited to private dwellings. The French ruling class was replaced by a foreign but similar type at the time of surrender to the British, and the latter allowed the same kind of relationship between the ruling and the lower classes to be perpetuated for another half century. If the lower class enjoyed little power during the old regime, it was to have its influence further eroded to the point of losing contact with the economy, and watching helplessly as industry fell under the control of others. This may partly account for the lower class's passivity and inability to manage the environment, a fact which is reflected in the lower-class urban neighbourhoods in the nineteenth and twentieth centuries. The francophone districts mirrored this reality at a time when the elegant anglophone neighbourhoods, with their spacious and individually designed homes, reflected the powers of a class in full control of its environment.

Some of the stifled collective attitudes displayed by the francophone classes during the whole evolution of Montreal may be attributed, in our opinion, to the influence exerted by religion on our society. Indeed, the clergy had created its basic institutions, moulded its traditions and its mentality, and had finally acquired full control over our society. Hence, a study of the role of the Catholic Church in Quebec, from the very beginning of French colonization, is vital to the understanding of the essence and extent of that role.[45]

One must bear in mind that the French colonists settled in America at a time when France was undergoing a religious renaissance of deep mystical fervour and was also actively participating in the counter-reformation of François de Sales, Berulle, Vincent de Paul, Jean-Jacques Olier, and others. The foundation of Montreal in 1642 by de Maisonneuve's group of proselytes was in keeping with this religious movement. There is little doubt that the king, the church, the soldiers, the peasants, and the religious orders were all imbued with this ambitious spirit and were hoping to establish in the New World a Catholic society after the image of the mother country.[46]

Judging by the following quotations from Arthur Lower, they did succeed to a degree: "On the religious and ecclesiastical side, New France came close to the cleric's dream, the perfect society which only the Church can provide."[47] Circumstances worked in favour of the church. The conditions it found in North America were very similar to those in the Middle Ages in Europe: an open territory ready for a new order. Its task was greatly facilitated by a population of peasant stock, with deep roots solidly entrenched in orthodoxy and conformity, carefully screened from any Protestant or heretic elements. The only obstacle to stand in the way of complete success turned out to be the secular ruling class jealous of its authority and privileges.

However, this obstacle was to disappear with the conquest of 1760. The near theocratic character of the French colony, marked by church control of education, cultural development, and social services, not only did not disappear but was reinforced when the regime changed. In exchange for unconditional loyalty, the church acquired absolute authority in these fields with the blessings of the victor who looked on this stabilizing framework for the lower classes as the best safeguard for its own interests.

The church took advantage of the collective return to the soil after the conquest and sought to foster a new ideal: a peasant Christianity, likening Catholicism to the calling of the land and this in turn to the calling of the nation.[48] Hence the city acquired a derogatory connotation, equating it with Sodom rather than with Jerusalem, and urban development became synonymous with dechristianization. This was not a very positive outlook for the rural population which would be forced, in order to survive, to emigrate to the city in the second half of the nineteenth century. As Falardeau pointed out: "This clerical–rural culture could not adequately prepare the people to meet the expectations and demands of industrial urban life."[49]

The consequences of this refusal to accept the city will be analysed in the course of this study. To complete the picture, we should describe an institution which was created by the church and was to become the basic structure of social organization of French Canadians, fulfilling at once religious, educational, and later on municipal functions: the parish. The first one appeared in 1722 and the institution has endured until today. The adherence of all members to the church's religious and social standards added to the stability generated by the natural cohesiveness of its members. Even though the urban parish appeared more impersonal than the rural one, it remained a dominant characteristic of the urban environment and constituted the first frame of reference with which a community could identify.

The physical legacy of this social framework would be impressive: the parish church, towering above the neighbouring landscape whether in rural communities, in villages, or in cities. In Montreal the number of parish churches would increase in direct proportion to population density. In 1874 there were no fewer than seventy-four churches for a population of some 150,000 inhabitants. Mark Twain said about Montreal that it was the only city he knew of where one could not throw a pebble without breaking a church window. It was more than a quip: it expressed a very distinctive reality in Montreal.[50]

Several features characteristic of Montreal and of its society at various epochs are rooted in the society of the old regime; this explains why, in this chapter, we have intentionally anticipated the chronological development of the city. Certain ideologies and attitudes which date back to the old regime would become the behavioural archetypes of the future. Let us now turn to the development of Montreal in its first century: a growth marked by the definite domination of the parish church.

4

The Frontier Town

> *It is pretty well fortified, and surrounded with a high and thick wall. . . . The long streets are broad and strait, and divided at right angles by the short ones: some are paved, but most of them very uneven. The gates of the town are numerous; on the east side of the town towards the river are five, two great and three lesser ones; and on the other side are likewise several.*
> PETER KALM, 1749[1]

Laying out the First Streets

On 12 March 1672 Dollier de Casson accompanied by, among others, Bénigne Basset, who was both surveyor and court clerk, went to Coteau Saint-Louis to lay out the first streets of Ville-Marie. Along the length of the upper crest of the hillside, roughly following a southwest-northeast direction, he lined up eight markers stamped with the seminary's seal to determine the boundaries of the first street, Notre-Dame Street. Its location on the crest and its width of thirty feet (French measure) made it the most important street projected for the small town. This is how Dollier de Casson meant it to be. This street was designed to lead in both directions from a parish church which he intended to erect right in the middle of the hill and in the centre of Notre-Dame Street. The actual construction of Notre-Dame Church started the next year. Two other streets were laid out almost parallel to this main street. The one toward the river was to be twenty-four feet wide and named Saint-Paul Street. At the time, it was but a path winding its way from the old fort of Pointe-à-Callières to the Hôtel-Dieu of Jeanne Mance and to Notre-Dame-de-Bonsecours Chapel. On the other edge of Coteau Saint-Louis, on the side of Saint-Martin Creek (also called Petite Rivière), St. James Street was laid out, to be eighteen feet wide. Later on, at the beginning of the twentieth century, it was to become the financial centre of the whole country.

Dollier de Casson lined up seven other streets perpendicularly to the first three, thus creating a relatively orthogonal grid of streets having rectangular parcels of land of unequal dimensions. They were from west to east: Saint-Pierre, du Calvaire, Saint-François (today's Saint-François-Xavier), Saint-Joseph (today's Saint-Sulpice), Saint-Lambert, Saint-Gabriel, and Saint-Charles. Three of these, Saint-Pierre, Saint-François, and Saint-Gabriel, all eighteen feet wide, connected Saint-Paul Street to Notre-Dame Street. Two others, Saint-Joseph and Saint-Charles, also eighteen feet wide, ran as far as St. James Street. Two more streets, du Calvaire and Saint-Lambert, both twenty-four feet wide, were designed to connect Notre-Dame with St. James, and to cross Saint-Martin Creek. However, du Calvaire would soon be abandoned, whereas Saint-Lambert would later become the famous St. Lawrence Boulevard, the major axis of demographic growth on the island. Except for du Calvaire, Saint-Charles (which would be absorbed by Place Jacques-Cartier), and Saint-Joseph (today's Saint-Sulpice), which was slightly re-routed, all the streets laid out by Dollier de Casson still exist today.[2] (Plate 11.)

Thus, as far back as 1672, Ville-Marie was planned according to a relative orthogonal grid, which would eventually take shape when built upon. In the southwest-northeast direction, the street alignment was dictated by the existing paths, like the future Saint-Paul, or by the natural topography of Coteau Saint-Louis. Perpendicular to the previous direction, the alignment of streets seems to have been ordained by the existence of land concessions granted by de Maisonneuve, such as those ceded to Pierre Gadois, Robert Cavelier, Jean Desroches, or Sieur Lambert Closse. For instance, the layout of Saint-Pierre Street follows the joint boundary separating the properties of Gadois and of Cavelier, the former being two arpents wide by fifteen long and granted in January 1648,[3] the latter being two arpents wide and twenty long and granted in 1654.[4] As was the custom, these concessions were perpendicular to the small Saint-Pierre River. The contract for Pierre Gadois's concession stipulated that "should the seigneurs require part of this lot to establish a town, they would be entitled to expropriate same and to replace it by a parcel of the same dimensions at the far end of the lot and would have to pay for cleared land in accordance with the estimates on the value of the land established by experts."[5] Another example is that of rue Saint-François, which follows the boundaries of the concession granted to Jean Desroches on 10 April 1655: "to take on the edge of the common a lot 3 perches wide and 31 perches and 6 feet long."[6] Rue Saint-Joseph follows the outline of the land granted to Le Moyne, Gervais, and Basset; rue Saint-Lambert, named "in memory of the brave major who died for his country"[7] and later known as St. Lawrence Boulevard, follows the western boundaries of the fief granted to Lambert Closse on 2 February 1658.[8]

Even though the alignment of several streets on the first plan seemed to be dictated by the constraints of occupation and of land use, Dollier de Casson's plan does reflect a desire for order in the physical, economic, and social development of the budding community. He would encourage the citizens to "erect buildings destined to embellish and decorate their town and to facilitate trade among the inhabitants as well as with foreigners."[9] In this sense, it was indeed a plan for development, the first for the City of Montreal, and as such it deserves closer study.

How good was the plan? What kind of urban environment was it creating? How was it to influence the development of Montreal? These are interesting topics. Unfortunately, few specialists in the matter gave it much thought and, if they did, only in a superficial manner. Some saw in Dollier de Casson's plan nothing but a poor copy of the checkerboard layout of Philadelphia. This is rather unlikely, since Holm and William Penn devised their plan in 1682, some ten years after Casson drew his for Montreal.[10] Others, like Raoul Blanchard, have exaggerated its importance and influence: "the whole plan for the huge city issued from the Sulpician's drawings."[11] It is true that there is a certain similarity between this first layout of streets and the typical grid of Montreal; it is also true that the alignment of a street like Saint-Lambert (later St. Lawrence Boulevard) was used as a guideline for the placement of several streets in the immediate neighbourhood. Yet, as we have attempted to show in chapter 2, we maintain that it was the permanence of the physical features of the côte and the mode of subdividing the land which created the street patterns of Greater Montreal. Most often though, the importance of this first plan (Casson's) has been either neglected or minimized, and reported as an event among many others in the history of the city. According to present day standards this first outline may not be very elaborate or cover a very wide area, but this

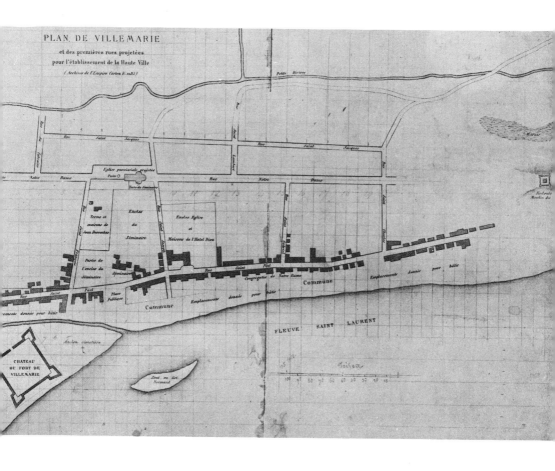

*11. Plan of the streets laid out by Dollier de Casson in 1672, at-
tributed to Bénigne Basset, sieur des Lauriers*

does not detract from its significance or from what we may learn from it.

The Dollier de Casson layout is very simple, with only a few streets demarcating several parcels of land of unequal dimensions. There is no attempt to further subdivide the lots as was done in Penn's plan for Philadelphia. A glance at the "terrier" of the Seigneury of Montreal will show that the lots inside the boundaries of the old fortifications varied in area and shape as a result of several mutations and transformations.[12] The only fixed feature on the plan, apart from the alignment of the streets, is the crossroad selected for the construction of the parish church. This point was connected by Saint-François and Saint-Joseph Streets to the Place du Marché (Market Square), which already existed near the mouth of the Saint-Pierre River. These two poles, one economic and the other social, would become the centres of development of the small town.

To understand the essence of this plan, one must follow its development in time and space, and the best way would be to trace the advent of Ville-Marie through the successive maps of the city. This is our only choice, since there does not exist a single contemporary view of the city between 1642 and 1760, not even a sketch of urban landscape, or of a street, or even of a building.[13] On the other hand, some unknown persons, some competent engineers like Catalogne or de Léry, and even a sculptor named Paul Labrosse have left us good sets of explicit plans, some of which have been authenticated and verified by Gustave Lanctôt.[14] Thus, from 1684 onwards, it is possible to retrace the topographical growth of the town as well as the transformations which, although slightly modifying Dollier de Casson's original designs, would eventually fulfil them.

A Century of Development

The first layout was drawn by an unknown author and bears the following inscription: "envoyé par Mr. Denonville le 13 novembre 1685." The Marquis de Denonville was governor of the colony from 1685 to 1689; this would tend to authenticate the document.[15] On this plan, the prominence of the parish church, erected in the middle of Notre-Dame Street, is evident. Baron de Lahontan, who visited Ville-Marie in 1684, states that the church is splendid and that it "is built after the Model of that of St. Sulpice at Paris."[16] One may wish to dispute such a flattering comparison; nevertheless, it reveals the importance and significance of this place of worship in the midst of the upper town. The comment is all the more revealing since Baron de Lahontan was well known for his anticlerical views. This can only attest to Dollier de Casson's determination to place the parish church in a prominent position. On the northwest side a public square was gradually developing: it was the embryo of today's Place d'Armes. (Plate 12.)

In spite of Dollier de Casson's exhortations to the citizenry, his initial scheme was barely beginning to take shape. A few buildings were built on four streets: Saint-Paul, Notre-Dame, Saint-Francis, and Saint-Joseph. These were sufficient to link the two essential poles of the small community: the church square and the market place. Indeed, every Tuesday and Friday, "the Inhabitants . . . rich in Corn, Cattle, Fowl, and a thousand other Commodities, for which they find a Mercat in the City" gathered in the lower town on Place du Marché, then also called Place d'Armes.[17] It was Colbert who wished that public markets were held for "the convenience of private citizens, who had to buy the provisions necessary for life, and also for the convenience of the inhabitants of the country, who wished to sell their farm produce or the products of their industry."[18] This location corresponds to today's Place Royale, partly occupied by the Old Customs building. It was the new city's true economic hub as well as the centre for justice. For the benefit of the population, it was considered normal that criminals be punished in public view, where the people would normally gather.

It is rather difficult to establish the exact number of inhabitants living at the time in Ville-Marie. Various researchers who have dealt with the matter do not always indicate whether their findings apply to the population of the whole island of Montreal, the district of Montreal, or the Coteau Saint-Louis alone. Thus, Lanctôt refers to a population of 1,500 inhabitants in 1684.[19] This figure seems large for Ville-Marie itself: the 1685 census of New France counted only 119 residences in the town, with 724 inhabitants, a number closer to reality.[20]

A second plan was drawn in 1704 by someone whose identity is not known for certain. It reveals the city's sizeable expansion both in area and in population.[21] The latter had doubled in twenty years to between 1,600 and 2,000 inhabitants.[22] Of the several reasons which account for this demographical and topographical growth, three are worth mentioning. First, as had already been noted by Baron de Lahontan, the côtes and neighbouring seigneuries produced enough food to sustain a large urban population.[23] At the same time, Ville-Marie was enjoying a flourishing economy as it had become the fur trade's centre as well as the military warehouse for the western territories.[24] Finally, an ordinance from the intendant, dated 15 June 1688, on the enlargement of the city and on the widening of its streets to thirty feet, made three demands on all

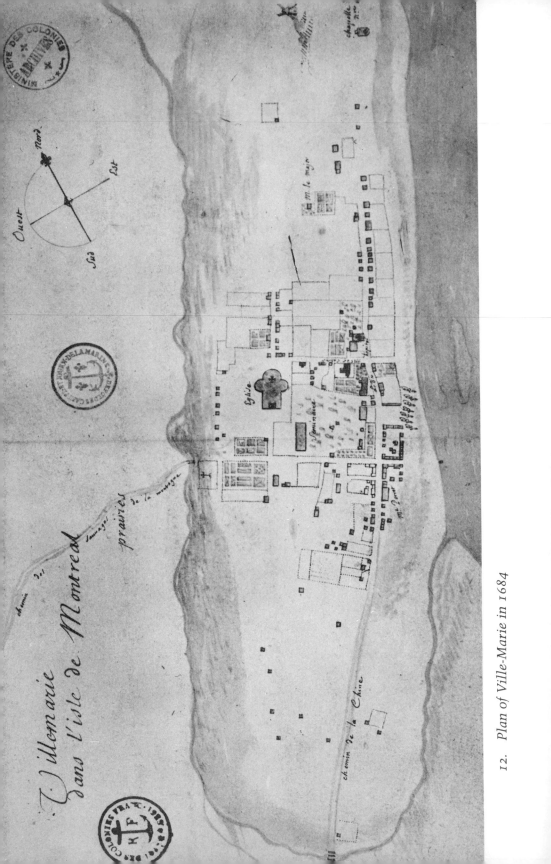

12. *Plan of Ville-Marie in 1684*

landowners living within the walls of Ville-Marie: they were to limit their lot to one arpent, start construction within one year, and respect the alignment of streets imposed by the city's bailiff.[25] (Plate 13.)

The 1704 plan reveals new elements. The city was surrounded by a wall made of wooden stakes and with bastions and curtains. Here is how Sister Morin describes it, around the same time, in her *Annales de l'Hôtel-Dieu*:

> there is at present a kind of town surrounded with stakes of cedar, five or six feet [French measure] high, bound together with heavy nails and wooden pegs, and this for the past ten years. This is how towns in Canada are surrounded; there are several large gates which are used as entrances and exits and are closed every evening by army officers maintained there by the King of France for our defence, should our enemy wish to worry us; they open both gates in the morning at regular hours, etc.[26]

The map shows that new streets have appeared since 1684: among others, those on either side of Saint-Gabriel and parallel to it, Saint-Jean-Baptiste (west) and Saint-Vincent (east). Monsieur Vachon de Belmont, who succeeded Dollier de Casson as head of the Seminary of Saint-Sulpice, also laid out rue de l'Hôpital in 1702 "for the embellishment and convenience of the public."[27] This street is one of the few in Ville-Marie which were not parallel to the original axis on the first layout, probably because it followed a long-existing path linking Côte Saint-Pierre to the Hôtel-Dieu hospital.

Even though the original layout by Dollier de Casson was slightly altered by the addition of these new streets, it nevertheless retained its original character. Notre-Dame Church maintained its predominant position and was now almost completely surrounded by a cemetery. Moreover, the church was increasingly committed to answer the various social needs of the small community: the Hôtel-Dieu had doubled the space occupied by its buildings; the Sisters of the Congregation, dedicated to education, had established their convent on the new Saint-Jean-Baptiste Street; the Jesuits and the Récollets, true to their rivalry, built at opposite ends of the town, on Notre-Dame Street. These structures were surrounded by large gardens which in time would constitute the green areas linking the various neighbourhoods. For the time being, "with gardens, vegetable gardens, and cultivated plots covering two-thirds of its area," as Lanctôt reminds us,[28] the city's landscape remained essentially rural.

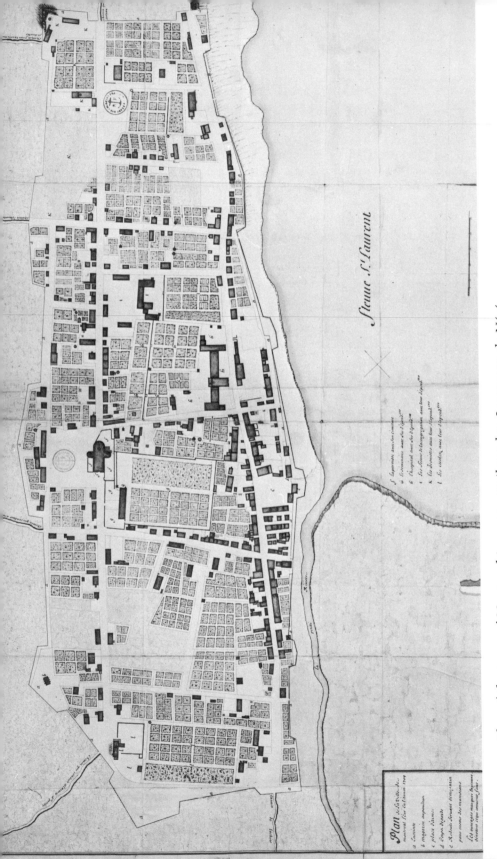

Fleuve S.t Laurent

13. *Plan of the town of Montreal in 1704, attributed to Levasseur de Néré*

Excellent plans, most of them by the king's engineers, were devised in the 1720s. One set, drawn in 1723 by de Catalogne, is remarkable for its neatness as well as for the wealth of information it supplies.[29] Another set, laid out the next year by Chaussegros de Léry, is astonishing for it produces a three-dimensional illusion.[30] The plan seems to have been used as a basis for others, among them one made in 1731 which is almost identical to it and whose author is not known for certain, unless it was the same Chaussegros de Léry.[31] The latter are important, for they enable us to see for the first time the stone fortifications of Montreal. They complement de Catalogne's plans and must therefore be studied together. (Plates 14 and 15.)

In the 1720s the small settlement had become considerably more urban in character than in 1704. Most streets were by now rather well delineated because of the continuous alignment of buildings. Around 1705 Ville-Marie had been renamed Montreal and now numbered 3,000 inhabitants.[32] Extending to the northeast to include Notre-Dame-de-Bonsecours Chapel together with "a sorry redoubt on a small spot,"[33] later to become the citadel, the fortified town had almost reached a size which would not change until the beginning of the nineteenth century. Some new streets made further cuts into the urban lots, probably on recommendations from Chaussegros de Léry. There were, in his opinion, still too many gardens inside the walls and the number of streets ought to be trebled to accommodate new arrivals. In the last twenty years several streets had appeared on the map, among them Saint-Alexis, Saint-Jean, and Saint-Sacrement in the west, Saint-Denis and Sainte-Thérèse in the east, and finally Bonsecours.

The lower town, centred around the Place du Marché, became more urban in character. Father de Charlevoix, one of the most serious observers and most prolific commentators who ever visited New France, noted that in 1721 the lower town was "the quarter in which the merchants for the most part have their houses."[34] This was to be expected, for trading took place on the Place du Marché, the annual fur traders' fair was held on the adjacent common, and the nearby St. Lawrence River remained the best means of communication with the neighbouring regions, with Quebec, and ultimately with France. On the map drawn by de Catalogne and de Léry, a similar concentration of functions by the civil administration is evident in the east end of this small town: the Château de Ramezay (1705) was the residence of the governor of Montreal and the Château de Vaudreuil (1723–26) was the official residence of the governor general in the town; the king's wharf and shed were located at the eastern extremity.

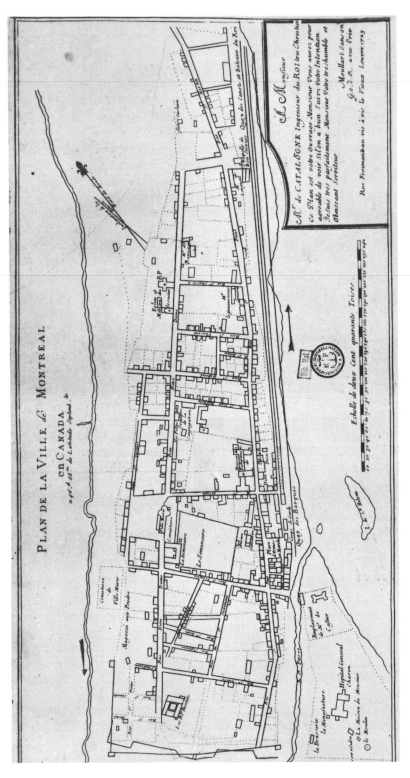

14.   *Plan of the town of Montreal in 1723, by Gédéon de Catalogne*

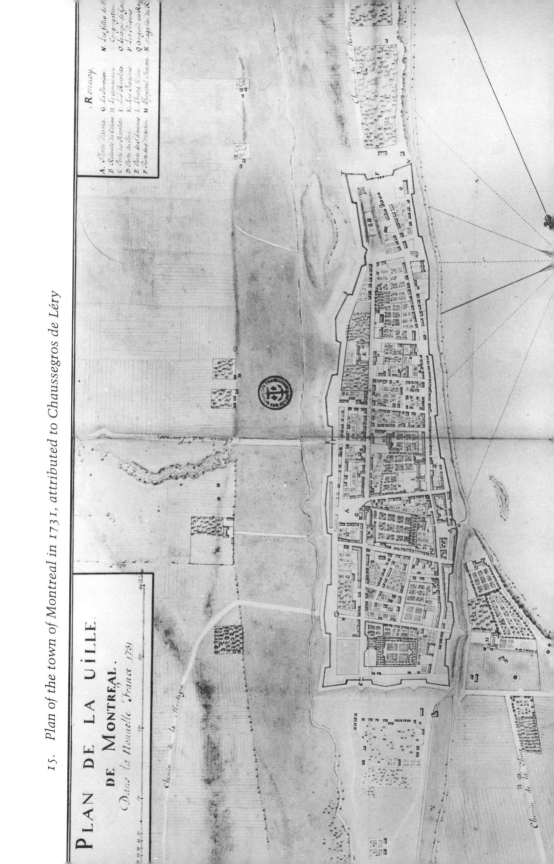

15. *Plan of the town of Montreal in 1731, attributed to Chaussegros de Léry*

Owing in part to the decisions and activities of the administrators, Montreal gradually lost its character as a simple trading post and assumed a more urban and permanent look as the second half of the eighteenth century approached. For instance, following a disastrous fire—the first in a long and grim list—which destroyed the Hôtel-Dieu and more than 130 houses on 19 June 1721, an ordinance signed by Intendant Bégon on 8 July of the same year forbade the use of wood for the construction of houses in Montreal and recommended that stones be employed, and that roofs be covered with nonflammable materials like slate, tile, or tin; new houses would have to respect the street alignments and be built with two storeys.[35] At the beginning these measures were poorly executed. Kalm, who visited the town in 1749, noted that most houses were made of wood. Later on, however, the ordinance must have been enforced, for the application of tin to cover roofs became such a visual characteristic of Montreal that it was nicknamed the "silver town."[36] Even today, roofs shining in the sun provide one of the most striking visual features of the old villages along both shores of the St. Lawrence River.

No study of Montreal in the 1720s would be complete without a description of the stone fortifications appearing on de Léry's plans: he had been in charge of building them since 1716. A simple stone wall, 18 feet high, 4 feet wide at the base, and 3 feet wide at the top, was built with curtain walls and 13 bastions; on the outside, the walls were protected by sloping banks and by a moat 8 feet deep. Four main gates gave access to the town: Porte des Récollets to the west, at the end of Notre-Dame Street; Porte Saint-Laurent, the only one on the Saint-Martin Creek side; Porte Saint-Martin to the east, at the end of Saint-Paul Street; and Porte du Port, on the St. Lawrence River side, giving direct access to Place du Marché. Later on, more gates would be added on the river side, a fact which reasserts the river's importance as a communication route. There would also be a gate at the extension of nearly every street: Porte Sainte-Marie at the end of Saint-Joseph Street and Porte de Lachine at the end of Saint-François-Xavier Street were the notable ones.[37]

It has often been said that these fortifications were modelled after Vauban's. This statement is not quite true and certainly does not do justice to the French engineer's genius. Louisbourg was much more likely to merit the title of New France's "Ville à la Vauban." Vauban's own works, whether Longwy, Neuf-Brisach, or any other fortified town, displayed such refinement of technique and were so vast and complex that they would by themselves provide all the protection a town needed. Lavedan cites Huningue as an example: the area represented by its fortifications was at least eight times that covered by the town proper.[38] This was not the situation in Montreal, where the fortifications could hardly stop an attack by the natives and certainly not assaults by an army equipped with contemporary weapons. Two reasons account for this fact. The walls were extremely fragile and extended too far and thus would require a considerable army to cover all points. Moreover, because of the steep topography of the Saint-Louis hillside, most buildings in the town rose above the top of the wall and were exposed without any defence to artillery shooting from either the river or the land.

Chaussegros de Léry should not be held responsible for the mediocrity of the fortifications. He was no genius, but he was a good engineer and revelled in military construction work. He was, after all, Sébastien Vauban's pupil and protégé. He had written an eight-volume treatise on fortifications with about one hundred drawings on "all that pertains to the manner of fortifying places, of attacking and defending them."[39] Only lack of money prevented him from publishing his treatise.

The real reason for the poor quality of construction was that Montrealers were not very interested in fortifications, mainly because they had to pay for a substantial part of the costs of erecting them. They were accustomed to skirmishes (typical of the new continent) in which personal adroitness was the decisive factor, and they were convinced that their valour was better than any fortification. Unlike the ruling class, with its typical European logic, they were unable to see Montreal as a link within a defence system which, in the mind of the decision-makers, took precedence over all group and private interests. To the inhabitants, Montreal's calling was not military but commercial. Aside from invasions by the natives, Montrealers would never resist foreign invaders; on the contrary, they seemed to welcome them inasmuch as their economic interests benefited.[40]

From 1730 until the British conquest, there are fewer good cartographical documents. There is a plan of Montreal from 1745 which Lanctôt mentions, but it appears to be a British copy of a French original, itself attributed to Chaussegros de Léry.[41] Except for the appearance of suburbs around the fortified town, there is little to be noted about the 1745 plan that has not already been said about the maps of 1723, 1724, and 1731.

There are some plans and views of Montreal dating back to the 1760s. Most of these documents, which are of uneven quality, were drawn by the British invaders for an obvious reason. They had just conquered New France and wanted the British citizenry to behold the prize of so many sacrifices, both in men and in money. Therefore, they were not above exaggerating the importance of the conquered booty, allowing imagination to compensate for the shortcomings of reality. Thus, the "View of the Town and Fortifications of Montreal, in Canada," published in the *Royal Magazine* in London, is pure fancy. It reduces Montreal to a strange cluster of military barracks protected by a powerful wall dotted with as many cannons as there are battlements, the whole picture dominated by the massive constructions of the Jesuits' establishment! [42] Certain other layouts should be read with the same caution; for example, the "Plan and View of the Town and Fortifications of Montreal in Canada," printed by the *Grand Magazine* of London in October 1760, is probably only a poor copy of the famous map by Thomas Jeffreys published in 1758, which was itself but a copy of a previous French one.[43] The last plan of Montreal of the old regime was drawn by the sculptor Paul Labrosse in 1761 and is considered authentic by several learned specialists, among them Massicotte.[44] (Plate 16.)

On the Labrosse plan new streets have appeared, such as Saint-Nicolas, Saint-Eloi, de la Capitale, Saint-Gilles, which were created to fulfil Chaussegros de Léry's wish to accommodate new citizens, without altering the original intent of Dollier de Casson's plan. One striking feature which shows up on this plan is that the city has begun to develop outside the fortified wall. Three main suburbs appear on the plan: Saint-Joseph, with access to the town via the Porte des Récollets; Saint-Laurent, on the street bearing the same name; and Québec, developing in the east and taking its name from its location on the road to Quebec. Streets outside the city gradually aligned themselves to certain main axes, for example Saint-Laurent, and according to the traditional subdivision of land.

Population density is but one of several reasons accounting for the fact that people settled outside the town walls. Was there in fact more building land inside the walls? Because of a lack of data it is not easy to determine the population density of the small town at the end of the French regime. The 1761 census enumerated 5,500 inhabitants in the town of Montreal and the 1765 census counted 900 dwellings therein.[45] Whether these figures refer only to the population living within the walls or include all or part of the population from the suburbs is not known, but they probably take in Montreal and the surrounding suburbs. Even if the total population were living inside the walls, its density would still not be excessive. The inner town covered some 36.5 hectares: this would mean a gross density of some 150 inhabitants per hectare. If one excludes the gardens and vegetable plots belonging to the various civil and religious institutions, covering at least 5 hectares, the net density rises to 175 inhabitants per hectare, a figure which is not excessive by modern standards, and is even less so by the standards of those days. Without making any formal comparison between Montreal and the small French towns of those days, we can show that the population density in Montreal was relatively low in the eighteenth century: cities like Rouen, Caudebec, Troyes, or Annecy numbered but 85 to 110 residences per hectare.[46] Even if all the 900 dwellings in Montreal mentioned in the 1765 census were located within the walls, the gross figure would still amount to only 25 residences per hectare.

The first realistic general view of Montreal was drawn by Thomas Patten, a skilled British officer in the army of General Amherst; it is dated 1762 and confirms the low population density of Montreal at the end of the French regime. On Patten's document, most dwellings are two storeys high, or two and a half including attics. Had the fortifications truly constituted an obstacle to expansion, the town would certainly have developed upward as did several fortified medieval towns in Europe, such as Edinburgh. In fact, even though Montreal was growing increasingly urban in character, the town nevertheless retained rural dimensions as well as some rural traits. To wit, the ordinances of Intendant Monrepos, as late as 1746, 1747, and even 1755, kept reminding the citizens not to allow their pigs to wander through the streets of the town.[47] This suggests that both agriculture and breeding were still practised to a degree in the town. Nevertheless, the beautiful and fertile land around the town must have tempted numerous inhabitants to settle outside rather than inside the walls, especially since the natives had not been a threat for the last fifty years and the Treaty of Utrecht of 1713 had established peace with foreign nations. The attraction of the rural suburbs was strong: indeed, the seemingly endless stretches of land were just outside the gates, with no insurmountable barriers to reaching them. (Plate 17.) Such was, in brief, the topographical growth of Montreal during the first century of its existence and the last century of French rule in America. The conquerors of 1760 would bring new cultural values, which would in time leave their imprint on the city's physical appearance. Before dealing with that subject, we wish to turn our attention to a more thorough analysis of the morphological character of Montreal during French colonization, in an attempt to bring out the various forces and influences which shaped the city's development.

Medievalism and Classicism

The fortified town of Montreal of the 1760s, as it appears on the Labrosse plan, was the result of the interaction of two dynamic compo-

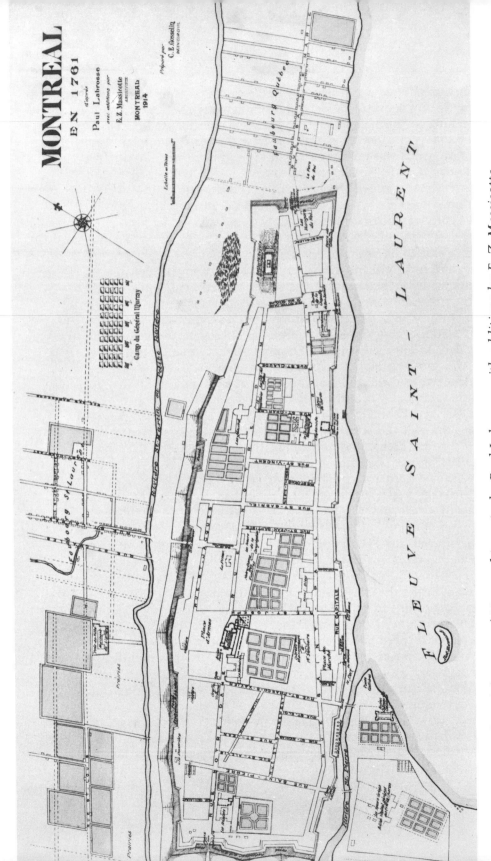

16. *Plan of the town of Montreal in 1761, by Paul Labrosse, with additions by E.-Z. Massicotte*

nents: an original layout and the ensuing development. The initial plan of 1672 by Dollier de Casson was the first element, an outline for development. Let us summarize that plan once more: an orthogonal grid of streets dividing the area into unequal rectangles, with the market place and the parish church polarizing their activities at either end of the town. This church, "which has much more the air of a cathedral than that of Quebec,"[48] to quote Charlevoix, was the most significant sociocultural determinant as well as the most imposing physical structure in the small town. This sociocultural significance was even symbolized by the dominant position of the church near the highest point of the crest of Coteau Saint-Louis. It was located in the middle of Notre-Dame Street, the most important street in town, which Dollier de Casson deliberately drew wider than any other. The convergence of such facts is not without meaning.

The second dynamic component is developmental. From the original scheme of 1672, the settlement progressed in a systematic manner with diversifying forms and functions. The various organs of collective life soon appeared inside the settlement: civil and religious buildings multiplied, clustering around distinctive centres, private dwellings progressively filled the urban lots, and streets gradually took shape.

As they appeared at the end of the old regime, when they had attained a certain degree of maturity, the morphological characteristics of the town resembled those of the small European towns of the Middle Ages. This result is hardly surprising, if one considers the kind of economic, social, and cultural climate in which New France took shape, and is not specific to the French colony, judging from the statement by Lewis Mumford:

> So far from giving birth to a new life, the settlement of the
> northern American seaboard prolonged for a little while the so-
> cial habits and economic institutions which were fast crumbling
> away in Europe, particularly in England. In the villages of the
> New World there flickered up the last dying embers of the medi-
> eval order.[49]

It is undeniable that the dominant structures of Montreal in the 1760s did in fact reflect the economic, social, and cultural structures of a medieval town: fortifications for the defence and protection of the community, a market place at the centre for trade and social interactions, and a parish church with its steeple rising above all other structures in town, attesting to the commanding role of the

17. *View of Montreal in 1762, by Thomas Patten*

church in society.[50] The church's role was not limited to the spiritual world. As in the Middle Ages in Europe, the church in New France and in Montreal took care of the physical and social welfare of the community. Religious institutions like the hospitals of the Grey Nuns and the Hôtel-Dieu, the convents of the Sisters of the Congregation, of the Récollets, and of the Jesuits, all dedicated to education and preaching, clearly point to the irreplaceable role of the church in the organization of the social structure of those days. The close links binding the civil and religious powers were another legacy of the medieval structures. Thus, the Sulpicians constituted both the spiritual and seigneurial authority in Montreal: their seminary, about which Charlevoix remarked that "you may, however, still discover it to be the manor-house," was located next to the parish church.[51]

The legacy of a medieval mentality and a medieval social organization may account for the organic development of Montreal as a homogeneous entity with the main characteristics of a small medieval town. Yet, when one considers the original plan of 1672, one may wonder why Dollier de Casson imposed this particular type of orthogonal grid of streets on the Coteau Saint-Louis, apart from the fact that the alignment of certain streets may have been dictated by pre-existing conditions. There is no satisfactory reply to this question, let alone a definitive answer. Eighteenth-century France may have been among the most advanced nations of Europe in the field of town planning but, unlike Spain, it had not laid out definite rules and principles for the construction of colonial towns and outposts.[52]

To trace the influences which governed the layout of French colonial towns in America, one must delve into the personality and intentions of the colonizers. Dollier de Casson, however, did not record his intentions. He had a rich, versatile personality and it would be difficult to find out what his aims were. Indeed, he first became a captain in the army, then a priest, later on an explorer in America, then Seigneur of Montreal Island, an excellent diplomat, and Montreal's first historian, then an architect and town planner of a sort, and even an engineer, becoming the first to elaborate projects and plans for excavating the Lachine Canal. There is no doubt about one particular point: he was familiar with the architectural and town-planning concepts of his time. He was a young nobleman, born in 1636 at the Château de Casson on the Erdre River in Lower Brittany, and hence probably received a solid education, which usually included some artistic training. He had been a captain in the cavalry under the great Turenne and his travels throughout Europe may have brought him in contact with past or contemporary architectural works. One must keep in mind that the classical Vitry-le-François ·was then only one century old and that the great Sébastien de Vauban (1633–1707) was a contemporary of François Dollier (1636–1701).[53] How were such probable or possible influences reflected in the plan he drew in 1672?

From the layout of some of the colonial towns, it appears that the checkerboard, or orthogonal grid, is particularly well suited for new urban settlements in a new or hostile environment. As examples, one could mention some of the Greek colonial towns like Miletus or Priene, Roman towns like Timgad, towns in Southern Russia, and certain European medieval colonial towns; colonial towns in America, like St. Augustine in Florida, founded by the Spaniards, or Philadelphia, founded by the British. Dollier de Casson, with his good military background, knew that the best way to pitch a military camp was to line up the tents in straight, parallel rows. Such a disposition makes for easier inspection, faster and more orderly assembling of troops, and swifter defensive action in case of attack. In the Middle Ages, the plans of new colonial towns called "bastides" point to an identical approach. In certain respects, the bastides resembled the original plan of Montreal.

The "bastide," which in the Provençal language means a fortress, is a small fortified colonial town. Most bastides were free towns with market privileges, where a prince or seigneur would attract colonists by granting them privileges. They were established with a definite purpose in mind: to bolster the financial assets of a seigneur or to allow him to extend his jurisdiction over foreign or hostile territories, to consolidate a military or political domination over conquered territories, or to protect borders. In Europe, bastides are found mainly in territories which have been contested by rival powers: in northern Spain and especially in southwestern France, between the Pyrenees and the Dordogne, in a country which had been for a long time the object of wars between the Dukes of Toulouse, the British (during the Hundred Years' War), and the French from the northern kingdom. They are also located on the borders which England shares with Wales and Scotland, and are even found in Northern Ireland.[54] There seems to be an interesting similarity between the conditions which prevailed at the time of the creation of bastides in the troubled Europe of the Middle Ages and the fashioning of certain French towns in North America, particularly Montreal on the St. Lawrence River. Indeed, the creation of Ville-Marie on the Coteau Saint-Louis in 1672, in the middle of a savage war with natives bent on ridding the island of the white invaders, does resemble the occupation of hostile territory.

One should not use the bastide of Monpazier in Dordogne, France, as a basis for a comparison between the European—and especially French—bastides and the town of Montreal under the French regime. That of Monpazier is exceptional, a fact which accounts for its fame. It was founded in 1284, and the rigidity, symmetry, and regularity of its plan reveal the ideal conditions of its well-planned settlement. Apart from the characteristic structures of a medieval town such as fortifications, a market place, and a church, it had few common features with Montreal.

According to Lavedan, the numerous French bastides present a great variety of plans and shapes, depending on the site or other conditions. Many, particularly among those founded towards the end of the thirteenth century, were laid out according to orthogonal plans but, unlike Monpazier, without any geometrical rigidity. Streets crossed more or less at right angles and the urban lots thus created were relatively regular in shape but of variable dimensions, as in Montreal. Ville-Marie's original checkerboard layout designed by Casson, the military Sulpician, resembled more closely the plans of bastides like Beaumont-en-Périgord, Monségur, Puymirol, Valence-du-Gers, Villefranche de Belvès, and several others.[55] (Figure 6.)

The location was often the determining factor in the layout of certain bastides: this is true of Montreal. The elongated, almost linear layout of the plan was determined by the Coteau Saint-Louis, with its steep crest locked between the river, Saint-Martin Creek, and swamp land in the northwest. On the other hand, when the site was free of any topographical limitations, the colonial French town in America tended to be closely patterned after the geometrical model of the bastide of Monpazier. This is somewhat true in the diminutive town of Trois-Rivières as it is depicted on an anonymous plan of 1704. The fort of Detroit, founded in 1701 on the Detroit River between Lake Erie and Lake St. Clair, provides a more striking example. It is a small fortified town, with an extremely regular layout and perfectly perpendicular streets forming rectangular lots of almost equal dimensions. As in Monpazier, there is a certain hierarchy in the width of its streets. Its founder, Antoine de la Mothe Cadillac, came from Gascogne in southwestern France.[56]

It is a remarkable fact that among French settlements in America, identical natural situations seemed to have dictated similar solutions to the town planners. Indeed, in most instances where a site displayed the same features and topographical restrictions as Coteau Saint-Louis, the plans for the town to be erected were similar to that of Montreal. This was true with Quebec's Lower Town, locked between the river and the cliff. This was also the situation, under the

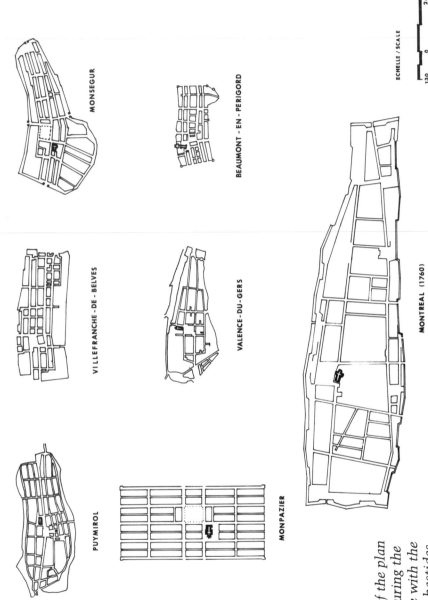

PUYMIROL

VILLEFRANCHE - DE - BELVES

MONSEGUR

MONPAZIER

VALENCE - DU - GERS

BEAUMONT - EN - PERIGORD

MONTREAL (1760)

ECHELLE / SCALE

130   0   260 M

Fig. 6
Comparison of the plan
of Montreal during the
French regime with the
plans of some bastides

French regime, with St. Louis, Mobile, and New Orleans. It is likely that the plans for these towns, founded later than Montreal, were inspired by Montreal's layout. This is hardly surprising, for the founder of Mobile and New Orleans, the Sieur Jean-Baptiste Lemoyne de Bienville (1680–1768), was born in Montreal and had lived there.[57]

If there was a connection between the plans and the layout of certain French bastides and those of Montreal under the old regime, there was however no mere transposition. They may have been similar on the whole, but they were marked by significant differences, one of which was scale. Chaussegros de Léry's fortified Montreal covered at least twice the area occupied by the bastides of Monpazier and Puymirol, three times that of Valence-du-Gers, and seven times that of Beaumont-en-Périgord. Dollier de Casson's initial plan was not so ambitious, but the lots between the streets were very wide. The plot which was originally bounded by Saint-Pierre, Notre-Dame, Saint-François, and Saint-Paul Streets covered an area of about four hectares, almost the total area of the bastide of Beaumont-en-Périgord, which was itself divided into about thirty blocks. Such a difference in scale may be explained by the fact that concessions to private citizens on Coteau Saint-Louis had been very generous. The grants made to Pierre Gadois in 1648 and to Robert Cavelier in 1654 were each two arpents wide and fifteen and twenty arpents long, respectively, as we have seen earlier. These concessions seem to have constituted decisive factors in the creation of several lots. In 1672 Ville-Marie must have been designed both as an agricultural centre and as an urban community. Only demographic pressures and the instigations of the authorities (Chaussegros de Léry, particularly) managed gradually to reduce the individual parcels inside the walls to proportions more in keeping with an urban settlement. It is interesting to note that the scale, the plan, the shape, and the very spirit of the traditional bastide find their natural place in the lower town, around the market place, where the merchants' activities are essentially urban in character.

It is in the upper town where we can distinguish the other fundamental difference between Montreal and the bastide: the placement and the importance accorded to the centres of collective life in the urban context. Indeed, the market place of a bastide covered an area near the centre of the town, which was considerable in comparison with the total area: this was one of the bastide's main features, especially in southern France. Moreover, the church was rarely built close to the market place, but usually on another square, or sometimes on a street relatively far away from the central market place.

Thus, in a bastide, the prevalence of trade was evident from the prominence of the market place.[58] In Montreal, under the old regime, the reverse was true. Although the market place closely resembled that of the typical bastide with its rectilinear outline and its streets located at the corners, it did not cover so large an area as the Place d'Armes adjacent to the parish church. Moreover, the very location of the market place in the lower town subordinated it to the church's public square. Dollier de Casson intended that Ville-Marie should be a religious enterprise, dedicated to religious ends. This is obvious from the location of the parish church and its square at the top of Coteau Saint-Louis, in the middle of the town's main street.

When he used an open space in the middle of a road to make a visual display of the parish church, the Sulpician was resorting to the town planners' language of his time, which was more a legacy of the Renaissance than of the Middle Ages. In a bastide or in a medieval town in general, no public square or street was ever used to show a cathedral, a church, or any structure. When it did happen, it was as a result of successive organic transformations, dictated by needs and opportunities rather than by preconceived intention. Thus, it appears that some people in New France were aware of the traditions of classicism both in town planning and in architecture. As a model, Ville-Marie had its limitation but, placed in its proper perspective as an achievement in the context of the colony, it deserves to be mentioned.

How did this Renaissance heritage find its way to America? As established earlier, it was part of the cultural background of the ruling class, the only group to intervene in the planning of the environment, and of which Dollier de Casson was a good representative. The Comte de Frontenac, as we have seen, was imbued with classical concepts of planning and he would certainly have made use of such notions had the opportunity arisen. There was, however, another source for the diffusion of the gospel of classicism in America, which may have left its mark in an indirect manner on the creation of French towns. It was the very significant Spanish colonial experience on the North American continent.

All the Spanish colonial towns in the New World were planned according to the principles and rules laid down in the "Laws of the Indies," a collection of royal ordinances promulgated by Philip II of Spain in 1573. They reflected the long urban tradition of Spain, which was being gradually infiltrated by the spirit of the Renaissance. To mention but one example, it was stipulated that when a coastal town was created, the public square was to be located near the shore, that the main structures representing the civil and religious authorities were to figure prominently on the public square, and so forth.[59] The orthogonal plan of the lower town in Quebec City, with an open market place in front of the church, reminds one of some of the ordinances from the "Laws of the Indies." A similar influence may be found in the first tentative plans for Sainte-Croix by Samuel de Champlain, who was later to found Quebec. Is there a causal relationship? One must remember that from 1599 to 1601 Champlain had visited the most important Spanish settlements in America, among them Mexico, San Juan, Vera Cruz, Porto Bello, Santo Domingo, Panama, and Havana. An eighteenth-century plan of the town of St. Augustine in Florida depicts an orthogonal grid of streets, a central market, and a parade square with a church prominently placed on it. Champlain's exact role in the planning of the Lower Town in Quebec is not known, but a glance at that map reveals noticeable resemblances to the plan of Quebec's Lower Town and, to a lesser degree, to that of Montreal under the old regime.

Did Dollier de Casson know the "Laws of the Indies" which governed the creation of Spanish colonial towns? He might have had in mind some of the French towns like Vitry-le-François or Charleville, or he might have remembered some of Vauban's achievements. The concepts behind the Spanish colonial towns were not all that different from Vauban's. He might also have been inspired by the plan of Quebec's Lower Town, which he had certainly seen. We have no information which would allow us to answer these questions. One thing is certain, though: there was a vast choice of sources of inspiration from which he might have drawn in order to establish Ville-Marie.

As mentioned in the previous chapter, two traditions prevailed in Montreal under the French regime. The initial plan seemed to issue from the concept of the medieval bastide. This characteristic is not limited to French settlements in America; it is also found in British and Spanish towns and outposts, a fact which is not surprising. Indeed, in the Middle Ages, various nations looked upon the bastides as a new way of dealing with the occupation of threatened, hostile, or newly acquired land. It was only natural for such nations to resort to a similar solution when faced with an analogous situation in America. In fact, without prior consultation, and one could say almost subconsciously, various colonizers seemed to have displayed a common attitude when faced with the task of creating towns and outposts in the New World. On the other hand, each one of these nations carried with itself the contemporary national tradition of its ruling class which, at the time, was influenced by the Renaissance and classicism. One must therefore expect to find some of these traditions in the physical structures of their colonial towns. Besides, one may ask, how much does the nature of a bastide differ from that of a "ville à la Vauban"? Might it not be said of Vauban's towns that they constituted a refinement of the art of the bastide? That remains to be seen. We now turn our attention to the architectural components of Montreal at the end of the seventeenth century and during the eighteenth century.

5

Architecture and Environment in the Frontier Town

Nos ancêtres étaient donc des hommes simples, réfléchis, prévoyants. Ils se sont créé un art à leur juste mesure; un art si compréhensible, si bien ordonné, fait de si peu de chose, qu'il a fleuri pendant près de deux siècles.
GÉRARD MORISSET [1]

The Architectural Heritage of the Old Regime
Contrary to popular belief, very few buildings in Old Montreal date back to the French regime. In fact, there are only five or six at the most. As it is sometimes difficult to discover the exact date of certain buildings, it is almost impossible to confirm this small number. For instance, a part of the old General Hospital of the Grey Nuns in the Normand/Saint-Pierre block, may date back to the French colonial era, to the early days of the Charron Brothers, around 1692 or 1694. However, this is true only of some of the walls; the hospital was destroyed in a fire in 1765 and only the undamaged walls were used for reconstruction.[2] One faces a similar problem concerning the Maison du Calvet (occupied today by Ogilvy's and restored by them in 1966). It is supposed to be one of Montreal's oldest existing residences and to have been built before 1725. An analysis of historical maps would establish that the northeast corner of Bonsecours and Saint-Paul Streets seems to have been occupied as early as 1723. Nevertheless, it is still difficult to say whether this is the same building. Finally, if Pierre du Calvet, who settled in Montreal in

1767, did in fact live there, this house must have been constructed before or around that period. One building which certainly belonged to the old regime is the old Seminary of Saint-Sulpice on Notre-Dame Street. The central part was probably erected around 1683 or 1684, and it is clearly indicated on maps of 1684 and 1704. However, the wings appear only on the maps of 1723 and 1724 that were drawn by the engineers de Catalogne and Chaussegros de Léry. One thing is certain: the 1740 engraved on the frieze of the central door indicates the date of construction of the classical style portico, rather than that of erection of the old main building.[3]

In fact, the famous Château de Ramezay is perhaps the only urban building in Montreal from the French regime for which we have a definite date for the start of construction, 1705. A masonry contract signed on 27 April 1705 between M. de Ramezay and Pierre Couturier, "master mason and architect," confirms this date, and stipulates that the "house shall be 66 feet long on the outside as well as 36 feet wide,"[4] all in French measurements,[5] which are much smaller than those found there today.

The solution to the enigma lies in another agreement, signed on 24 August 1755, between the Sieur Paul Texier La Vigne, master mason and contractor, and M. Deschambault, general agent for the Compagnie des Indes, which had owned the château since 1745. Indeed, the latter contract refers to "the restoration and enlargement of the Company's mansion situated in this town, on Notre-Dame Street, to 92 feet in length by 48 feet in width,"[6] measurements which approximate the present dimensions, although excluding the ugly extensions of 1830 and 1906.[7] What is left of the original construction of 1705? How did the 1755 renovations alter the architectural features of the previous building? These questions would be hard to answer and, at any rate, are not of great significance for this study. It is often claimed that the style and architectural features of the Château de Ramezay date back to 1705, whereas in fact they most likely go back only to 1755; such claims may lead to erroneous conclusions. One might surmise that the château, far from being the first known example of a detached house with fire-break gables, typical of the Montreal region according to Traquair,[8] would in fact be a more prestigious example of a kind of domestic architecture already widespread at the time in Montreal and in the vicinity.

People tend to believe that several buildings still existing in Old Montreal date back to the French colonial era, probably because they display the features of the distinctive popular architecture of that era, although they were in fact built up to a century later. The Maison du Patriote on Saint-Paul Street, the Maison de la Sauvegarde on Notre-Dame Street, and the Maison Truteau on Saint-Gabriel Street are among the best examples of this type. Others include the d'Youville Stables, built around 1820, and the pleasant cluster at the northeast corner of Place Jacques-Cartier and Saint-Paul Street which was probably built between 1800 and 1850.

These buildings are the products of an artisan tradition which extended far beyond the conquest. Indeed, if the character of public architecture had been altered by the change of allegiance, it would be wrong to think that popular architecture also was suddenly modified. The contemporary fashions in French architecture had been unable to alter a traditional art deeply rooted in centuries of an educational system controlled by the guilds. In like manner, the British takeover did not have any immediate effect on the way of conceiving and building private dwellings. On the contrary, apart from forcing an already conservative population to further strengthen its bonds, the conquest caused some of the acquired traditions to crystallize. Some residences did reflect the influence of the new occupants, like McTavish House, but most perpetuated the ancestral attitudes and ways until the middle of the nineteenth century and beyond. For this reason such urban dwellings will be integrated into our study of the architectural heritage of the French regime.

Finally, a word about Notre-Dame-de-Bonsecours Chapel. Contrary to popular belief, it does not date back to the French colonial period. The present chapel was erected on the location of the previous one which had been built in 1675 and was destroyed by fire in 1754; at best, only parts of the first walls were used for reconstruction. The new chapel, slightly larger than the previous one, was erected from 1771 onwards and must have looked like its predecessor; the same restraint, the same soaring volume, and the same architectural expressions resulting from the happy marriage of two traditions prevailed. There were pointed gables, arched doors and windows, protruding corner stones, a circular bull's eye, basket vaults, and the interior was decorated in the traditional manner of our sculptors in wood. Unfortunately, its simplicity of form and taste was vulnerable to the rules of romanticism at the end of the nineteenth century. Moreover, the chapel was a place of pilgrimage and, as such, became a particular symbol for a nation which made no distinction between faith and nationalism. As could be expected, the symbol was enlivened at the expense of architecture. From 1886 to 1894, it suffered repeated alterations meant to embellish it, but which in fact were an insult to good taste. The interior was rough-cast plastered and redecorated; the exterior was loaded with towers, turrets, bell-turrets, statues, galleries, ex-votos, and other frills.

With the blessing of the church it ended up looking like a bazaar; it was now a credit to the lack of taste of the romantic period and no longer characteristic of French colonial architecture.[9]

Outside the boundaries of the old fortified city there are few structures dating back to the French regime on Montreal Island. The oldest are the two towers of the Grand Séminaire, on Sherbrooke Street West, which are the last vestiges of the Fort des Messieurs. Erected in 1694 by the Abbé de Belmont, the turrets were part of a group of four located at the corners of a stone wall which protected the Sulpician's mission on the mountain. The Maison de la Ferme Saint-Gabriel, discussed later in this chapter, is located in Pointe Saint-Charles; the central part was built in 1698, and constitutes another legacy from the end of the seventeenth century. Some time later, early in 1700, a windmill was built in Pointe-aux-Trembles, but it is in a deplorable state today. Finally, one of the only other structures from that era is the Church of the Visitation at Sault-au-Récollet, with its main building of stonework dating back to the year 1749–50.

It is probable that sections or even whole buildings constructed in the French regime still exist, mainly among the old houses found along the old king's ways of the island's côtes, such as Côte Saint-Antoine. Short of patient searches through notaries' records to trace building contracts and property transfer documents, it would be difficult to date the old dwellings. In the country as well as in the town, old concepts and methods of construction for private dwellings were perpetuated until the 1900s. The relative degree of adaptation of such buildings to the environment and to climatic conditions would constitute the only valid criterion of reference to establish the date of construction.

A word of caution, before undertaking a more intensive study of such buildings. They must not be judged according to the criteria of conventional aesthetics. Such an excessively exclusive approach accounts for Traquair's assertion that Montreal "never seems to have had any public buildings of any architectural importance, and today very little survives from the French regime. The old seminary of St. Sulpice . . . is a plain building with only an amusing little clock belfry and an ionic doorporch. The Château de Ramezay is simply a big house."[10]

Architecture with a capital "A," a subtle blend of functionalism, solidity, and beauty, is too rigidly tied to established rules for it to apply to colonial architecture. After all, Montreal under the old regime was not exactly a cultural centre. It was a frontier town, a pioneer settlement, exposed to the harshness of the continent and to the hatred of the natives; it was a trading post, a transit centre where people tried their luck and often saw their hopes dashed. Compared with Quebec it was the new town, and its traders were setting an example of daring and boldness for the industrialists of the future, rushing to the conquest of new values under the aegis of men, ideas, and influences which seemed out of place in such a small settlement. How different from Quebec! Quebec was the capital, the administrative centre, the seat of the episcopate, a port through which all ideas, fashions, and European influences filtered before reaching Montreal. Quebec was the guardian of the values of an old civilization attempting to tame the new continent: Quebec was essentially traditionalist and conservative. The colonist who had visited Quebec with its ramparts, its Jesuit church and college, and the bishop's palace must have found Montreal very rough indeed! Quebec was nostalgic Old France; Montreal, less ostentatious and more down-to-earth, was the developing New France.

We are most interested in the changes brought about by the adaptation of the old European architecture to the new physical environment. Any building displaying such characteristics should be considered for a study of this nature and we intend to select a few examples in the field of public and domestic architecture, each of which shall be examined on its own first and then within the context of its own urban environment.

Public Architecture

The parish church of Notre-Dame was designed by François Dollier de Casson and built by a contractor and master mason named François Bailli,[11] but only a few sketches by Lambert, Drake, and Sproule are still extant. Construction started, in the middle of Notre-Dame Street, in 1672 and the church was completed some ten years later. It became the second most important church in the colony after the cathedral of Quebec. As noted, Father de Charlevoix, who visited Montreal in 1721, after the church had been enlarged in 1708 by Vachon de Belmont, wrote that "it has much more the air of a cathedral than that of Quebec."[12] It was one of the most significant monuments of French colonial architecture in Montreal, a perfect example of the dichotomy of traditions described in chapter 3. The construction of the present Notre-Dame Church on Place d'Armes, from 1824 to 1829, constitutes a breach with the cultural and artisan traditions of French Canadians. A study of the previous sanctuary will reveal the extent of this rupture.

The first Notre-Dame Church was the embodiment of the perenniality of medieval traditions, appearing in its strong structure as well as in the materials used in the construction. The church's ability to adapt and to evolve through successive alterations reinforces this feeling. Indeed, the nave had to be enlarged to accommodate the rapid population increases in Montreal. In 1731 three chapels were inserted between the transept and the tower on the right; three years later, the left side underwent the same alterations. Such free, organic growth dictated by the needs of the times is indicative of medieval concepts rather than of the formal principles of classic tradition. The architecture of the first Notre-Dame Church was dynamic and, to a contemporary observer, it seemed to grow with the city. In spite of architectural features borrowed from classicism, such as arched windows and dormers and quoins (dressed corner stones), the building was true to the medieval spirit, and the sanctuary was enlarged without detracting from the style or infringing on any canon. Yet, the front of the church seems to have been inherited from a completely different tradition. (Plates 18 & 19.)

In fact, important alterations were made to the church after 1722, not the least of which was the remodelling of the front according to designs by Chaussegros de Léry. The front, in common Jesuit style, was compressed between two massive towers and had two levels separated by an entablature. The lower storey was decorated with pilasters in the Tuscan style framing a central arched door and two windows placed symmetrically on either side of this axis. The upper storey, smaller in size than the lower one, was connected with it, in traditional Jesuit style, by two wings. This storey was also decorated with pilasters framing a large arched central window and supporting an entablature adorned with triglyphs and crowned with a classical triangular pediment. Two identical steeples had been provided for in the original plan, but only one was finally completed (on the side facing Place d'Armes) and late at that, in 1782.

If the sketch by John Drake (1828) depicting the façade is a faithful representation of Chaussegros de Léry's intentions, it confirms a previous contention that the latter was above all interested in military architecture. The façade he designed for Notre-Dame in Montreal is in fact severe, without great refinement of details, displaying rather clumsy military rigour. Leaving aside aesthetic considerations, Chaussegros de Léry's façade, attached to a less exclusively classical structure, is nevertheless symbolic of the influence of the ruling class which, in those days, was familiar with the current fashions in architecture; de Léry, as a king's engineer, was both the envoy and the promoter of that fashion. The two founding classes of New France's society did not mix. In like manner, the façade designed by the king's engineer did not fit in with the church's nave: it

18. *Façade of the parish church of Notre-Dame. Watercolour by John Drake, 1828, after a project by Chaussegros de Léry, 1721*

was irrelevant in many ways, but especially because of its formalism and its identifiable style. Juxtapositions of this kind are frequent in Europe: a façade with three classical orders has been added to the western side of the sixteenth-century Gothic nave of Saint-Gervais–Saint-Protais in Paris (1616–21): they reflect the passing of time with its corresponding changes in fashions and architectural ideals. In Notre-Dame of Montreal, though, both constructions are almost contemporary and are the simultaneous expression of two architectural traditions. In fact, when Chaussegros de Léry designed the front, it appeared more as a curb on popular tradition than as the logical and chronological attainment of its evolution. One should hardly be surprised to find that when the old church was demolished in 1830 to clear the parvis for the new Notre-Dame, the "Jesuit" style front was carefully dismantled and rebuilt to ornament the old church of the Monastery of the Récollets in Montreal (1706).[13] Once more, the ruling class was imposing its own brand of classicism on a construction built in the popular tradition.

In a certain way, the plan drawn by Chaussegros de Léry was an innovation. It provided for two bell-towers, although only the foundations for the second were laid. Before his project, twin bell-towers were unknown to religious architecture in New France, and even in France they were a rare occurrence in the seventeenth century. Moreover, in a colony with very limited resources, such luxury did not fulfil any functional need, not even that of accentuating the predominance of the church in the social organization. It could very well be that the Sulpicians were attempting to surpass the splendour of Quebec's cathedral, for the rivalry between Quebec and Montreal was an old one. It could also have been a legacy from the great Romanesque abbeys in Normandy or from the majestic Gothic cathedrals on the Ile de France. It might also have been inspired by the legitimate desire of the Gentlemen of Saint-Sulpice to recreate in Montreal a new architectural feature which highlighted the mother church in Paris. Even though its famous Paris façade by Servandoni was completed some years after that of Notre-Dame of Montreal—in 1749, with one tower finished only in 1788—plans for the Saint-Sulpice Church in Paris had been prepared as early as 1660 and Dollier de Casson, Vachon de Belmont, and other Sulpicians of Montreal must have been aware of them. Whatever the facts, the two-tower plan as a means of pointing out the importance of the church was to have a significant influence on the architecure of parish churches in New France and in Quebec and set a trend that would last until the twentieth century. Thus, from the beginning of the eighteenth century onwards, Montreal set the tone in Canadian architecture, a position which the city has held until now.[14]

19. Parish church of Notre-Dame, Place d'Armes, after a drawing by R. A. Sproule, 1830

The old Notre-Dame Church is not the only public building of the old regime in Montreal to have displayed features borrowed from the two architectural traditions. The old Seminary of Saint-Sulpice on Notre-Dame Street is another example, and has survived to this day in a reasonable state of repair despite the disappearance of one of the two original wings, a fact which lessens its character.[15] Several features of medieval tradition are apparent in the seminary: the staircases in the corner towers, the turrets erected at both ends of the back of the building but no longer extant, the solid foundations with cradle-vaults, the predominance of full spaces over open spaces, and the artisan building techniques. On the other hand, even though the seminary was not built all at once, several features dear to classicism are obvious: a U-shaped plan, with turrets, lateral wings, and doors symmetrically located about a central axis, a balanced vertical and horizontal alignment of windows, arched crowning of some of the dormers, and the ashlar framework of the openings. The seminary is usually attributed to Vachon de Belmont, who was Dollier de Casson's successor as head of the institution and who largely financed its construction from his own fortune. At any rate, whoever the architect was, he showed himself capable of blending contemporary ideas with the more humble traditional architecture. The whole structure seems somewhat squat, the storeys are low, and the windows small, but this is an adaptation to the climate. On the other hand, its strength, its naïve confidence, and the fineness of its clock and bell-turret lend the structure a great deal of character. (See figure 7 and plate 20.)

To further satisfy their need to identify with the classical tradition, the Seigneurs of Montreal Island adorned the seminary with a most charming main door leading to the old building. The casing of the door is composed of ionic pilasters topped by a very simple entablature with the date 1740 engraved on the frieze. Whoever designed this small classical portal knew his business. Some maintain it was Chaussegros de Léry. Others, among them Morault, are of the opinion that Monsieur Normant, then superior of Montreal's seminary, had it designed by the Chevalier de Beaucourt, captain and king's engineer.[16]

The seminary's small formal garden "à la française" is the oldest in the metropolis, the only significant green space to have survived in Old Montreal, which today is nothing but stone, asphalt, and concrete. The historical maps are not clear on this matter, but it seems that the plot was originally intended to be a vegetable garden. In this, it follows the tradition of the medieval cloister gardens which were used as vegetable plots, as spaces to walk through or to rest in,

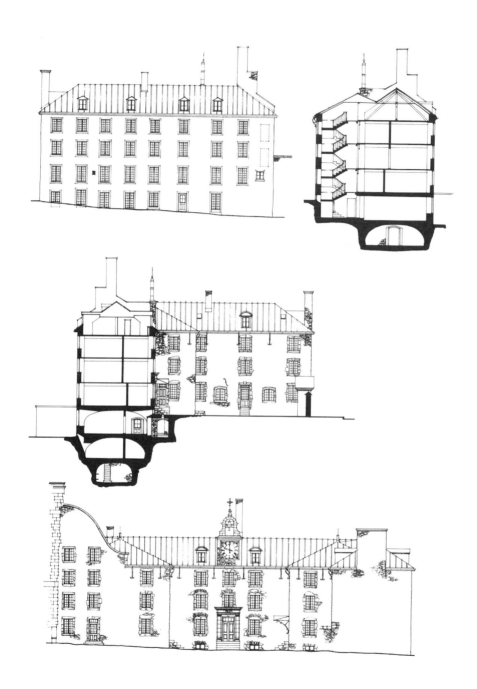

Fig.7 The old Seminary of Saint-Sulpice, central part built in 1683–84

20.   *The old Seminary of Saint-Sulpice towards the end of the nineteenth century*

even as cemeteries, but rarely as an ornament for the monastery it-self or for any other building. Such spaces were usually enclosed, as was that of the old Seminary of Saint-Sulpice in Montreal. Even to-day, one may not be aware of its existence as one walks along the neighbouring streets. It may be reached through a long dark corridor running along the western wing. Upon entering the garden, one is struck by a feeling of intimacy reminiscent of European medieval towns.

The architecture of the old Seminary of Saint-Sulpice was a blend of two traditions, but such was not true for the Château de Vau-dreuil. It was located at the foot of today's Place Jacques-Cartier and, together with the Jesuit building facing it on Notre-Dame Street, was destroyed by fire on 6 June 1803. Luckily, authentic sketches by James Duncan and by others enable us to describe its appearance. It was designed to be the residence in Montreal of the colony's gover-nor, and the Marquis de Montcalm as well as the Duke of Lévis spent some time there. Such a function required a certain decor: the château was meant to highlight the prestige of the ruling class.

It was therefore the most classical of public buildings in Montreal under the old regime and perhaps also the most elegant. Gaspard Chaussegros de Léry drew the plans in 1723 and they turned out better than the ones he had made for the façade of Notre-Dame Church. Volumes and openings were distributed symmetrically about a central entrance, in a manner reminiscent of the small clas-sical portal of the Old Seminary. A formal staircase "à la Fontaine-bleau" led to the entrance. The storeys were separated horizontally by mouldings and by a cornice on the roof, and the reception room was designed so as to show a generous view of the outer esplanade. The château was Montreal's modest contribution to the classical and Baroque canons which governed public architecture in contem-porary France. Unlike the cloistered garden of the Old Seminary, the formal garden of the château was purely ornamental, meant to high-light the prestige of its functions. Although it may not have com-pared favourably with the most significant of private mansions of eighteenth-century Paris, the Château de Vaudreuil seems to have been equalled only by the bishop's palace in Quebec.[17]

Domestic Architecture
Domestic architecture was the most likely to be influenced by environment and climate. As indicated earlier, the popular class was made up of ordinary people who came from the rural regions of France. They had little self-awareness, but brought with them the legacy of an ancestral way of building whose main purpose was to

satisfy the basic needs for security and comfort against outside elements. Heaven knows that in Canada the need for security and comfort in the face of hostile natives and harsh winters was more bitterly felt than in "douce France." Moreover, domestic architecture was receptive to the various influences of the new continent, inasmuch as it represented the most common type of construction and also the least likely to submit to the culture-centred currents of architectural fashions. By comparison, public buildings, whether secular or ecclesiastical, were much fewer in number and were meant to reflect the ideals of the ruling class. Therefore, they were much less likely to lend themselves to experimentation and adaptation. This is what appears to be revealed by the slow evolution of the Quebec house from its original European models.

What were these models like? It has repeatedly been stated that the prototypes for domestic architecture in the Montreal region came from the northern provinces of France, more specifically from Maine, Anjou, and especially Brittany. Robert-Lionel Séguin has said that:

> the Montreal house has the appearance of a small square domestic fortress; it is massive, flanked by heavy chimneys, and built with large fieldstones drowned in mortar. The windows in the walls are recessed behind heavy shutters reinforced with iron. . . . Such a house seems to find its origin in Brittany.[18]

Any visitor to the French provinces can vouch for the accuracy of that statement. In Lower Brittany, in the departments of Loire-Atlantique and Morbihan, the peasant house is robust, squat, gloomy, and anonymous, and is solidly anchored in the ground like a solitary menhir. The stone walls have small openings, and small dormers are perched on a simple double-slope or ridge roof. Two chimneys, one at each end of the building, tower over gables which are often windowless. All in all, these houses look like those which were built in the Montreal region at the beginning of the colony and of which several specimens are still extant.

The best example is perhaps the Maison de la Ferme Saint-Gabriel in Pointe-Saint-Charles. It was built in 1698 and enlarged in 1726 and 1728. The elongated plan of the house already shows a large common room; the first floor is almost level with the ground; the massive walls are two feet thick. The roof, with a slope of 50 percent, has small dormers and the eaves do not protrude more than six inches beyond the outside walls. This dwelling appears to be the prototype for the Quebec rural house.[19] (Plate 21.) Weather condi-

21. *Maison de la Ferme Saint-Gabriel, built in 1698, with extensions in 1726 and in 1728*

tions and new patterns of activities dictated by the contingencies of the environment as well as the inhabitants' contacts with other American colonies enabled this type of house to reach a state of perfect adaptation during the nineteenth century (1780–1920). The rural house was more affected by this evolution than were the town dwellings. The stone foundations progressively rose above the ground level to fend off snow accumulation in winter; a porch became the functional link between the ground floor and the soil; the slope of the roof was progressively reduced to a practical 45 degrees while its edges were extended more and more to protect the walls better and to cover the porch; a stove replaced the open fireplace, thus diminishing the size of the chimneys to the point where the second one was reduced to an ornament. Improvements in the heating system and the use of double panes allowed for more and larger windows. The interior remained simple: a large common room serving both as a kitchen and as a living room, a parlour, and one or two other rooms; the storey below the roof was divided into rooms or kept for storage, or both. A summer kitchen was often added to the most exposed wall; it was cool during the summer and could be used for cold storage during the winter.[20] Several good specimens of the Quebec rural house may still be found on the island of Montreal in places not yet affected by the urban sprawl: for example, in Sainte-Geneviève, Cap Saint-Jacques, or Senneville. Whether made of wood or of stone, they have adapted to the environment in a similar manner.

The urban house developed in a different manner, as may be seen from surviving homes in Old Montreal: the Maison du Calvet, probably built around 1770; the Maison du Patriote, constructed around the same time; the Maison de la Sauvegarde, from around the end of the eighteenth century; and the Maison Del Vecchio (1807–9). Indeed, these structures show few if any traces of a significant elevation above the ground, or of a porch and protruding roof edges; on the other hand, floors and fire-break walls became characteristic features. Even though none of these houses dates back to the French regime, they nevertheless are characteristic of the urban dwelling inherited from that period. One may exclude the city residence of the Marquis de Lotbinière, located at 221 Saint-Sacrement and probably erected around 1755, and the Maison Papineau, part of which had been built around the same date, because restorations have altered their domestic architectural features.

Here again, Brittany had provided the models for eighteenth-century Montreal urban dwellings displaying some features found in the austere alignments of city dwellings in Guingamp, Châtelaudren, Saint-Brieuc, or Lamballe, on the north coast of Brittany. A sloping roof with the ridge parallel to the street is one of the most important features common to houses in the towns of Brittany and in Montreal. This seems to be the reason why the arrangement was used here, even though the climate did not favour it. Indeed, in Canada's harsh weather it would have been more logical to place the ridge of the roof perpendicular to the street, as in Flemish, Rhenish, or Dutch houses, to protect the street and passers-by from falling water, snow, or ice.[21] This aspect of the matter did not worry the sparse population of eighteenth-century Montreal; moreover, it may have been overlooked because it was foreign to the building traditions of the inhabitants.

Other differences between the traditional rural houses and the urban dwellings may be accounted for better by the interventions of the ruling class than by cultural legacy or the natural influences of the environment. The citizens often accepted the interventions with reticence, a fact which indicates that the changes ran contrary to acquired tendencies and attitudes. The "Ordinance ruling on the reconstruction of houses [destroyed by the fire of 19 June 1721, in the town of Montreal] in fireproof materials and on other purposes; dated 8 July seventeen hundred and twenty one" was the first important intervention. It was Intendant Michel Bégon's immediate intention to prevent, through both inducement and coercive regulations, the repetition of a blaze like that of 19 June which had razed more than 130 buildings in the town.[22] This ordinance, confirmed and completed by a second, "ruling on the construction of houses in fireproof materials in the towns of the colony; 7 June 1727," by Intendant Claude-Thomas Dupuy, constituted a true abridged construction and town-planning code and deserves a closer look.

First of all, the intendant forbade anyone "to build a house in towns and large villages, where stone is easily found, except in stone; we forbid [anyone] to build them in wood, piecemeal, or with timber framing," and he further ordered that all houses should be built with two storeys. Judging from remarks by Peter Kalm, who wrote in 1749 that "some of the houses in the town are built of stone, but most of them are of timber, though very neatly built,"[23] it does not seem that the obligation to build in stone was ever followed to the letter. This would also account for the small number of houses still extant today.

The ordinance further recommended that "cellars and storerooms be as vaulted as possible, to prevent beams and floors which are placed above them from rotting." Such vaults are found here and there in Old Montreal, notably at the Château de Ramezay and in a building located at the southwest corner of Saint-Laurent and Saint-Paul Streets; the arched vaults of its foundation today serve as a background for a discothèque. Concerning cellars or storerooms located above the street, the intendant ordered owners to move "the stairs from the outside to the inside of the house, in order that no more than three steps at the most should protrude either in height or towards the street." Some people found even these few steps to be a problem. This is what E. A. Talbot has to say:

> The streets are in general very narrow; and, to add to the inconvenience which this occasions, the side-paths or causeways are rendered almost impassable, by a barbarous practice which prevails in every part of the city, of erecting outside the doors wooden steps which project from three to four feet into the streets. If only two persons meet opposite one of those cumbersome piles, they will inevitably be obliged either to retrace their steps, or out of hasty complaisance to descend into the channel, probably up to their knees in snow, or to their ankles in mud.[24]

It is easily understood that the porches common to rural dwellings were not found in the cities where space was at a premium.

Then follows a series of regulations designed to lessen the risks of fire. It is forbidden "to include in the construction of outside walls and gables of houses any apparent wood"; it is strictly forbidden "to cover with shingles any house at present built in towns and suburbs"; it is forbidden to build "curb-roofs [mansard] . . . which burden the buildings with forests of wood"; it is forbidden "to lay or rest any chimney or stove pipe on partitions, wooden partitions or studworks." These interdictions are followed by suggestions like the following: "to build on the floors of attics and garrets a pugging or layer of lime and sand, at least two inches thick, so that when the upper floor is protected from fire, it would be easier to dismantle and cast down the roof of these same houses, should fire start in the house or in the neighbourhood of such houses." Such fire-break floors are found in the old Saint-Sulpice Seminary and the Château de Ramezay. One suggestion in particular would leave a visual mark on Quebec houses: the construction of "internal partitions which extend beyond the roofs and divide them into several sections, or separate them from neighbouring houses, so that fire is less likely to spread from one to the other."

The common wall with a fire-break gable extending above the roof line and leaning on corbels would become one of the most distinctive features of urban Montreal in the eighteenth century and in the beginning of the nineteenth century. And it is obvious that the style created by this functional characteristic, which was originally designed to prevent fire from spreading from one roof to another, survived its original purpose. Thus, although the western wall of the Maison du Calvet is not a common wall but overlooks Bonsecours Street, it is topped by an imposing fire-break gable made of stone and surmounted by two chimneys linked by a straight parapet (figure 8). The same is true of the Château de Ramezay which has always been completely isolated from its urban surroundings. Moreover, rural houses in the Montreal region were often built with fire-break gables, a feature borrowed from the urban dwelling, even though the need to prevent the spreading of fire never existed. As is often true in architecture, the form long outlived the function for which it was imposed.[25]

The ordinance by Intendant Dupuy is as much a code for town planning as it is for construction. As specified by the intendant himself: "one must consider the proper placement and embellishment of the town as much as the durability of its buildings." Consequently he ordered that "no new building should be located . . . unless the owner of the house to be built or to be rebuilt has aligned it on the lot itself and has accordingly a writ from the Sieur de Bécancourt, chief road surveyor of Canada" and this "under penalty of a fine for the master masons and contractors and at the risk of the owners being ordered to demolish their houses at their own expense." The intendant further ordered that

> no building should overhang on the street, or encroach on public squares, whether it is the main building or the stairs, which should both be properly aligned; that no house should be built too close to the gates of the town, to the ramparts, to the batteries in public places and other places reserved for the defence and embellishment of the towns; that squares and streets should be wide enough and sufficiently sloped to permit the drainage of water, and to satisfy the needs for convenience, safety, and public health.

This ordinance of 7 June 1727 ends on a note of fairness:

> We order, to ensure just compensation and provide the seigneurs with adequate indemnity, that those who have lost part of their land for having conformed to the prescribed alignments, should be exempted from payment of the taxes and rents owed to the seigneurs in proportion to the amount of land lost; those whose

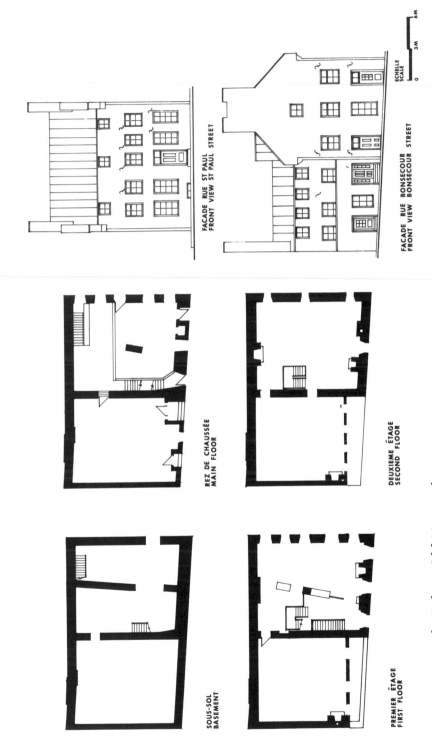

FACADE RUE ST PAUL
FRONT VIEW ST PAUL STREET

FACADE RUE BONSECOUR
FRONT VIEW BONSECOUR STREET

ECHELLE
SCALE

0   3 M   6 M

REZ DE CHAUSSÉE
MAIN FLOOR

DEUXIEME ÉTAGE
SECOND FLOOR

SOUS-SOL
BASEMENT

PREMIER ÉTAGE
FIRST FLOOR

Fig. 8   Maison du Calvet, Old Montreal

lands have been extended by the realignment will have to pay the taxes and rents to the seigneur in proportion to the additional land they have acquired.[26]

This type of ordinance reveals that the foundation and principles for state intervention, whether by an absolute or a democratic state, in the organization and development of the environment and the control of its constituent parts have, all in all, not changed much in the last two and a half centuries. Present-day regulations governing construction and development, although respecting the rights of all parties, aim at upholding certain standards judged necessary for the public good. Likewise, ordinances like those of 8 July 1721 and 7 June 1727 had the same objectives in mind. Inasmuch as they were likely to change or modify certain acquired attitudes or tendencies in the face of development and to create differences between the urban and rural house, the latter was much less affected by the rulers' concern.

We shall now attempt to complete the picture of the urban house in eighteenth-century Montreal with a study of a few dwellings that have survived from the end of that century. The plan was rectangular or oblong, but some of the older houses—for example, the Maison de la Sauvegarde—were sometimes as long as they were wide. The layout was always a simple one, normally divided vertically between day activities and nocturnal rest, and horizontally between front and back rooms. This division was often reflected in the two chimneys linked by a parapet, as in the Maison du Calvet and the Château de Ramezay. The walls were thick, usually made of fieldstones or roughly cut stones; ashlars would be used at the beginning of the nineteenth century. On the front, solid surfaces covered a wider area than the openings, and windows varied in dimensions; some were even rather large, as in the Maison Del Vecchio. Dormers were small. Sloped roofs were most common, bounded by fire-break gables, and surmounted by "chimneys which are like buttresses at each end of the building and contain as many outlets as there are rooms to heat."[27] According to Morisset,[28] the pitch of the roof seems to have diminished with time. For instance, the slope is 45 degrees for the Maison du Calvet and the Maison de la Sauvegarde, 40 degrees for a house located at number 160–170 on Saint-Amable Street, and 35 degrees for the d'Youville Stables. The interiors must have been covered with pine boards, such as the ones recently restored in the Maison du Calvet and the Maison Del Vecchio.

A concern for aesthetics inspired by classicism and probably to a

certain extent by the presence of public buildings like the Old Seminary and the Château de Vaudreuil seems to have influenced the
construction of these urban dwellings. Solid surfaces and openings
were equally distributed about an axis on the front of the house;
openings were placed at regular intervals and the windows of the
first or second floor were usually on the same axis as the corresponding doors and windows of the ground floor. Even dormers were
placed either on the same axis as the solid surfaces or on that of
openings. Some buildings were graced with an overall symmetry, as
appears from the plans of the Maison du Patriote with doors at each
end of the building.

In some domestic construction, the pursuit of forms had been carried even further and shy attempts at applying a principle of Italian
Renaissance architecture were evident. It was the custom to highlight one floor, usually the ground floor, by designing it more carefully. The ceilings were placed higher and this hierarchy was given
prominence on the front of the house by varying window dimensions. This was done at the Maison du Calvet, the Maison du Patriote, the Maison Truteau on Saint-Gabriel Street, and a few other
houses. Another expression of classicism could be found in the ornamentation of doors and windows with lintels placed at the same
level and in frameworks of ashlars or of relatively well-squared
stones.

Who were the architects of these residences? Ordinarily, where
public structures, either secular or ecclesiastic, are concerned, the
answer is easy to find for contracts were usually recorded. Such was
not true for domestic architecture. Today's architect is different
from his counterpart in the seventeenth or eighteenth century. In
those days of traditional, popular architecture, the artist and the
craftsman were but one man: he designed the building and usually
built it. He was also a master mason or a contractor and it was difficult to find out where one field of activity ended and the other began. Indeed "a master mason was equally versed in the theory and
the practice of the art of building; in those days, thought and hand
were inseparable."[29] Thus, the first contract for masonry work (on
27 April 1705) for the Château de Ramezay was granted to Pierre
Couturier, "master mason and architect."[30] Sieur Paul Texier La Vigne, "Me Maçon & Entrepreneur," would be asked to restore and enlarge the château in 1755.[31] During the old regime, several "architectes, entrepreneurs, maçons" operated in Montreal, but it is not
known whether they had any training in their trade or were im-
provising. In "Mémento historique de Montréal," Massicotte mentions about twenty of them, including people with such diverse vo-

cations as Dollier de Casson, Vachon de Belmont, and Chaussegros de Léry.[32] It is quite possible that a man like Pierre Janson-Lapalme, stonecutter and master mason, who worked on Notre-Dame Church and built the portals for the Chapel of the Récollets (1712) and for the Jesuits' Chapel (1719), did in fact spend some of his talent on domestic architecture.[33] The same is probably true of his son, Dominique, architect and mason who was contractor for the fortifications of Montreal.[34] J.-B. Testard de Montigny, who appeared on the Montreal scene in 1754, carried the title of "author of plans for houses."[35] Names and titles meant little, for the popular traditions in the construction trade were transmitted from father to son, from master to apprentice. Even if a century separated the Maison du Calvet from the Maison Truteau, the concepts and methods of construction and the materials used were almost the same in both dwellings.

This analysis would not be complete without a glance at the Château de Ramezay, Montreal's best known and most appreciated specimen of French colonial architecture. Yet, it has not always been so: it has been threatened with demolition and a good deal of its character has been destroyed with the building of a parking lot around it. It has been saved, nevertheless, and it stands opposite City Hall as a symbol of the authority of the old regime and as the only large residence of the French era which has survived to this day.

The Château de Ramezay's history is rather complex. It was the residence of the governor of Montreal, M. de Ramezay, and his family. It was sold in 1745 to the Compagnie des Indes, which used it to store cloth, spices, liquors, and pelts. At the time of the conquest, it regained its position as Government House and the British governors stayed there, except for a short interval when the Americans drove them out and established their headquarters for the occupation troops in the château (1775–76). Around 1784 Baron de Saint-Léger restored the château and lived in it for a while. It was once more linked to the country's history when the Special Council held its sessions there between 1838 and 1841. It then became the gathering place for deliberations during the stormy sessions carried out between 1844 and 1849. In the fall of 1849 it became a court house. From 1856 to 1867 it was used by the Ministry of Education, housing the Normal School from 1856 to 1878. Next it harboured Université Laval; from 1889 to 1893 it was once more used as a court house. The City of Montreal bought the château a few years later and subsequently turned it over to the Antiquarian and Numismatic Society of Montreal, which changed it into a museum.[36] (Plate 22.)

That the château's original character should have been altered by a succession of different landlords who used it for numerous purposes is hardly surprising. As mentioned earlier, it was enlarged and restored in 1755 by the Compagnie des Indes. Doors and windows were cut in the walls and at other times filled in, fireplaces and chimneys were added, others dismantled. Around 1830 ugly additions were constructed on the east side, including turrets (1906–?) to enhance its appearance as a "château." In early 1972 an attempt was made to restore it to its 1755 appearance.

As a specimen of architecture, the Château de Ramezay is interesting, for it represents an intermediary stage between the typical urban house and the rural house then found in the Montreal neighbourhood. Its rectangular plan (15.25m by 30.5m) is basically that of an urban row house, with the characteristic heavy wall dividing the whole length of the building into front rooms and rear rooms. In line with this typical division, there are two chimneys on the west side joined by a straight parapet. The two end walls with gables projecting beyond the roof line take their inspiration from the fire-break common walls separating urban row houses. The Château de Ramezay appears to be a synthesis, within a single detached dwelling, of some of the forms which were borrowed from the urban row house and which outlived their original purpose to become fashions. The fact that the building was impressive for its quality, as well as the prestige of its functions, and that it looked somewhat like a private mansion in Paris may have significantly contributed to the success of this type of house. Indeed, the nineteenth century saw a proliferation of this sort of detached rural house in the Montreal region.

The building rests on the powerful, Romanesque cradle-vaults of its foundations. The floors of the attics are covered with slabs of stone ten centimetres thick resting on solid cedar beams, closely joined. As explained earlier, such floors were meant to prevent fire from spreading to or from the attics. Tenons, mortises, and wooden pegs hold the truss-frame of the roof together. From these few details it is obvious that the château is solid in construction and represents the state of the art in the various fields of seventeenth-century craftsmanship.

The Environment of the Frontier Town

It is difficult to imagine what the character and the quality of the urban environment were like in Montreal in the middle of the eighteenth century. The actual situation has been so altered that there is little left on which to base an opinion. The grid of streets may have deviated little, but drastic changes in the various functions of the urban environment, in building techniques, and in modes of trans-

22.   *The Château de Ramezay around 1920. Paul Texier La Vigne,
master mason and contractor, 1755*

portation have altered the essence of its original design. The town no longer appears to belong to its urban fabric, and impersonal buildings ten or twenty storeys high are cramped on a grid designed for family dwellings one or two storeys high. Only two sectors, which suffered fewer alterations because they were developed later and built of more enduring materials than wood, may give us a vague idea of what the original environment was like. They are the Bonsecours block, bounded by Saint-Paul, Berri, and Notre-Dame Streets, and Place Jacques-Cartier, and the d'Youville block, a triangle formed by Place d'Youville, de la Commune Street, and Normand Street. But even there, they are forever separated from the whole whose foremost quality was its homogeneity. In order to recreate the picture, we are forced to refer to historical maps, to ordinances and other authentic documents, and to brief descriptions of the town by contemporary observers such as Thomas Patten (1760).

Judging from the tone as well as from the number of ordinances on the matter, Montreal during the French colonial regime seems to have suffered from deplorable hygienic conditions. For instance, the decree promulgated in Montreal on 22 June 1706 by Intendant Jacques Raudot forbids "any inhabitant, whatever his quality or condition, to throw refuse, soil, or manure on to the streets . . . to keep any pigs in his house . . . or to allow any horned cattle to wander into the streets."[37] This state of affairs does not seem to have improved with time. On 24 April 1745, Guiton de Monrepos promulgated an ordinance compelling "all the inhabitants of Montreal, whether landlords or tenants, to collect in front of their lot all manure, refuse, or garbage lying there every day and to pile them up on the side of the street, so as not to be in the way of carriages."[38] This kind of regulation was systematically repeated every spring, which suggests that the harshness of Canadian winters prevented citizens from properly clearing their refuse which piled up in the yards and on the streets until spring. In New France, such poor hygiene was not unique to Montreal; the other towns and villages in the colony seem to have suffered the same conditions. To wit, Quebec's Superior Council ruled on 1 February 1706 that in the capital landlords, tenants, and house builders should "build latrines and privies to prevent infection and stench from dung left on the streets."[39]

Such poor sanitary conditions are hardly surprising. Public hygiene is a relatively recent practice. The Quebec or Montreal resident who relieved himself on the street was hardly less civilized than the nobles at the court of France who, at that same time, did the same thing in the staircases and the corridors of Versailles! Sanitary conditions in the small town of Montreal were not worse—perhaps they were even better—than those prevailing in most European cities in the eighteenth century. In those days, according to J. H. Plumb, in many towns and villages in England, most cellars sheltered not only people but also their pigs, poultry, and sometimes their horses and cattle. Even worse, all residents, merchants, and craftsmen used the streets as a dump; even butchers would throw scraps to rot there.[40] Such conditions may very well have been worse in England because of the impact of growing industrialization, but they remained a significant feature of life in France. With the installation of aqueducts and public sewers, we have undoubtedly made great progress in that field. Yet, we have not progressed very far. We have managed to get rid of our garbage and refuse with elegance and refinement, but we have also polluted our atmosphere and natural waterways within a radius of 160 kilometres around Montreal. In 1760 a fifteen-minute walk away from his house or place of work would take the Montrealer into nature's wilderness and he was able to draw much of his food from fishing in the river. Who could have believed that two centuries of progress were to transform the wide, clear river into a revolting sewer and push back nature to a distance of more than an hour by car from the city?

Similar deficiencies appear in the development and maintenance of public areas in eighteenth-century Montreal, as indicated in this statement from Intendant Raudot:

> When I arrived in this town, I became aware of the untidiness in all the streets: they were almost impassable in any season, not only for pedestrians but even for carriages and carts because of the quagmires in their midst, caused as much by the nature and unevenness of the terrain as by the refuse thrown daily by the inhabitants.[41]

These conditions seem not to have improved with time, for as late as 1785 Joseph Hadfield noted in his diary that unpaved streets made the town unpleasant during poor weather, and that walking in the streets at any time was always hard on the feet.[42] During the French regime, the authorities did try to alleviate these conditions by compelling the inhabitants to build and maintain sidewalks during the winter months. An ordinance dated 10 November 1744 compelled "every landlord in Montreal to cut or cause to be cut all the wood necessary to build passages in front of the houses so that pedestrians might safely walk on them when there is ice."[43] Such conditions are hardly shocking either: they were normal for the time. Plumb, who was quoted earlier, reminds us that in those days streets were unpaved in the towns of England. Many of them were particularly narrow and congested to a point that in Bristol, for instance, carriages could not pass through them and goods were transported on sleds.[44] One should keep in mind that aqueducts, sewers, and night lighting are recent additions to the comforts of life in the city. Even in large capitals like London, such improvements were carried out, in main arteries only, from the second half of the eighteenth century onwards.[45]

In spite of such negative features, the small town did in fact function quite adequately. It is in the nature of organic growth to integrate urban development at the rhythm of needs and opportunities. During the pre-industrial era, the pace of growth and urbanization was very slow: integration took place smoothly and a balance was achieved between the needs and interests of the community and those of the private citizens. Documents issuing from the authorities of that time give no indication of any major flaw in the basic plan for development drawn up by Dollier de Casson. The various ordinances relating to urban life in Montreal tended to improve rather than to alter the practical application of that plan. Various legislation attests to this fact: rulings on the width of streets and on their alignment, on reducing the area of city lots, on improving drainage, on the construction and maintenance of sidewalks, on garbage and snow removal.

Montreal in the eighteenth century was a fortified town with some distinguishing features of spatial relationships between the various facets of urban life. Trading took place in the lower town, because of its proximity to the river. The market place was there and, all along Saint-Paul Street, the merchants' district. In those days, the place of work and the living quarters were located in the same house, and merchants lived and worked in this specific district. The administrative and political centres were located in the east end and included the Château de Vaudreuil, the Château de Ramezay, the intendant's palace, the king's wharves and sheds, and the Citadel. As we have seen earlier, religious organizations took care of the physical, social, cultural, and spiritual needs of the small community. These institutions were located around the parish church and on the high crest of the Coteau Saint-Louis along Notre-Dame Street. The buildings of the religious orders and the civil administration were located in their own districts, but they stood out against the more humble private dwellings around them by their very size and also because of the open green spaces surrounding them. The latter were like buffer zones separating these buildings from the rest of the built-up environment. In 1749 Peter Kalm remarked:

The priests of the seminary of St. Sulpitius have a fine large house, where they live together. The college of the Franciscan friars is likewise spacious, and has good walls, but it is not so magnificent as the former. The college of the Jesuits is small, but well built. To each of these three buildings are annexed fine large gardens, for the amusement, health, and use of the communities to which they belong.[46]

This was an environment made up of solid buildings and empty spaces, of masses and hollows. Montreal in the middle of the eighteenth century was a homogeneous ensemble which had developed along a constant and uniform scale. The streets were "broad and strait, and divided at right angles by the short ones."[47] From them a contemporary observer would have beheld austere rows of solid, anonymous houses, all built to about the same height; here and there, around a corner, were gardens and public places, dotted with distinctive, larger structures which attested to the town's main aspirations as well as to the ideals of the ruling class. The overall picture was articulated in a free, well-proportioned, harmonious manner generating contrast and variety in the middle of a homogeneous ensemble bounded by its fortifications. Such an environment looks conspicuously like that created by the medieval towns of pre-industrial Europe!

6

Years of Transition

We should judge of the beauty of our city, more from its impression on strangers, than on ourselves.

ANONYMOUS CRITIC, *American Journal of Science and Arts*, 1830[1]

A City of Merchants

Historians generally consider the cession of New France to Great Britain a major event in the history of Canada. And rightly so, for the conquest heralded the upheaval of economic, social, political, ideological, and mental structures. If 1760 marked a decisive turning point, it was not an incision but a link. There was a gradual period of transition between the old and the new regimes. In the field of architecture and urbanism at least, Montreal's character would not change overnight and façades on buildings would not be altered just because of the surrender. They underwent progressive transformations which, for all their significance, did not match the upheavals brought about by the industrialization of Montreal in the middle of the nineteenth century. This is the reason why the years of transition are more characteristic of the frontier town than of the Victorian city.

In the first decades following the cession, Montrealers of that period scarcely noticed any difference in their urban surroundings. The suburbs expanded, but inside the old walls there were the same austere streets and the same public buildings attesting to the same social pretensions. British governors merely replaced French ones at Château de Ramezay, and Notre-Dame Church continued to dominate the silhouette of the city. As late as 1795, Count de Colbert Maulevrier described this city in a manner that could easily be attributed to an observer at the end of the French regime: "Three roads running parallel to the river, about one mile long each, crossed at right angles or almost, by about ten streets, constitute the town which is partly surrounded by an old wall."[2]

The following year, Isaac Weld described the town as seen from the heights of Mount Royal: "On the left below you appears the town of Montreal, with its churches, monasteries, glittering spires, and the shipping under its old walls."[3] There is hardly any significant difference between the view of eastern Montreal depicted by Thomas Patten in 1762 and that of Richard Dillon dated 1803. It is in all aspects the same town, undoubtedly slightly more densely built up, but with the same scale and the same silhouette marked by the same steeples pointing skywards; but from now on it would be partly inhabited by anglophones. The latter, however, formed only a very small part of the population, and those who think that a massive invasion of Britons followed the cession would be surprised to learn that there were only about one hundred Protestants in Montreal in 1765.[4]

In fact, at the end of the eighteenth century, Montreal was a town undergoing slow transformation. In more ways than one it had retained the mentality of the old regime. Indeed, men's reactions to the call of the vast continent were the same as under the French regime. Montreal was still looking to the west for its destiny. More than ever, its position at the crossroads of the St. Lawrence River network gave it prominence; the only difference was that its realm had changed hands. Thus, as Creighton emphasizes, the first British Canadians were adventurers attracted by the promises of the river.[5] Alexander Henry's reaction was typical: he was a prosperous merchant in the American colonies but he rushed to Montreal as soon as he learned that a new market was opened to British ventures.[6] The most tempting attraction of the river was that it provided an access to the virgin territories that abounded in fur.

For another half-century, under the almost fanatical impetus of anglophone merchants, Montreal remained the North American capital, if not the world capital, of furs. Among the merchants figured Englishmen like Lee, Molson, and the Frobisher brothers; Americans like Price, Alexander Henry, and Pond; Scotsmen like Lymburner, McBeath, McGill, Mackenzie, and Simon McTavish. From around 1784, grouped into a powerful association called the

North West Company, these merchants spread across the hinterland from Montreal to the Pacific Ocean.

In fact, just as the great discoveries under the French regime had been stimulated by the search for furs, the same motives led to the discovery of the Canadian West. It was in order to open new territories for the Montreal merchants that Alexander Mackenzie, partner in the North West Company, reached in 1789 the great river which bears his name, and later, in 1793, made his way to the Pacific Ocean. For the same purpose Simon Fraser, also a partner in the company, followed in his footsteps and explored the territories west of the Rockies and named the Fraser River. In 1811 it was Thompson's turn to survey British Columbia on behalf of Montreal's interests, while John Jacob Astor, owner of fur stores in New York and Montreal, became the true father of Oregon. All these inroads into the west originated in Montreal. In 1812 the North West Company alone employed more than 1,300 persons and Montreal was living off the profits of the beaver trade as it had never done before, even in the most prosperous days of New France.[7]

The years of transition marked the last attempts by Montreal merchants to bend politics to suit the geographical and economic realities of the continent. With the conquest, the British had inherited a homogeneous economic empire centred on the rivers as a communications network. However, a major event, the insurrection of the American colonies against England, was to precipitate the network's disintegration, and Montreal gradually lost its continental leadership.

Thus, the Treaty of Paris in 1783 sanctioned the victory of the colonies over the mother country, and heralded drastic changes for Montreal. The new frontier with the United States cut through Montreal's natural hinterland, depriving it of the huge territories south of the Great Lakes, between the Ohio and the Mississippi Rivers. This new border also cut across the traditional roads of the fur traders, which explains why the trade expanded towards the Arctic and the Pacific. The new orientation did not favour Montreal: the gradual increase in transportation costs made it less competitive and the North West Company was absorbed by the Hudson's Bay Company in 1821. Later on, the beaver trade moved to Hudson Bay and Montreal lost its main commercial activity after having led the fur trade for almost two hundred years.

On the other hand, the American War of Independence by the thirteen colonies caused an exodus of Loyalist emigrants who came to settle in British America, especially in Upper Canada along the St. Lawrence and the Ottawa Rivers. The new colonization pushed back the forests and more land was cultivated; a new export market developed, mainly for timber and wheat. The Napoleonic wars and the continental blockade created a need for wood, and between 1800 and 1820 the timber trade suddenly soared. At the same time, Montreal ceased to be a frontier town buried in the midst of the continental forest and gradually assumed a new economic significance as the shipping point for new resources and a receiving port for manufactured goods. The latter became increasingly necessary as the population of Upper Canada grew from 158,000 inhabitants in 1825 to 347,000 ten years later.[8] From the status of key-town in a continental empire, Montreal in the nineteenth century became the national port of a growing country.

Yet, the consequences of the American rebellion did not end there. It was more than a struggle for freedom from imperial ties: it concealed a confrontation between social classes, a collision of the new capitalist bourgeoisie with the aristocracy and the perpetuation of the feudal structures it stood for. This conflict was carried over into Canada by the merchants.

It started immediately after the conquest. Two groups were facing one another: on one side the anglophone merchants, American and British, were rushing in to reap the profits of a new market and to participate in the administration of public affairs; on the other side, the officials of the British crown, recruited from the ranks of a conservative aristocracy, were determined to maintain their position and the privileges of their class. Governors like Murray or Carleton would not hear of demands made by merchants like Walker or du Calvet who were clamouring for a new social order in which all individuals would be equal. In fact, Murray and Carleton were merely replacing Frontenac and Vaudreuil: the absolute rule of the old regime gave way to a similar structure in the new, and a society based on the social usefulness of groups tended to perpetuate itself on the shores of the St. Lawrence. The Catholic Church now had absolute power in its field and, much to its benefit, preached this static conception of society to the small French-Canadian nation. The anglophone bourgeoisie would soon fashion its future after its own ideals.

The history of the years of transition in Montreal clearly shows that the real power gradually moved from the Château de Ramezay, residence of the governors, or from the Old Seminary, residence of the Seigneurs of Montreal Island, to the suburban "châteaux" of the rich merchants. One of these was the Château Saint-Antoine, where William McGillivray, nephew of Simon McTavish, and like him a powerful fur magnate, lived like a lord and enjoyed a magnificent view of the city and the river. Beaver Hall (at the corner of Beaver

Hall Hill and de La Gauchetière Streets) was another mansion where Joseph Frobisher gave many a reception; it was surrounded by about sixteen hectares of forests and apple trees. Simon McTavish, Montreal's king of the fur trade, often called the "First" or the "Marquis," built a large stone château more than 126 feet wide, near the top of the street which today bears his name. It is most unfortunate that these three bourgeois residences have disappeared, for they would have remained as historical landmarks of the take-over of power in Montreal by a capitalist bourgeoisie. A study of their architecture could have informed us better of the aspirations of that particular class.

These great merchants left their mark on the city's evolution. They were the first to have a residence separated from their place of work, and for the first time the rich were separated from the poor. The fur magnates withdrew from the city as if the human beehive were but a means of providing for their comfort on the virgin, airy slopes of Mount Royal. The rich bourgeois had merely borrowed from the aristocrats the external marks which identified the latter's status, namely the château and a large estate. The anglophones settled in the most beautiful spots, thus starting a trend, characteristic of Montreal, towards the subdivision of the city along ethnic and social lines superimposed on the geography of the metropolis.

To understand better the influence of the great merchants on the life and development of the city, we might look into the activities of one of the most famous among them, James McGill, who was born in Glasgow on 6 October 1744. He registered at Glasgow University but apparently did not stay there very long, for he was soon involved in the fur trade in the American colonies. He became very prosperous and settled in Montreal in 1776, where he was to play a major part in Canada's fur trade. But he did not stop at that: he distinguished himself by his philanthropy and by his civic spirit. One way or another, he was connected with just about every improvement brought to Montreal during the years of transition. He was one of the commissioners in charge of the demolition of the old fortified wall, a task which he brought to completion and on which we shall comment later. He was a prison administrator, chairman of the volunteer fire brigade, a member of the building committee of Christ Church Anglican Cathedral, representative for Montreal West at the Legislative Assembly, and a member of the Legislative Council. It was mainly his Burnside estate, however, which would link his name to the city's history. Like most rich Montreal merchants, McGill had acquired a vast estate of some 18.6 hectares. A few years before his death, which occurred on 12 December 1813, he bequeathed his estate and a substantial sum of money for the purpose of promoting education in the province. McGill University was the outcome of that gift and it soon acquired an international reputation. A large section of its magnificent campus is located on the old Burnside estate (north of Sherbrooke, between McTavish and University Streets): it is still one of the most positive contributions to the urban landscape of our metropolis.[9]

Architecturally, the years of transition saw certain interesting contributions. Official and social styles revealed the variety as well as the rivalries of ethnic groups living in Montreal. At first glance, the architecture of each group appeared to have inherited the same classical spirit, but neither the motivations nor the designs were identical.

Imperialism was the predominant characteristic of the British ruling class. It was only natural, for this group never doubted the superiority of British institutions: England was, after all, the most powerful nation in the world as well as the seat of power of the largest empire the world had ever known. About the golden age which, in England, followed the Peace of Paris in 1763, John Summerson said: "It was an age which combined confidence and vitality, security and adventure."[10] Hence, it was only natural for colonizers to import from the mother country their architectural models, selected from the vast classical repertoire of the eighteenth century. Thus, Christ Church, the first Anglican cathedral in Montreal, followed the great architectural tradition of churches designed by Sir Christopher Wren (1632–1723) and by James Gibbs (1682–1754). The model for the Anglican cathedral in Quebec City was the famous Church of St. Martin-in-the-Fields (1721–26) on London's Trafalgar Square, a masterpiece by Gibbs. It was no accident, for in the mind of Quebec's Anglican bishop, Jacob Mountain, St. Martin-in-the-Fields constituted the most representative piece of religious architecture erected by the virtuous and perfect English society of the eighteenth century.[11] In the province, the British espoused a kind of colonial classicism, healthy, conscious, and rather heavy, extolling the virtues of strength, confidence, and superiority in which the colonizers believed at the time. Architecture was envisaged as a symbol. In the same period, a similar attitude prevailed in American architecture.

The Americans, some of whom came to Canada after the War of Independence (208 in Montreal in 1779), were familiar with the traditions of British classical architecture which had reached the American coast as early as the first decades of the eighteenth century. From 1720 on, Boston became the centre for the diffusion of the architectural ideas and theories of Wren, Vanbrugh, Nicholas

Hawksmoor, and James Gibbs.[12] The American War of Independence and the triumph of the middle classes over aristocracy changed many things. The colonies' armies had defeated proud England and a republic was declared. This new nation would no longer seek its architectural models in defeated England, now considered corrupt, but in the ancient republics of Athens and Rome, idealizing their virtues and moral strength. Lewis Mumford defined this state of mind: "It was the Revolution itself . . . that turned the classical taste into a myth which had the power to move men."[13] This explains why works like James Stuart's (1713–88) *Antiquities of Athens* (1762) were appreciated by the Americans. They quickly abandoned the Palladian and Georgian idioms for those of ancient architecture with a predilection for "la maison carrée" of Nîmes which, through imitation, would be reproduced again and again on this side of the Atlantic Ocean.[14] In the Montreal region, the influence of American popular classicism was not so pronounced as in the areas where Loyalists had settled, namely Nova Scotia, New Brunswick, and Upper Canada. At the beginning of the nineteenth century, waves of Americans who were acquainted with the post-revolutionary period settled in Canada. With them came a form of romantic neo-classicism, inspired by Greco-Roman models, which soon found its way into Montreal's public architecture, particularly as the Greek Revival style.

French-Canadian architecture of that time showed signs of the influence of the classical traditions of the eighteenth century. As we have seen earlier, it was the preferred mode of architectural expression of the ruling class; we even saw to what extent its influence had pervaded the humble domestic urban designs as attested by the Maison du Patriote or the Maison Del Vecchio. The Maison Papineau, on Bonsecours Street, which has recently been restored to its original splendour (circa 1830), provides a better example. The balance and harmony of full and empty surfaces as well as its good proportions, the accent on horizontal linearity, and the interior decoration are all elements which contribute to make this house a specimen of domestic architecture belonging to this tradition.[15]

After the conquest, the Quebec elite remained faithful to the classical tradition. It flourished particularly in religious architecture, a further proof of the predominant role of the Catholic Church in French-Canadian society. Two men who complemented each other extremely well, Jérôme Demers and Thomas Baillargé, were responsible for this trend. The former was a priest and director of the Seminary of Quebec from the beginning of the nineteenth century on. He was an avid theoretician and a protagonist of a classical architecture that was rational, gracious, refined, lighter than the heavy classicism of the conquerors, and closer to the French institutional classicism of Louis XVI. His main sources were Vignole, Blondel, d'Aviler, and the *Book of Architecture* by Gibbs; he wrote *Précis d'architecture*, the better to spread his doctrines among the students of the seminary.[16] The second, Thomas Baillargé, was the last representative of the Baillargé dynasty of architects, sculptors, painters, and contractors from Quebec. He was the executor of Demers's ideas. He took his apprenticeship within the framework of the traditional craft of the province and was associated with his father François who had studied in Paris. With Abbé Demers, he acquired a deep knowledge of classicism and put his learning into practice in a most creative manner. His name and his art are linked with some of the most valuable achievements of religious architecture in Quebec during the first half of the nineteenth century. In the Montreal region, he built Sainte-Geneviève Church in Pierrefonds, construction of which was started in 1849. The purity and universality of Thomas Baillargé's classicism have survived in spite of the many alterations the church has undergone.[17]

Demers and Baillargé came originally from the Quebec region, where traditions were more solidly entrenched than in Montreal. In the metropolis, classicism was regarded as provincial and antiquated, and the church wardens of Notre-Dame turned down a plan by Thomas Baillargé for the reconstruction of their church. Indeed, to maintain its rank and prestige, the Catholic Church of Montreal had to counterbalance the cold, imperial classicism of Christ Church Anglican Cathedral, built but a short distance from the venerable parish church of Notre-Dame. Demers and Baillargé's French classicism must have seemed both too bare and too timid; upholding the superiority of Catholicism over Protestantism demanded a style altogether more convincing and more symbolic of the ongoing struggle for the protection of existing values. At this time, there occurred an event that was to mark the history of architecture in Montreal and in Canada: the building of Notre-Dame in a neo-Gothic style. This action officially inaugurated the era of Victorian architecture in the province and it is rather surprising to see the most conservative of all ethnic groups coexisting in Montreal taking the first step.

The Plan of the Commissioners
If we set aside the old grid of streets inherited from the Sulpician Dollier de Casson, a visit to Old Montreal and to its neighbourhood reveals that urban development seems to have occurred spontaneously. Place Jacques-Cartier, Place d'Youville, the Champ-de-Mars,

Saint-Antoine (Craig) Street, McGill Street, Victoria Square, all familiar landmarks making up an urban landscape, appear to have developed out of the successive transformations of a growing organism rather than according to a set plan. Moreover, as in other large American cities, land speculation seems to have been the sole spur to physical development in Montreal. Yet, evidence shows that this was not quite true as far as the years of transition are concerned.

As early as 1799 the Parliament of Lower Canada introduced a resolution aimed at the orderly development of Montreal and Quebec. This legislation called for the naming of an inspector responsible for the drafting of plans for the town and its surroundings, for the opening of wide streets, and for the preservation of land for public squares. Parliament had already acknowledged that it was

> necessary and of utility to the Public, that the said Divisions should be parcelled out agreeable to a regular plan, and that commodious Streets should be opened, and convenient places reserved for Squares in time to come . . . [and] that from and after the day such Plan shall be homologated, it shall not be lawful for the Proprietors of any part of the Tracts of Land aforesaid to sell the same, for the purpose of dividing them into building Lots, Orchards, or Gardens, unless they conform, in every respect, to the said Plan, nor shall they reserve to themselves the Streets or Squares which shall be therein laid down or described.[18]

All this sounds very modern and very much like today's town-planning practices.

Two years later, a unique opportunity to apply the resolution presented itself: the demolition of the old walls of Montreal which by then were hindering development of the city. On 8 April 1801 the lieutenant governor gave Royal assent to a bill entitled "An Act for removing the old Walls and Fortifications that surround the City of Montreal and otherwise to provide for the salubrity, convenience and embellishment of the said city."[19] To the mover of this bill, convenience and embellishment or the functional and aesthetic aspects happened to go together.

To complete the task, three commissioners were appointed: the Honourable James McGill, the aforementioned public-minded merchant; the Honourable John Richardson, born in England, who had first immigrated to the United States, then to Canada (1787) where he gained quite a reputation for his prosperity as well as for his dedication to civic duties; and finally, Jean-Marie Mondelet, a notary by profession who, like many representatives of the new French-Canadian elite, distinguished himself in politics as a member of Parliament for Montreal West. They were to look after the demolition of the old walls and fulfil two obligations. First, they were to return to their legitimate owners or their legal heirs all land expropriated for the construction of the fortifications under the French regime. Secondly, they were to submit a plan for subsequent improvements and to establish the cost of such improvements.[20]

We shall be particularly interested in this plan, which would have later repercussions on the physiognomy of Montreal. Joseph Bouchette, surveyor general of Lower Canada, knew the plan well. He was born in the colony in May 1774; as an adolescent, he had already shown great talent in the art of drawing geographical maps and landscapes. When only thirty years old, he became head of the surveyors' offices and held this position until his death in Montreal in 1841. He had a passion for statistics; he spent his life gathering data on the province and other parts of British North America. He published the results of his compilation in several books among which were *A Topographical Description of the Province of Lower Canada* (1815) and his important topographical and statistical study of the British provinces, issued in London in 1831. He received congratulations from the Prince Regent, two medals, and the envied title of corresponding member of the London Society of Arts and Sciences, but his expenses ruined him financially. All this attests to his zeal and dedication to public interest.[21]

Joseph Bouchette was full of praise for the improvements suggested by the commissioners. Here is what he said in his detailed *Topographical Description*:

> When the act that passed the provincial parliament, in 1801, "for removing the old walls and fortifications surrounding the city of Montreal, and otherwise to provide for the salubrity, convenience and embellishment of the said city" shall have been carried into effect, according to the plan projected, none of the external possessions of England, excepting its eastern dominions, will embrace a town of so much beauty, regularity, extent, and convenience as this.[22]

An elevated terrace was to extend along the river from Pointe-à-Callières to the Faubourg de Québec. It was to be used as a street and to serve as a rampart against icefloes which covered the common every spring; it would also be used as a barrier against fire which could start at any moment amid the huge stocks of lumber stacked permanently on the shore. This was to be a welcome improvement over previous conditions, for several observers had described the pitiful state of the shore. Compared with the present, one can dream of an esplanade where one would be able to walk and, at last, admire the river. Another improvement concerned the small Saint-Pierre River separating Pointe-à-Callières from the Coteau Saint-Louis. A road was to be built on either side of the river to reduce its width to twenty feet. The plan provided for a similar canal in the middle of Saint-Augustin Street (today's McGill Street) which was to link the Saint-Pierre Canal with a canal yet to be dredged in Saint-Martin Creek. The old town thus would be physically separated by water from the adjacent suburbs, except on the Faubourg de Québec side. The projected improvements were imperative, judging from a comment by Count Colbert de Maulevrier, who in 1798 mentioned that "behind the city's walls, to the north, runs a muddy creek which could easily be changed into a canal which would benefit the salubrity of the place instead of harming it as at present."[23] Circular basins were to be dug out at the intersections of the canals, and buildings on the shore were to stand thirty feet away from the edges of the canals in order to form airy lanes eighty feet wide.

Among other improvements, St. James Street was to be extended from the Faubourg des Récollets to the Faubourg de Québec and widened to 60 feet. Another street, 24 feet in width, was to be opened midway between St. James Street and the future Saint-Antoine (Craig) Street. It is today's Ruelle des Fortifications to the west and rue du Champ-de-Mars to the east. A public square, measuring 174 feet by 208 feet, was projected for the location where the old Quebec Gate stood. Another square, measuring 180 feet by 468 feet, was projected for the southwest corner of Saint-Antoine (Craig) and Saint-Augustin Streets; this would later become the Marché aux Foins (Hay Market). Today, this square has been pushed northwest to Vitré Street and is called Victoria Square. The old Place d'Armes was to be enlarged to 344 feet by 392 feet and lengthened as far as the Craig Street Canal. The Champ-de-Mars was to be extended to the Craig Street Canal and was to constitute an esplanade of 114 toises by 57 toises (684 feet by 342 feet), in order to be large enough for military drills and parades. At the time of Bouchette's writings, these improvements had almost been completed; trees had been planted and benches installed in an open invitation to the citizens to come and admire the magnificent panorama of Faubourg Saint-Laurent and the cultivated slopes of the island's second terrace (today called Sherbrooke Terrace). All that now remains of the redesigned Champ-de-Mars is a huge, faceless parking lot. A last important improvement concerned a new market place to replace the old one which had become too small for the growing population. This new market was to be located in the eastern section of the small town, where the Château de Vaudreuil and its gardens used to stand. It is today's Place Jacques-Cartier, a long rectangle stretching from Notre-Dame Street to Commissioners Street.[24] (Plate 23.)

For commissioners who were working for nothing and whose only claim to competence in the field lay in their dedication to their civic duties, carrying out so many improvements was quite an accomplishment. In their plan, the commissioners were aware that the old town constituted a homogeneous entity and that the most recent suburbs had to be hinged on to it in a structurally identifiable manner. Thus, the old town was connected to Faubourgs Saint-Antoine and Récollets by a public square (Victoria) and the wide Saint-Augustin Street; to Faubourg Saint-Laurent via Saint-Antoine (Craig) Street and its canal; and to Faubourg de Québec via Dalhousie Square.

However, the commissioners' plans were drawn to the scale of Montreal as it then was, without as much as a hint of how industrialization in the second half of the nineteenth century would upset that very scale. McGill and Saint-Antoine (Craig) Streets may have been splendid in 1800: today they are quite ordinary. It is unfortunate that the commissioners allowed the area west of McGill to be developed and that Saint-Louis, Champ-de-Mars, and des Fortifications Streets were opened. The fortifications had been built on land which, after their demolition, should have been kept by the city and returned to its natural state. A green band extending along the old town, between St. James and Saint-Antoine (Craig) Streets would have created a feeling of space. Coming back to McGill, Richardson, and Mondelet, let us now see how their projects were executed.

A map of the city and suburbs drawn by John Adams in 1825 constitutes a good working document. Only a few of the projected improvements were not carried out or were treated in a different manner. Thus, no canal ever ran in the middle of Saint-Augustin Street, later renamed McGill Street in honour of the commissioner. Place d'Armes was never extended to Saint-Antoine Street. This is unfortunate, for an enlarged Place d'Armes would have been more in proportion to the forthcoming, enormous new Notre-Dame Church that was built along one of its sides. A better visual relationship would have been achieved between that monument and the rest of the city, namely the Sherbrooke Terrace. However, all other improvements were carried out, with only the odd minor change. (Plate 24.)

23. *Plan of the town of Montreal in 1815, by Joseph Bouchette, showing the projected town improvements*

This does not mean that the commissioners had only to impose their will to achieve their ends. They often had to seize upon opportunities to bring about certain improvements, as with the creation of the new market, later named Place Jacques-Cartier. It all started, as so often happened in Montreal, with a disastrous fire. On Monday, 6 June 1803, fire started in a house in Faubourg Saint-Laurent; driven by strong winds, it spread to the buildings on Coteau Saint-Louis after destroying dozens of structures in the faubourg. The prison burned down, as well as a large section of the Jesuits' establishment, a dozen houses, and the College de Montréal which used to be the Château de Vaudreuil. Some time later, two fairly rich bourgeois gentlemen, Joseph Périnault and J.-B. Durocher, whose only bond lay in their business acumen, brought about interest in the ruins, for they had engineered a neat speculative deal. On 14 December of the same year, they bought the ruins of the old château with its outbuildings and gardens. Then, with calculated generosity, they presented the city with about one third of the land they had bought on the express condition that the city erect a public market on the site. As soon as the offer was accepted, the two speculators subdivided the remainder of the land into seven building lots which they offered for sale at a high price, for they would now border on the new Market Place. Within two days, all the lots were sold: Périnault and Durocher had made a small fortune and Montreal had a new public square.[25] (Plate 25.)

The creation of Dalhousie Square, which the commissioners had intended to locate near the old Quebec Gate, took a very different turn. The old Citadel, perched on a hillock at the end of Notre-Dame Street, became redundant following the demolition of the fortifications between 1801 and 1817, and also as a result of the purchase by the imperial government, in 1818, of St. Helen's Island where a military post overlooking the entrance to the Port of Montreal would be built. As the hill hindered any further development of the city, it was decided to level it and a contract was signed for that purpose on 14 August 1819 with the Bagg and Wait Company. The soil removed would be used to complete the Champ-de-Mars esplanade and to fill the swamps of Faubourg Saint-Louis. Once the hillock had disappeared, Louis Charland, a surveyor and roads inspector for the city, was ordered by the commissioners to draw up plans for the utilization of that land by the city. After an amusing series of incidents involving influence peddling, Jacques Viger, the future first mayor of Montreal, stole the limelight from Charland and managed to have his own plan accepted. The latter consisted of extending Notre-Dame and Saint-Paul Streets to a public square,

24. *Plan of the town and suburbs of Montreal in 1825, by John Adams*

later named Dalhousie, after Lord Dalhousie, who would offer it as a present to the municipality in September 1823. It would soon become an elegant residential district, much sought after by rich citizens. But not for long: in July 1852 a fire levelled all the buildings. A few decades later, the square was to disappear altogether, as it was dug to a depth of nine metres to accommodate Viger Station. This site had been the town's highest elevation during the French regime: it was now the lowest point of the industrial city. Such a fate was symbolic of the transformations which Victorian Montreal was to undergo.[26]

During the years of transition, public squares multiplied in the city and suburbs. Dalhousie was one. Place d'Armes became a square, in the proper sense of the term, when the old Notre-Dame Church was demolished and the new one was built on the edge of the square. The Hay Market would become Victoria Square. In Faubourg Saint-Laurent, Viger Market would become Viger Square after being considerably enlarged. At the far end of Faubourg de Québec, Papineau Square was built at the end of Papineau Avenue. In 1830 Chaboillez Square was created in Faubourg des Récollets and Richmond Square in Faubourg Saint-Antoine.

Squares proliferated under the influence of the British, for they had perfected this particular urban concept, especially during the Georgian era (1714–1830) when London acquired its most beautiful squares. In terms of utilization of space, there is a great deal of difference between the continental squares, like the ones Montreal had inherited from the French regime, and the typical British version. A comparison of Place d'Armes under the old regime with its counterpart around 1840 shows the difference. Under the French colonial regime, the church was located in the middle of the square, on the axis of Notre-Dame Street. This manner of highlighting a monument by placing it at the far end of a visual perspective is more characteristic of the classical continental square than of the British. The reaction of John Duncan, an Englishman who complained about the location of the old church, is very revealing indeed. Said he: "Notre-Dame Street . . . is however unfortunately broken into separate portions by the principal French Church, which . . . has been awkwardly set down in the very centre of the street."[27] The typical English square is an intimate open space, self-contained, located without any didactic intention; it is meant only for the enjoyment and satisfaction of its residents. This is more or less what Place d'Armes would look like in the nineteenth century, when the new Notre-Dame Church was built on the edge of the quadrangle. Trees were planted in 1848, and the year after a fountain graced the plaza which was then surrounded by a high cast-iron fence.[28]

25. *Place Jacques-Cartier in 1896*

There are many other areas where the influence of the new masters altered the city's development and image. Thus, for instance, under the French colonial regime, the parish church of Notre-Dame had been the focal point of the town and Place d'Armes one of the most significant centres for social contact. One hundred years later, the picture was radically altered. Place d'Armes became a simple residential square with a church on one of its sides, whereas the Champ-de-Mars, an artificial esplanade turning its back to the old town, became a meeting place for the citizenry, "a favourite promenade in the summer evenings, and the principal scene of military displays," according to the same John Duncan.[29]

New suburbs appeared and the old ones were extensively developed during the years of transition, as the Adams map of 1825 indicates. According to a census taken the same year, out of a population of 26,154 (14,830 francophones and 11,324 anglophones) only 5,316 inhabitants were living inside the old fortified town; this represented 20 percent of the total figure.[30] The census covered the whole territory of the new administrative boundaries of the city: some 413 hectares versus 40.5 hectares for the old fortified town. This new administrative entity was established on 7 May 1792 by a proclamation of the Parliament of Lower Canada. It resembled a parallelogram bounded by the river and by an imaginary line drawn 100 land chains (660 feet) away from and parallel to the old fortified walls. Today, the same boundaries would correspond roughly to Atwater on the west, Pine Avenue on the north, and d'Iberville Street on the east. The same proclamation of 7 May 1792 stipulated that the town would henceforth be divided into two districts, the western and the eastern, with St. Lawrence Boulevard as a demarcation line between the two.[31] This is how the custom of dividing the city into an east end and a west end originated, even though geographically speaking it is an absurd distinction. Indeed, Montreal is shaped like a boomerang, and what we call the east end of the city lies in fact more to the north, and St. Lawrence Boulevard runs more from east to west than from north to south.

Five of the suburbs had now grown to respectable size. Saint-Laurent, the largest and also the most populated, lay along the axis of St. Lawrence Blvd., thus named because originally it led to the village of Saint-Laurent. Faubourg de Québec was the most aristocratic of the five, but only for a time, for later on it would be referred to as the "Faubourg à la mélasse" (molasses suburb). It was centred on Sainte-Marie Street, which was itself a northeast extension of Notre-Dame Street. In the opposite direction, two suburbs developed: Saint-Antoine along the extension of Saint-Antoine Street, and Faubourg des Récollets, also called Saint-Joseph, along the southwest extension of Notre-Dame Street. There was also Griffintown that arose south of Pointe-à-Callières. It used to belong to the nuns of the Hôtel-Dieu and was then leased to an Irish Protestant, Robert Griffin, who would subdivide it and name it after himself. The land was marshy, rather unhealthy, and regularly flooded. It attracted mainly poor immigrants, most of them Irish, who settled there because industries employing cheap labour were established in the district.

A closer study of one of these suburbs, Saint-Laurent, reveals some interesting facts. Urban development was gradually veering from a northeast-southwest orientation, parallel to Notre-Dame Street, to one perpendicular to the latter, that is, northwest-southeast and parallel to St. Lawrence Boulevard. This thoroughfare would henceforth be the axis of demographic growth whereas the river banks and the parallel arteries like Notre-Dame, St. James, and Sainte-Catherine became the axis of economic growth. The regularity, uniformity, and anonymous character of the grid of streets was remarkable; by now it looked like a construct: as it reached the steep second terrace of the island, it did not seem adapted to the natural topography. Unlike the old town, the new suburb of Saint-Laurent was not centred on the facets of community life; it was the result of a uniform, amorphous development. The erection, from 1823 on, of St. James Cathedral and the Bishop's Palace on the northeast corner of Saint-Denis and Sainte-Catherine Streets could have constituted a strong polarization centre. Unfortunately, after the fire of 1852 which razed the whole area, both the cathedral and the palace were rebuilt on the side of Dominion Square. Another attempt at reviving the district by locating the Université de Montréal there failed miserably at the turn of the century. At present, a new attempt is being made by centralizing the Université du Québec in that same area.

In this suburb, as in others, there were as yet no lanes. Most houses were one-family dwellings, wider than they were deep, like the ones analysed in the previous chapter. Such a building pattern was still possible because the front of the lots was wide enough to allow passage, often through a gateway, to the back of the property. With time, demographic and economic pressures would reduce the frontage to a minimum of 7.6 metres, and houses would have to be oriented towards the back of the lot. The lane became the new way of reaching the far end of the lots. This way, more dwellings could be lined up on the same street and the cost for equipment and services was kept down. As we shall see in the next chapter, however, it had marked disadvantages.

The quality of life had been greatly improved during the years of transition. From 1801 on, a system of aqueducts brought drinkable water to Montreal, whereas before that date it was only available from a few wells. At the beginning, spring water was collected from the mountain by means of wooden ducts; from 1819 on, they were replaced by cast iron ducts. Protection against fire was also better organized, still on a voluntary basis, but in a more efficient manner which would gradually evolve into the present-day system. Street lighting also progressed rapidly. Because of pressure from merchants, Saint-Paul Street became the first in Montreal to be lit with oil lamps, from 1815 onwards. Others would follow, and gas light was introduced in 1830. In 1818 the municipality got its first contingent of twenty-four policemen or "night watchmen." All these innovations seem trivial today. Nevertheless, they were essential landmarks in the development of normal urban life.[32]

The Image of the City
In those days, how did visitors react to Montreal, when they saw the city for the first time? Most of them agreed that viewed from the river it was a very striking sight. In 1807 George Heriot, who had travelled across both Upper and Lower Canada, published in London an account of his journey. In his opinion, Montreal was best seen from St. Helen's Island.[33] A landscape painted in 1828 by James Gray, in the manner of Epinal, gives us an idea of the exceptional background provided by Mount Royal with fields and orchards all over the hill. Another Englishman, John Lambert, who visited Montreal probably in the same year, was impressed by the city's unusual profile, by the light grey hues of the houses, and by the sun's reflection on the tin roofs.[34] This impression of the town was shared by J. E. Alexander: "Montreal had a most inviting appearance as we approached—the high and varied roofs, covered with shining tin, rivalling in brightness the broad and sparkling mirror of the St. Lawrence."[35] Another traveller, John Duncan, a Glasgow University graduate whose travelogue expressed sound and sometimes stern judgements, was also very much impressed by the sight of Montreal. In 1818 he wrote: "From the opposite bank the town has a showy appearance, and in summer the circumjacent scenery is exceedingly beautiful."[36] Adam Fergusson, another Scotsman touring Canada in 1831, was even more articulate:

> The city looks very handsome, as it is approached from Prairie; and the glistening tin-roofs of houses, nunneries, and churches, give it an appearance of splendour, rarely equalled, while the

mountain, with its woods and rocks, its orchards and villas, forms a beautiful and romantic background to the picture.[37]

However, the enthusiasm of some visitors often cooled once inside the town. They were dismayed by its dark, narrow streets, which appeared grim and dull. Isaac Weld, an Irishman from Dublin, whose account of his visit to North America in 1796 met with considerable success, noted that the houses of the lower town were gloomy and reminded him of a prison.[38] In 1820 Edward Talbot, whose opinion can be trusted since he spent five years in Canada, gave what is perhaps the most upsetting description of the city:

> It is impossible to walk along the streets of Montreal on a Sunday or other holiday, when the shops are all closed, without receiving the most gloomy impressions. The whole city appears one vast prison; and at every noise which salutes the ear of the passing stranger, he imagines that he hears the clanking of a malefactor's chains, or the pitiful moanings of an incarcerated debtor.[39]

Théodore Pavie, who seems to have been a very keen observer, explained this in a much simpler way when he wrote in his *Souvenirs atlantiques*, published in Paris in 1833:

> The houses are all made of grey stone so that the long narrow streets look very dark. What first strikes the stranger's eyes is the white colour of the roofs which are covered with tin while the shutters are lined with sheet iron, as a protection against fire. This method of building conveys an impression of great monotony.[40]

Fortunately, such unfavourable opinions were not shared by everybody. Joseph Bouchette, for one, was not so reticent. According to him, the streets, especially the new ones, were airy and reasonably wide; and though the houses were indeed made of grey stone, he had seen several large, attractive modern ones. In 1815 he wrote: "In its present state Montreal certainly merits the appellation of an handsome city."[41] Since the surveyor general of Lower Canada was Canadian born, he naturally did not see the city from the same angle as a foreigner, nor did he consider it with the same critical eye.

His testimony, however, corroborates the view of Benjamin Silliman, whose observations are noteworthy, for he was a distinguished geologist from Yale University. Silliman maintained that the quality of a landscape and the mentality of the people it surrounded were closely related to the geological characteristics of the land; he was also one of the first to give a valid geological description of the province of Quebec. Open-minded and well travelled, he had a solid basis for making comparisons when he visited Montreal in 1819; he had been to England, Holland, and Scotland and had published an account of his travels there.

In *Remarks Made on a Short Tour between Hartford and Quebec* he noted that Montreal had the appearance of a European town and, more specifically, of a continental one, because it was built of stone after the old fashion. He did not hide his admiration: "I was, I confess, much gratified at entering, for the first time, an American city built of stone." He praised the quality of the limestone used in Montreal, adding that it was just as handsome and durable as the famous Portland stone in England and that "a number of the modern houses of Montreal, and of its environs, which are constructed of this stone, handsomely hewn, are very beautiful, and would be ornaments to the City of London, or to Westminster itself."[42] As a geologist, he may have been prone to professional bias. Silliman willingly admitted that the American visitors, more familiar with brick and lumber, were likely to find Montreal dark and gloomy. Still, he stated his marked preference for stone because of its structural and plastic qualities. He was perhaps the first American to find something in Canada he wanted to imitate: "Montreal is certainly a fine town of its kind, and it were much to be wished that the people of the United States would imitate the Canadians, by constructing their houses, wherever practicable, of stone."[43]

Silliman's remarks were echoed a few years later by J. E. Alexander, a widely travelled man who stayed for a while in Montreal after visiting the two American continents. He too regarded it as "interesting because it has an air of stability and antiquity about it, and does not savour of the shavings and paints of the new cities in the States."[44]

Such contradictory testimonies might lead us to believe that Montreal, during the years of transition, was not, after all, so grand and impressive as Bouchette and Silliman had depicted it, nor was it so dull and depressing as Weld and Talbot had described it. On the other hand, visitors from Europe certainly viewed it differently from American-born travellers. To the former, the small town had preserved some of the characteristic features of the traditional village, whereas in the eyes of the latter Montreal held the promise of a unique future. This difference in perception is still noticeable today, depending on whether visitors are coming from the Old World or from the New World.

At any rate, there is no lack of positive data. Bosworth, for in-

stance, found that Saint-Paul Street, the main business thoroughfare, could easily have been wider but that it could nevertheless
compare with "some of the central streets in London, but without
their fog and smoke."[45] Most observers agreed with Joseph
Bouchette when he praised Notre-Dame Street for being "by much
the handsomest street in the place,"[46] and described it as the rich
merchants' residential area and the site of most of the public buildings in the town: the Church of the Récollets, the parish church of
Notre-Dame, the Anglican Christ Church, the Court House, the
prison, and the Château de Ramezay. They also commended the
commissioners for the improvements they had brought about, such
as the spacious Place Jacques-Cartier, the elegant Dalhousie Square,
and especially the Champ-de-Mars, considered in those days as the
ideal place for walks on a summer evening. Lambert extolled the
view one could enjoy over Faubourg Saint-Laurent and Faubourg
Saint-Antoine from that particular spot,[47] while Théodore Pavie
hailed it as "one of the loveliest places" he had ever seen in any
city.[48] (Plate 26.)

Let us now turn to private buildings. Except for a few large mansions, belonging to rich merchants, which have long ago disappeared
and about which we have but scarce data, the average house had no
architectural pretensions. We have described in the previous chapter
the Maison du Patriote, the Maison Del Vecchio, the Maison de la
Sauvegarde, as well as other houses. The old-town houses were generally made of stone, in the traditional way, but ashlar was used increasingly. In Hadfield's opinion, only a few of these residences
could boast of any elegance.[49] In his journal of 1785 he wrote that in
the suburbs, where houses were generally made of wood, they were
quite insignificant. Weld agreed on their lack of elegance but found
them at least very comfortable.[50] One suburban villa worth mentioning is Monkland House. According to Massicotte, it was built at
the end of the eighteenth century after the plans of a castle in Scotland.[51] In the middle of the following century, it was considerably
altered and decorated in the Italian fashion by the architect Browne
in order to turn it into a suitable residence for Lord Elgin, then governor general. Later, in 1854, it was purchased by the Sisters of the
Congregation of Notre-Dame who converted it into a select board-
ing-school under the name of Villa-Maria. Today, its significance is
somewhat blurred by the success of the institution it continues to
house and by the additions made to the original building.[52]

This brings us to the subject of public buildings: are there any
that may be traced back to the period after the cession? Few were
built and fewer still deserve our attention. From an architectural

26. *View of the Champ-de-Mars in 1830, after a drawing by R. A. Sproule*

point of view, the following may yield some valuable information: the new parish church of Notre-Dame, Christ Church Cathedral, the Bank of Montreal, the Hôtel-de-France, the Old Customs House, the Court House, and the prison. Except for the Old Customs House and Notre-Dame Church, they unfortunately have all disappeared. Leaving Notre-Dame Church for the end of the chapter, let us look briefly at the other buildings, referring to engravings and contemporary writings when needed.

From an architectural standpoint, they are of unequal quality. In John Duncan's opinion not one of them could even be described as elegant, and we tend to agree. According to Duncan, the most "upright" and interesting were the Court House and the old prison,[53] a view which was shared by Lambert, Bouchette, Silliman, Fergusson, and Sir Bonnycastle.[54] Another visitor, James Silk Buckingham, went so far as to say that the Court House was "one of the best ornaments of the town."[55] Both buildings were erected on Notre-Dame Street, on a former property of the Jesuits which, following the cession, had been declared crown land. They stood approximately on the site shared by the present Old Court House and Place Vauquelin. Built in 1800 and 1806, respectively, they were typical of British colonial classicism: quiet and stately, with an air of aloof self-confidence. Their location, adjacent to the Champ-de-Mars, was largely responsible for their prestige; had they been placed in different surroundings, they might have failed to attract any attention.

There is no reason either to praise unduly the Bank of Montreal Building erected in the spring of 1818 on St. James Street, even though Talbot described it as "by far the finest edifice, either public or private, in the Canadas."[56] As the first building in the country especially designed as a bank, it retained the air of an upper-middle-class residence. Its architect remains unknown but he must have come originally from Scotland or Ireland, for the austere ashlar façade and interior decoration of this building are strongly reminiscent of a Georgian style prevalent in both countries. A sketch by John Murray, drawn around 1850, shows the good proportions of the façade, although its vaguely Doric portico seems out of scale. In 1847 the bank was transferred to neighbouring premises, and in 1870 the original building was pulled down to make room for the General Post Office.[57] (Plate 27.)

The same Georgian spirit prevailed in the Hôtel-de-France, but here the inspiration came more directly from England. Built on Saint-Gabriel Street, in front of the Champ-de-Mars, it was pulled down in the 1960s. It may tentatively be dated to the early nineteenth century, for it appears on "Vue du Champ-de-Mars," an 1830

27. *St. James Street in 1850, after a watercolour by John Murray*

engraving by Sproule. It was somewhat heavy-looking and showed influences of the Georgian square-plan house with hip roof and a central staircase. (Plate 26.)

The example of the Old Customs House is more interesting. To-day it houses government offices. First of all, its location in the middle of the old Market Place is symbolic of a change in the values prevailing at the time. Under the old regime, only the parish church could have claimed the right to such a location. Now it was the Customs' turn—a clear reflection of the merchants' growing importance in the life of the city. Designed in 1836 by John Ostell, it was rather a small building; today it retains most of its original architecture despite certain alterations.

John Ostell, with Victor Bourgeau, was one of the most prominent architects of nineteenth-century Montreal. He was born in London in 1813 and he probably undertook some study of architecture, engineering, and surveying before coming to settle in Montreal around 1835, apparently remaining there until his death in 1892. Ostell was never short of work in his adopted town. In addition to the Customs House he is responsible for the towers of Notre-Dame Church, the façade of the remarkable Church of the Visitation at Sault-au-Récollet, the Church of Notre-Dame-de-Grâce, the Grand Séminaire on Sherbrooke Street, the Episcopal Palace, destroyed by fire in 1852, the rebuilding of St. James Church after it was levelled by the same fire, and, finally, the Asile-de-La-Providence. He has also been credited with a number of other designs, including the Church of Sainte-Anne, in Pointe-Saint-Charles, which has been recently pulled down; a few buildings of McGill University as well as the general planning of the campus itself; and, finally, the plan for the Côte-des-Neiges cemetery. With his nephew, H.-Maurice Perrault, Ostell set up what was to become the oldest firm of architects in the country. Together they designed the Old Court House on Notre-Dame Street, to which we shall return later. If we compare this building with the heavy Gothic style of what remains of his work in St. James Church, it seems that John Ostell was more successful with the classical orders than with any other style.[58]

The Customs House was his very first work in America; moreover, it was built within surroundings where the vernacular architecture was predominant. Ostell seems, therefore, to have wanted to show off his skill in the field of classical architecture. Even though few people realize this at first, much to the credit of the architect, this small construction displays almost the whole gamut of the characteristic features of classicism: Tuscan pilasters; triangular pediments and arched windows on the side overlooking Saint-Paul

Street; ashlar courses with strongly marked joints; lovely porticos with Tuscan columns; entablatures crowning the openings over-looking Commissioners Street; Venetian or Palladian windows on the other façades, and so forth. We need to emphasize the British influence evidenced here in every detail although it is specially apparent in the Venetian windows and triangular pediments; the latter, Palladio's favourite devices to enhance main entrances, had been adopted by his English followers. At a closer look, we find the small Customs House rather overcrowded with architectural details, but there is little doubt that it answered the Montreal merchants' quest for a symbol of their growing importance in the community. (Figure 9.)

The merchants were not alone in their determination to see their rights and pretensions acknowledged. The official Anglican Church was indeed quite eager to assert its presence by way of a symbolic building, all the more so since it had to take root in a predominantly Roman Catholic town. For Anglican Montrealers, it was therefore a matter of rivalling the old Notre-Dame Church. This may be the reason why they chose to build their temple on a nearby lot on the northern side of Notre-Dame Street and halfway between Place d'Armes and St. Lawrence Blvd. As for the building itself, after several architects had submitted their plans, they eventually selected those of William Berczy, a German traveller and sometime painter and amateur architect. Thus, on 21 June 1805, the first stone was laid by the Anglican bishop of Quebec. Originally, the building was to accommodate about eight hundred people at a cost of some £7,500. Construction, however, was considerably delayed for lack of funds and the building's capacity was subsequently enlarged to meet the increase in the Protestant population of Montreal. The church eventually cost far more than expected and was not completed until 1821.[59] (Figure 10.)

Silliman liked the church and did not hesitate to call it the most beautiful building in Montreal.[60] Talbot was also much impressed, particularly with the steeple "which is acknowledged to be superior to anything of the kind in British North America," and which he found very slender and elegant. The inside of the church, in his opinion, attested to the taste and refinement of its designers.[61] Joseph Bouchette, in his 1831 description of British North America, wrote that he regarded the church as one of the most splendid specimens of modern architecture in the province.[62]

Notwithstanding what Bouchette had to say, the first Anglican cathedral in Montreal was not at all modern. Its models, the magnificent churches of Christopher Wren and James Gibbs, had been in existence in London for over a century. Like the Anglican cathedral of Quebec with which it had much in common both in spirit and in form, it was meant to reflect the consciousness of a self-confident church and the virtues of a society faithful to its traditions and code of ethics. And what could be better than a society which had restored the Anglican Church and the monarchy? And since Wren had been the first architect to adapt the temple to the new Anglican liturgy, his architectural designs rested on solid grounds.

The design of Christ Church with its rectangular plan and extension to accommodate the altar[63] resembled the design for St. Bride's on Fleet Street and St. James, Piccadilly, in London. Its inside volume was divided into three sections: a central nave with a semicircular arched ceiling resting on an uninterrupted entablature, itself supported by Corinthian columns; one lateral nave on each side, with typical flat ceilings and galleries also supported by columns. In brief, a good illustration of Wren's principles for "a convenient auditory in which everyone should hear the service and both hear and see the preacher."[64] Incidentally, these galleries were an innovation devised by Wren for his churches and later were perpetuated by Gibbs in his own designs.

With its main façade and its three doors corresponding to the three inside naves, the Anglican cathedral of Montreal resembled more St. Martin-in-the-Fields by Gibbs. From the outside, the latter is conspicuous for its unique combination of a classical portal and a soaring, almost medieval, steeple. Christ Church strictly speaking, had no portico as such, but gave the illusion of one by its Tuscan-style pilasters supporting a Doric pediment. Its main feature was certainly its steeple, set in the same way as its counterpart in St. Martin-in-the-Fields, though not quite so elaborate. It consisted of a square tower built of stone and brick, topped by a wooden bell-tower covered with tin, with its pinnacle rising to sixty-two metres.

More classical in style than the Anglican cathedral of Quebec, thanks mainly to a parapet crowning the building and emphasizing the horizontal volume, Christ Church, as a monument, was intended to symbolize self-confidence. However, considering the site where it was erected, it probably did not convey a very comfortable feeling. In this respect, the Anglican cathedral of Quebec and the Old Customs House in Montreal were erected on lots which were in keeping with their message. Christ Church, symbol of the stereotyped values of an idealized society, should have had a clearing on all sides, like a funeral monument standing in a cemetery. This purpose was to be achieved half a century later when the second Christ Church Cathedral was erected on Sainte-Catherine Street, in lieu of

Fig.9   The Old Customs House, view from Saint-Paul Street and view from the western side of Place Royale. John Ostell, architect, 1836

Fig. 10 The first Anglican cathedral, Christ Church. William
Berczy, architect, 1805–21

its predecessor which had been entirely destroyed by fire in December 1856.

The latter nevertheless had provided Montreal with an important landmark. Its steeple was right there competing for sky and heaven with the steeple of the old Notre-Dame Church. The two sanctuaries, built almost side by side, reaffirmed the existence of two communities divided at the religious as well as at the cultural level. Christ Church was a challenge to the French-speaking Roman Catholic community, and even more so to the Sulpicians of the Old Seminary who were in charge of the parish of Notre-Dame and were seigneurs of the site. Already roused by the construction, against their will, of St. James Church, in Faubourg Saint-Laurent, which was to become the first Catholic cathedral in Montreal, they met the challenge in the most unexpected way: they built the new Notre-Dame Church.

The New Notre-Dame Church
The present Notre-Dame Church is too familiar a sight to bear description here. It is so much a part of the city's image that it is impossible today to imagine Place d'Armes without this huge neo-Gothic monument. On the other hand, when one is over-familiar with a building one tends to forget its main features, whether they be qualities or defects. Who, for example, is aware today of the monumental scale of this church, especially since it has been completely dwarfed by the presence of nearby skyscrapers? We have to remind ourselves that its towers are 66 metres high and its nave about 78 metres long by 41 metres wide; measured under the vault, the nave is some 25 metres high. At the time it was built (1824–29), it was the largest building in both Canadas and perhaps in all of North America. Of course, any comparison with the great Gothic cathedrals of Europe would be futile. However, because bad habits prevail, its portico has been compared with that of Peterborough cathedral, its towers with those of Westminster Abbey, and its façade, as incredible as it may seem, with that of Notre-Dame in Paris. True, its vault is as high as that of Peterborough cathedral; its towers are almost as high as those of Westminster and fall short of equalling those of Notre-Dame in Paris by only two and a half feet. Although the new Notre-Dame is not so long as the last two churches mentioned, it is wider than the former and almost as wide as the latter. (Plate 28.)

Comparisons of this kind are superficial, but they are the only ones we can safely make. From a strictly architectural point of view, a confrontation between Notre-Dame in Montreal and the Gothic masterpieces of the Middle Ages would only highlight the absurdity of Montreal's achievement. The authentic Gothic style was primarily a dynamic construction contrived to balance the thrust of the vaults through devices such as crossing ogives, flying buttresses, and abutments, which allowed the walls to be hollowed out and adequate lighting to reach the interior of large structures. Our church is obviously only a caricature of such a style. Indeed, its vault is a mere ceiling hanging from the roof. Its structural principle remains essentially the traditional box, including inside galleries, which prevailed in the classical English churches of the late seventeenth and the eighteenth centuries built by Sir Christopher Wren and James Gibbs. In the nave, instead of the brightness and vitality offered by an authentic Gothic approach, there was, originally, gloom and obscurity. This reflects the almost unanimous opinion of contemporary observers. The present interior is, indeed, very different from the original design. It was transformed in the 1870s by Victor Bourgeau, a Canadian architect. The large stained-glass window rising, as in Yorkminster, at the apse of the church, dispensed a harsh light to the choir but hardly any illumination elsewhere. It was therefore pulled down and three rose-windows were cut through the hanging vault and the roof in an attempt to provide the main nave with adequate lighting. Similarly, the initial grey-blue imitation-marble whitewash was removed and replaced by a polychrome surface similar to that decorating the Sainte-Chapelle in Paris and the fortress-cathedral of Sainte-Cécile in Albi. The complete renovation of the high altar is another alteration completed around the end of the last century. (Plates 29 and 30.)

On the other hand, Notre-Dame is a pioneer achievement of Gothic Revival in North America. It is certainly the only example of such monumental proportions. Gothic components were used in a decorative rather than in a structural way since the architects involved in that movement were trying, at first, to recapture the "atmosphere" of the style rather than the logic of its construction. In this light, Notre-Dame assumes a much more significant place in the history of Canadian and Montreal architecture than is generally acknowledged. As a matter of fact, the architect James O'Donnell did not try to re-create a Gothic monument, nor did he draw his inspiration from the genuine sources of that art in Europe. He seems to have contented himself with reminiscences of monuments seen in his native Ireland or in England, a country with which he was well acquainted. According to Franklin Toker, O'Donnell's direct sources of inspiration were his own achievements in the United States, notably Christ Church in New York (1823) and the First Pres-

28. *Notre-Dame Church, Place d'Armes, around 1870. James O'Donnell, architect, 1824–29*

byterian Church in Rochester (1824), where he had resorted to the use of certain Gothic features. He also borrowed from the contemporary work of American architects such as the First Unitarian Church (1817–18) by Maximilian Godefroy in Baltimore, Christ Church (1816) by Charles Bulfinch in Lancaster, Massachusetts, and St. Paul's Church (1817–18) by Benjamin Henry Latrobe, in Alexandria, Virginia.[65]

Observations and reactions to Notre-Dame by contemporaries enable us to understand that they were not looking for old-style Gothic as such; rather, they were seeking the image for which that style had always stood: a symbol of faith, majesty, and beauty that not even the very real defects of this church have managed to blur: Théodore Pavie, whom we have already acknowledged as a sensitive observer, wrote in 1830 that Notre-Dame was a "large and beautiful monument," the most remarkable he had ever seen in all of America.[66] Coke, in *A Subaltern's Furlough*, an excellent work published in 1833, was even more emphatic when he claimed that the "Catholic Cathedral" (*sic*) of Notre-Dame was probably superior to any other monument of its kind in North America and even to any other structure of the nineteenth century. Strangely enough, his short description of Notre-Dame is mainly concerned with its weaknesses and with some details of poor taste.[67] A few years later, a Scotsman, Hugh Murray, was to react in a similar way. He felt a strong dislike for the large stained-glass window but this did not prevent him from appreciating the style and the surprising dimensions of the church. He thought that its altar resembled that of St. Peter's in Rome, its pulpit that of the cathedral of Strasbourg, and he concluded that "the new Catholic Cathedral . . . is undoubtedly the most splendid, and is, in fact, superior to any other in British America."[68] Walter Henry's reaction is also typical. He was a seasoned traveller who spent a whole year in Montreal. He readily acknowledged Notre-Dame as the most majestic church on the continent and a dignified monument but he did not have a kind word for its inside decoration; he found it pitiful and an example of bad taste. He was, however, most impressed by the vast dimensions, the lamps that never ceased burning, the sumptuous altar, the madonnas on the walls, and the constant presence of kneeling penitents.[69]

Considering such evidence, it becomes obvious that the criteria for assessing architecture had lost a great deal of sophistication since the classical period. Notre-Dame, for instance, was not so much appreciated for its intrinsic architectural qualities as for the sentimental emotion derived from its stunning dimensions and other striking features, as well as for the "message" conveyed by its

29. *Interior of Notre-Dame Church, as it looked around 1838. Drawing by William Henry Bartlett*

30. *The present interior of Notre-Dame Church, after alterations by the architect Victor Bourgeau around 1870*

style or by its other functions. We were now entering the romantic era and Notre-Dame was gradually becoming a symbol. O'Donnell, its architect, addressing the members of the Church Construction Committee wrote: "Gentlemen, you should keep in mind that you are not erecting a temporary building but rather a monument that will bring glory to yourselves, to your assembly, and to your country. . . . I can assure you that the story of your church will be passed on to generations of the future."[70]

James O'Donnell himself was a romantic artist, as may be gathered from biographical notes by Maurault and by Toker. Born in Ireland in 1774, he studied architecture there, and then completed his education by travelling to some European countries. He never set foot in France, however. He emigrated to the United States of America in 1812, without having achieved anything remarkable in his own field. Once settled in New York, he does not appear to have emerged in any outstanding way except that he produced plans for a dozen buildings, including renovations and additions to Columbia College and to the two neo-Gothic churches already mentioned. He was also the only architect to have been elected a member of the American Academy of Fine Arts in New York, a distinction in which he took great pride. A confirmed individualist, he attached the utmost importance to his status as a professional; he was openly conscientious and ticklish in matters involving his honour.[71] He seemed unable to conceal his boredom and impatience when confronted with unintelligent laymen or with opinions contrary to his own. A letter he wrote to François Antoine La Rocque, a member of the Notre-Dame Construction Committee, and reproduced in the appendix to Franklin Toker's excellent book,[72] is very revealing in this respect. Some time later he complained: "Alas! there are so very few people here to appreciate the work of an architect." This sounds like the echo of many a romantic complaint.[73]

On the other hand, James O'Donnell had every right to claim credit for his work in Montreal. Toker reminds us that he had been called upon to design a church two or three times larger than any other on the continent, to build it on a prestigious but somewhat awkward location, and to do so in a new style that would challenge entrenched traditions.[74] As for the construction itself, he was very successful: he completed this considerable work in only five seasons, thus demonstrating his skill as an engineer, especially in the structural devices provided for the roof. Considering the site chosen, O'Donnell had grand ideas, and his portico with three monumental arches proves that his church was designed to be viewed from as far away as Sherbrooke Terrace. If Place d'Armes had been extended down to Saint-Antoine Street, as advocated in the plan approved in 1801 by the commissioners and as intended by O'Donnell himself, the scenery we would enjoy today would be much more in keeping with the monument's scale than the view we now manage to get from Place d'Armes. From an architectural point of view, he was more successful with the exterior of the church, which does not lack vigour, than with the interior, which seems to have disappointed everybody. We cannot, however, accept at face value all the opinions voiced on this subject, including the following statement by J. E. Alexander: "Its tawdry internal decorations, its blue compartments and spotted pillars, caused the death of the unfortunate architect, who died of a broken heart, disgusted at the bad taste which had spoiled his handiwork."[75] O'Donnell had accepted poor working conditions and a lower salary out of dedication to his work, but it eventually impaired his health; he must have truly believed in the importance of his venture. An artist seldom cares for his work to the point of asking to be buried therein after his death. It was perhaps with this thought in mind, since he had already expressed the wish before, that O'Donnell renounced the Protestant faith to become a Roman Catholic some time before his death which occurred on 28 January 1830. His wish was granted; he lies buried under his church, at the foot of the first pillar on the side to the right of the altar.

The Gothic Revival came into fashion in England around 1750–70, that is, at the time Robert Adam and his followers completed the renovation of Strawberry Hill, the residence of Horace Walpole. The new style had certainly reached its climax as early as the beginning of the nineteenth century, for the delightful Church of St. Luke, in Chelsea, London, designed in 1820 by James Savage, gives ample proof of its perfection. In America, however, the new trend was still in its infancy at the time. In the United States, examples can be counted on the fingers of one hand. To the already mentioned buildings designed by Godefroy, Bulfinch, Latrobe, and O'Donnell, we must add St. Mary's Seminary, in Baltimore, designed in 1817 after the Gothic fashion. However, the most famous examples of the style, such as Trinity Church in New York (1841–46) by Richard Upjohn, were to be completed much later. In Upper and Lower Canada, the new mode made its first appearance in the Maritime provinces in the early nineteenth century. At that time, it only amounted to a few Gothic devices grafted onto Georgian or neo-classical wooden buildings. One may therefore imagine the tremendous impact of a monument of the size and importance of Notre-Dame in Montreal, built entirely in the neo-Gothic style, especially since that church was closely identified with the established values propounded by the prestigious clerical order. Notre-Dame launched the fashion and neo-Gothic evolved into the only proper style for places of worship; it became synonymous with Christianity, as if one could pray better in a church decorated with ogival arches and crowned with pinnacles. Carried away by this example, many parish priests throughout the province would not hesitate to "gothicize" some delightful churches built in the vernacular style, sometimes pulling down what had been a delicate masterpiece to replace it by some Gothic elephant. The bells of Notre-Dame were now tolling for the old French architectural tradition in Quebec.

A few alert people, such as Abbé Jérôme Demers and Thomas Baillargé, who had been preaching the gospel of classicism throughout the province, were quick to realize that the style of Notre-Dame was about to deal a mortal blow to the classical tradition. Baillargé even submitted an alternative plan, presumably a cruciform church of classical inspiration. But their opposition carried little weight: time had already moved ahead. O'Donnell simply answered that the Gothic style seemed to him "more suitable to your materials, workmen, climate, wants and means, etc."[76] This meant nothing except, perhaps, that the idea had put down roots and from now on, the Gothic style was going to be an acceptable alternative to classicism, even in the eyes of the layman. When Thomas Baillargé, by now a recognized architect, was approached by the church wardens of Montreal to take into his hands the construction of the future cathedral, he answered to the point in a letter: "Since your building is to be in the Gothic style, and since I have only studied Greek and Roman Architecture, which I thought was sufficient for this country, my knowledge of the Gothic is only superficial. I therefore believe I would be unequal to such a task."[77]

He was not the only one to feel unequal to the task of building the new Notre-Dame. According to O'Donnell, all the workers on the site were in the same predicament: they were "universally careless, and inattentive in obeying orders."[78] What was mainly lacking, he complained, was a "system," forgetting that a "system," as such, was foreign to Quebec craftsmen's tradition. Indeed, in the eyes of the latter, conception was rarely dissociated from execution. A man like Thomas Baillargé thought, conceived, drafted, and built his own plans. And now, for the first time in Montreal, a professional architect had appeared on the scene to deal with a large project. He was bringing in a new style, borrowed moreover from the English tradition. He was imposing a monumental scale to which the Quebec workers were not accustomed. He used materials that had to be assembled in a new way, and insisted on working techniques that would deny the craftsman any autonomy or creative ability because he was forced to complete steps ordered from above by a total stranger. The industrial era was dawning.

This second part of our study of the development of Montreal started with the vision of the first Notre-Dame Church, proudly standing as a beacon in the heart of the small town. It ends with the vision of a church which steadily holds the same position. But not for long, for a new era was about to be born. Tremendous changes were in the offing for Montreal, as the city was about to experience unprecedented topographical growth. This new world was to extend vertically and horizontally all at once, with railways and skyscrapers as its symbols. The merchant and the industrialist were to triumph over the "seigneur" and the "craftsman," as we shall see in the third part of this study.

Part III

VICTORIAN MONTREAL: 1840–WORLD WAR I

Les rues y sont larges et bien mieux entretenues qu'à Québec; les magasins vastes et superbement bornés, les institutions de crédit abondent, et quelques-unes des banques principales—situées pour la plupart dans la rue Saint-Jacques—sont installées dans de véritables palais. Les journaux anglais et français écrasent par l'ampleur de leur format et l'abondance des renseignements leurs plus modestes confrères de Québec; les maisons particulières elles-mêmes affectent les prétentions architecturales des plus grandes cités du continent américain. Vingt sectes diverses ont édifié des églises, dont un bon nombre, avouons-le, sont bâties dans ce style hybride et désagréable, semi-gothique et semi-rocaille, qui fait la joie des cockneys anglo-saxons et le désespoir des véritables artistes. Dans cette débauche de bâtisses religieuses, le clergé catholique tenait à ne pas se laisser distancer. Non content de posséder une cathédrale qui passe cependant pour l'une des plus belles d'Amérique du Nord, l'évêque de Montréal a entrepris, à grand renfort de souscriptions, d'ériger une basilique nouvelle qui sera la réduction, mais une réduction grandiose encore, du premier des temples chrétiens: Saint-Pierre de Rome aura sa copie sur les bords du Saint-Laurent.

H. DE LAMOTHE, 1879[1]

7

New Forces

---

*It is revolution that has done most to change
the places where men live, not the revolution of
politics but the revolution of economics and
technics.*
HENRY S. CHURCHILL[2]

The Transportation Revolution

Queen Victoria ascended the throne of England in 1837 and ruled for
sixty-four long years until her death in 1901. Her reign witnessed a
great many discoveries, inventions, and technical and scientific developments which marked the beginning of the industrial revolution and turned England into the first and most powerful industrial
nation in the world. As far as the evolution of Montreal is concerned, her reign might have been less noteworthy had it not also
witnessed the impact of the economic and technical revolution on
architecture and on the urban environment.

One of the first achievements of technology in the colony was the
launching in 1809 of the *Accommodation*, which was the first
steamboat to navigate the St. Lawrence River and which had been
completely built and fitted in Montreal. The use of steam to propel a
ship had shortened distances and proved that commercial navigation on the St. Lawrence was both possible and economically feasi-
ble, a fact which sailing ships had not established. This was to stimulate the launching of huge projects to improve the great waterway.
In 1825 the Lachine Canal was opened; it was further transformed
and enlarged in 1836–37 and again in 1844. The Lachine Rapids

were thus no longer an obstacle. As early as 1848 a network of canals as well as the dredging of the river permitted navigation on the
waterway from the Atlantic Ocean to the Great Lakes. The first
ocean steamer to sail up the St. Lawrence, the S.S. *Genova,* docked
triumphantly at Montreal harbour in May 1853.[3] (Plate 31.)

Montreal, with its privileged geographical location, was to benefit
significantly from steam navigation. This is evident from the spectacular development of port installations. At the turn of the century,
the few ships which ventured through the St. Mary's Current had
only a muddy beach at the foot of the Market Place along which to
lower the anchor. Here is what John Lambert had to say about this
"natural" harbour in 1807:

> The shipping lie close to the shore, which is very steep, and
> forms a kind of natural wharf, upon which the vessels discharge
> their cargoes. About twenty yards back, the land rises to the
> height of 15 or 20 feet; and an artificial wharf has been con-
> structed, and faced with plank; the goods are, however, all
> shipped from, and landed upon, the beach below.[4]

This state of affairs soon improved. Between 1832 and 1838 the
average number of arrivals a year was 100 ships for an overall tonnage of 23,137. In 1842 there was scarcely one mile of stone piers. By
1850 there were two miles of piers and both arrivals and tonnage
had doubled to 222 ships and 46,000 tons. Ten years later, tonnage
rose to 261,000 tons for ocean-going vessels and 530,000 tons for
riverboats. In 1877 colonization expanded into the western territories, now politically unified under Confederation. This growth was
reflected in the progress and development of Montreal Harbour. Its
piers and jetties by now extended from the entrance of the Lachine
Canal to the eastern limits of the city (the level of today's Frontenac
Street). There were over four miles of installations and tonnage had
reached the million and a half mark. Montreal was a transit point
between ocean-going vessels and riverboats and the most important
Canadian trading centre between the Old and New World.

Towards the end of the century, Montreal Harbour, although operating for only seven months of the year, received about one thousand ocean-going vessels a year. It was by then the second most important port in North America after New York, surpassing both
Boston and Philadelphia on the Atlantic seaboard. By 1914 the tonnage reached nine million tons. During these first years of the twentieth century, important changes were made to the port facilities for
the storage of western wheat. The huge grain elevators, which today

31. *The entrance to the Lachine Canal towards the end of the nineteenth century*

partially hide the outline of the city, date back to that time and are as characteristic of the industrial era as are the large factories and the first skyscrapers.[5] (One elevator was demolished in 1978.)

The use of steam to power rail transport was to constitute the greatest event marking the Victorian era and, as an achievement, it would be even more significant than steam navigation. Together with the improvement of the port facilities and the navigable channels of the St. Lawrence River, the railway would prove to be the most precious ally of the metropolis in its quest for a national destiny. Indeed, the railroad was able to reach areas not accessible by boat and, unlike the rivers which freeze, it was not susceptible to the rigours of winter. In 1836, a mere six years after history's first railroad linked the cities of Liverpool and Manchester in England, the colony inaugurated its first rail line which was also the first in all the British colonies. It was named the Champlain and St. Lawrence, and it linked Saint-Jean on the Richelieu River to Laprairie; it was meant to facilitate communications between Montreal and New York. A second railroad, inaugurated in November 1847, united Lachine to Montreal and complemented the Lachine Canal. In 1853 a connection with the Grand Trunk line associated Montreal with Portland, on the coast of Maine, and gave Montreal its first link with an ice-free port. The same company would, some years later (1855–56), lay the tracks for a rail line between Toronto and Montreal. Around the same time, the construction of the first bridge over the St. Lawrence River was planned and was eventually completed within the framework of the Grand Trunk project. The bridge, to which we shall return in a later chapter, would be called Victoria, a symbolic name for the era. In 1876 the Intercolonial Railway linked Montreal to the Maritime provinces and a decade later, in May 1887, the first transcontinental railway, the Canadian Pacific Railway, extended the line from Montreal to Vancouver. With the advent of the Canadian Pacific, two monumental railway stations were erected in the metropolis: Viger and Windsor. They became the railway's architectural symbol and Montreal developed into the hub of Canada's entire railway network. Once more, the city resumed its role as a link between the East and the West.

Although less spectacular than the transcontinental railway, the secondary network of railway lines was equally important to Montreal's economy. Looking like a spider web, the rails spread out in every direction to points like Quebec City, Joliette, Saint-Jérôme, Hull, Valleyfield, and other localities, as well as to national and intercontinental connecting points, functioning both in winter and in summer and thus complementing the river network.[6]

The revolution in the means as well as in the equipment of land and sea transportation, together with other influences such as natural, human, and financial resources, became a determining factor in the rapid industrialization which was to mark the development of Montreal in the second half of the nineteenth century. Without Montreal's port facilities and without the railways, industry certainly would not have progressed to the point of becoming the city's most important field of economic activity from 1870 onwards. Although coal and steel were the catalysts of economic development, both materials were lacking in the Montreal region and had to be brought in by boat and rail. The same carriers introduced other raw materials to Montreal. Grain became an important commodity; large amounts of it were stocked in the huge silos on the harbour for later export. Some grain was processed on the spot, in breweries and distilleries, in the Ogilvy Mills on the pier of Windmill Basin, and at the St. Lawrence Flour Mills established in 1910 near the Lachine Canal. Cane sugar was transported to Montreal to be refined at the John Redpath Plant and at the St. Lawrence Sugar Plant in Hochelaga. Later, oil refineries would occupy a considerable amount of space on the island's east end. The new industries generated many new jobs, and hundreds of men were also employed in the shipping and handling of raw materials. Design, construction, and maintenance of the new means of transportation became a growing industrial sector of the economy. Thousands of workers were now employed at various shipyards and steel plants manufacturing steam engines, vessels, and rolling stock. There were numerous factories located near the harbour and the Lachine Canal: Canadian Car and Foundry with workshops in Saint-Henri, La Salle, Pointe Saint-Charles, and Longue-Pointe; Montreal Locomotive Works in Longue-Pointe; Canadian Vickers and the Angus Shops in Maisonneuve; and many others. Their employees were also numerous: in 1880 the repair yard of the Grand Trunk Railway in Pointe Saint-Charles engaged some 3,000 people, whereas the large Angus workshop of Canadian Pacific, which built and maintained the rolling stock, had some 7,000 workers towards the end of the century.[7]

To understand the other aspects of Montreal's industrialization let us now turn our attention to the human element involved in this process.

Two Solitudes

The revolution in the means of communication and intercity transportation—steamboats, railways, soon followed by the telegraph—generated a centripetal force which resulted in a concentration of most of the Dominion's economic activities in Montreal. This gathering of economic, financial, commercial, and industrial activities turned the city into a powerful centre of attraction towards which thousands of immigrants converged, sometimes looking for instant fortunes but more often in search of their daily bread. The new sources of energy as well as technological progress created a need for the division and interdependence of labour, which in turn forced the centralization of manpower and production. In turn, the increasing concentration of population in the city stimulated the growth of industry, trade, and services, resulting in a growth of both consumption and manpower. Thus the process of urbanization, which until then had been rather slow, suddenly accelerated. For the first time since the second half of the nineteenth century, the ratio between the urban and rural population and between grouped and scattered dwellings had been upset. In 1825 Montreal and Quebec, which were British America's most important urban centres, had only 5 percent of the territory's population; in 1851, for the province of Quebec alone, the percentage of urban population had risen to 14.9. In 1881 the percentage rose to 23.8. The steepest increase occurred at the beginning of the twentieth century: 36.1 percent in 1901, 44.5 percent ten years later. Over the forty-year period from 1881 to 1921 the percentage of urban dwellers doubled to 51.8.[8]

In less than a century the process of urban growth completely upset the balance between rural and urban populations, and Montreal became the first point of agglomeration as well as the most dynamic and most insatiable city, not only in the province of Quebec but also in all of British North America. As transportation improved and production was rationalized and mechanized, population growth showed parallel acceleration. In the seventy years following the British conquest, from 1761 to 1831, Montreal's population grew by 21,797, which is not surprising considering the natural demographic process and the influx of British as well as Loyalist immigrants. In the next seventy years, however, from 1831 to 1901, the population rose by more than 300,000 individuals, a figure which cannot be accounted for by the normal demographic processes and which is more consistent with a large-scale immigration.[9]

Who were these immigrants and where did they originate? Many came from the British Isles in three main waves: the first, composed mainly of soldiers who had been discharged after the Napoleonic wars, reached its peak around 1820; an economic crisis in Europe in the 1830s set off a second wave; and Irish immigrants fleeing the famines of the 1840s made up most of the third. It is not known exactly how many immigrants landed and stayed here, for Montreal was both a national harbour and a point of entry into America, thus a transfer centre for people arriving on the continent, and many of the new arrivals went on to Upper Canada or to the United States. Even without the availability of information, it is obvious that those coming from Britain made a significant contribution to the land from the point of view of both numbers and quality, especially during the second wave. Indeed, the British brought with them technology as well as capital at a time when the United Kingdom had gained an enviable position in the fields of science and technology. The wealthiest, most astute, and most daring among them—Scots, most of them—soon gained control over the means of production and began to exploit the new methods of transport and communications.[10]

Many worthy men followed in the footsteps of McGill and McTavish. The names of a few Montreal families that acquired large fortunes in the second half of the nineteenth century illustrate this fact. John Redpath had been very successful as head foreman during the construction of Notre-Dame Church and as contractor for Victoria Bridge (the most daring structure of the era); at fifty years of age he ventured into sugar refining and was even more successful. McGill University owes its most beautiful buildings to the generosity of the Redpath family. The Ogilvies were farmers on Côte Saint-Michel who became the most enterprising flour-millers in the country. McGill University also benefited from the generosity of another man, Sir William Macdonald, who was somewhat of an eccentric and who made millions in the tobacco industry while openly deploring the use of tobacco. Hugh Allan founded the Montreal Ocean Steamship Company in 1852 and projected the Canadian Pacific Railway Company; he left a personal fortune assessed at six to eight million dollars—an astronomical figure for the time—and his old residence of Ravenscrag on Pine Avenue bears witness to his wealth.[11] The importance of Scottish immigrants in Montreal is best shown by a visit to the Protestant cemetery on Mount Royal, where their tombstones surpass all others in number as well as in opulence.

Not all immigrants from the British Isles, however, were qualified, audacious, or destined to great fortunes. A majority of them were poor, starving people coming from Ireland. Between 1845 and 1848 about one hundred thousand Irish immigrants came to Canada to escape the great famine of 1845–46. So many of them set up residence in Montreal that the Cheneville Street neighbourhood was nicknamed "Little Dublin" and the old Griffintown district was almost exclusively settled by the Irish. The large population increase

(56 percent) in Montreal between 1851 and 1861 probably reflects this massive Irish immigration. Many of them managed to survive as construction workers for the canals or on Victoria Bridge, or as labourers at the shipyards of the Lachine Canal.

The city's census of 1851 clearly reflects the larger proportion of British among immigrants from overseas. Indeed, of some 57,715 inhabitants living in the city at the time, hardly two-thirds (38,514) were born in Canada, whether of French or other origin. Of the 19,201 remaining, 11,736 were born in Ireland, 3,150 in Scotland, 2,858 in England, 919 in the United States, a mere 133 in France, and 405 in other countries.[12] In time, though, the preponderance of British settlers would diminish in favour of a more varied immigration, which would herald the multiracial and cosmopolitan aspect of twentieth-century Montreal. Russian Jews—6,000 of them in Montreal in 1900—Syrians, Italians, Chinese, and others came to live in Montreal. Gradually they developed strong communities, often residing in specific districts as exemplified by Chinatown.[13]

Overseas sources alone cannot account for the remarkable growth of population in Montreal in those days. The number from foreign sources was more than equalled by strong local migration of French-Canadian country dwellers attracted by the city. In spite of a lack of precise figures one may nevertheless assume that local movement towards the city surpassed all other types of immigration. This would explain why the great rural plain of Montreal counted fewer inhabitants in 1931 than in 1861, and why the city, which was mostly populated by people of British origin in 1840, regained a French majority from 1870 onwards, even though immigration from France for the whole period between 1861 and 1931 numbered a mere 4,000–5,000.[14] As Cooper pointed out, the seven French Canadians, namely Rivard, Beaudry, Beaugrand, Grenier, Desjardins, Villeneuve, and Préfontaine, who were mayors of Montreal between 1879 and 1902, were all born outside the city.[15]

This migration to the city of a large number of French-Canadian country dwellers accounts for the soaring growth as well as for the main features of Montreal's manufacturing industry. After the conquest, French Canadians retreated to the countryside where the church held them in the bondage of parochial structures, preaching to them rejection of the city and of material riches. Without money, instruction, or technical knowledge, without tradition or experience in business or industry, these future city dwellers were in no position to take over the control of industrial development. The latter would completely escape their grasp to the benefit of immigrants, mostly British, who imported both capital and technology.

French Canadians, on the other hand, constituted the ideal source of manpower for low-technology and low-salary industries such as those producing common consumer goods (food, clothing, and other items), especially in view of the fact that there was a great demand for such goods in Montreal, which was by far the most populous city in Canada. To quote Cooper: "No people [were] better adapted for factory hands, more intelligent, docile, and giving less trouble to their employers."[16] If we exclude from these considerations industries linked to transport, the existence of such abundant, capable, and not very demanding manpower, together with the ready availability of raw materials, fostered towards the end of the last century the creation in the Montreal region of a whole range of industries: flour mills, refineries, cotton and other textile mills, clothing, shoe, and tobacco plants, breweries, and others, most of them processing industries for agricultural products.[17]

The 1871 census reveals that of 22,784 workers from the Montreal district engaged in the manufacturing industries, almost half were employed in plants making shoes, clothes, and tobacco. In 1911, at the very end of the Victorian era, 78,000 people worked in Montreal's various plants; the clothing industry, in first place, employed over 10 percent of that manpower and was responsible for two-thirds of the total Canadian output in that field. Metalworks, stimulated by the needs of the transport industry and new steel-processing techniques, came second. Next were tobacco plants, flour mills, refineries, and cotton mills. These are revealing figures.[18]

The division of the city into two poles of concentration was further accentuated by the influx of immigrants from the aforementioned two sources: the British from overseas and the rural French Canadians from the Montreal Plain. Moreover, social segregation had been intensified by the industrialization of cities worldwide. Disraeli, the British novelist and politician of the nineteenth century, refers to "two nations" coexisting in the industrial cities of his days. The same reality was expressed by the great Dr. William Channing of Boston who wrote in 1841: "In most large cities, there may be said to be two nations, understanding as little of one another, having as little intercourse as if they lived in different lands."[19] In Montreal, though, Disraeli's or Channing's "two nations" are no longer a metaphor expressing the cleavage between the social classes according to economic strata: they represent two groups separated along racial and linguistic lines as well as along social and economic planes. The ruling class of the "haves" is usually anglophone, whereas the proletarian "have-nots" are usually francophone. Even worse, this division is physically imprinted into the soil and is reflected in the quality of the buildings. Gabrielle Roy appropriately described this reality in these words: "Here wealth and poverty stare each other in the face, Westmount from above, Saint-Henri at its feet. Between them rise the belfries."[20]

Montreal is divided into two distinct cities, or even three, if one takes into account the existence of a mixed, shifting, predominantly Jewish population, centred on St. Lawrence Boulevard and serving as a buffer zone between the two linguistic groups. This division has not gone unnoticed by most of the observers and visitors who re- corded their impressions of Victorian Montreal. The theme of "two solitudes," on which C. H. Farnham expanded in an important arti- cle on Montreal written in 1889, usually underlies such remarks.[21] To wit, these few lines from a description of Montreal published in the 1882 issue of *Picturesque Canada*:

> There is no fusion of races in commercial, social or political life, the differences are sharply defined, and appear to be perma- nent. . . . It is easy to trace the two main divisions of population of Montreal. Taking St. Lawrence Main Street as a dividing line, all that is east of it is French, all that is west of it is English speaking. The two nationalities scarcely overlap this conven- tional barrier, except in a few isolated cases.[22]

We shall now follow the topographical development of the city dur- ing that period of its history in order to uncover the patterns of set- tlement of these human groups.

The Impact of Industry

In the 1830s, when O'Donnell's neo-Gothic church surprised the colony and inaugurated the era of Victorian architecture in Canada, Montreal was still a small town centred on its original commercial nucleus and first hub of economic activities. True, it was sur- rounded by suburbs, principally Saint-Antoine, Saint-Laurent, and Quebec, but they did not reach out very far. Moreover, their expan- sion was limited by the necessity of remaining within accessible reach of the centre of economic activity. There were few employ- ment opportunities in the suburbs as industrial development was in its infancy: several tanneries, the small soapworks of Griffintown, and Molson's Brewery, to name but a few. This explains why urban development was still confined to the lower terrace and did not reach much beyond the limits of the legal and administrative terri- tory of the town; these margins had been set in May 1792 and, as stated earlier, they corresponded roughly to today's Atwater Avenue to the west, Pine Avenue to the north, and Frontenac Street to the east.

Industrialization would soon transform the landscape. Industry created employment and thus attracted both manpower and population. But at a time when adequate means of transport and communication within the town did not yet exist, industry had a direct influence on the very structure of population settlement and on the topographical orientation of the urban development. The need for a defence system had played a part in the pattern of human settlement on the island, but industry would now take over.

The Lachine Canal district was the first to be industrialized. This was to be expected, as the site was at the hub of water and rail transportation and the canal's locks provided the necessary hydraulic energy. Ogilvy's flour mill and the Redpath sugar refinery were established at the mouth of the canal for these very reasons. Extending south of the old Griffintown district, on either side of the canal, a workers' district quickly developed; it would be called Sainte-Anne but was sometimes referred to as "Little Lowell" or "Fall-River." Most of the district's inhabitants were poor Irish immigrants who found jobs in shipyards and other industries which, like flour mills, did not require very skilled manpower. The construction of Victoria Bridge—a gigantic project for that time—and the establishment of the Grand Trunk Workshops at Pointe Saint-Charles contributed to the settling of the district, which by 1871 already harboured 18,639 inhabitants. By 1911 Sainte-Anne could justifiably be called the capital of industry: the number of people (19,000) employed in its shipyards, factories, and other plants was greater than its population forty years earlier. In fact, one quarter of all labourers engaged by industry in Montreal worked in Sainte-Anne.[23]

The industrial development of that section of the Lachine Canal, however, was not confined to the one district. It moved further to the southwest, outside the municipal boundaries of Montreal, probably because Sainte-Anne soon became overcrowded, but also to escape the burden of municipal taxes. The new territory, invaded by industrial development, would eventually be organized into three distinct municipalities—Saint-Gabriel, Sainte-Cunégonde, and Saint-Henri—and the labour force would be predominantly employed in heavy industries. The population in the new districts rose to 15,770 inhabitants by 1881 and three times that figure twenty years later (48,063).[24]

Even today this industrial "valley," seen from the heights of the Turcot Interchange, presents a picture of gloom. The district became a festering ground for social vices and the environment was degraded to an extent that was unfortunately all too characteristic of nineteenth-century industrial cities. In Montreal, as elsewhere, long hours of work, low salaries, and the exploitation of women and children as a source of cheap labour became a common practice. In Montreal, as in other parts of the world, slums became the Victorian era's most dominant feature in the city.[25] Herbert Brown Ames was a shoe manufacturer, who, like many of his contemporaries, was also a social reformer. He carried out a sociological study, rather advanced for the times (1897), entitled *The City below the Hill*; this "city" covered about 2.6 square kilometres, including parts of the Sainte-Anne and Saint-Antoine districts. Some of the facts revealed in the book attest to the harsh circumstances in which the population lived. Ames's study shows that on some streets the population density varied between 495 and 740 inhabitants per hectare, that half the living quarters within the confines of the area were overcrowded (more than one person per room), that half the occupied lodgings were not equipped with inside toilets, and that for a large section of the district, rather symbolically called "the swamp" and harbouring some 15,000 inhabitants, there was but a single green space, namely Richmond Square, which covered barely half an hectare. Such living-and-environmental conditions in the area covered by the study may be related to the mortality rate which averaged 22.47 per thousand inhabitants, with "black districts" where the rate climbed to 40 and 44, whereas the same year deaths in the wealthy districts of the "city on the hill" (for example, Westmount) counted for a mere 13 per thousand inhabitants.[26]

More recently, in her novel *The Tin Flute*—of some international renown—Gabrielle Roy described the Saint-Henri district with these same images of poverty, misery, boredom, human degradation, and deterioration of buildings and of the environment:

> At one time the suburb had ended here; the last houses of Saint-Henri looked out on open fields, a limpid, bucolic air clinging to their eaves and tiny gardens. Of the good old days nothing is left now on St. Ambroise Street but two or three great trees that still thrust their roots down under the cement side walk. Mills, grain elevators, warehouses have sprung up in solid blocks in front of the wooden houses, robbing them of the breezes from the country, stifling them slowly.[27]

Inevitable as this vision of despair and injustice may seem, it fits an era when "laissez faire" became a doctrine, and when housing developments grew everywhere in utter chaos, driven by blind, commanding forces: on the one hand, the appetite for profits and comfort of a daring class, made up of people speculating in consumer goods, manpower, and land, and, on the other hand, human hordes seeking their daily bread, a class of workers who were poorly paid because they were too numerous and too poorly qualified. It is small wonder, then, that working-class districts had to do without the most elementary community services. Blanchard points out that Sainte-Cunégonde was without an aqueduct until 1879 and without sewers until 1887.[28] It is not surprising that the spontaneous growth of the suburbs did little to transform the structures of the invaded rural domain. The uniform and monotonous orthogonal grid of streets was merely superimposed on the old pattern of land division of the rural côtes. This topic has been dealt with in chapter 2.

Like Saint-Henri and Sainte-Cunégonde, another working-class suburb—Hochelaga—would rapidly burgeon to the east and outside the boundaries of Montreal. It too owed its growth to an industrial development which the advent of electricity had accelerated. The village of Hochelaga extended east of the old Faubourg de Quebec and it was an ideal location for heavy industry because of its proximity to the port and to the Canadian Pacific Railway tracks. When the Angus Shops were established there, the railway became one of the most important sources of employment. After Sainte-Anne, Hochelaga–Maisonneuve became by 1911 the most dense industrial district with some 15,000 workers.[29]

Inside the administrative boundaries of the city of Montreal, the old suburbs of Saint-Antoine, Saint-Laurent, and Sainte-Marie (as the old Faubourg de Quebec was now renamed) were subdivided into boroughs or at least referred to as such, and were experiencing a remarkable industrial growth, parallel to that of Sainte-Anne and the outside suburbs. Light industry for ordinary consumer goods like clothes, for which the rigours of the climate created a great demand, was not too dependent on rail or water transport. These districts supplied the necessary manpower as well as a ready and expanding market. Thus, Saint-Antoine became the shoe district. Its population rose from 23,925 residents in 1871 to 48,638 in 1911. By then, Saint-Antoine had already encroached on the beautiful slopes of Mount Royal, towards Côte-des-Neiges, Côte Saint-Antoine, the future Westmount, and Notre-Dame-de-Grâce, all of which would become autonomous municipalities in 1881. The suburb of Saint-Laurent, the centre of the garment industry, was subdivided into several boroughs: Saint-Laurent, Saint-Louis, Saint-Jacques, and part of Saint-Antoine. Saint-Laurent was the first district to have deeply penetrated the Sherbrooke Terrace. St. Lawrence Boulevard, which became the main artery as well as the backbone of this north-westerly development, opened the way, followed closely by Bleury, Saint-Urbain, and Saint-Denis. A number of streets were drawn per-pendicularly to the latter, gradually consolidating the encroachment of the city on the rural territory. The district of Sainte-Marie became the gathering point of French Canadians seeking work, as the shoe factories and tobacco industry were looking for a capable but unde-manding and unskilled source of manpower. Like Sainte-Anne and Saint-Henri, it became a working-class district, generating a uni-formly boring urban environment; its population grew from 13,695 residents in 1871 to 54,910 in 1911. A similar demographic growth rate would cause the population of the adjacent districts of Saint-Jacques and Saint-Louis to double over the same period.[30]

From the preceding description it appears that industry played a major role in tearing apart the traditional framework of Montreal and in shaping urban development. Two other factors also came into play. In 1865 Bishop Bourget divided the old Parish of Montreal into several smaller ones. This decision accelerated the settling of the suburbs, as newcomers would now be assured that parishes—which were ecclesiastical administrative units as well as bases for social organization—could be established when necessary. There was an obvious need to be fulfilled in this respect, for within the next two years Saint-Jacques, Saint-Patrice (1866), Notre-Dame-de-Grâce, Saint-Enfant-Jésus du Mile-End, Saint-Henri, la Nativité in Hoche-laga, Saint-Vincent-de-Paul, and Sainte-Brigide (1867) became au-tonomous parishes. In 1876 the law on municipal corporations, passed in Quebec City, would allow parishes to become incorpo-rated as civil municipalities if they so wished; this would accelerate the process of decentralization. The second factor which favoured the gradual dismemberment of the traditional framework relates to the constant technical progress in the organization of public util-ities, such as the use of iron and cast-iron pipes for aqueducts and sewers, of gas for lighting of streets, and so forth.

Decentralization, however, was still limited. Indeed, lack of ade-quate means of communication and of inner-city mass transporta-tion forced the inhabitants to stay close to sources of employment, the plants and factories, a fact which accounted for the high popula-tion density of the first industrial districts such as Sainte-Anne and Saint-Henri. This explains why there were no strictly residential suburbs or districts until the end of the nineteenth century.

Definitive changes appeared in 1861 following the inauguration by City Passenger Railway of a horse-drawn omnibus system. In spite of its inherent limitations, this service rapidly expanded, and for the first time workers were given a chance to live away from their immediate but often sordid and degrading places of work. This explains why districts like Saint-Laurent would rapidly expand up to the second terrace, a magnificent site which until then had been preserved for the rich suburbanites who could afford to keep a carriage. In 1888 this omnibus service carried over 8.5 million passengers. The rate of change was further accelerated from 1892 onwards when an electric tramway system was inaugurated, quickly relinquishing the horse-drawn omnibus into the realm of memories. By the end of their first year in service, the electric tramways had already carried twice as many passengers as the omnibus system in 1888. The speed and regularity—even in winter—of the new system were its greatest assets. Moreover, regional (in those days) lines soon linked Montreal to distant communities. Thus, Park and Island Railway would run between Lachine and Sault-au-Récollet while the Montreal Island line would serve the east end, Maisonneuve, and Bout de l'Ile.[31]

Whereas on a national and regional level the transportation revolution had fostered the concentration of economic and productive activities in Montreal as well as the onset of urban growth, on a city level transportation would be a primary factor of greater dispersion and of population growth outside the city; this process would be further accentuated by the coming of the automobile. With the advent of electric tramways and, in 1879, of the telephone,[32] distance and communication difficulties, which had been limiting factors in the frontier town, were no longer an obstacle in the way of building expansion. The consequences were immediate: the strictly residential suburb became a reality. Thus, in the rich upper-class suburb of Westmount the population rose from 3,000 residents in 1891 to 8,856 in 1901 and to 14,579 a decade later. In this particular instance, it was not so much the increase in population which was noticeable as the number of "châteaux" which were erected on the side of Mount Royal. Outremont, another residential suburb having affinities with Westmount, was almost non-existent in 1881, but by 1911 it harboured 4,820 residents. This shortening of distances did not benefit only the elegant suburbs. The county of Maisonneuve, which was subdivided into industrial townships, experienced a prodigious growth: from 65,178 inhabitants in 1901 to 170,998 ten years later! Verdun is another example. The development of the old fiefdom had been thwarted by frequent inundations in parts of its territory as well as by its distance from Montreal's centre of activities. As soon as a dike had been built to protect the area from the rising of the river and when mass transportation brought the suburb within reach of sources of employment and economic activities, Verdun's population grew accordingly: 296 inhabitants in 1891, 1,898 in 1901, 11,629 in 1911. Finally, Lachine also became the site of an extraordinary boom, attracting a large population as well as very important and technologically advanced industries, such as Dominion Bridge in 1882 and Canadian General Electric ten years later.[33]

The chronology of the creation of parishes following the division of the Parish of Montreal in 1865 is indicative of the rhythm of urban growth throughout the island. For instance, from 1870 to 1900, seventeen French parishes and three English parishes were founded on Montreal's territory; between 1900 and 1920, this number doubled: thirty-eight French, eight English, and three New Canadian.[34] Since the law on municipal corporations of 1876 allowed each parish to be incorporated as a municipality, that which had always been an ecclesiastical unit of administration now became a territorial civil entity. The precincts within the judicial and political boundaries of Montreal were subdivided into small autonomous municipalities. In 1871 there were but four towns and three cities on the island; by 1901 there were already eleven towns and eight cities.[35]

Many of these municipalities would be short-lived: Hochelaga and Saint-Jean-Baptiste, for example, were too close to the City of Montreal; others such as Saint-Henri, Sainte-Cunégonde, or Maisonneuve shared identical interests with Montreal. Most of these small municipalities were in no financial position to offer the services and assume the costs of public utilities for proper urban living, so many would gradually be annexed to Montreal. It would be pointless to list all the annexations: for instance, between 1883 and the end of World War I about thirty municipalities were absorbed, from the populous cities of Saint-Henri with 21,000 residents or Saint-Louis with 35,000 residents to small villages, such as Côte-des-Neiges or Villeray. One must remember, however, that it was through annexations that the City of Montreal grew out of its old 1792 boundaries to the point of completely surrounding some municipalities which had remained autonomous, such as Westmount and Outremont, and of extending its jurisdiction to the shores of the Rivière-des-Prairies.[36]

The abolition of distances, the prodigious growth of population, the considerable extension of its administrative territory, all these factors affected the very character of the old city. It was launched on a process of morphological transformation which would leave it totally different from the small town designed in the early nineteenth century by the Commissioners McGill, Richardson, and Mondelet.

The city progressively lost its residents and surrendered its social duties to the sole benefit of commercial and administrative functions. The latter took over the entire territory of Coteau Saint-Louis. Saint-Paul Street, which had been the privileged artery of retail merchants, became the centre of wholesale trade and of warehouses, close to the harbour and to the railway services. The retail trade moved first to Notre-Dame Street, then to St. James Street, and finally, under the impetus of Morgan, Birks, Ogilvy, and Dupuis, who were the first merchants to establish their stores in the early 1890s, to Sainte-Catherine Street which would become the most prominent commercial street in the metropolis. At the same time, the rich homes on St. James Street relinquished this artery to the banks, the financial institutions, and the newspapers and moved to the Sherbrooke Terrace. St. James Street became the Dominion's Wall Street while Sherbrooke Street took on an appearance of wealth and distinction and some travellers, in search of a comparison, likened it to the Champs Élysées in Paris! Public administration grew in importance as the governed territories expanded; the population grew in numbers as a result of the concentration of economic and productive activities. Hence, new buildings had to be built: City Hall, the Court House, the Post Office, and many others. Together with the commercial and financial institutions they transformed Dollier de Casson's "cathedral" town into a modern city. (Plates 32, 33, 34.)

Victorian Architecture
From the foregoing paragraphs it is obvious that Victorian Montreal no longer reflected the influence of the seigneurial class. Moreover, by 1838, the Sulpicians had, in theory if not always in practice, renounced their rights to the property of the island. Under the French regime, they had been the ruling class and they attempted to maintain their social status, after the Anglo-Saxon merchants landed, through a tacit agreement with the Tory aristocracy. Now they would shy away from this rising class of merchants and industrialists, for this new bourgeoisie was active and hard-working and intent on promoting the new order. Of the five mayors who ran Montreal's administration from 1850 to 1860, namely Fabre, Wilson, Staines, Nelson, and Rodier, only Nelson represented the old order; the others were either merchants or industrialists.[37] The new ruling class had its own gospel, the aim of which was wealth and comfort; the means to achieve these goals were free enterprise, audacity, and ambition.

The previous era had left its own contribution to architecture in the form of the two Notre-Dame Churches in succession on Place d'Armes; the new era would produce new monuments attesting to the new values, for the bourgeoisie would soon monopolize architecture for its own purposes. Was it mere symbolism that the factory chimneys of the industrial districts should henceforth rise as high as the church steeples and the huge grain elevators along the harbour tower over the bell-towers of O'Donnell's Notre-Dame Church? Equally revealing is Montreal's City Hall, with its mass and prolific decoration, towering over the Château de Ramezay across the street. The fact that Bonaventure, Windsor, or Viger Stations should accommodate more people than Place d'Armes or the Champ-de-Mars, and that one of the greatest architectural successes of the time should be a bank (John Wells's Bank of Montreal) is hardly surprising.

The architectural image of Victorian Montreal is obviously more complex than that of the previous era and could not be restricted to a description of the few buildings which are the expression of social pretensions. Unprecedented progress had been achieved during that era in the scientific and technical fields; revolutionary developments had transformed the fields of communications, transport, and production; organization and the first large concentration of population had altered the shape of the towns. Such an era had to find new solutions for the new functions and problems. Indeed, the first bridge across the river, the Victoria, was a railway bridge built according to new concepts and with new materials. Increasingly specialized functions needed appropriate architectural programs as well as suitable structures. Warehouses, commercial buildings, factories, and railway stations appeared for the first time. For the first time also, buildings began to rise in height, first levelling off at five or six storeys, then pushing higher with the advent of the elevator. With the exception of the residences of the wealthy, which would remain symbols of the latter's prosperity, human habitations would lose their individual, family-centred character and become a consumer item, subject to criteria of economic profitability as well as to standardization and industrial prefabrication.

Architecture, however, is more than a function or the expression of a technology: it is a reflection of cultures and ideologies; it is both form and spirit. Thus, moving from a rural world still in the bonds of a medieval way of life to a modern urban world, French Canadians would attempt to maintain their ancestral and traditional values as a protection against the anonymity of the urban environment. Religious architecture was still the best way to express this concern. Farnham, who wrote a sociological study on Montreal's two soli-

32 & 33. Montreal around 1870, view towards the mountain

34. *Montreal around 1870, view from the mountain*

tudes, pointed out that parish churches in French-speaking districts were noticeable not so much for their architecture but because they revealed a kind of religious life still imbued with medieval traditions that were maintained with great vigour until the nineteenth century.[38] With little command over the economy, French Montrealers would follow rather than shape trends of development, a fact that is evidenced by the aspect of the environment in their districts. With a few rare exceptions—for example, the new St. James Cathedral erected on the edge of Dominion Square, City Hall by the architect Perrault, and the National Monument (headquarters of the nationalistic Saint-Jean Baptiste Society and a pretentious building) —banks, commercial structures, railway stations, large residences, and other buildings of architectural value expressed the ideals of a rich ruling class which was almost exclusively Anglo-Saxon. When studying Victorian architecture in Montreal, one should know something about the mentality and culture of these Anglo-Saxons who were all too often depicted as "committed to commerce and valuing modernity, progress."[39]

Historians teach us that nineteenth-century romanticism counteracted the excesses of eighteenth-century rationalism with its own excesses. This is in accordance with history's pendulum, motions which usually apply to human thought also. The Victorian era, as opposed to the rationalism of the classical period, would hence be plunged into a turmoil of passions, feelings, and emotions. Victorian man, inasmuch as he had attained fame and fortune, was an individualist who was greatly aware of his personality and eager to express himself in his own manner. The prevailing attitude towards architecture would differ from that of previous centuries when criteria of order, harmony, and "Beauty with a capital B" had presided over architectural creations. The new architecture would express the Victorian man's strengths and virtues, his eccentricities, his individuality, or his wealth. For the first time, perhaps, architecture would not be regarded as a form of art subjected to its own rules but rather as a symbol of an admired and coveted reality. Thus, in England, Pugin would link Gothic architecture to his passion for Catholicism, and the Cambridge Camden Society would try to revive the religious fervour of the Middle Ages through the new architectural style. In a like manner, when authoritarian Monseigneur Bourget of Montreal wished to erect a tangible symbol of the attachment of Quebec's population to the Holy See, he borrowed St. Peter's Basilica in Rome as a model for his new St. James Cathedral (now called Mary Queen of the World). Victorian man would choose his symbols from the historical styles, ranging from Greek to Baroque.

At first the integrity of each style would be respected, but towards the end all would be shamelessly mixed in a last attempt to carry the message through visual stimulation.

This complacency towards an idealized past may seem surprising for an era which had tamed the power of steam and had mass-produced steel. It may seem rather strange for a society to make use of very modern structural principles (tubular form) and materials to build a span like Victoria Bridge across the St. Lawrence River and at the same time to revel in Christ Church's neo-Gothic style, in St. James Cathedral's neo-Baroque, or in the "Château de la Loire" architecture of the Viger station and hotel complex. Does the explanation lie in the fact that the bourgeoisie who achieved power and wealth lacked cultural roots? Centuries of culture had shaped the old regime's aristocracy. Thrilling at the wonders of travelling and learning about past architecture through reading, engravings, and archaeological research are signs of cultural insecurity and point to people who may have started their lives in poverty and with a total lack of culture. This characteristic of the ruling class appeared more pronounced in British colonies, and especially in Canada, than in the mother country.

As Arthur Lower pointed out, for the British Canadian ruling class, the era's romanticism was more like the kind of nostalgia only an exiled people could experience.[40] They yearned for Britain and its Empire, the greatest one man had ever known, which dominated the world with its scientific progress and its virtues; they attached as much importance to archaeology as to futurology, and could appreciate London's Parliament buildings and the Crystal Palace at the same glance. This nostalgia made most British Canadians more British than the British themselves. To quote Murray Ballantyne, one of those sons of Albion who lived in Montreal's own bastion of British descendants, known as the "Square Mile": "We were not a mere minority in the midst of a sparsely populated colony. We were proud citizens, builders of the largest and best empire the world had ever known."[41] It is therefore not surprising that, in an epoch when everyone was entitled to his emotions and feelings, those who had earned power, prestige, and wealth in a distant colony should have looked towards the mother country, the "Land of Hope and Glory," for architectural forms which would best express their nostalgia and sense of belonging. Distances had been considerably reduced by steam navigation, and cultural influences from Great Britain would soon be felt and welcomed in the Dominion. Thus, Ottawa's Parliament would be built in the neo-Gothic style of London's House of Parliament and Christ Church would remain faithful to the canons set up by the Cambridge Camden Society; Montreal would erect its own poor version of the Crystal Palace a mere decade after that of London, and would build its own mediocre tubular Victoria bridge a decade after Britannia Bridge was constructed on Menai Strait.

Victorian architecture in Montreal, however, was no mere copy of the British version. Depending on the buildings—and on the point of view—it was enriched or impoverished by many external pressures which highlighted Montreal's geographical location as well as its cosmopolitan nature. Influence from the southern neighbours would mark several buildings, and as the Americans were beginning to produce excellent architects, such as Richardson or Sullivan, these ideas would yield happy results. As a rule, though, Montreal's Victorian architecture, both public and domestic, tended to be more ostentatious than in Great Britain; at times it was even vulgar in its display of the financial success and prestige of the newly rich.

This was unavoidable in a city where all immigrants had to land before deciding whether to settle permanently or to stay only temporarily on their way to seek their fortunes throughout North America. During that period of its history, Montreal was a cosmopolitan centre for business deals, influences, and ideas which caused Arthur Lower to compare it to a Canadian Shanghai.[42] And as many immigrants, particularly the Scots, prospered beyond their dreams, they felt compelled to exhibit their success for everyone to see. Indeed, the best reward for one's risks is still the display of the fruits of one's initiative and audacity. To quote an observer:

> In perhaps no section of the Colonies, have Englishmen and Scotchmen made more of their opportunities than in Montreal. There is an air of prosperity about all their surroundings which at once impresses the visitor. Taken all in all, there is perhaps no wealthier city area in the world than that comprised between Beaver Hall Hill and the foot of Mount Royal, and between the parallel lines of Dorchester and Sherbrooke Streets in the West End.[43]

This was the district of the audacious men who built Canada. They were wealthy merchants, founders of international seafaring lines and of international commerce, railway entrepreneurs, industry magnates; they were the princes of the New World and of the New Era who, in an attempt at self glorification, were to borrow from the old regime the outward signs of noble birth: the châteaux, the gardens, and the large greenhouses, all designed to perpetuate summer in this Dominion of the North.

Within the framework of the study of architecture and of the environment in Montreal during the Victorian era, we shall first analyse public and religious buildings. We shall then turn to commercial architecture, which, at a time when structures became increasingly specialized, is of growing interest. Finally, we shall study man's dwellings and environment, in an attempt to discover what was the heritage of the metropolis. One must keep in mind, however, that some of the buildings deemed worthy of our attention may not seem to be so from an aesthetic standpoint. We are mainly concerned here with the kind of architecture most likely to help us discover the essence of Montreal. We shall not limit ourselves to buildings erected during Queen Victoria's reign, for even before her accession to the throne O'Donnell's Notre-Dame was already pointing to a very Victorian attitude towards architecture. This mentality unfortunately would far outlive the Queen's reign.

Somewhere Between Good and Mediocre: Public and Religious Architecture

> *One thing is certain—there is something in*
> *architecture generally, and Canadian architecture*
> *in particular, for everyone to enjoy.*
> ALAN GOWANS [1]

Neo-Classical and Neo-Gothic Architecture

Notre-Dame Church, by the Irish architect James O'Donnell, had inaugurated, in a naïve but convincing manner, the era of Victorian architecture in Montreal as well as in the province. One cannot draw the conclusion, however, that Victorian architecture was solely comparable to the renaissance of the Gothic style, even though this rebirth was particularly successful in Canada where it constituted the first national expression of architecture. Far from being a style in itself, Victorian architecture is above all a particular attitude towards the art itself; it is a state of mind which expresses itself by resorting to historical styles. In fact, as R. F. Jordan stressed, no other architecture informs us better about its creators, and about their arrogance and doubts, than Victorian does. [2] In Montreal, the neo-Gothic style was only one among many, but one which had won the favour of religious orders. The design of public buildings continued for the time being to be inspired by a romantic classicism imbued with Greek Revival; Bonsecours Market and the Old Court House are good examples of this style. (Plates 35, 36, 37.)

We know very little about the construction of Bonsecours Market and not much more about its architect, William Footner. He had spent a part of his life practising in Montreal; he designed, among other buildings, the Court House in Sherbrooke which, incidentally, shows some affinity of style with Bonsecours Market. The latter cost approximately 70,000 pounds sterling, a sum considered extravagant for that period. However, in the words of contemporaries, the "striking beauty" of the building compensated for this expense.[3]

The building has survived in an acceptable condition after suffering floods and fires—in 1946 (and again in 1976) fire completely destroyed the dome—as well as the onslaught of merchants who propped their stalls against the exterior walls. It is a structure of great architectural value with a place in the history of the city and the nation; indeed, it once served as the Town Hall and as Parliament.[4] During the past years, it has been restored at great expense to its former splendours, at least on the outside, for the interior has undergone alteration to accommodate the building's new administrative functions.

The building, begun in 1842, is of considerable dimensions (over 152 metres in length) and with its three storeys and its soaring dome dominates the rue des Commissaires and the adjacent port.[5] Footner undoubtedly kept the exceptional site in mind when he conceived the design: in fact, when one approached the town from the river, it was the first important building that came into view, and a quick glance at the engravings of that period is sufficient to convince us that the architect succeeded in creating the desired effect. However, he did not neglect the façade on Saint-Paul Street: the slight recess of the building with respect to the alignment of other structures on the street strongly contributes to highlight its presence. This may be a better solution than the extended perspective of a straight façade, customary for this type of building. The latter disposition usually emphasizes the portico and the dome at the expense of the whole.

Bonsecours Market itself does not lack character. It is not so refined or culturally pretentious as other similar contemporary buildings such as Kingston's Court House or City Hall, but it possesses its own picturesque charm. Its portico with magnificent Doric columns, made of cast-iron smelted in England, closely resembles that of St. Andrew's Presbyterian Church at Niagara-on-the-Lake (1831), and its soaring dome confers a naïve but proud air which must have been characteristic of the young metropolis during this period of hope and remarkable prosperity at the beginning of the second half of the nineteenth century. (Plates 35 and 36.)

The Old Court House was duller and more classical in appearance. It was constructed following the destruction by fire of the pre-

35. *Bonsecours Market and the harbour around 1870*

36. *Bonsecours Market around 1870. William Footner, architect,
building started in 1842*

vious building in July 1844, on the same site, adjacent to Champ-de-Mars. It was designed in the classical British colonial style of Province House (1811–19) in Halifax and Osgoode Hall (1829) in Toronto. It was the work of architects John Ostell and H.-Maurice Perrault, who won the competition opened by the government to that effect in October 1849, but it was never a very successful building from a functional point of view. One must add, however, to the credit of the architects, that the gentlemen of the bar had changed the plans frequently and substantially. They even went as far as attempting to change the style of the Court House by demanding a portico copied from that of the Bank of Montreal by John Wells or from that of Notre-Dame Church by O'Donnell. Quite a Victorian attitude, indeed.

The Court House was completed in February 1857 and complaints were soon made about its poorly lit rooms, its humidity, and its inadequate ventilation; moreover, before long there was insufficient space to meet the growing needs. The latter inadequacy was overcome by the worst possible solution, namely, the addition in 1890–94 of another storey, adorned with a dome, which contributed towards complete negation of the work of Ostell and Perrault. Moreover, it was all to no avail, for scarcely two years after the addition of this storey, which had required an almost complete reconstruction of the original building (excluding the exterior walls which had not been changed) and which cost over twice as much as the construction of the Court House itself, there were again complaints about the shortage of space.[6] (Plate 37.)

Of this odd ensemble so typical of the kind of errors of Victorian taste also apparent in the restoration of the Chapel of Notre-Dame de Bonsecours, only the original portico with its Ionic columns is worthy of attention. Yet, it cannot compare with that of the Bank of Montreal. This bank, situated on Place d'Armes and designed by the architect John Wells, is among the most elegant monuments of the metropolis. (Plate 38.)

As with Footner, we know very little about John Wells. He was an Englishman by birth, and John Bland suggests that he was good enough as an artist to have exhibited his architectural sketches at the Royal Academy in London in 1823 and 1828.[7] This claim has not yet been proven. In Montreal he designed the Bank of Montreal Building as well as Sainte-Anne's Market which was later transformed into the Union's Parliament and subsequently burned down during a dramatic fire in April 1849. He also planned a post office on St. James Street; other buildings bear his mark, but it is not known whether he just restored them or actually designed them. He and his

37.　*The Old Court House around 1864. John Ostell and H.-Maurice Perrault, architects, 1849–57*

son worked together as architects, landscape architects, and surveyors; among other assignments, they undertook the subdivision of the old McTavish estate. The manner in which they advertised themselves showed that they lacked neither knowledge nor modesty: they were prepared to execute works "in every variety of ancient and modern taste . . . as practised in Europe during the last century."[8] This was exactly what ambitious Victorians were looking for.

Moreover, one may safely assume that the very fact that John Wells was hired to build the new Bank of Montreal Building indicates that he did enjoy a good reputation in his profession. Indeed, this bank was jealous of its prestige as the first and most powerful institution of its kind in the country. It was decided that the new headquarters would be built right beside the building it had occupied from 1819 to 1848, and that the new edifice should stand as a witness to the bank's achievements. It was the same reason which prompted the bank at the beginning of the twentieth century to call on the renowned firm of McKim, Mead, and White to enlarge Wells's building.

Of this latter building, only the façade on Place d'Armes remains today. This provides enough, however, for one to appreciate the scale and the good proportions of the structure as well as the strength of the stonework details which were obviously the work of an agile and expert hand. It was a remarkable achievement; so would be—both in plan and in elevation—the alterations completed in 1903 by McKim, Mead, and White, especially the façade on Craig Street. Percy Nobbs, who was an honest architect as we shall see later, referred to the latter as one of the finest achievements of its kind in Montreal and perhaps even in America.[9]

Today, next to the anonymous but imposing skyscraper of the Banque Canadienne Nationale, the venerable façade by John Wells shyly seeks its place in the sun. But at the time of its completion, it was certainly worthy of its position facing Notre-Dame Church on the old Place d'Armes. Both the church and the bank were indeed very good expressions of the Victorian era: the former because it symbolized religious fervour through its neo-Gothic style; the latter because it adorned a bank with a style which had always been a symbol of grandeur and conquest.

With John Wells's bank building, Montreal approached international standards of architecture for the first time. In its own right, the bank's façade may be compared to that of the famous Bank of the United States (1818–24) erected in Philadelphia by the architect William Strickland. During the same decade, another building would confirm the excellence of architecture in the Canadian metropolis: Christ Church, the new Anglican cathedral. Before analysing the latter, let us comment on St. Patrick's Church (1843–47), another church built in the same style and marking a further step in the neo-Gothic evolution in Canada. (Plate 39.)

Following the great Irish migration of the middle of the nineteenth century, the Irish population of Montreal quickly expanded: there were some 6,500 of them in the town in 1841. St. Patrick's Church was erected on a magnificent site which since then has lost some of its splendour because of nearby skyscrapers. At the time of construction, it was the most significant neo-Gothic church after Notre-Dame Church. Other reasons, though, make it worthy of our attention; indeed, it marked a significant step in the understanding of the formal principles of the Gothic style as well as the end of the classical box-construction adorned with Gothic details.

The church was built by the French architect Pierre-Louis Morin (1811–86), who worked in close collaboration with another Frenchman, the Jesuit Félix Martin (1804–86). It is not known which of the two men made the most significant contribution. Judging from Morin's comments on Notre-Dame, he certainly had a better grasp of the Gothic style than did O'Donnell. Yet, St. Patrick's does reflect the art of a conscientious amateur like Father Martin. He was the founder of the Collège Sainte-Marie, for which he drew the plans. It was a solid but somewhat naïve piece of work, probably inspired by Ostell and Perrault's Court House.[10] Actually, the school acquired its fame for the quality of its teaching rather than for its architecture. Father Martin, though, was well equipped to work in the Gothic style. His main source of information in this field was his brother Arthur who had made his fame through his monumental book on the windows of Bourges cathedral; moreover, he was much in demand as a specialist in the field of restoration of Gothic cathedrals.[11] To return to St. Patrick's Church: it is a structure of remarkable simplicity on the outside—the apse in particular—built of carefully chosen materials and well adapted to the climate. It is somewhat heavy, though, and the bell-tower lacks a certain spirit. These shortcomings do not seem to be attributable to the architects, but rather to a Monsieur Quiblier who, as the superior of Saint-Sulpice, was their client. The original plans provided for a structure without a steeple and measuring 55 metres by 27 metres; Quiblier had these dimensions extended to 68 metres by 32 metres and asked for a steeple which, much to the architects' chagrin, would never reach the height they had recommended for it.

Luckily, the interior of the church makes up for its somewhat

38. *The Bank of Montreal around 1870. John Wells, architect, building completed in 1848*

39. *St. Patrick's Church. Pierre-Louis Morin and Félix Martin, ar-chitects, 1843–47*

heavy outside appearance. The volume is airy, vast, and elegant. The author of an article in the 28 April 1866 issue of *Minerve* uttered a Victorian profession of faith when he approved of Gothic architecture because "it fulfilled the demands of worship as well as those of the great thoughts it was meant to represent." He had indeed understood the dominant characteristic of St. Patrick's when he wrote: "Upon entering the church, one is struck by its beautiful, neatly divided proportions."[12]

Gothic Revival in Montreal reached its highest point with the new Christ Church Cathedral, which was built on Sainte-Catherine Street facing Phillips Square. Completed in 1859 and dedicated in 1867, it had been erected to replace the previous Christ Church, on Notre-Dame Street, which was destroyed by fire in 1856 and of which we spoke in Chapter 6.

The almost archaeological reproduction of the Gothic style achieved in the new Christ Church reflects the influence of the Camden Society of England on the style of Anglican churches from the 1840s onwards. Founded in Cambridge in 1839, this society of learned men who were preoccupied with church matters became interested in religious architecture not because it was a form of art with its own set of criteria, but rather because they were looking for a symbol to identify the true Catholic Church of England. At a time when Gothic architecture was considered by the British as an essentially indigenous and very Christian form of art, it naturally became the most appropriate mode of expression. Yet, to consider Gothic as the only true Christian architecture was not enough; for a variety of reasons, one particular period of the Gothic style was considered to be more truly Christian and more worthy of symbolizing the Anglican Church; it was known as "ornate" or "Edwardian" Gothic. Hence, with all the intransigence for which it became famous, the Camden Society held that only that style should be accepted for the construction and restoration of Anglican churches.[13]

For the next fifty odd years, nearly all the Anglican churches in England and throughout the world would be built according to the precepts and instructions of this ecclesiological society. Christ Church Cathedral was the new church of a community anxious to assert its identity in a mostly Roman Catholic society, to reaffirm its links with Great Britain, and to display its cultural pretensions in the midst of a French cultural environment. It is therefore not surprising to see the design of the church conform to the instructions and intransigent attitude of the Camden Society. Yet, it was not the only Christ Church in Canada to have accepted the dictates of the Camden Society. A similar structure, probably the most remarkable of its kind in America, was built in Fredericton from plans revised by the great Victorian architect William Butterfield, the Cambridge Camden Society's favourite designer. The Anglican cathedral of St. John's in Newfoundland is another example of an imported design: even the stones were brought from Scotland!

Exeter and Salisbury's Frank Wills, who made the preliminary designs for both Fredericton's and Montreal's Christ Church Cathedrals, was a propagandist for this type of church architecture. In 1850 he published a book in New York entitled *Ancient English Ecclesiastical Architecture*. He certainly did not lack practice, for between 1840 and 1856 he built no fewer than twenty churches in the United States. Even though his death in 1857, before the foundations of Montreal's Christ Church were even laid, prevented him from directing the work on the church, his plans were followed to the letter. It was only under this condition that Thomas S. Scott was allowed to carry on his work.[14]

Although as an architect Frank Wills was inferior to Butterfield and Scott, who were later consulted for the construction of the Canadian Anglican cathedrals, his work in Montreal, which was modelled after fourteenth-century English churches with a regular cruciform plan, points to a sound knowledge of ornate Gothic. Too sound, in fact, because, despite a few original details such as the capitals of the nave's arcades which portray the foliage of different kinds of Canadian trees, the church looks more like a refined and carefully detailed scale model than like an original and consistent creation. The best view of the church is obtained from the tower of Place Ville-Marie, from where it resembles a tiny, delicate exotic jewel set in a patch of grass. Yet despite its pretensions as well as its real qualities, Christ Church is not inspiring. A building like St. Patrick's, where an amateur has used his imagination to avoid the pitfalls of an exact copy, is more likely to move us. The steeple of Christ Church, however, is worth mentioning. One of the few to have been built of stone in Canada, it numbered among the most elegant, rising 39 metres above the tower. It was torn down in June 1927, because its weight caused fissures in the foundations. In 1940 it was rebuilt on a light steel frame covered with aluminum slabs which had been especially treated to imitate stonework.[15] (Plate 40.)

Neo-Baroque Architecture

The Gothic Revival style was particularly appreciated in Canada. In fact, it became a truly national architectural style in the same manner as the classical renaissance in the United States in the years 1820 to 1830. This accounts for the fact that Ottawa's Parliament

Buildings are neo-Gothic. In Montreal, where the style had been inaugurated with O'Donnell's Notre-Dame Church, it would enjoy a great success. Yet, apart from some secular buildings of no great architectural value, such as Morrice Hall at McGill University or the later "College" style buildings of the medical faculty at the same university, the neo-Gothic mode applied mainly to churches and other religious buildings.

Between 1850 and the beginning of 1900, many neo-Gothic churches were built in Montreal and the neighbouring municipalities. Although they do not possess the architectural qualities of St. Patrick's or Christ Church, they nevertheless lend the community a character all of its own which caused Baron Hulot to write at the end of the century that above "the shimmering silvery roofs rise the towers of Notre-Dame, St. Peter's dome, and the steeples of about thirty churches, all of them more or less Gothic in style."[16] These sanctuaries belonged to various denominations and were built in the neo-Gothic style, but with slight variations. The Church of Scotland asked the architect G. H. Smith to build St. Andrew's in 1850–51 on the present-day site of Bell Telephone on Beaver Hall Hill. The new St. Paul's Church, located at the corner of Dorchester and Sainte-Geneviève Streets, was to be the pride of the Presbyterian community.[17] It was inaugurated in 1868 and was the creation of Frederick Lawford, who had been a student of Sir Charles Barry; it was probably the most interesting after Christ Church and St. Patrick's. Unfortunately, this church was demolished at the time the site was developed for Canadian National Railway's Central Station. But it was rebuilt, stone by stone, at Collège Saint-Laurent. Lawford and his partner Nelson built other churches in the same style, among them St. James in 1863 (at the corner of Sainte-Catherine and City Councillors). It has a nave with rather fluid lines and galleries on either side, but its façade is today partially hidden behind storefronts on Sainte-Catherine Street. In 1865 they erected Saint-Sauveur Church, which was originally an Anglican church on the northwest corner of Saint-Denis Street and Viger Square; it was inspired by English primitive Gothic. St. George's Anglican Church is another good example: it rises, small and delicate, facing the massive Windsor Station. It was built by the architect William Thomas—we shall return to him later—who had won the competition set up for that purpose. Another Anglican neo-Gothic church, better known for its location than for its style, is the Church of St. James the Apostle on the northwest corner of Sainte-Catherine and Bishop Streets. Protestants remained fond of this design; the Presbyterian Church of St. Andrew and St. Paul, at the corner of Redpath

40.   *Christ Church Anglican Cathedral around 1870. Frank Wills and Thomas S. Scott, architects, 1857–59*

and Sherbrooke West, was built in 1932 in the same neo-Gothic fashion.

Compared with the temples of the Protestant faith, the Catholic churches were generally not so refined or historically faithful. It was John Ostell who drew the plans for St. James Church after the great fire of 1852. All that is left of it today is the rigid façade and the very high steeple (84 metres), which was erected only in 1880, but according to Ostell's plans. This unique steeple has since been an excellent landmark in the downtown area, and for that very reason it has been saved. As a whole, the architectural qualities of the Catholic churches vary from a naïve use of neo-Gothic styles (as attested by Saint-Joseph's Church on Richmond Street, Sainte-Catherine d'Alexandrie [now demolished] at the corner of Robin and Amherst Streets, or Saint-Edouard at the corner of Saint-Denis and Beaubien Streets) to the great vigour displayed by churches such as Saint-Joachim (Pointe-Claire) and Saint-Pierre Apôtre on Visitation Street, at the corner of Dorchester Boulevard, and built in 1851–53 by a versatile architect named Victor Bourgeau. We shall return to Bourgeau later.

The French Catholics soon reacted against the Gothic Revival. Whereas the beginning of the Victorian era witnessed a war of styles, in Quebec this conflict reflected the rivalries between the Roman Catholic religion and the other faiths. The use of Gothic forms for O'Donnell's Notre-Dame had already stolen the limelight from the first Christ Church which had been built in a classical style. There is little doubt that the proliferation of neo-Gothic temples of the Protestant faith—which reached its peak with the erection of the second Christ Church—was an important factor accounting for the gradual loss of interest expressed by the Catholics for that particular style. The neo-Baroque would fill the gap, thanks to the influence of one man in particular: Monseigneur Ignace Bourget.

Monseigneur Bourget (1799–1885) succeeded Monseigneur J. Jacques Lartigue in 1840 as bishop of Montreal; he was a man of his era. An astute, ambitious, and conservative man—some say reactionary—he was hard-working and his mind, for want of being very broad, was very clear; he headed the religious rebirth which marked this era. Heir to the ultramontanist tradition of Montmorency de Laval and his successors, with an unlimited admiration for Rome as the symbol of authority of the Catholic Church in Montreal, Bourget went so far as to demand that some churches in his diocese— among them, his own cathedral, a copy of St. Peter's—be built as replicas of churches in the Eternal City.

The history behind the construction of the Gesù on Bleury Street exemplifies the influence of Bourget on the religious architecture of his time. In 1842 he secured the return of the Jesuits to Canada and urged them to build a college (the future Collège Sainte-Marie) and a chapel to exercise their ministry. The chapel was at first built inside the school but soon proved too small, so the Jesuits decided to erect a larger church next to their institution. Plans were drawn in 1861 by Father Arthur Jones who had learned the art from Father Martin. He chose the Gothic, "the beautiful style of Saint-Louis, the Sainte-Chapelle, the cathedral of Amiens, and especially the cathedral of Cologne."[18] Eclecticism was alive and well during the Victorian era! Jones's project seemed too expensive; it was a polite way of expressing fear over his lack of experience. The firm of Lamontagne and Perrault was then asked to prepare plans for a church "in pure twelfth-century Gothic"; the emphasis was on "Gothic."

The plans, prepared by Lamontagne and Perrault to the Jesuits' satisfaction, were firmly refused by Bourget. In his mind, a Jesuit church in his diocese had to take its inspiration from the Gesù in Rome. In fact he was not so much interested in the architecture of the Gesù as in the symbol represented by this church of the Counter-Reformation. In a copy in Montreal of the Gesù, he saw the opportunity of impressing the "foreigners," that is, the non-Catholics of the metropolis. This explains why the architects Lamontagne and Perrault were asked to modify their plans to satisfy the bishop.

The new plans must have aroused his apprehensions, for they were again modified by an architect from Brooklyn, a Mr. Keely, who had built some two hundred churches and who prided himself with knowing the Gesù like the back of his hand. The church thus was built according to his plans in 1864–65.

The claims of the New York architect notwithstanding, Montreal's Gesù in no way resembles its Roman counterpart except for a particularly horrible imitation of its "trompe-l'oeil" decoration. Apart from that aspect, there is no similarity in plane, elevation, or volume. Few elements, if any, from the exaggerated transept and the basilica-style aisles to the non-existent dome and the almost complete obscurity, are reminiscent of the powerful unified volume of the original Gesù with its light filtering down to the marble and the sensuous colours of its decoration. As for the main façade, for which Keely had designed two bell-towers—they would never rise above their foundations—it bears no resemblance to that of Rome's Gesù, except perhaps for the use of the Italian Baroque style. Could it be that the very name Gesù applied to any building held sufficient magic for Bourget, just so long as it was not Gothic? At any rate, the only redeeming quality of Montreal's Gesù lies in the fact that it heralds the Picturesque style that would later enhance Victorian architecture.[19] (Plate 41.)

The construction of the Gesù was not Bourget's first experience with neo-Baroque; as early as 1852 he was considering building his cathedral using St. Peter's of Rome as a model. Nevertheless, the Gesù venture attests to the bishop's significant influence on the religious architecture in his diocese. He never hid this fact and would openly state that it was "up to the bishop alone to set the plan and the dimensions of churches to be built in his diocese," and that he exercised this right "under the sole authority of the Pope."[20] The Anglican Christ Church may have been under the architectural dictates of the Cambridge Camden Society, but Montreal's Catholic Church could only rely on the bishop, who was infinitely less competent in the field of architecture than the ecclesiological society, but certainly not less intolerant.

John Ostell and Victor Bourgeau were, each in his turn, Monseigneur Bourget's favourite architects. It is therefore not surprising to see both producing neo-Baroque buildings during that time. Thus, Ostell overloaded the new Episcopal Palace with a façade and a heavy dome in the Baroque style,[21] and in 1852 he added a powerful but austere façade, in a very English Baroque style, to the delightful Church of the Visitation at Sault-au-Récollet. In the early 1850s, he designed two almost identical churches, in eighteenth-century Jesuit style: Notre-Dame-de-Toutes-Grâces and Sainte-Anne, located in the districts of the same name. Only the former remains today, as Sainte-Anne was recently demolished; the façade resembles that of Rome's Gesù more than does that of Montreal's own Gesù and seems to have been inspired by the one Chaussegros de Léry had added to the parish church of Notre-Dame in 1721. Like the latter, it is cold, solid, and austere. There is, alas, little to be learned from the interior which has been altered in the doubtful post–world war "modern" manner.[22]

Victor Bourgeau (1809–88) seemed to have been more favourably inclined towards his bishop's penchant for the Baroque. He was the son of a farmer from Lavaltrie and had been educated as a sculptor in the tradition of Quévillon and Baillargé; although he did not have the theoretical background of Ostell or Wells, the sureness of his taste made up for this shortcoming. He had a remarkable career as an architect and built no fewer than twenty churches and remodelled another twenty-three. In Montreal, Sainte-Brigide, the Hôtel-Dieu, and the large convent of the Grey Nuns (on Dorchester Boulevard) with its splendid chapel figure among his creations. His whole architectural output is characterized by three great qualities: simplicity, solidity, and economy. He originally started working in the neo-Gothic style—his first assignment was the sculpture of the Gothic details for O'Donnell's Notre-Dame—and then he used it in building Saint-Pierre Apôtre (1851–53) in Montreal and the cathedral of Trois-Rivières in 1858. Subsequently, under Monseigneur Bourget's influence, he became interested in Italian Baroque. The church he erected in Sainte-Rose in 1850 was vaguely Baroque. In 1856, at Bourget's instigation, he went to Rome for an on-the-spot study of St. Peter's Basilica, which left him deeply impressed. The façade of the Church of the Assumption which he drew in 1859 was a modified version of that of St. Peter's Basilica. In 1866–67, for the Church of Saint-Barthélemy in Berthier, he would combine the portico of Notre-Dame on Place d'Armes with the same façade copied after St. Peter's.

When Monseigneur Bourget sent Bourgeau to Rome in 1856, it was not to allow him to complete his study of the Italian Baroque. He had a more immediate purpose in mind: to study and measure St. Peter's Basilica in order to build a scaled-down version of it in Montreal as a replacement for the old cathedral (on Saint-Denis Street) which, together with a large section of the city, had burnt down in 1852. The bishop had indeed decided to go all out with his new cathedral and to prove the attachment of the Canadian church to the Holy See by creating a faithful copy of St. Peter's Basilica. As he wished to display the glory of the Catholic faith in a more forceful manner, he went as far as attempting to impress the Protestant community of Montreal in its own quarters and to defy Christ Church on its own grounds. He chose a site for the new cathedral near the Canadian Pacific's new Windsor Station, right in the middle of the Anglo-Protestant section of the city, much to the detriment of the French-Catholic districts which this church was to serve. The choice of both site and style incurred many objections. Bourgeau himself opposed the project. In his mind, one just did not copy St. Peter's Basilica, least of all scaled down. He obviously judged the project with the critical sense of an architect for whom the rules of scale, proportion, harmony, and beauty inherited from the ancestral classical tradition still prevailed. Monseigneur Bourget, just as obviously, saw the whole enterprise from a totally different angle and in a more Victorian spirit: architecture was first and foremost a symbol. Besides, if he had St. Peter's Basilica copied, it would be the best safeguard against the possibility that the Protestants might imitate it first!

The obstinate bishop bided his time until he could realize his

41. *Du Gesù Church. Keely, architect, 1864–65*

project. The opportunity presented itself in 1871, during the period of euphoria brought about by the calling to arms of the pontifical zouaves in defence of the Vatican against the Italian nationalist army. It was a unique occasion: what greater proof of attachment to the Holy See was there than the reproduction on Canadian soil of St. Peter's Basilica? Work began in 1875 under the direction of Father Michaud, an amateur whom Bourgeau, against his own principles and objections, felt compelled to help with his competence and experience. The result was a strange monument, a historical curiosity rather than an architectural achievement, which nevertheless became an essential component of the familiar environment of Dominion Square.[23] (Plate 42.)

With the dedication of St. James Cathedral in 1885, the neo-Gothic mode in religious architecture finally yielded to the Italian styles in Montreal as well as in the province. Religious architecture had now been released from its yoke, for the variety of expressions of the Italian styles allowed for a greater freedom of interpretation. In turn, this liberty would contribute to the emphasis on the visual aspect of architecture rather than on the symbolic or spatial. From then on, the Picturesque would rule the field, in a quest for visual and plastic effects through the use of motifs borrowed from various historical styles, in order to create attractive ensembles.

Unfortunately, this quest for visual stimulation would at times be responsible for a certain degree of superficiality, vulgarity, and bad taste. There are many examples of this among Montreal churches built at the turn of the century, particularly with respect to façades, for Victorian architecture proved unable to ensure any degree of unity between façades, volumes, and plans. To mention but a few: Saint-Charles and Saint-Gabriel on Centre Street in Pointe Saint-Charles, and Saint-Enfant Jésus (corner Saint-Dominique Street and Saint-Joseph Boulevard), whose only redeeming quality is its setting on a lovely square. The last achievement of this pedantic trend would be completed with the erection of Saint-Joseph's Oratory on Mount Royal, a project which was started in 1925.

Second Empire and Beaux-Arts Styles

A survey of public and religious buildings erected during the Victorian era would show that many of them do not belong to the various categories of styles that we have analysed thus far: neo-classical, neo-Gothic, and neo-Baroque.[24] Buildings such as City Hall, Windsor Station, or Saint-Sulpice Library belong to different categories. Like the structures previously studied, they are not masterpieces, but are sufficiently numerous and distinctive to justify a more thorough analysis.

42.   *St. James Cathedral under construction. Joseph Michaud and Victor Bourgeau, architects, 1875–85*

City Hall, the new Post Office, Windsor Hotel, and other less important but architecturally significant buildings such as Molsons Bank, the Banque des Marchands, or the Dominion Block all display common features.[25] They are all massive; they are firmly and heavily anchored to the ground. One feature, in elevation, which characterizes their tridimensional composition is the mansard roof, which constitutes a strong visual statement; it is often placed at varying levels in order to accentuate different parts of the building. The outer skin is usually decorated in a rich mixture of Renaissance and Baroque elements, which Hitchcock labelled the pompous modulation of a Renaissance revival.[26] Elements from the Georgian period are sometimes found, as in the Windsor Hotel, but as a rule motifs borrowed from the Florentine and Roman palaces of the Renaissance are predominant and lend these buildings an easily identifiable texture.

These structures constitute the North American version of the Second Empire style which originated in France and which gained universal popularity. Whether it reached Montreal directly from France or indirectly through England and the United States is open to question; the latter route is more likely for the style in Montreal has seemingly lost a great deal of its strength. From a standpoint of design, Montreal's City Hall is closer to the Department of State, War, and Navy Building in Washington (built in 1871 by A. B. Mullet and perhaps the best example of this style in the United States), and Windsor Hotel is closer to Chicago's Palmer House than to Visconti and Lefuel's Nouveau Louvre, a building which launched the new vogue in Paris.

The old City Hall, built in 1872–78 by H.-Maurice Perrault (the architect who, with John Ostell, had won the bid for the Court House in 1849), was more elegant than the later version. Perrault's building burned down in 1922 and only the walls remained, to which another floor and a high mansard roof were added. The volumetric composition originally was articulated around a central tower and set within corner pavilions, but the new structure presented a more monolithic aspect and an almost cubic figure. (Plates 43 and 44.)

In 1873, while building City Hall, Perrault completed the new Post Office, located on the northeast corner of St. James and Saint-François-Xavier Streets, which was later altered and finally demolished to make room for the present Bank of Montreal Building. It was probably the best example of Second Empire architecture in Montreal. Of a homogeneous composition, with powerful convex mansard roofs, it was vigorous and not without a certain monumental scale which seemed to fit its function. There were few buildings

43.   *Montreal City Hall. H.-Maurice Perrault, architect, 1872–78*

44. *Montreal City Hall under reconstruction in 1923*

in the same style that could rival it; the others were relatively minor and only interesting because they blended well into the picturesque and lively spectacle of Victorian streets. Molsons Bank nevertheless deserves mention, for it is a credit to the honest talent of George Browne who, together with William Thomas, was the most prolific anglophone architect of that period.[27] (Plate 45.)

The Windsor Hotel was an example of the many luxury hotels across the world which celebrated the glorious, cosmopolitan image of Paris in the days of Napoleon III. Built on Dominion Square, along Dorchester Boulevard's high plateau, it constituted an appropriate background for the city's largest square. The publicity for the hotel during its most glorious years proves that this palace was first and foremost a setting for the rich, nostalgia-prone bourgeois. There were large halls "defying description" and salons "frescoed and furnished in strictly Egyptian style."[28] This palace of Victorian splendours, where princes and other great people of this world used to stay, fell victim in part to dynamite in order to make room for the Imperial Bank of Commerce skyscraper.[29] (Plate 46.)

France was to launch another international fashion which would gradually supplant that of the Second Empire. The new style would be called "Beaux-Arts" because it originated in the architectural teaching dispensed at the time at the Ecole des Beaux-Arts in Paris. From the second half of the nineteenth century Paris, somewhat like Rome in the eighteenth century, became the mecca of architects, a fact which accounts for the Beaux-Arts influence, especially on those from the New World whose training was normally complemented by a stay in Paris.[30]

The Beaux-Arts style was based on the premise that contemporary architecture was to take its inspiration from the monuments of the past, using the resources of the present to improve on them. This form of eclecticism, however, was not left to the fancy of the architect. Symbolism somehow came back to the fore and it was decided that contemporary buildings were to take their inspiration from the historical styles which could best express the spirit of their functions. Thus, for example, the Romanesque would apply to abbeys and monasteries, Gothic and Byzantine to churches, and Roman and Renaissance to public, commercial, and domestic architecture.[31]

It was easy to forecast that the Beaux-Arts style would enjoy a great popularity in Montreal, as a large section of the population had both cultural and sentimental links with the French metropolis; Montreal's School of Fine Arts would soon follow the trend set by the Paris school. This influence, unfortunately, would be long lasting.

45.   *The Post Office. H.-Maurice Perrault, architect, building completed in 1873*

One of Montreal's first proponents of the Beaux-Arts style was J.-Omer Marchand (1873–1936), the first French Canadian to have studied at the Ecole des Beaux-Arts in Paris, between 1893 and 1903. He then returned to Canada and specialized in church architecture. The Catholic cathedral he built at St. Boniface, Manitoba, is a typical example of his work in the Beaux-Arts style. Some of his achievements in Montreal include Sainte-Cunégonde Church (1906), the Chapel of the Grand Séminaire on Sherbrooke Street West (1905–7), the interior of which was considered at the time to be one of the most serious and most attractive in town,[32] and especially the Mother House of the Congregation of Notre-Dame (1907), also on Sherbrooke Street West. The last-named building, of monumental proportions, is a good example of the use of Romanesque and Byzantine forms to express the religious character of the convent.

The list of Montreal buildings constructed in the Beaux-Arts style at the turn of the century is a long one, from the Town Hall of the old municipality of Maisonneuve to the pretentious Masonic Temple at the corner of Saint-Marc and Sherbrooke Streets. As a rule they are rather mediocre and only a few deserve to be mentioned as typical examples of public architecture. (Commercial and domestic architecture will be analysed in subsequent chapters.) Eugène Payette built two libraries: the Municipal and the Saint-Sulpice, which is now the National Library. The former, with its powerful, monolithic, granite columns, presents a monumental Roman façade on Sherbrooke Street; the latter, which looks more like a private Paris mansion, is delicate and refined; its plan reflects the influence of the French school. The Museum of Fine Arts, again on Sherbrooke Street, was also designed in the Beaux-Arts antique style by Edward and William Maxwell; it was inaugurated in 1912. The old Stock Exchange Building (1904) on Saint-François-Xavier Street reminded one of imperial Rome because of its architectural features and the marble and precious wood used in the interior decoration.[33]

The attractiveness of a building like the Saint-Sulpice Library by Payette should not allow us to forget that the Beaux-Arts style would have a rather negative influence on Montreal's architecture, as it had elsewhere in the world. It came at a time when new structural materials were available, when new building techniques had proved their worth, and when the new architectural programs were to be radically changed to answer the unprecedented needs which had arisen, at never imagined scales, from the urban phenomenon. This pseudo-style imposed a yoke on architecture, reducing it to an ill-fitting cladding surrounding functions totally alien to the eclecticism of forms and the architectural symbolism of a bygone era. The

46. *View of Dominion Square and Windsor Hotel, beginning of the twentieth century*

Ecole des Hautes Etudes Commerciales, facing Viger Square, provides a striking example of this type of pretentious architecture. Built by Gauthier and Daoust, it was considered at the time of its inauguration "the finest and most dignified structure to that purpose in North America."[34] Today, one would think exactly the opposite. Commercial architecture would reach the same dead end; even though it was supposed to answer the growing demand for space, it would nevertheless remain enslaved to the forms and concepts of the High Victorian tradition. This, however, is the subject of another chapter.

The Influence of Shaw and Richardson

It is a difficult task to trace the cultural influences which marked public and religious architecture in Montreal. This is due mainly to the city's privileged geographical situation as well as to its history. Thus, for instance, we have already learned that neo-Gothic and neo-Baroque styles appeared partly as the result of the religious rivalry between Catholics and Protestants. The Second Empire and Beaux-Arts styles which originated in France were particularly well received in this city, where a large section of the population was francophone. One must, however, not neglect the fact that this land was also receptive to British and American influences. This might explain why the Royal Victoria Hospital on Pine Avenue, built in 1887–93 by a London architect named Saxon Snell, was a replica of the Royal Infirmary in Edinburgh, and why Frank Lloyd Wright's very personal style was shamelessly plagiarized, even for fire stations.[35]

The British and American influences at the turn of the century may be reduced to three main streams. One is the ill-labelled American Romanesque, which is in fact an extension of the work of the great American architect Henry Hobson Richardson. A second current originating with the British architect Norman Shaw—who was to England what Richardson was to the United States—found more followers and was also more varied than Richardson's. Facing the two giants, who both resorted to one form or another of eclecticism, a reaction took place leaning towards a more discreet and purer form of classicism, a response which Hitchcock nicknamed the Academic Reaction; its best interpreters were undoubtedly McKim, Mead, and White.[36]

Apart from commercial and domestic architecture, two interesting buildings were built in Montreal according to the precepts of the Academic Reaction. One is the annex to the Bank of Montreal, to which we have already alluded. This building, with a rather typical and even remarkable façade on Saint-Antoine Street, was designed by McKim, Mead, and White at a time (1903) when they had mastered their architectural precepts as well as the means of implementing them. Redpath Museum at McGill University is another building which interests us in this sense. Inaugurated in 1880, it was designed by the architects Hutchison and Steel, and constituted a romantic version of Greek Revival. Highlighted by its magnificent site, it has an imposing mass; its proportions are fair, even though the portico's entablature is somewhat heavy. It looks better, however, from a distance; a closer examination reveals a lack of restraint in the decoration and a curiously curved back. This did not prevent the building from being included in Ferguson's *History of Modern Architecture*.[37]

As far as the influences of Norman Shaw and of Richardson are concerned, they are best exemplified by buildings found on the McGill campus. Indeed, towards the end of the century, McGill University was undergoing a great expansion and aspiring to the world reputation it would attain some decades later. As McGill was the hub of anglophone intelligentsia, its class of intellectuals would naturally try to identify with buildings which reflected the architectural excellence of the day, and, of all the structures on the campus, Redpath Library is the best example. Its design was inspired by the very personal touch of one of the best architects America had ever produced: Henry Hobson Richardson. His style—which would be enormously popular between 1875 and 1890—took its inspiration from a form of Romanesque that owed little to archaeology. It was not simply a revival of Romanesque or just neo-Romanesque. Richardson went beyond eclectic juggling: his formal expression is logical and functional and shows an intuitive feeling for the nature and characteristics of materials which would cast him as one of the forerunners of modern architecture and an essential link in the explanation of the works of Root, Sullivan, and Wright.[38] Some of these qualities are apparent, to a certain degree, in the Redpath Library. The building is asymmetrical and as rigorous and solid as a fortress; its assertive semicircular arches are characteristic of Richardson; the stonework is robust and gives a feeling of permanence. The interior, which lacks any great continuity with the exterior, has its own character. The various masses of the building do not, however, seem sufficiently articulate: the belfry is not high enough for its mass, and the whole structure looks somewhat stiff. (Plate 47.)

The library was built in 1890–91 by Sir Andrew Taylor and Gordon, enlarged a first time in 1901, and then again in 1921 according to plans drawn by Nobbs and Hyde. As an architect, Taylor was very

47.   *Redpath Library at McGill University. Sir Andrew Taylor and Gordon, architects, 1890–91*

active towards the end of the nineteenth century. He was awarded many contracts to build branch offices for the Bank of Montreal and became involved in designing the heavy-looking residences fashionable in those days. One of his contributions to architecture in Montreal seems to have been the use of colourful construction materials like red and brown stones.[39] In 1890, while he was an associate of Hogle and Davis, he started another structure for McGill University, the Macdonald Physics Building. This latter is also reminiscent of Richardson's influence, although to a lesser degree; the organic unity found in the Redpath Library has yielded to a version of the Picturesque based on a sophisticated juxtaposition of medieval forms and themes.

The Macdonald Engineering Building was erected near the Macdonald Physics Building in 1907 by the architect Percy E. Nobbs. It took its inspiration from British architectural traditions, in particular from the work of Norman Shaw, who practised his art with a great deal of success in England during the second half of the nineteenth century. It is difficult to pinpoint Shaw's style: on the whole it is an eclectic mixture of seventeenth-century Dutch and of English William and Mary as well as of Queen Anne; it exudes charm, sensitivity, imagination, and a wish to please. The Macdonald Engineering Building, with its rising Dutch gables, is somewhat reminiscent of Shaw's style.

Two years earlier, on Sherbrooke Street, Nobbs had completed the McGill Student Union Building (now the McCord Museum) which, with its characteristic bay windows, also showed the influence of Shaw's work and in our opinion is the best example of Nobbs's style. It is unpretentious, simple, and well proportioned. Another structure inspired by Shaw's work and displaying the same simplicity as the former McGill Student Union Building is the Central Fire Station on d'Youville Square in Old Montreal. It was designed in 1903 by the architects Perrault and Lesage. Although not a masterpiece, this diminutive building with its small watchtower adds a decorative note in the midst of the square.

Royal Victoria College is another structure on the McGill campus built in the Shaw tradition. Giving an attractive perspective to the end of Union Street, it was completed in 1899. Although not presenting any outstanding features, it carries the characteristic themes of rising Dutch gables and shallow bay windows. Its architect was the celebrated Bruce Price. Price (1845–1903) was undoubtedly one of the most influential American architects in Canada, together with his compatriots McKim, Mead, and White. His all-too-brief career as an architect was typical of the opportunities for success which the Victorian era thrust onto talented, ambitious, hard-working individuals. Rather poor during his youth, he was the breadwinner of the family but spent his spare time studying architecture. He had a pleasant, attractive personality and was much sought after as a guest among high society; he soon became one of the most prolific and prosperous architects in America. He did not limit his activities to the United States; he was commissioned by several other countries and did a lot of work in Canada. Indeed, he contributed to the launching of the "Château de la Loire" fashion for the construction of stations and hotels for the Canadian railways. His first achievement in this style was the famous Château Frontenac in Quebec City, drawn up in 1890 after the outlines of a French sixteenth-century château.[40] The Château Frontenac, with its turrets and dormers, would become the prototype for a number of railway hotels in Canada, where the best known of them is still the Banff Springs Hotel, also designed by Price.[41]

In Montreal Bruce Price is remembered not only for Royal Victoria College, but also for the two railway stations he left us, Viger Station (since renovated to accommodate the administration of the City of Montreal and now known as the Jacques-Viger Building) and Windsor Station. The Viger station and hotel complex had been built in the same style as the Château Frontenac: it was picturesque, somewhat exotic, colourful, and, although somewhat stiff-looking, highlighted by its setting on Viger Square. It was typical of the architecture which became Price's trademark and which was so much in demand at the end of his career.

His Windsor Station, along with the old Toronto City Hall which was built in 1890 according to the plans of Edward Jones Lennox, best reflects the influence of Richardson in Canada. Both buildings also constitute landmarks, for they signal the beginning of the growing American pressure on Canadian architecture, to the detriment of the European influence.[42] They seem to draw their inspiration from a structure which did much to contribute to Richardson's reputation: the Allegheny County Court House in Pittsburgh, completed in 1887. The connection is not without foundation, for Price started construction on Windsor Station the very next year.

Windsor Station possesses the assurance of a medieval castle. It was completed by the architects Taylor, Watts, and Painter; its tower, sixteen storeys high, was built around a steel frame. Price's semicircular arches extending over three storeys helped to maintain the building's unity of style during later enlargements, in spite of the difficulties presented by the pronounced unevenness of the site. This device had been used successfully by Richardson for his Marshall Field Wholesale Building in Chicago (1885–87). The choice of rustic stones to lend vigour to the semicircular arches, as well as to the arches of the windows on the floors above them, adds to the feeling of power and strength which characterizes the station today and as conceived then by Price. To quote an observer of his time (1889):

> The new station and general offices of the Canadian Pacific is in many respects one of the most interesting buildings in the city. In it the common grey limestone of Montreal has been used with a truer perception of its character as a building material and with better effect than ever before. It has been given a texture which not only prevents it from being unpleasantly cold but is admirably suited to the size and power of the building it composes.[43]

During subsequent enlargements, a large hall was added to the station; although not very high, it lends a feeling of spaciousness which is further enhanced by the light pouring in from the huge skylight. (Plate 48.)

Windsor Station is a natural ending for this chapter on public and religious architecture in Montreal during the Victorian era. Indeed, this period would be marked by the imprint of steel and steam and ultimately by the spirit of capitalism which was to erect the instruments and the symbols of its activities and of its power wherever it prevailed. Productivity, efficiency, and profitability are all part of the capitalist way of imposing its demands which would be sufficiently reflected in the commercial architecture of the day to warrant a chapter on the latter.

48. *View of Dominion Square and Windsor Station around 1930*

9

Hopes and Disappointments: Commercial Architecture

We should never be able to perceive the real nature of the period from a study of public buildings, state residences, or great monuments. We must turn instead to an examination of humbler structures. It was in routine and entirely practical construction, and not in the Gothic or Classical revivals of the early nineteenth century, that the decisive events occurred, the events that led to the evolution of new potentialities.
SIGFRIED GIEDION [1]

"Stone Skeletons"

Commercial architecture in Montreal in the nineteenth century is sufficiently distinctive to warrant a separate chapter. As the chapter title indicates, this architecture was at first interesting, but became disappointing as time went on. Why this happened, we intend to find out by looking at some of the structures still standing today; other examples which may have been more appropriate have since disappeared. Indeed, these "practical constructions," to use Giedion's term, were extremely vulnerable, for their survival depended solely on their economic usefulness. As soon as the latter was outlived they would be torn down to make room for better, economically adapted buildings.

At its best, this commercial architecture may be described as a structural system of beams and pillars with the austere "stone skeletons" of the façade separated by glass areas. One of the most interesting examples of this type of construction in Montreal is located at 417 des Récollets Street. As is usual today, its façade has been disfigured by the presence of an emergency staircase; apart from this unfortunate feature, one is struck by the building's powerful simplicity, its good proportions, and the quality of the copings. What is even more interesting is that its inner structure of beams and pillars allows for an open plan on every floor, something reflected in its façade. This kind of architecture is very common today, but one must keep in mind that this particular building was probably erected in the early 1850s, when architecture was still a slave to supporting partitions and walls as well as to historical styles. Both the structure and the design concepts of this building are reminiscent of the "architectural functionalism" brought to the forefront by Sullivan and picked up by Le Corbusier and his disciples in the twentieth century to form the basis for the International Style: it was undoubtedly the archetype of our modern office buildings.[2] (Plate 49.)

In Montreal the kind of commercial architecture exemplified by this building on des Récollets Street was both vigorous and audacious. It seemed like the spontaneous, logical, and economic answer to commercial and industrial functions which had thus far been unknown in the city, at least to such an extent. In earlier days, such pursuits, limited to local exchanges and handicrafts, were located on the ground-floor of traditional residences from which there was no need to separate work from living. However, with the division of tasks and cooperation in labour, with the gradual mechanization of the means of production, and with the considerable expansion of markets, these undertakings rapidly assumed a new character and were considerably enlarged. They became more specialized, more complex, and put greater pressure on the demand for space. There was a need for unobstructed space which could be easily organized to harbour a variety of operations such as the manufacture of clothes, furniture, shoes, or leather goods, all of which required many types of machines; to accommodate functions like wholesale trade or the stockpiling of goods; to house administrations with their increasingly defined and necessary operational functions. Builders answered these demands for space with the open plan: a structure of beams and pillars offering a maximum of flexibility with a minimum of obstruction, as well as plenty of natural light through glass façades. It was a clear, practical, and unpretentious solution, and was good architecture. Although not exclusive to Quebec, it was one of the authentic types of architecture in the

49.   *Commercial building located at 417 des Récollets Street*

province, together with that of the traditional rural and urban dwellings, so well adapted to the land, and that of the sober industrial housing.

Unfortunately, we do not possess much information on this original and worthwhile commercial construction in Montreal. We hardly know anything about the architects or builders of these edifices or even when they were built. This is to be expected, for it is difficult to become interested in an architecture which made no claim to that name. At times, we may be fortunate enough to find an inscription such as the one engraved on a cornerstone of a building located at the corner of d'Youville and Saint-Pierre and which reads: "Bâtisses des Soeurs Grises construites par E. Plante & Dubuc en 1871." Faced with a lack of evidence, we can only hypothesize as to where this revolutionary commercial architecture originated or why such advanced concepts were gradually forgotten and neglected, only to be rediscovered and appreciated late in the twentieth century.

This type of architecture seems to have originated on the American continent, more precisely in New England. Structures using cast-iron beams and pillars may be traced back to the first half of the nineteenth century in Great Britain. This feature, however, was not reflected in their façades, which were usually built in the traditional manner with supporting walls made of masonry. The monolithic stonework skeleton was an American innovation and the art historian Hitchcock traces its origin back to Boston and to the Quincy Market stores erected in 1824 by the architect Alexander Parris. During the same year, the stone-skeleton structure was used for the construction of the Granite Block and the Roger Williams Bank in Providence; some decades later it was commonly found in several buildings in Philadelphia.[3] Since the large cities on the American eastern seaboard became industrialized before the Canadian ones, it is quite probable that this type of commercial architecture appeared in those centres before crossing the border. Other influences also may have prevailed: it is quite possible that the military engineers of the king's army, stationed in Montreal, may have had some effect, for they had a practical and direct way of dealing with construction problems.

Whatever their origin may have been, the stone-skeleton façades were particularly well suited to the construction of commercial buildings in the heart of the old town. Indeed, most of them were erected on already densely built-up streets, like Saint-Paul, Notre-Dame, and Saint-Pierre, to replace more traditional structures which had been judged inadequate for the new functions. As most of the individual lots, which had been cleared by destruction of the original occupancy, through natural causes, or otherwise, were narrow and deep strips of land locked in between other buildings, the skeleton façade with its large glass windows was the only structure capable of providing enough natural light to such buildings which were often 27.4 to 30.5 metres deep and set between two blind common walls. Thus, the building located at 7–9 Notre-Dame Street West is about 3.5 metres deep by about 7.6 metres wide, yet is not unusual. Except for very slim columns, the space between the common walls of such structures is free of any obstruction on every floor. We still possess some engravings depicting the interior arrangements of some of them. One published in the *Canadian Illustrated News* of 21 November 1874, representing the interior of the Merchants' Exchange Refreshment Rooms on de l'Hôpital Street, shows the kind of flexibility provided for by these structures.[4] (Plate 50.)

Stone-skeleton façades were applied not only to buildings which were locked in between common walls but also to some large autonomous structures such as the Sisters of Saint-Joseph's Warehouse (1862), built on a block bounded by Saint-Sulpice, Saint-Dizier, de Brésoles, Le Royer, and Saint-Paul Streets,[5] and the Grey Nuns' Buildings erected in 1871 and 1874 on the block bounded by Normand, d'Youville, and Saint-Pierre Streets, and d'Youville Square. The architectural features of the façades were remarkable for the times. Strong arcades braced the ground floor while powerful masonry pillars rose between every third bay through the other floors, clearly reflecting the inner structure.[6] These buildings already contained the main architectonic principles which would be at the origin of the success of the Chicago School at the end of the century. (Figure 11.)

The features of these façades lead us to another fundamental characteristic of this first attempt at commercial architecture in Montreal: not only are the stone-skeleton façades a technical innovation, but they point to research of a purely architectural nature in the realms of composition, proportion, articulation, and scale. Unlike modern commercial buildings where all floors are identical and which generally look like a production line, these structures were designed to be seen and appreciated by the passers-by on the street. Therefore the façades were usually vertically modulated, and the height of each floor gradually diminished towards the roof. This is obvious in the building on des Récollets Street as well as in others located at 410 Saint-Vincent Street, 120 Saint-Paul East, 215, 221–231 Saint-Paul West, and also the magnificent edifice at 438–442 Place Jacques-Cartier. (Plates 51 and 52.)

50. *Interior view of the Merchants' Exchange Refreshment Rooms,
de l'Hôpital Street*

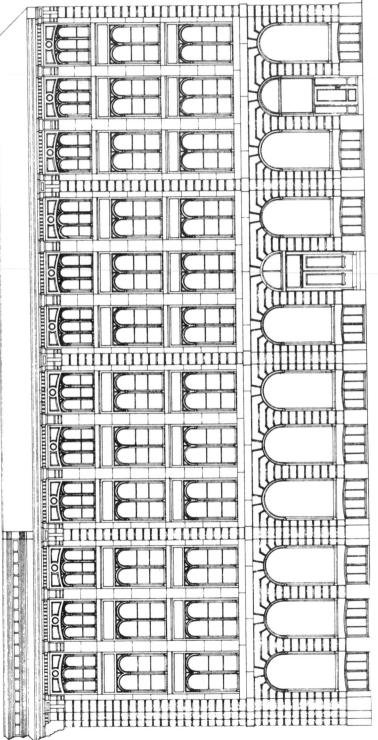

Fig.11   The warehouses built from 1862 onwards on the site of the old Hôtel-Dieu of Jeanne Mance. Partial view of the façade on Saint-Paul Street

Even the roofs of these commercial buildings seem to have drawn the attention of the builders. When the structure was topped by a mansard roof, strongly protruding dormers would highlight the fact. This appears to be so in the buildings on the east side of Saint-Pierre Street, between d'Youville Street and d'Youville Square. However, mansard roofs represented a loss of space in a building where space meant money. The use of tar would permit the construction of flat roofs from the 1880s onwards and soon many mansard roofs were to be replaced to create an additional floor. Yet, the buildings looked incomplete with flat roofs. The remedy suggested by architects and builders seems to have been the use of imposing cornices. This architectural solution had made its first appearance during the Italian Renaissance, and although it may not have been very original, it was nevertheless both effective and interesting, as the Chicago School would prove. The previously mentioned edifice on Place Jacques-Cartier attests to this fact, as do those located at 430 Sainte-Hélène Street, 434 Saint-Pierre Street and, among numerous others, 92 – 100 Saint-Paul East and 7 – 31 Notre-Dame West.

It would be a mistake to look at these commercial buildings without considering the manner in which they were integrated with the streets on which they were erected. There is little doubt that the architects who designed them did attempt to integrate the façades into the "spectacle" of the Victorian street. Opposite the Grey Nuns' Building on Saint-Pierre Street the same ground-floor arcades and the same rhythmic pattern of pillars at every third bay as in the Grey Nuns' Building unify the whole street by imposing strong horizontal lines on its perspective. Horizontal lines are also apparent in the buildings at 7 – 39 Notre-Dame Street West. In the two buildings at 215 – 31 Saint-Paul West, vertical lines predominate: powerful pillars rise uninterrupted from sidewalk to cornice. As they project beyond the windows, and cast long shadows, these façades appear solid and blend well with neighbouring buildings. This emphasis on vertical lines is most strikingly exemplified by the building at 430 Sainte-Hélène; here six storeys are vertically divided by uniform pillars into three thin strips which accentuate a soaring feeling and create a link with adjacent buildings. Other façades, in which neither vertical nor horizontal lines predominate, appear to be well-proportioned rectangles or squares of stones (120 Saint-Paul East; 374 – 84 Saint-Paul West; 367 – 73 d'Youville Square) or plain glass surfaces with a barely perceptible framework (47 – 55 des Commissaires West). Almost always these stone skeleton façades participate in the spectacle of the street either by integrating with the dominant lines and textures or by running squarely against these features. (Plate 53.)

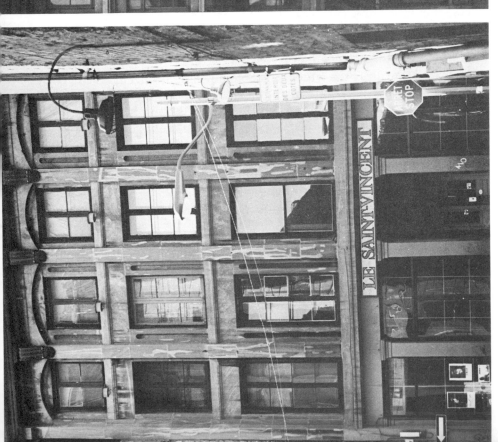

51 & 52.   Façades with skeleton stonework

If the stone-skeleton façades preceded metal-frame architecture, they are also precursors of the latter method of construction which likewise involved the prefabrication of some of the building elements. There is so much affinity in the spirit of these two methods that they are sometimes applied together to the same façade. We do not know for certain, however, whether some elements of cast-iron or iron were originally combined with the stone framework of the façades or whether they replaced parts of the latter at a later date. The second hypothesis is likely to apply in the building located at 177–83 Saint-Paul Street East which was probably erected in the early 1860s. The gable with its dormers suggests that its façade of stone and cast-iron may be the result of the alteration of a traditional stone course. Whatever its origin, this remarkable façade is probably among the most bare and most "glassed-in" of all the structures we have studied thus far. In fact, the ratio of glass-covered to solid surfaces is so high that it may just surpass that of our modern skyscrapers. (Figure 12.)

Façades with stone frameworks were nevertheless predominant in Montreal's commercial architecture. Whereas in the United States the cast-iron frames were very popular from 1850 to 1880—the St. Louis business centre was probably the best proof of this [7]—cast-iron was seldom applied to façades in the Canadian metropolis. It is not known whether fear of the effects of climate on the raw material or apprehension about the cost of prefabricated cast-iron elements was responsible for this fact. Yet, the use of stone in the creation of avant-garde architecture confirmed the preference of Montrealers for stone (available throughout the island) and reinforced the picture of a "town built of stone" which had so much impressed Benjamin Silliman a few decades earlier.

The Italian Forms
It is likely that the stone-skeleton façades we have just studied were not appreciated at the time they were built. Strictly for commercial purposes, they were regarded as utilitarian and without architectural pretensions. We are now in a better position to judge these buildings, for they were the forerunners of our contemporary architecture which we have learned to esteem for some of its qualities. Yet, for someone used to looking upon architecture as the nostalgic image of the past and accustomed to appreciating the picturesque in architecture, the stone skeletons must have looked bare and devoid of interest. The romantics at the end of the nineteenth century certainly would have preferred Perrault's Post Office and Browne's Molsons Bank to the Grey Nuns' Building by the little-known

53.   *Saint-Paul Street, Old Montreal*

Plante and Dubuc. This reaction must have influenced the merchants, bankers, and insurance company heads for whom prestige was the cornerstone of success and who were particularly anxious to see this reputation expressed through the architecture of their office buildings. The block located at 445–49 Saint-Pierre Street is a good example. The façade itself, made of a stone framework with sharply defined glass surfaces, in general reflects the logic of the structural system. However, mouldings decorate the lintels, capitals enhance the pillars, and copings and triangular pediments cap the doors as well as some of the bays. Such ornaments are ill-conceived and the overall impression is ghastly, but one can feel the tendency to adapt the stone skeleton to the tastes of the day.

Luckily, an acceptable form of "dressing-up" this type of architecture would soon appear and do away with the kind of monstrosity we have just described, to make way for a number of coherent shapes and details borrowed from the Italian Renaissance palace style. This type of commercial architecture "à l'italienne" flourished in Britain during the years 1840–60: Karsapian's Warehouse on Leeds Road in Bradford, with its Roman details, is a famous example. America would soon follow in Great Britain's footsteps, as we may see in Philadelphia.[8] No matter how this influence reached Canada,[9] it would leave its mark on a number of buildings in Montreal; one of these is the Bell-Rinfret Building (366–68 Notre-Dame West). This Italian style was not exclusive to commercial architecture; after the revival of Greek and Gothic motifs, it became the Victorian era's most important mode of architectural expression and had already started to influence religious architecture (neo-Baroque) in the province. (Plate 54.)

A closer look at the façade of the Bell-Rinfret Building tends to show that the Italian fashion was perhaps the best way of decorating the skeleton façades without damaging them too much. In this building, the internal structure is still perceivable because the horizontal and vertical supports are apparent; the arcade here is a simple ornament set between them. There is a slight loss of glass surface and of natural light inside the building, but this is compensated for by the freer articulation of the façade's various components and by the richness of its texture.

The decoration in the Italian manner makes the façades look livelier, which is more than one can say about the austere stone frames. When the articulation and liveliness of the various components are held in check by the very structure of the building, or when decoration is limited to an attempt at enhancing elements which reflect the internal composition, this type of commercial architecture becomes interesting. Every street in Old Montreal possesses at least one of these structures. While keeping in mind that the value of this kind of architecture lies in its honesty, one realizes that not all these buildings are equally worthwhile; indeed, many have been altered or disfigured in the most brutal manner. We would like to point to some of them before they disappear under the plough of "progress." There is a building located on the northeast corner of St. James Street and Place d'Armes which was probably erected around 1870 for the Life Association of Scotland. Three floors have been added since, to replace a rather original mansard roof that had arched dormers. Its façade reflects the main themes of the Italian style, with arched windows and with columns lending a vertical rhythm to the floors. One sour note, though: the proportion of glass to plain surfaces is almost equal, a fact which represents a regression compared with the stone skeletons previously analysed.

Another building has attracted our attention, even though its ground floor and its roof were poorly altered: it stands at the northwest corner of McGill and Saint-Maurice Streets. In this instance,

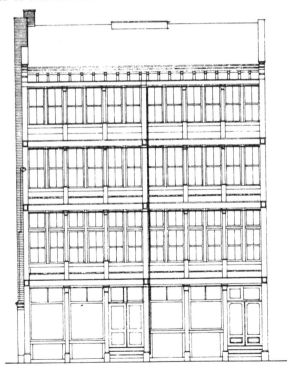

Fig. 12 Commercial building, 400–402 Saint-Paul Street West. Combination of cast-iron elements and stonework on the façade

the columns themselves are enhanced, thus lending both structural logic and texture to the façade. Such visual effects would evolve into strictly decorative motifs, however, without any reference to a logical structure. This may be observed on the façade of the building located at the northeast corner of Notre-Dame and Saint-Jean Streets, and particularly on that of the structure located at 380–84 St. James Street West (the Pub Saint-Jacques occupies the ground floor), where the columns are protruding and strictly decorative, lending a rather Second Empire look.

The search for the Picturesque did not, alas, stop at the few examples just given. The streets of the old town are littered with nineteenth-century commercial buildings whose façades are an orgy of decoration, the unfortunate result of various blends of styles, predominantly Italian. In such instances, structural considerations as well as climatic conditions have been ignored: only the picturesqueness of the "attire" matters.

Three contiguous buildings located at 38–60 Notre-Dame Street West provide a good example of this often heavily pretentious type; another is on the southwest corner of Notre-Dame and Saint-François-Xavier Streets, appropriately named the British Empire Building. Other structures display extremely superficial textures. Many a Montrealer must have been struck by the look of the façade of a building located at 157 Saint-Paul Street West, across from John Ostell's serious Customs House; it is covered with faked rustic stones whose motifs change with every floor. However, when it comes to decorative extravaganza, the building located at 451–57 on Saint-Pierre Street is unsurpassed. Its overloaded façade defies description: it may rival that of the most exalted Venetian palace.

In an age which prides itself on being rational, it is quite easy for us to criticize the style of some of these buildings; taken individually, many are in very poor taste. As a group, however, they do reflect the presumption, the vigour, the imagination, and the creativity of the golden age of capitalism and free enterprise. A visit to short Sainte-Hélène Street allows one to grasp the essence of this dynamic period at the end of the nineteenth century (plate 55). To participate in a unique experiment, one should stand at the corner of Sainte-Hélène and des Récollets Streets and look around at the four corner buildings. It is the best spot to take the pulse of the commercial city of the last century.

On the northeast corner of these streets stands a building which does indeed mark the gap existing between the commercial architecture of the end of the nineteenth century and that of the middle of the century, which was characterized by the stone-skeleton façade. This original architecture was both revolutionary and logical and had managed to rid itself of the bonds of the styles of the past, which were ill-adapted to modern materials and to new functions; it was now replaced by a heavy, powerful, purposeful, and complacent Italian Renaissance palace where all the progress achieved in the field of open plans and proper natural lighting was sacrificed on the altar of the romantic mania for plagiarism. Constructed in 1870, it is one of the few commercial buildings of the time whose architect is known to us. William Thomas practised in Montreal from 1860 to 1890 and distinguished himself by his preference for the Italian styles which he handled well. Everything he built, though, whether palace-like buildings or residences—with the exception of his delicate neo-Gothic St. George's Church—tended to be massive, square, and formal.[10]

The First Skyscrapers
The tragedy in the evolution of commercial architecture, in Montreal as elsewhere, is that it reverted to obsolete concepts. This happened at the very time when the specialization of functions required more appropriate structures, and when new materials (such as structural steel) and new technical improvements (the elevator, for example) made such building possible. There was a widening gap between technique and art, between construction and architecture. It is all the more unfortunate since open-plan buildings and façades based on a stone structural framework had already paved the way for a revival. We should compare, for instance, the buildings of the Grey Nuns from the early 1870s with the strange construction of the head office of the Grand Trunk Company erected in 1900 at 360 McGill Street. The former is an open plan, enjoys maximum natural light, and projects its functions to the outside. The latter was first conceived as a decor (perhaps Egyptian or Assyrian?); it is hard to reconcile its volumes with the expected functions, and natural light is sacrificed because the façades are decorated with all the architectural ornaments and motifs that one finds in a Dictionary of Art. One cannot be mistaken as to the purpose of the Grey Nuns' Buildings, whereas the Grand Trunk headquarters could easily be a palace or a hotel, but hardly an office building. One is genuine, the other ambiguous. Indeed, this ambiguity and this emphasis on architectural style and visual concepts, to the detriment of function and logic, are chiefly responsible for the poor reputation of Victorian architecture, in Montreal as elsewhere.

We can draw another comparison, this time between the Customs House built in 1833 by John Ostell and the gigantic eight-storey

54. *Commercial building located at 366–68 Notre-Dame West,
now Bell–Rinfret Building*

55. *Sainte-Hélène Street in Old Montreal*

mass (40 metres by 125 metres) of the new Customs House started in 1912 and occupying the entire block bounded by Place d'Youville, Normand, d'Youville, and McGill Streets. A whole century separates the two buildings, during which time new techniques and materials appeared which required new forms of expression. From the standpoint of architecture, however, there is no basic difference between these two Customs buildings except their scale. We must remember that John Ostell's purpose was to display his mastery of classical themes. The architects of the new Customs House seem to have entertained the same hopes. The use of steel and concrete does not alter the fact that this 1912 structure is an old-fashioned frame in an ill-fitting "Beaux-Arts" attire. John Ostell had but little choice in the means at his disposal; the architects of the new Customs House had the opportunity to construct a building much more in keeping with its functions. Unfortunately, they remained enslaved to the same architectural vision which had inspired Ostell some hundred years earlier.

One must not conclude that commercial architecture at the turn of the century was all poor. It has, indeed, left us a few good structures and we shall analyse them in due course. Yet, as a whole, it is disappointing. Let us consider, for example, the first skyscraper built in Montreal: the New York Life Insurance Company Building (today the Société de Fiducie du Québec) erected in 1887 by the architects Badcock, Cook, and Willard, on Place d'Armes at the southeast corner of St. James Street. It was the first eight-storey commercial edifice in Montreal; it was somewhat symbolic, for no commercial building, until then, had ever risen beyond five or six storeys (in fact, never beyond the number of flights that customers would be willing to climb) because of the lack of adequate vertical conveyance. In 1850 a safe passenger elevator designed in the United States was to radically change the picture. At the end of the century, Gustave Eiffel with his Tower and Contamin and Dutert with their Galerie des Machines (structures erected for the 1889 International Exhibition in Paris) were demonstrating the potentialities of structural iron. At the same time William Le Baron Jenney in Chicago was discovering (with the Leiter Building in 1889) the first clear and logical answers to the construction of iron-structured skyscrapers. The first Montreal example, therefore, appeared rather conservative for its time. Though steel had been used for its floors and roofs, its supporting walls, 80 to 100 centimetres thick, were still made of masonry and carried the weight of the floors on each storey. In this respect, the previous buildings with their structure of beams and columns and their façades of monolithic stone frames were, once more, much ahead of their time.[11] (Plate 56.)

The gradual use of new methods of construction such as concrete or steel skeletons, however, was not going to save commercial architecture from its apathy and mediocrity, for the academic concepts which had inspired the New York Life Insurance Building in 1887 were going to prevail unabated until the 1930s. There are many examples to confirm this statement, ranging from the Canada Cement Building on Phillips Square to the Dominion Square Building with its Atlantic City flavour, and the Bell Telephone Building on Beaver Hall Hill, designed by the architect E. Barott. The stubborn affection for the picturesque and for an obsolete symbolism at the expense of a more contemporary approach to architecture is even better demonstrated by two other skyscrapers: the Royal Bank of Canada Building—which covers the whole block bounded by Notre-Dame, Saint-Pierre, St. James, and Dollard Streets—and the Sun Life Building on Dominion Square.

The Royal Bank Building was erected in 1928 by the architects York and Sawer. Its monumental ground floor, in the manner of a Renaissance Florentine palace, makes it quite conspicuous and confirms the triumph of mercantile classicism in Montreal. This elegant ground floor serves as a base to support a dull and massive tower, although there is no real connection between the two volumes; this expedient simply reflects a municipal regulation which then limited the height of office buildings to 335 metres above which further floors had to be recessed.[12] The Sun Life Building was built along the same lines but in different stages, during the last of which, in the late 1920s, the present tower was added by the architects Darling and Pearson, thus making it for a time the highest and largest office complex in the British Empire. Its steel skeleton is covered with Stanstead granite, a beautiful material. It was hailed at the time as the most impressive and the most ornate of all the new buildings in the city—but certainly not the most novel. It is undoubtedly an impressive mass, enhanced by its location facing magnificent Dominion Square. It has monumental Corinthian columns on the ground floor, parapets on the several roofs, and a colonnade running from the seventeenth to the nineteenth floors (in the manner of Perrault at the Louvre); all these are picturesque features which were already obsolete at the time. By comparison, the Aldred Building is much more modern. It was built by the architects Barott and Blackader at about the same time as the last additions made to the Sun Life Building.[13] Almost as high as the latter or as the Royal Bank, it is definitely more contemporary in the architectural expression of its volumes, reflecting the structural system and the function of the building. Unfortunately, its many recessed segments

56.   *The first skyscraper built in Montreal, the New York Life Insurance Co. Building, now the Société de Fiducie du Québec Building. Badcock, Cook, and Willard, architects, 1887*

would be better suited to a skyscraper with a floor area three or four times larger, as in the Palmolive Building in Chicago which may perhaps have inspired the architects of the Aldred.

Fortunately, the commercial buildings of the late nineteenth and early twentieth centuries did not all follow the style of the Sun Life, the Royal Bank, or the Canadian Bank of Commerce (built in 1907 on St. James Street by Darling and Pearson) which remained slaves to the academies. Some edifices were spared the eclectic disguise, such as the Jacobs Building at the corner of Sainte-Catherine and Saint-Alexandre Streets, a seven-storey concrete building covered with varnished tiles, erected in 1909. It somehow resembles the Leiter II Building of Le Baron Jenney in Chicago. Built in the same spirit, Ogilvy's department store at the corner of Sainte-Catherine and Mountain Streets has a steel structure and concrete floors; it is framed on the façade by a monumental arch rhythmically structured. Another building located on the north side of Sainte-Catherine Street, west of Drummond, also reflects the influence of the Chicago School. However, it is the Unity Building (plate 57), completed in 1912, on the southwest corner of de La Gauchetière and Saint-Alexandre Streets which, except for the ornaments, is the most reminiscent of the Chicago commercial architectural style, for it resembles what may be considered as Henry Sullivan's most striking skyscrapers: the Wainwright Building in St. Louis (1890) and the Guaranty Building in Buffalo (1894).

The construction of the Royal Bank and the Aldred Buildings deprived Notre-Dame Church of its title and prestige as the highest edifice in that area, at the same time as the Sun Life cast its shadow over the dome of St. James Cathedral. In the span of a few decades, Montreal had become a powerful commercial and industrial city, a fact confirmed by the number of skyscrapers. In the course of this very rapid transformation, however, the city had lost many of the environmental qualities it had gradually acquired during the two first centuries of its existence. For the pre-industrial town had left behind the imprints of some form of organic planning with its perfect hierarchy of social functions translated into structures that were physically identifiable within the urban framework. Notre-Dame Church towered over the city, the Court House bordered the Champ-de-Mars, whereas the Château de Ramezay and the Château de Vaudreuil were connected to the urban fabric by their gardens which acted as buffer zones. In every instance there seems to have been a concern for the setting of a building and for the meaning it assumed in the general context of the town; this even applied to the humble private dwellings. This humanized concept of urban space has tragically disappeared from the industrial town. Space is no longer perceived as the orderly reflection of a way of life governed by cultural and social ideals but rather as a means of exchange and a common consumer good.

This downgrading of the quality of urban space in the commercial downtown area follows two different but consecutive patterns: first, the space was infiltrated; then, there occurred a siphoning phenomenon. At first commercial buildings expanded horizontally to compensate for their inability to rise upwards for lack of efficient means of vertical transport; they infiltrated everywhere, occupying every available space, swallowing up green areas and public land, and only stopping at the street because they found it practical to do so. It is not surprising then that these commercial functions should have displaced most of the other operations on Coteau Saint-Louis. In fact, they simply dislodged them without changing anything in the existing structures or in the grid of streets. This explains why the avenues planned by Dollier de Casson, to service a low-density residential settlement, were converted into narrow corridors completely out of the sun's reach. It was "Wall Street" revisited. Then, with the invention of the elevator and all the modern techniques in the fields of construction, heating, and ventilation, the reverse phenomenon took place: the skyscrapers siphoned up their immediate neighbourhood, creating vacuums around them; they dismantled the urban space, transforming the downtown area into an asparagus field. More about this later, for it really belongs to our own time rather than to the Victorian era.

The Grain Elevators and Victoria Bridge

We could hardly conclude this chapter on Victorian commercial architecture in Montreal without a few words about the bridge, named specifically after Queen Victoria, and about the grain elevators, for these are characteristic monuments of that period. Victoria Bridge was under construction from 1854 to 1859 and was to undergo transformations after 1897. It was the first span to cross the wide St. Lawrence River and it aroused the same feeling of awe that had accompanied the first railways a few decades earlier. Indeed, at the time of its inauguration, this bridge was considered the greatest scientific achievement and the largest project—the eighth wonder—of the world. As for the grain elevators, they were remarkable for the complexity of their operation which is expressed in a variety of forms, from the geometrical shapes of the silos to the linear dynamics of the conveyors.

The new construction techniques and materials developed during

57. *Unity Building, completed in 1912*

the Victorian era had a definite impact on those structures. For example, Elevator number 2 (now demolished) erected in 1912 for the Harbour Commission, by the engineers of John S. Metcalf, was the first of its kind to be built of concrete. It was 139 metres long, 30.5 metres wide, and 61 metres high, with a capacity of 2,662,000 bushels; it was a purely functional mass, visually out of scale in relation to the buildings of Old Montreal and it stole the limelight from nearby Bonsecours Market as well as completely obliterating the view of the river.[14] These elevators are perfectly anonymous and without pretensions of any kind; they do not even bear names but simply numbers (Elevator number 1, number 2, number 3, etc.) and they are connected to the quays, and sometimes to each other, by conveyors operating high in the air. For those able to appreciate them they are marvellous pieces of functional architecture, and therefore they confirm a principle dear to modern architecture: form follows function. Seldom has cybernetic architecture been better heralded than by those huge tentacular structures hovering above the quays like octopuses. They have even been a source of inspiration for formal architecture and Le Corbusier was one of the first architects to admire and perceive the design potential behind those austere structures. By 1925 he had already included photographs of the grain elevators of Montreal in an important book he wrote, entitled *Vers une architecture*.[15] (Plate 58.)

Victoria Bridge was also, at the time of its inauguration, a striking example of the potentialities of the new techniques and materials. Unfortunately, from a strictly architectural point of view, it was a failure which can in large part be blamed on the cultural dependency of the colony on the mother country.

To build this bridge over the St. Lawrence, the Grand Trunk Company had commissioned the great British engineer Robert Stephenson, son of George Stephenson, the "father of the railways." Robert had acquired a considerable reputation for having constructed the famous Britannia Railway Bridge (1845–50) after three years of research in the laboratory. This bridge, across Menai Strait, joined the island of Anglesey to Wales; it was remarkable for its tubular structure, for the maturity of its design, and for its pure and simple lines. Credit is also due to Francis Thompson, a talented architect who had joined Stephenson in this venture. Britannia Bridge was essentially based on two structural rectangular tubes made of wrought-iron plates riveted to each other; they were reinforced at the floor and at the roof by I-beams, and were supported between the two shores of Menai Strait by three geometrically designed masonry pillars.

Stephenson used the same tubular structure for Victoria Bridge.

Although the Britannia Bridge could be considered as "the greatest and boldest civil engineering feat of the early Victorian era"[16] and also as the most beautiful span at the beginning of the present era, Victoria Bridge, though a remarkable piece of engineering, unfortunately did not possess the qualities which turned Britannia Bridge into a piece of art. The main reason for this is that a structure perfectly suited to the Menai Strait was adopted without any alteration for a completely different site. Another reason is that in this instance Robert Stephenson had not benefited from the precious collaboration of a man like Thompson.

Menai Strait filled all the prerequisites for a harmonious relationship between the steep shores of the strait, the vertical volumes of the pillars, and the horizontal lines of the bridge; but the place selected on the banks of the St. Lawrence was exceedingly flat and the river looked more like a lake than a waterway. At Menai Strait, the distance to be covered was short and the site dramatic: the total length of the bridge between the entrance gates—signalled by two huge lions carved out of stone—was 457.2 metres. The distance was covered by four spans: the two main ones measured 141 metres and the tubes themselves were suspended some 30.5 metres above the high tide waters.[17] In the Montreal bridge, the length of the tube was more than four times that of the Britannia, about 2,011.7 metres, whereas the total length of the bridge, including the access ramps, was 2,799.3 metres. The distance between the two abutments was covered by 25 spans, each measuring 73.8 metres (except for the central one which was 100.6 metres), and the elevation of the tube above the water, at the highest point under the central span, was 18.3 metres.

The harmonious proportions of the Britannia were evidently not duplicated in the Victoria Bridge, for here one dimension definitely prevailed over the others: the seemingly endless length. And to extend this linear aspect even further, contrary to the Britannia which had two tubes side by side, Victoria Bridge had only one tube (5.5 metres by 7.6 metres) with only one railway track running inside it. So, in spite of the wish expressed by the officials of the Grand Trunk Company who had wanted to provide their railway with a bridge "of the best and most substantial character," only the pillars made of black limestone had some character, for they were indeed adapted to the local conditions. They were constructed with a sharp edge facing the current in order to break the drifting ice during the spring thaw. Yet, their masonry, as well as that of the abutments, did not have the distinction, discretion, or ingenuity of the Britannia's. (Plates 59 and 60.)

58.   *The grain elevators at the harbour*

Such a monumental task, the greatest venture in the world at the time, had indeed caught the eyes of the whole world. Yet, the overall impression conveyed was everywhere the same: the principal merit of Victoria Bridge seems to have been its length. These feelings have been very well summed up by de Lamothe:

> We must admit that this masterpiece of engineering makes a deeper impression on the mind than on the eye, for the distance strangely dwarfs its gigantic proportions. Seen from a distance, the long, rigid line of the gallery, the slender and equally rectilinear arches give the bridge the humble appearance of a bridge on trestles.[18]

New York's Brooklyn Bridge, designed by Roebling Engineers, would show the world what original results could be achieved in the United States by local talents using their own imagination.[19]

Faced with the overwhelming size of structures like Elevator number 1, which with a capacity of four million bushels was at the time the largest port elevator in the world, and with Victoria Bridge, which in spite of its "humble appearance of a bridge on trestles" was still the longest bridge in the world, one cannot help but draw comparisons with what Geddes and Mumford have called the Paleotechnic era which is indeed characterized by gigantism, a conquering spirit, ruthlessness, lack of respect for human values, and a devotion to power and money. Thus, those elevators crushed the old city with their mass, depriving it of any view or access to the river which was once upon a time its raison d'être and the charm of its site. Thus, Victoria Bridge, which had cost the lives of twenty-six people during its construction, crossed one of the most beautiful rivers in the world without providing the slightest chance of admiring it. Like a cave, the tube was totally dark inside—"an Egyptian darkness" according to one witness!—with, from time to time, a few tiny openings through which the odd ray of light would filter. Moreover, the tube retained smoke, noise, and vibrations, at the expense of the passengers' comfort. On the day of its inauguration, 25 August 1860, Prince Albert Edward (the future Edward VII) and the officials who were attending the ceremony were almost suffocated by the smoke from the locomotive.[20]

59. *Britannia Bridge, Menai Strait. Robert Stephenson, engineer,*
and Francis Thompson, architect, 1845–50

60. *Victoria Bridge around 1878. Robert Stephenson, engineer,*
1854–60

10

From Extravagance to Indigence:
Domestic Architecture

Si l'on veut retracer l'évolution d'une authenti-
que architecture moderne au Québec au cours
de la seconde partie du XIXe siècle et de la pre-
mière moitié du XXe, c'est dans les rues qu'il
faut la chercher.
   MELVIN CHARNEY[1]

The Residences of the Rich
Domestic architecture is not only one of the most authentic reflections of the ideals of an era but also the faithful mirror of the social
and economic conditions of a population. The rich have always been
able to follow the fashion in the way they dress as well as in their
choice of residences, whereas the poor have had to make do with the
type of shelter their limited income could provide. Thus, Victorian
Montreal was divided into two distinct poles: the rich areas and municipalities encroaching on the hillsides of Mount Royal and the
poor sectors and municipalities spread out on the lower terrace and
in the east end of the metropolis. However, the distinction between
rich and poor areas in Montreal was not limited, here as well as in
most towns, to a mere difference between social classes and incomes. Differences in ethnic origins added another variable to the
picture: the rich sections were populated chiefly by anglophones,
whereas the poor were inhabited mainly by francophones. Domestic
architecture, as we shall see, reflected the differences between "having" and "being."

In the rich areas, the type of housing varied with the state of one's fortune, not to mention extravagances such as the Hispano-Moorish residence at 1374 Pine Avenue. In the poor sectors, an original type of housing did eventually develop, but only through a long process of evolution. Upon careful inspection, one may uncover here and there buildings inspired by foreign models, whether English, American, Russian, Ukrainian, or other. They are discreet witnesses to the cosmopolitan character of the metropolis. The amazing wooden residence on the southeast corner of de Bullion and de La Gauchetière Streets is a good example of this phenomenon.

We chose to leave aside those particular examples in favour of an overall vision of domestic architecture in the past century. This image rests on the basic assumption that the residences of the rich reflect primarily the pretensions and the cultural imitations of a privileged colonial group and that housing for the underprivileged classes reflects an adjustment—most of the time compulsory—to social and economic realities. We shall begin with the study of the first type, the easiest to analyse, as it espouses all the styles and fashions we have already identified in the study of our public and religious architecture, namely neo-classical, neo-Gothic, Picturesque, or Shaw's style.

A look at the residences selected by the privileged of that time— the big landowners, bank presidents; industry, shipping, and railway magnates—would reveal the main features of those types of dwellings. In the days of Queen Victoria, they were all gathered in a restricted and exclusive perimeter, on the territory where merchants of the nineteenth century, like McGill, McTavish, and other fur magnates, had carved out for themselves aristocratic estates. Later on, under the pressure of urban development, this belt was somewhat dislocated and extended along a southeast axis, including certain avenues such as Dorchester and Sherbrooke, as well as making an assault on the mountain. Around 1900, a large number of interesting, palace-like residences were located between Sherbrooke Street and the side of Mount Royal and between Côte-des-Neiges Road and Bleury Street. At that time about 70 percent of Canada's wealth was in the hands of the 25,000-odd residents of this territory, measuring approximately one square mile, a fact for which it earned the name "Golden Square Mile." Today, all that remains of the past glory of the original Square Mile lies along McGregor (Docteur-Penfield) Avenue, once Montreal's Consulate Row.

Stephen Leacock, in his usual incisive language, has left a penetrating picture of the Square Mile, the abode of the "Sirs," "Lords," and the nouveau riche. He describes it as the sanctuary of hypocritical Victorian virtue: quiet as a cloister, where summer never came to an end in the large private greenhouses, where private collections of paintings such as that of William Cornelius Van Horne were the envy of museums around the world, and where "the rich in Montreal enjoyed a prestige in that era that not even the rich deserve."[2] At the top of this sacred territory stood Ravenscrag, the pompous residence of the richest of the parvenus of the Square Mile, Sir Hugh Montagu Allan.[3] New York had its Vanderbilts, Philadelphia its millionaires from Rittenhouse Square; Montreal was now entitled to have its Allans, as this era of steam and iron had skimmed its bath of sweat, poverty, and squalor to create the fortunes of the few.

It might have been appropriate to start our tour of the Square Mile with a look at the Prince of Wales Terrace. Unfortunately, these rows of residences, located on Sherbrooke Street West at the northwest corner of McTavish Street, were pulled down in the fall of 1971. There was nobody there to protest such an act of vandalism which was perpetrated with the blessing of the university authorities. Yet, among the neo-classical row houses of this type found in Canada, mainly in Quebec City, Kingston, and Hamilton, the Prince of Wales Terrace stood out for its dignified grandeur, its well-balanced appearance, and its sober taste, inside as well as outside. Less opulent and more severe looking, it was reminiscent of the style of John Nash in London, although the use of ashlar for the façade and the austerity of the design were more reminiscent of the classical mansions in Edinburgh. They were built in 1859–60 for speculative purposes and had been commissioned by Sir George Simpson, who was then governor of the Hudson's Bay Company. The plans were by two talented architects, William Footner, whose fame rested mainly with Bonsecours Market, and George Browne, who had designed the excellent Molsons Bank as well as other buildings.[4] (Figure 13.)

Remarkable as the architectural qualities of these neo-classical residences may have been at the time they were built, they must have appeared slightly behind the trends of the second half of the nineteenth century. One building which is more up-to-date and representative of the tastes of this period is the solid, red brick house with stone framed doors and windows located at 3015 Trafalgar Avenue and known as Trafalgar House. This name, by which several streets in the neighbourhood are called, comes from Trafalgar Farm. The land was formerly part of a farm owned by John Ogilvy, who had named it in memory of Admiral Nelson for whom he professed the greatest admiration. The splendid residence was built in 1848, as indicated on the carved stone above the door, and it was designed by the Toronto architect John George Howard. He was an excellent

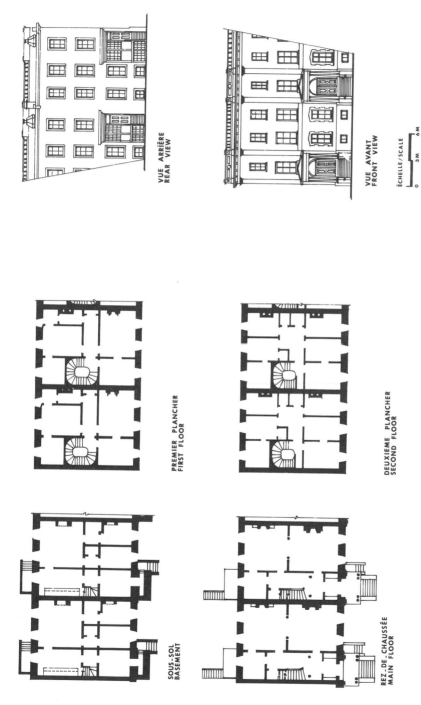

VUE ARRIÈRE
REAR VIEW

VUE AVANT
FRONT VIEW

ÉCHELLE/SCALE

0   3M   6M

PREMIER PLANCHER
FIRST FLOOR

DEUXIEME PLANCHER
SECOND FLOOR

SOUS-SOL
BASEMENT

REZ-DE-CHAUSSÉE
MAIN FLOOR

Fig. 13   Prince of Wales Terrace. William Footner and George Browne, architects, 1859–60

draughtsman as well as an engineer, and after emigrating from England he practised mainly in English Canada, and at one time taught design at Upper Canada College. As an architect, he started with delightful residences in Regency style, but he soon decided to join the neo-Gothic and the Picturesque movements for he had a very alert mind and was always eager to experiment. He designed the Toronto Prison, inaugurated in 1840, in the neo-Gothic style, and also the old Arts Building at Bishop's University in Lennoxville, which shows almost the same characteristics as Trafalgar House. The latter is remarkable for the feeling of solidity it conveys, its interesting blend of Gothic and Tudor features, and the quality of its construction. Unfortunately, the interior, where the walls of some rooms were upholstered with leather, has been ruined for lack of care and by utter misuse of some of the rooms.[5] (Plate 61.)

The enthusiasm for the neo-Gothic, which resulted in some valid religious buildings such as St. Patrick's Church, Christ Church, and St. George's Church, left us few domestic structures. Interest in neo-Gothic was probably on the wane at the time private wealth became well established. Whatever the reason, the return to the Renaissance (especially Italian) in architecture was undeniably an ideal answer to the ambitions of the rich merchants and industrialists.

The architect William T. Thomas, whom we mentioned in the previous chapter and who is responsible for the large commercial palace on Sainte-Hélène Street, built his reputation with the construction of this kind of opulent, upper-middle-class residence. He designed more than a dozen, but most of them are gone today, including the dwelling of George Washington Stephens (originally at 363 Dorchester). It was built in 1867 and showed some interesting imitations of the Roman and Florentine palaces of the Renaissance. Of Thomas's domestic structures still existing today, there is the residence occupied formerly by the Engineers' Club and now a restaurant on Beaver Hall Square. (Plate 62.) It was probably erected around 1860 for it appears on a map of the city printed in 1872; however, it seems to have been enlarged in the meantime. Although the years have not altered its scale or its Italian opulence, they have considerably changed its environment. Today this aristocratic mansion is completely surrounded by high buildings and no longer cuts a very impressive figure. Lord Mount Stephen's house, at 1440 Drummond Street, now occupied by the Mount Stephen Club, is perhaps not so elegant, but of all the classical residences designed by Thomas it is the most opulent, the most impressive, and the richest. Inside, the central staircase is made of mahogany, the mantelpieces of marble and onyx, the panelling of precious wood, the doorknobs are

61. *Trafalgar House. John George Howard, architect, 1848*

62. *The former Engineers' Club, Beaver Hall Square. William T. Thomas, architect*

plated with 22-carat gold, and so on. Notman, the great Montreal photographer of the end of the century, has left us some splendid photographs of the drawing-rooms and of the greenhouse of this residence.[6] In accordance with the taste of the times, the features of architecture literally disappear under a mass of paintings, vases, trinkets, and bric-à-brac. Built around 1880, this mansion gives us a fair idea of the opulence and extravagant tendencies of the ruling class of Montreal barely a hundred years ago.[7]

These mansions were among the true examples of their style, for, in spite of their heavy aspect, they retain an air of dignity which was probably not very common in this well-to-do neighbourhood. We need only look at the huge building on the northwest corner of Mc-Gregor (Docteur-Penfield) Avenue and Drummond Street, the former residence of Charles Hosmer, a director of the Bank of Montreal and the Canadian Pacific. Probably built around 1905–6 in a pretentious style reminiscent of the Second Empire, it is a showpiece of excessive wealth. The lavish use of brownstone does not make the building appear any lighter—on the contrary. We cannot help but think of Mumford's "Brown Decades," and of the meaning he attached to the use of brownstone as a symbol of the autumn of an art which had lost the freshness of spring and the vigour of summer.[8] In every respect, this house is oppressive, it is out of scale, and its architecture is completely alien to the splendour of the surrounding site. In fact, it reflects the deep lack of confidence of this class of parvenus in their own artistic taste: they always appear ready to barter original and creative solutions in exchange for safe and reassuring values, and to despise the suggestions of their environment, the better to welcome foreign influences, whether European or American.

This very Victorian tendency of a colonial society to show off in public their success or money and to cling to the familiar values of styles belonging to the past found its ideal vehicle in the Picturesque. There are several residences in this mode within the Square Mile; they have a well-fed, pretentious look about them, but no definite style of their own in spite of their contribution to "image architecture"—which is really what "Picturesque" is all about. It is surprising, exciting, thrilling—and eventually tiring! There was, at one time, the house belonging to Senator George Drummond, a large mansion of red stone built in 1889. Its architect, Sir Andrew Taylor, had designed it to convey the feeling of some haunted manor in Scotland. Here is how a visitor described it at the time: "The general design of the house is strong and good. The strong corner tower, which is still the tower of a house not of a fortress, and the two gables rising steeply to the grotesque 'beastes' that terminate them, produce a most admirable effect in the mass."[9]

This house, originally located on Sherbrooke Street West, almost opposite the Prince of Wales Terrace, has since disappeared. We can console ourselves, however, by regarding "Ravenscrag," the former residence of Sir Hugh Allan, a man who had accumulated the largest fortune ever made until then by a Canadian. Its site, towering over the McTavish reservoir, is quite exceptional and conveys a feeling of power, of mystery, and of legend. The house itself, which was perhaps inspired by the "Ravenscrag" of the Marquess of Lorne, in Ayrshire, Scotland, is a mixture of rather indefinite forms with most of its features borrowed from the Italian Renaissance.

While discussing the Picturesque, let us mention a little masterpiece of its kind, combining English bay windows with Dutch gables and with turrets dear to the heart of Viollet-Le-Duc: the house located at 438 Sherbrooke Street East, now occupied by the Canadian Club. There is another reason to refer to this house: it used to be the home of the Dandurands, the first family in Montreal to own an automobile, an omen of the deep transformation of the urban environment.

As for the interior of these sumptuous mansions, we need not describe them here for everyone has probably had the chance as a child to visit parents, grandparents, or family friends and experience the hushed and cushioned atmosphere of similar large rooms overcrowded with furniture and ornaments and whose worst enemies were simplicity and sunlight. As Lewis Mumford pertinently puts it: "No house was thought fit to live in that did not contain truck loads of ornament and bric-à-brac."[10]

Aside from the Picturesque, several residences built at the turn of the century reveal the influence of the Beaux-Arts style. There is a parallel between the delightful library of Saint-Sulpice, by Eugene Payette, and the Parisian-type residence at 430 Sherbrooke Street East; its façade is one of the most harmonious on this long street. Another dwelling on Sherbrooke Street belongs to the same style though it is more pretentious; it used to be the private residence of Sir Hugh Graham, then owner of the *Montreal Star*, and is located at the southwest corner of Sherbrooke and Stanley Streets. The Mortimer B. Davis House (now Arthur Purvis Memorial Hall, McGill University) was even more monumental, more austere, and more classical. It was built at the beginning of the century on the southeast corner of Pine Avenue and Peel Street, one of the most privileged sites in Montreal. We have here a perfect example of the cool balance and the well-calculated symmetry of the Beaux-Arts style. We know of only one residence (in fact, a duplex) that can rival the latter construction; it is the Château Dufresne, located on Sherbrooke Street, at the east end near Pie IX Boulevard. Designed by Marius Dufresne, a Montreal architect and contractor of the first quarter of the century, the mansion was a joint venture of Marius and his brother Oscar to launch a select residential district in that part of the town. They failed, perhaps because the east end of Montreal was already too identifiable with the French town and its poor people. The Château Dufresne was later converted into an educational institution, and is now a museum of decorative arts.

To conclude, we should briefly note that even temporary architectural fashions, such as those launched by the architects Norman Shaw and Henry Hobson Richardson, found their place in the Victorian domestic architecture of Montreal. The two houses on 3465–71 Drummond Street, now demolished, for instance, were made of splendid red brick and were typical of Shaw's style with their graceful design, their Dutch gables, and their slightly protruding bay windows. As for Richardson, we can trace his impact—even through the mixture of foreign influences the era was able to contrive—in the magnificent row houses located on the north side of Dorchester Boulevard, between Saint-Mathieu and Saint-Marc Streets. The Ordre des Architectes de la Province de Québec has established its headquarters in one of these buildings (now partly demolished).

Towards Standardized Housing

The houses we have analysed in the Square Mile are almost all detached residences; they show but one small aspect of domestic architecture during the Victorian era: they are dominated by individualism and heavily loaded with pretentious features borrowed from foreign cultures. This factor has influenced residential development to this day in municipalities and well-to-do areas such as Outremont, Westmount, and Hampstead, except that a search for comfort has gradually replaced a concern for style. If we are interested in the other facets of domestic Victorian architecture, we should turn our attention to the rows of houses built along Montreal's traditional grid of streets. Depending on whether they are located in the west end or in the east end, these row houses may be found in low, middle, and high-income areas, and differ accordingly.

Victorian row houses may be seen inside the Square Mile and in its immediate periphery; they are derived from the British models, conceived as rows of individual units with rooms distributed over several storeys. These rows follow the same concept as the Prince of Wales Terrace except that their façades, almost always made of stone, are usually decorated with ornaments and bear witness to the impact of the Picturesque trend. This kind of dwelling may be found on Sainte-Famille Street: three-storey houses (with the third floor usually fitted under a mansard roof) built on lots 15.2 metres by 27.4 metres (two housing units per lot); some have outside staircases to reach the main floor. The same kind of row houses, two or three storeys high, with grey or brown stone façades and often with bay windows, may be found on Crescent Street, or on Peel Street north of Sherbrooke Street. In the latter, they are built on lots about 7.6 metres wide and 30.5 to 39.6 metres long. This type of housing seems to be exclusively confined to the richer areas or to the anglophone municipalities; they are seldom encountered in the francophone areas where only a few isolated examples exist on Laval Avenue near Saint-Louis Square. This is easily explained: besides being of British origin, these dwellings required a fairly high income which was rare among French Canadians.

Once outside the Square Mile, going eastwards, one cannot fail to notice a type of vertical housing, with several flats set on top of each other, which seems to prevail everywhere. The first examples of this kind are found on Hutchison Street with its two-storey houses and its stone façades with superfluous Picturesque features. Similar façades are also noted in the east end, on the main thoroughfares, and on the more prestigious streets where the residential density is generally higher. Saint-Hubert and Saint-Denis, for instance, between Sainte-Catherine and Sherbrooke, are lined by sturdy apartment houses with stone façades, some of which are very austere and others quite pleasant. There are also similar houses on Cherrier and Berri Streets and on that part of Laval Avenue immediately north of Sherbrooke. The important thing about the latter examples is that access to the second floor is most often provided by outside staircases.

The further one penetrates into the populated areas of Rosemont, Saint-Edouard, Plateau Mont-Royal, or Verdun, the more one notices the predominance of a characteristic type of dwelling consisting of brick houses set in a row with two or three storeys of flats invariably provided with balconies, porches, and outside staircases in the front as well as the back. In the nineteenth century, every country, and perhaps even every large city, produced its own type of housing, suited to the economic, social, and cultural conditions of the majority of its population. It then became a standard that hardly seems original because of the very fact that it is so common; it covers large areas of the towns and bestows on them a part of its own identity and character. In the large cities of Continental Europe, as well as in Scotland (Glasgow and Edinburgh) or in New York, the most common type of housing at that time seemed to be the five- or six-storey apartment. In Boston it was the famous "Three-Decker"; in St. Louis and in Chicago it was the two- or three-storey type. On the other hand, in London, England, and in certain American cities such as Baltimore and Philadelphia the prevalent type is the one-family house built on a terrace, generally with two or three storeys, or sometimes four or five, depending on the financial status of the occupants.[11]

This kind of standardized housing appeared in Montreal at the turn of the century. Its origin, unfortunately, is not quite clear but we shall try to retrace it here. We are interested in discovering how and why the urban type of dwelling analysed in chapter five (that is, the one-family stone or wooden house, built in a row, with two or more storeys, and rooms distributed breadthwise) evolved into this new type of urban housing, usually made of brick, with flats built on top of each other and rooms distributed lengthwise.

First of all, it is obvious that the phasing out of the one-family house and its replacement by the apartment building can be explained by the need to cope with a rapidly growing population attracted by the employment opportunities in Montreal following the acceleration of industrialization. The increase in residential density, however, was related not only to the general rise in population but also, more specifically, to the growing number of workers who had to find a house close to job opportunities or at least close to public transport—tramways first drawn by horses, then by electricity—enabling them to commute to their place of work. This need explains why the first vertical type of apartment houses appeared in the early industrial areas of Montreal or in sectors reasonably close to employment concentration. Some of the latter areas happened to be ready for redevelopment, for they had been devastated by the great fires which ravaged Montreal in the middle of the nineteenth century, especially in 1845 and 1852.

According to Cooper, who obtained his information from rather inaccessible sources, the first vertical housing units were built in Pointe Saint-Charles to accommodate workers employed in the construction of Victoria Bridge and in the workshops of the Grand Trunk. These houses were built in rows, on vacant lots which were of uniform dimensions: 7.6 metres by 30.5 metres. Their façades were flush with the sidewalks. At the back, there was space for the washrooms (built outside the house at that time), the community wells, laundry facilities, and sheds to which small alleys provided access.[12] Their occupants were mostly Irishmen driven from their own country by the Great Famine; the very names in this embryonic development reveal the identity of its residents: Forfar, Conway, Britannia, and Menai Streets. Nothing remains today of this small settlement; the Autostade (now dismantled) and a part of the Bonaventure Expressway were built on its site.

On the other side of the marshalling yard of Pointe Saint-Charles, however, there are still several residential streets, such as Sébastopol, de la Congrégation, Sainte-Madeleine, Bourgeoys, Charon, Favard, and Le Ber, which probably developed at about the same time and along the same lines as the Irish settlement just described. This other residential section was built on virgin territory originally owned by the Sisters of Charity of the Hôpital-Genéral de Montréal, and by the Sisters of the Congregation of Notre-Dame. It apparently was developed with the same kind of concern for order and standardization as in the previous situation. The only difference was that there were no back alleys in the original plan and the land was subdivided into uniform plots about 14.3 metres wide by 26.5 to 29 metres long. It must be noted; however, that here we usually find two houses, each 7.15 metres wide, per lot; these dimensions therefore are similar to those which would become standard for this type of housing in Montreal. Sébastopol Street (undoubtedly given its name to commemorate the victory of Sebastopol in 1855, thus allowing us to give an approximate date to its development) can be considered as typical of its kind, with its dull rows of two-storey brick houses, their two-room flats built on top of each other and distributed lengthwise. All the houses are identical, a fact which leads us to believe they were built by the same contractor.

This type of multiple-family dwelling also emerged at the same time in the periphery of the downtown area. It probably started in the sectors that were redeveloped following the great fire of 9 and 10 July 1852, which raged for twenty-six hours, destroying almost half the houses in Montreal: all of the territory bounded by Saint-Laurent, de Maisonneuve, Saint-Denis, and Craig Streets, and that between de La Gauchetière Street and the St. Lawrence River from the Champ-de-Mars to the foundries of Sainte-Marie, which stood approximately at the level of today's Papineau Avenue. Unfortunately, we cannot rely on these places as witnesses, for they have since undergone many changes. The Faubourg à la Mélasse, for instance, a picturesque residential area which had developed east of the Champ-de-Mars after the 1852 fire, was in turn partially demolished (and the rest eventually faded away) to make room for Viger Station, the harbour facilities, and in the fall of 1963 the Maison de Radio-Canada.[13] One can best reconstruct the process that led to the first stage of standardized housing by considering an adjacent sector, bounded by Amherst and Sherbrooke Streets, Papineau Avenue, and Dorchester Boulevard. The latter district has hardly changed since it was first developed; it is therefore possible to retrace the gradual standardization of the urban blocks, building lots, and of the dwellings themselves and finally to arrive at a typical model of streets and housing of which Wolfe Street is undoubtedly a good example.

The first streets to originate in this sector were Champlain, de Maisonneuve (today Alexandre-DeSève), Plessis, Panet, and de la Visitation. They look like long corridors lined with uninterrupted rows of houses following the somewhat irregular outline of the cadastre. A closer examination reveals that the urban blocks bounded by these streets are 61 to 70 metres deep, without any inside lanes, and that within the blocks there used to be—and still are to a certain extent—median rows of houses standing back to back. Services for and access to these dwellings were normally provided through passageways or carriage gates cut through the houses that bordered the streets. So, beneath the apparent uniformity conferred by the orthogonal traffic grid, this urban fabric is textured like Gruyère cheese. Inside the blocks there is plenty of room for the unexpected and the mixture of heterogeneous constructions provides an interesting experiment in spatial relationships.

The houses themselves display a number of characteristics that are relevant to the evolution of the anonymous domestic architecture in urban Montreal. Most of them consist of a wooden framework covered by a layer of brick and are built right against the sidewalk. Their façade is quite simple; they have no balcony but usually have two doors side by side on the same landing, one leading directly to the ground floor, the other to an inner staircase climbing to the floor above. There are usually two storeys, but where there are three the two top ones usually belong to the same apartment and the third floor is then laid out under a mansard roof. There are three types of roof: flat, mansard, and composite. In the last-named, a steep sloping side with dormers faces the street whereas the other side is only slightly slanted. The dormers, together with other components of the roof, such as the cornice, are usually the only ornaments on these rather austere and classical façades. The apartments, usually two rooms deep, are quite small but full of light. Access to the inner courtyard through an interior corridor cuts down the space allotted to the ground floor apartments, which usually consist of only three rooms.[14]

There are, as a rule, galleries and an outside staircase at the back of these dwellings. Later on, these vertical and horizontal means of communication would commonly be provided on both ends of this type of house. It seems, however, that this practice dates back to earlier days. Indeed, outside stairs leading to the upper rooms were first built within the inner courtyard and garden of the traditional urban house. Then, because of demographic pressures and the ensuing scarcity of building lots suitably located in the vicinity of available employment or of the facilities provided by the community, people started to build apartments above the sheds and the stables in the courtyards, or simply converted their traditional houses into separate apartments. The outside staircases, which were but elaborate versions of the ladder, seemed to be the easiest and cheapest way to reach those lodgings. This was really nothing very new. Mitchell and Leys, in their fascinating book on everyday life in London, remind us that, towards the end of the Middle Ages, craftsmen and workers used to live in apartment houses of a kind, where ladders were used to reach the upper floors. The use of ladders or outside staircases was quite frequent, even in comfortable houses, for only the rich could afford the luxury of an inner staircase.[15] There is no doubt that wherever such contrivances appear, the economic factor played a predominant role.

When the vertical-housing concept was first applied to apartment houses in Montreal, as in the working-class residential developments of Pointe Saint-Charles, or in the type of dwellings in the St. James and Bourget areas, the outside stairs became the most suitable means of linking the apartments on the upper floors to the washrooms, the wells, and the laundry facilities located in the backyards. The apartments were individually heated and it was essential to provide access to the coal supply normally stored in the backyard and to ensure easy disposal of the ashes. An inside staircase leading to the backyard would have been equally suitable. However, since the floor space of these apartments was itself strictly limited to save costs—46.5 square metres is an average surface area for a four-room apartment in the St. James and Bourget districts—and since a part of this precious floor space was already wasted to accommodate the inside front staircase, outside stairs solved the problem of these occasional, though quite essential, activities. The porch now became a necessary link between the outside staircase and the apartment. As it was often impossible to place the outside stairs in front of the door of the upper floor, this landing became very useful for temporary storage, for resting, or for other specific purposes. Galleries appeared as the natural extension of already cramped lodgings, and they would eventually be perfected to lead directly to a shed used as a storage place for coal or personal belongings.[16]

Moving slightly to the west, towards Wolfe and Christophe-Colomb Streets for instance, without leaving the area we have selected, we observe a gradual standardization of the urban house as well as of its topography. Here, the development lots have regular and identical dimensions: 6.4 metres by 20 metres and 6.7 metres by 22 metres. Moreover, a back-alley runs through the block. Compared to the 61- or 70-metre depth of the previous blocks, the 47.2-metre depth of these blocks eliminates any waste space and discourages any attempt to build on the inside of the block. The service alley eliminates the need for passages through the houses bordering on the street. The ground-floor apartments are the first to benefit from the space thus regained. These houses, and the ones on the west side of Wolfe Street in particular, although inspired by the previous examples, were built according to a standard, repetitive pattern: a two-storey structure with flats on top of each other, a flat roof, entrances in the front, through two adjoining doors, one leading to the ground floor, the other to a staircase reaching the second floor; at the back, access to the second floor is gained through an outside staircase and a gallery. The construction has also been standardized: a wooden frame covered by red brick. This type of urban block is undoubtedly the work of one sole controlling agent, a developer or a contractor perhaps, who directed the planning of the site as well as the construction of the dwellings according to a definite plan and with a definite purpose in mind—probably maximum profit. (Figure 14 and Plate 63.)

Maximum utilization of space through planning appears to have been systematically achieved on Sherbrooke Terrace, on the virgin territories caught up in urban development in the last quarter of the nineteenth century. A typical example is that of the subdivision of the rural lands of Messrs. William and Logan and of other adjacent estates, partially in the former village of Saint-Jean Baptiste and on the former Côte Saint-Louis, today referred to as Plateau Mont-Royal. There, the size of the building lots is standard almost everywhere: 7.6 metres wide by 24.4 to 30.5 metres deep. No regulations have ever determined these dimensions: they seem to have been established by custom.

The type of housing which developed in this sector, and which was to become typical in Montreal, was also designed for profit. However, compared with the houses on the lower terrace which we have just described, they differ in several respects because they were built at a time when there was a need to increase the density of residential development. With the large growth in urban population, mainly due to the immigration of large rural families, it became imperative to concentrate the greatest number of people on the shortest lines of access. This was aimed at reducing the cost of the transport (still dependent on rather primitive means) of people as well as the goods indispensable to their existence; it was also aimed at bringing down the cost of equipment such as sidewalks, aqueducts, sewers, and of gas and electricity services. This need for concentration was a determining factor in the orientation of the rooms which would be laid out between two common walls running parallel to the length of the lot instead of being oriented across its width as they used to be in earlier models.

The first of several distinctive features to attract our attention is the outside front staircase. At that time houses were set back from the line of the sidewalk, leaving vacant but unused space; this provided an opportunity to build the staircase leading to the upper floors on the outside of the house. The space thus saved inside the apartment was then put to good use. For houses with three floors, the staircase from the balcony of the second floor to the flat on the third floor usually remained inside. Even then, however, there are many examples of outside stairs of all kinds with several flights climbing up to the third-floor balcony. Another distinctive feature of this type of house was the front balcony which was made possible when the structures were set back from the sidewalk. Just as with the galleries at the back, the balcony served as a landing between the flats and the outside stairs and was the natural extension of an apartment. Since most of these houses were designed to accommodate people who had recently arrived from the country, where porches and verandahs were quite common, these features were possibly considered as something necessary, a fact which certainly did not escape the notice of speculators, developers, and contractors. Front balconies may also have been an attempt, whether conscious or not, to imitate the houses of the rich where the main entrance was often protected by a porch whose roof was used as a balcony for one of the rooms on the second floor.

Inside this type of housing the layout of the flats distributed lengthwise is also standardized. For instance, when a flat occupies the whole width of the lot, which is normally true on the ground floor, often occupied by the owners themselves, the six or eight rooms follow each other lengthwise on each side of a central corridor. In front, on one side there is a double living room and on the other a bedroom and a boudoir or a double bedroom. Proceeding towards the back, we enter a kitchen, with or without its adjacent windowless dining room, and on the other side there is a single or a double bedroom. When the apartment has an L-shaped plan, with an extension reaching almost to the end of the lot and generally leading to a shed, this wing usually contains the dining room, the kitchen, a

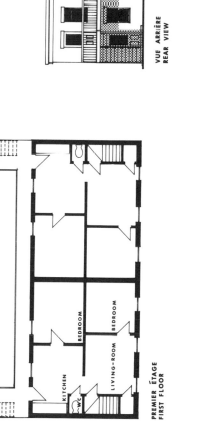

PREMIER ÉTAGE
FIRST FLOOR

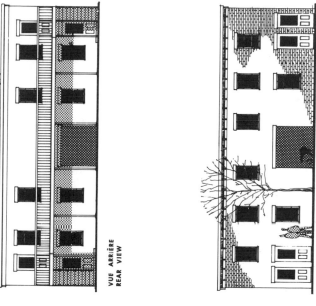

VUE ARRIÈRE
REAR VIEW

REZ-DE-CHAUSSÉE
MAIN FLOOR

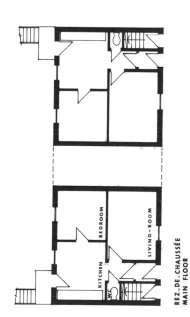

VUE AVANT
FRONT VIEW

ADRESSE
ADDRESS

2094 / 2106 MONTCALM
MONTRÉAL

ÉCHELLE
SCALE

0   1,5 M   3 M

Fig. 14   Typical house on Ontario Terrace, end of nineteenth century

63.   *Wolfe Street, Ontario Terrace*

bedroom, and sometimes bathrooms. On the other side there is a windowless room, occasionally equipped with a small alcove.

The flats on the upper floors follow the exact plan of the apartment on the ground level, inasmuch as they cover the same area. They are generally smaller, however, for one of several reasons: they do not follow the extension provided for on the ground floor; they lose one room or have a smaller room to leave space for the inside staircase leading to the third floor; or again—and this is so with most second and third floors—because the area is split into two separate flats with four rooms on either side of a passage: a double bedroom, a bathroom, a windowless living or dining room, and a kitchen. Every apartment has access to the back galleries which open into the sheds and to an outside staircase leading to the service alley. The staircase is often housed in the shed itself.[17] (Figures 15 and 16.)

There are, of course, a few variations of this type of apartment. The ones just described seem common enough to be considered typical of the housing popular in Montreal at the end of the nineteenth century and in the first quarter of the twentieth century, especially in the large francophone areas. As late as 1948, John Bland said about these houses that "for most Montrealers, a flat in a three-storey block is a home."[18]

Standardized Housing: Pros and Cons

The standard Montreal house just described was severely judged by nearly all critics, whether town planners, geographers, architects, or artists. They objected to its small size and poor layout (the bedrooms and living room are located on the noisy side, facing the street, whereas the utility rooms look on to the quiet backyards), as well as to its poor natural lighting and ventilation. They also criticized the obvious weakness of its construction, its flat roof, tin cornices, balconies, galleries, sheds, outside staircases, in fact, all its distinctive features.[19] The outside staircases, in particular, were universally disapproved. We could quote critics ad nauseam, but we shall cite only Victor Barbeau who sums up almost all the unfavourable comments in a few pointed words on the subject: "those corridor-flats reached by a ladder improperly called a staircase . . . those outside staircases history will never deny us."[20]

The time has come to revise those judgements, to forget the stereotyped concepts of architecture and beauty, and to be more concerned about the social, economic, and cultural conditions which generated this kind of house. Following the lead of commercial architecture with its open plan and stone-skeleton façade, which in the same era seemed to be an original solution to new needs, the Montreal duplex and triplex appeared as an emergency solution at a time when rural migrants were flocking to the big city. From 1891 to 1921 the population of the city of Montreal nearly tripled, rising from 219,616 to about 618,506.[21]

Such a flow of population and its concentration inside the town tended to increase the economic value of the land, but most of these rural migrants were particularly poor. The result was that the density of these new areas and the kind of housing available created a state where an equilibrium was reached between the cost of housing (including land) and what the potential residents could afford to pay. The fluctuations followed the growth curve of the urban population, which explains the gradual move from the sturdy and comparatively expensive colonial, urban one-family homes to the kind of low-rent housing found in sections of the lower terrace, and finally to the high-density duplex and triplex of later Victorian areas. The latter type of housing was particularly well suited to the rural migrant who had only a small amount of capital to invest in urban property. It also answered the needs of those who only required temporary shelter until they could afford better accommodation.

This type of urban housing offers its owner about the same return and presents the same operating characteristics as the rural farm itself. In the first place, the capital expenditure for building or purchasing is not very high and involves almost no risks; it requires neither a thorough understanding of the financial markets nor particular managerial skills. On the contrary, this kind of investment provides the owner with a stable income that does not conflict with other profitable activities. As with the rural farmer, he can live in his own house, provide for its maintenance, and keep better control over his assets. Finally, he can bequeath the building and the land to his heirs.[22]

As for the tenants, who make up the majority of the occupants of these houses, this kind of lodging is so popular that one can only conclude that it is the best they can hope for, considering their social and financial standing. Hans Blumenfeld reminds us that in every country it is the most common type of building that proves to be the most inexpensive as it constitutes a frame of reference for the building industry and for construction codes.[23] A succinct analysis of the structural features of this kind of housing would show that as far back as the end of the nineteenth century modern techniques of standardization and prefabrication were already being used.

First of all, the structural wooden frame covered with bricks had replaced the supporting walls made of stone, brick, or brick covered

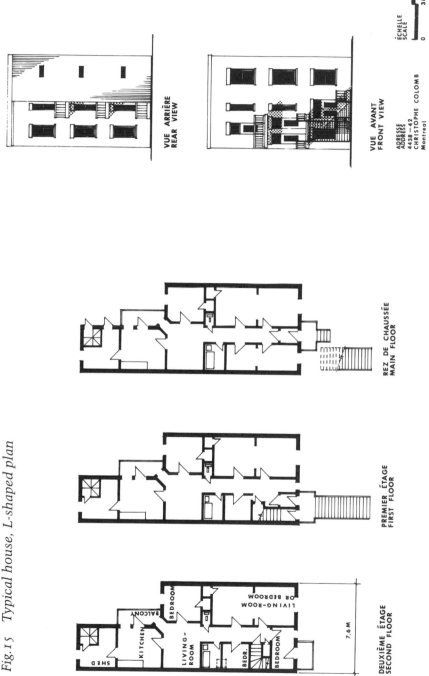

Fig.15 Typical house, L-shaped plan

VUE ARRIÈRE
REAR VIEW

VUE AVANT
FRONT VIEW

ADRESSE
ADDRESS
4438–42
CHRISTOPHE COLOMB
Montreal

ÉCHELLE
SCALE

0   3M   6M

REZ DE CHAUSSÉE
MAIN FLOOR

PREMIER ÉTAGE
FIRST FLOOR

DEUXIÈME ÉTAGE
SECOND FLOOR

SHED

KITCHEN

BALCONY

BEDROOM

LIVING-ROOM

BEDR.

BEDROOM

LIVING-ROOM
OR BEDROOM

7,6 M

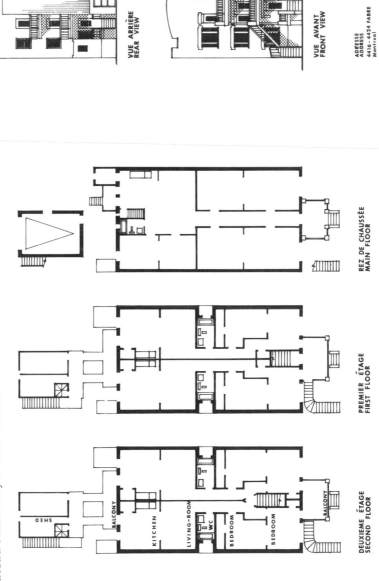

Fig. 16   Typical early-twentieth-century house, especially prevalent in the wards of Plateau Mont-Royal and Verdun

VUE ARRIÈRE
REAR VIEW

VUE AVANT
FRONT VIEW

ADRESSE
ADDRESS
4416 - 4424 FABRE
Montréal

ÉCHELLE
SCALE
0   3 M   6 M

SHED

BALCONY

KITCHEN

LIVING-ROOM

WC

BEDROOM

BEDROOM

BALCONY

DEUXIÈME ÉTAGE
SECOND FLOOR

PREMIER ÉTAGE
FIRST FLOOR

REZ DE CHAUSSÉE
MAIN FLOOR

with stone. These two materials combined (wood plus brick) need total standardization to be efficiently used. The beams must have the same dimensions and characteristics when they reach the building site. The same applies to the use of brick, the cost of which is considerably less than that of the transporting, handling, setting, and cutting of stone. The application of brick to a wooden framework eliminates the drawbacks inherent in wooden construction (fire and storm hazards and year-round maintenance), while retaining the latter's advantages: cheapness and warmth. Another good point is that the sloping or mansard roofs are replaced by a flat surface with a sheet covering, thus saving space, materials, building costs, and time, and also economizing on maintenance and heating. Indeed, sloping or mansard roofs with their many surfaces exposed to the natural elements allow ice and icicles to form in winter. Water from flat roofs is easily collected and drained through the heated building, and the snow accumulating on top of the roof provides an excellent insulation. A flat roof, however, requires a type of prefabrication and standardization for tarpaper, joints, vents, drains, and so on.[24] Vertical communications provide another cost-saving device: the outside staircase economizes on the space for a stairwell and on its heating. Here again there is a high level of standardization and prefabrication in the manufacture of all the components of vertical and horizontal communication: stringers, steps, and hand-rails for the stairs, guard-rails for the balconies and galleries. The need for prefabrication even extends to the decorative components of the façades such as the sheet-iron cornice ornaments which are made in a workshop. Again, there are other factors which contribute to economy in construction: the blind common walls, the repetition of the same plan, and the superimposition of the service equipment and plumbing units. While this kind of standardization and prefabrication certainly answered the need for the immediate accommodation of thousands of people, it also served the interests of builders and contractors, eager to minimize investment and maximize profits, by allowing them to know ahead of time the quantity of materials required as well as the machinery and labour necessary to assemble them.

Let us now turn to the outside staircase, which has been so widely criticized. A more objective look may disclose some unsuspected qualities. It has been said repeatedly, for instance, that it was ill-suited to our hard winters. We must admit that standardized housing shares the blame in this respect with all Victorian architectural production. Is there any building of that period, from the neo-Gothic to the neo-Baroque, from the Second Empire to the "Beaux-

Arts," that is truly suited to our climate? We could look at the matter the other way around and say that the outside stairs are better suited to our stifling summers than are the inside staircases; and the same applies to our balconies. For one thing, the outside staircase provides residents with more privacy, with a feeling of greater security, than the inside stairwell leading to several apartments. One has only to live in an apartment building with an inside staircase, such as the ones built since the late forties—when the regulation forbidding the building of stairs outside the house was adopted—to realize that those towers of vertical communication carry all the noise and smells everywhere (imagine what might happen during a fire!), that they are expensive to maintain, that they can shelter hooligans and other unwelcome visitors, and finally that they bring about unplanned encounters. In this respect, the outside staircase and the individual balcony provide greater flexibility in that they encourage social communications from one staircase to another, from one balcony to the next one, without making such encounters unavoidable.

Even the sheds do not deserve the contempt in which they are usually held. Apart from the fact that they used to be indispensable as depots for stove and furnace fuel, they were and still are very essential adjuncts to the small apartments that appealed to average-income families. Furthermore, some tenants were obliged to store away their belongings for later use. As with the outside staircase, these sheds perfectly illustrate their function: indeed, they are usually quite distinct from the apartments and are built from light, less durable materials. They are not even that displeasing to the eye, for, at times, the interplay of their masses with the galleries creates interesting visual relationships. Lack of maintenance is the main cause of their shabby appearance. A good coat of colourful paint would probably convert them into attractive urban fixtures.

The most valid reproach we can make against this type of housing is that it lacks both air and light, since the rooms are laid out in a line between two common blind walls. It is quite usual to find four such windowless rooms in a row, or a room sharing a skylight shaft with the bathroom or without any light whatever. There are also all sorts of devices, such as three-quarter glass doors, to dispense light to the staircase, the corridors, and the dining room.

To make matters worse, most of the streets where this kind of housing can be found are poorly oriented. They follow the structure of the côte, the colonial unit of territory analysed in chapter 2, which left the Victorian house to deal with an inadequate pattern that has remained unchanged and is responsible for the typical grid of streets in Montreal. The great majority of those streets run more or less from east to west; this is true of Longue-Pointe, Hochelaga, Maisonneuve, Plateau Mont-Royal, Rosemont, Villeray, Ahuntsic, Notre-Dame-de-Grâce, Verdun, and others. As a result, only one side of those uninterrupted rows of houses receives sunlight during the greater part of the year: on the odd-number side of the street, the front of the houses is favoured, whereas the back of those on the even-number side is exposed. Thus at least half of the rooms hardly ever get any sun. These already unfavourable conditions are not improved by the position of the outside staircase blocking the front windows and by the permanent shade projected at the back by the various galleries, stairs, and sheds. Tragic as it may seem, there are apartments which never receive the faintest ray of sunshine: usually on the ground floor of houses built with their back to the sun. Moreover, because of their orientation, these dwellings face the prevailing winds, a fact which explains why the snow accumulates on the galleries and balconies during winter storms.

Thus, the typical house with its "long" plan, its usually narrow, poorly lit and poorly ventilated rooms is certainly not without defects. Yet, it would be wrong to blame architecture for these flaws, for they stem from poverty and lack of resources, both of which prevailed long before this type of construction came into being. On the contrary, this house, which is a true illustration of an architecture without architects, is quite remarkable for its high degree of prefabrication, for the frank, overt layout of its functions and for its communications potential expressed through its balconies, galleries, passages, and outside staircases, all of which are reminiscent of the aerial conveyors of the grain elevators at the harbour. These original houses have generated an equally original environment which has deeply marked the identity and the image of Montreal. This aspect will be dealt with in the next chapter as a typical feature of the Victorian legacy. (Plates 64 and 65.)

64. *Garnier Street, north of Saint-Joseph Boulevard, Plateau Mont-Royal*

65. *A typical dwelling. Fabre Street, south of Mont-Royal Avenue*

11

The Victorian Legacy

The building of the cities was a characteristic Victorian achievement, impressive in scale but limited in vision, creating new opportunities but also providing massive new problems. Perhaps their outstanding feature was hidden from public view—their hidden network of pipes and drains and sewers, one of the biggest technical and social achievements of the age, a sanitary "system" more comprehensive than the transport system. Yet their surface world was fragmented, intricate, cluttered, eclectic and noisy, the unplanned product of private enterprise economy developing within an older traditional society.

ASA BRIGGS [1]

Discovering a Legacy

Industrial towns are generally blamed for the environment they generate. This dismal reputation seems justified when we think of the chaos, the short-term expediency, and the "laissez faire" which have come to replace the order, the organic unity, and the clarity that used to characterize the pre-industrial urban environment. It is as if the essence of the city had been diluted and had lost its flavour following the explosion of the traditional urban structures under the pressure of demography.

The comments of critics like Lewis Mumford, on the distur-
bances in the habitat and the social failure they most often reflected, have largely contributed to identify most of the industrial
agglomerations with one single model, Coketown, an infamous
town full of ugliness, squalor, and despair.[2] We are tempted, at first,
to applaud this comparison, for the dreary images of factory towns
seem to match the prototype only too well. In our own country, the
conditions described by Herbert Brown Ames in *The City below the
Hill* were far from being ideal and seem to have been very similar in
all the working-class urban areas of the industrialized world. For instance, what difference was there, at the time, between our Irish
communities, clustered in the district of Sainte-Anne around the
oppressive factories of the Grand Trunk Company, and the "Little
Ireland" in Manchester described by J. P. Kay? Kay was a doctor who
had practised there and, in 1832, he wrote that it was "surrounded
on every side by some of the largest factories of the town, whose
chimneys vaunt forth dense clouds of smoke, which hang heavily
over this insalubrious region."[3]

The fact that the same territory harboured "the City below the
Hill" and the opulent Golden Square Mile further emphasized the
inequitable and dilapidated areas. The wealth of the Square Mile
and the squalor in Sainte-Anne, Saint-Henri, or Sainte-Cunégonde,
in those days, were the two extremes in an age with very little sense
of proportion; an age which could just as easily generate weaklings
and wretches, such as those on whom Dickens lavished his compas-
sion, or men like the heroes we read about in Kipling; an age that
could build dark, cramped, and stuffy houses as readily as it could
construct palaces for its railways.

Asa Briggs suggests a number of arguments[4] to support his contention that, on the whole, the record of the industrial town is not
all negative. In his opinion, the industrial town was the result of unprecedented technical revolutions and the fact that the latter did not
always happily fit into the urban fabric does not mean that they
failed to contribute to progress. For instance, electricity—used for
artificial lighting, for the tramway, and for the subway, and later on
for telegraph, telephone, radio, and television communications—
and the railways are achievements of the Victorian era from which
we still benefit today. It is true that, at the time, communication
and transportation services were in the hands of private enterprise
and that the latter were more concerned with profit than with the
welfare of the community; it is also true that railways have often
wreaked havoc with the urban fabric, and that the ugly poles carrying electric wires have defaced monuments and landscapes alike.

Yet, fast and even instantaneous means of communication have provided man with a fantastic tool which would utterly change his urban style of life, usually for the better. To mention only electric light and easy communications, who would dream of going back to the state of pre-industrialization? And are we, at the present time, in a position to condemn the effects the steam engine had on urban life in the past when the impact of today's internal combustion engine (in itself a minor invention when compared to the steam engine) is literally destroying us?

Communications—railways, tramways, the telephone, the telegraph—and electricity services providing energy were "visible." "Hidden" services, such as sewers and aqueducts, in the opinion of Briggs,[5] were part of an even more advanced system than the transportation network itself. In Montreal, for instance, the few rather dilapidated wooden ducts which, in the early nineteenth century, distributed water through gravity-feed were replaced at the beginning of the twentieth century by a strongly structured and ramified system with powerful mechanical pumps and huge tanks distributing more than 310 million litres of water daily to over half a million citizens (1912). During the same period, the sewer with its 390 kilometres of brick ducts seems to have functioned equally well.[6] Were it not for excellent networks of that kind, the existence of important urban settlements like Montreal would have been uncertain, if not impossible. That part of the Victorian legacy became so essential to modern urban life that we took it for granted and soon forgot its legator.

Most nineteenth-century towns, whether on this continent or in Europe, have undergone these technical and economic revolutions, enjoying their benefits and suffering their unavoidable consequences. Yet, they did not subsequently merge into stereotyped patterns. On the contrary, except for certain common social characteristics, each town developed its own sense of identity from this exceptional period. Montreal, like Baltimore or Pittsburgh, Birmingham or Manchester, inherited some distinctive features from the Victorian era which have marked the city's identity and character. It is that legacy we intend to analyse in the following pages.

One could easily be misled by these features, however. At first sight all the public or religious monuments described in chapter 8— the Catholic and Protestant cathedrals, the courts, the banks, and the stations—may seem characteristic of Montreal. With the possible exception of some elements which are more regional in character, like Victor Bourgeau's steeples and churches, this is not true. Gothic renewal, neo-classicism, the eclectic and Picturesque styles influenced nineteenth-century architecture in every western country. Montreal's Christ Church Cathedral, for instance, may be considered a prototype reproduced in almost every Canadian provincial capital, in several towns in the United States, and all across the British Empire, including probably Australia. In the same way, every large American town has a bank with a classical pediment like the one designed by our own architect John Wells.

We are more likely to find the distinctive features we are looking for in the overall environment of these monuments or in certain characteristic projects, as for instance in the working-class residential area. Although it is true that Notre-Dame Church in Montreal finds its counterpart in New York's St. Patrick's Cathedral and that the Bank of Montreal is a twin to the Bank of Philadelphia (now the Customs Building) by William Strickland, the fact remains that those Montreal monuments acquire their particular identity from their confrontation on Place d'Armes, where they stand out against one another. One could also contend that Windsor Station presents nothing indigenously unique since it was inspired by the works of Richardson, the great American architect. Standing on the edge of Dominion Square, however, and linked by a green buffer-space to St. George's Church, to Mary Queen of the World Cathedral, and to the romantic Sun Life Building, it represents a unique sample of Victorian architecture.

To learn more about the Victorian legacy, therefore, we must now turn to the study of whole environments and to their structural elements: the street, the square, and the park.

The Environment as a Legacy

Compared with the town of the early nineteenth century, Montreal at the dawn of the twentieth century had changed beyond recognition. The old pattern of development no longer prevailed. The preindustrial city had been static, entirely centred on the physical symbols of religious and civil power. This emphasis, in a way, explains why the parish church of Notre-Dame stood in the middle of Notre-Dame Street, the main thoroughfare: it was the true heart of the city. Then, with the spread of industrialization, the traditional framework exploded, symbolically and physically, to make room for mobility. From now on, the way the city developed would depend more exclusively on economic trends and the dictates of geography. As we have already learned from chapter 7, the people would begin to settle where industries had been established. This move, however, was only temporary, for with the advent of public transport, horsedrawn at first and later electricity-driven, the population scattered across the territory.

The dispersion, eagerly encouraged by real estate and land speculators, was neither planned nor controlled; although public transport services did their best to answer this spontaneous demand, they were not much concerned about orienting it. Thus, farmlands were invaded by the process of urbanization and the original cadastres with long narrow lots grouped into côtes were incorporated into the developing urban environment. As previously established, such was the origin of our grid of streets, which explains the uniformity that was later to prevail in the speculators' developments.

Although we may deplore the permanence of this uniform grid and take exception to its many defects, the fact remains that, in the circumstances, it was probably the simplest possible model and the most appropriate to contain the urban flood within orderly limits. Settlement, henceforth, would no longer be distributed according to a comprehensive pattern centred on the symbols of power; it would be structured in relation to one sole criterion: the access to one's place of work or trade. The physical town no longer illustrated common social and cultural interests inherited from the previous era, and it soon became a huge, anonymous machine, conditioned by the needs for dwellings and for labour. Speculation on land and housing played a significant part in this process. Even though the orthogonal grid superimposed on Montreal was not the outcome of conscious planning, it served the purposes of speculators no less than the grid designed for the streets of New York, for instance, which was the result of a deliberate decision. The plan drafted in 1811 by the Commissioners of New York City was quite explicit in this regard: "A city is to be composed principally of the habitations of men, and that strait sided, and right angled houses are the most cheap to build, and the most convenient to live in."[7]

Though the orthogonal grid in Montreal, as well as in New York, seemed to be the best way to reap dividends for speculators and contractors, it was not flexible enough to follow the natural topography of a rather hilly territory and to make room for some of the social and cultural values cherished by certain communities. What logic was there in maintaining the same grid of streets to ascend Sherbrooke Terrace and the mountain and in extending it through the level surface of Plateau Mont-Royal? The pattern was also bound to generate monotony in urban developments, for it cut across certain contrasting features which might have been utilized more advantageously. We are indeed struck by the fact that except for the cemeteries, Mount Royal Park, and Maisonneuve Park, the city has inherited very few green spaces from its Victorian days, and as for those salvaged from former farming land, they were quite small and subjected to the straitjacket treatment of the grid. Although they may fulfil a useful role nowadays for recreational purposes, their impact on the surroundings, in terms of the contrast they provide, is insignificant when compared with that of wide-open spaces.

One last implication of the grid is its inability to provide public or religious buildings with a site commensurate with their real or symbolic status in the city. Concerning religious buildings, it is common knowledge that the parish has been the foundation of all community life in Quebec, and that the parish church was the physical reflection of that social reality. This is the reason why, in traditional villages, the church is the focal point of the community. Although parishes which were engulfed by the city may have retained some of their rural spirit, as Stuart Wilson pointed out in his comments on the Ontario Terrace,[8] the churches themselves lost some of their grandeur. The building now looked uncomfortable in the middle of rectangular blocks which had little to offer in terms of the right setting for the important social and cultural role of the church. In our view, two distinct realities are intertwined in those situations: one is a sociocultural actuality of communities sharing the same language, the same culture, and—until recently, at least—the same beliefs, which identify with specific institutions such as the church and the school. The other is a physical and economic reality comprising a series of almost identical houses connected to an orderly and anonymous traffic network. These working-class areas, with a high density of approximately 370–495 inhabitants per hectare, used to be and still are "housing machines." They are like a functional organism with interchangeable cells which is dependent on a rigid system of communications.

The Street as a Show
Long, endless streets, looking like impersonal service corridors, are one of the most striking features of Victorian Montreal. There are exceptions, of course, even in the most populated areas; architects like Wilson and Anderson have helped us to discover bits of streets and odd dead ends such as Delorme and Lartigue Avenues which are quite remarkable for the feeling of privacy they convey, for the architectural variety they display within a basic unity, and for the village characteristics they retain right in the heart of the metropolis.[9] These few examples are not numerous enough, however, to dispel the feeling of tension and standardization prevailing in many of the streets of these destitute Victorian districts, especially those located at the foot of the Sherbrooke Terrace or in Pointe Saint-Charles. These streets have obviously been built by speculators and contractors; we are here referring to Champlain, Alexandre-DeSève,

Plessis, Panet, de la Visitation, Beaudry, Montcalm, Wolfe, and so forth, on the one hand, and to Sainte-Madeleine, de la Congrégation, Bourgeois, and Charon on the other hand. One can sense a conflict between the rigid standardization of space, construction, and even colours, and life ready to explode. Some streets in Plateau Mont-Royal as well as some sections of Rivard Street, for instance, seem to bristle with the same tension.

Yet, these areas do not provide a total picture of the Victorian residential world. Those who criticize the industrial town are usually too prone to dwell on a few selected details which they do not take the trouble to relate to an otherwise abundant subject matter. Undeniably, the first industrial areas are quite striking and we find them practically everywhere in towns with similar characteristics. If they are perhaps more conspicuous today, it is probably because they are located mainly in dilapidated zones deprived of any social liveliness by the collapse of the first industries or the encroachments of downtown. The ones that have survived are now at an advanced stage of decay. Anyhow, they show only one facet of the Victorian reality and we cannot ignore other areas which developed around them at that time or later on, and which present rather different kinds of environments, from the very poor to the very prosperous.

Sherbrooke Street is perhaps the best example of an environment which is totally different from what can be seen on Wolfe, Montcalm, and Sébastopol Streets. Today, it has lost its main Victorian features but at the turn of the century it was lined with rich and pretentious residences, competing with each other in idyllic, almost pastoral surroundings. It was very much a green boulevard, a prestigious avenue inspired by the French Second Empire as well as, directly or indirectly, by the residential avenues built in the same style in most large American cities in those days. For this reason Sherbrooke Street has often been called the Fifth Avenue or the Champs Elysées of Montreal.

Off Sherbrooke, there were other equally prestigious streets: Crescent, Hutchison, Sainte-Famille, Laval. Today, residential high-rises have marred this opulent environment, breaking the unity and continuity of its façades, and, sadder still, the trees that used to grace the streets have gradually disappeared. It was Stephen Leacock who recalled that these avenues reminded him of the vaults in a Gothic cathedral.[10] Reverend Borthwick resorts to a similar comparison when he writes that Saint-Denis, below Sherbrooke, "is finely bordered both sides with healthy trees and in summer, looking down, you seem to be entering a long avenue of some sylvan forest or a grand entrance to some ancient castle."[11] Original photographs, taken in the early twentieth century, give us but a faint idea of the visual effect of the leafy domes suspended over thoroughfares like Park Avenue or Drummond Street.[12] Today, de Lorimier Avenue between Sherbrooke and Saint-Joseph is one of the few residential streets to have preserved a sufficient number of tall trees to recreate the feeling of this vanished environment.

Another important characteristic of rich Victorian residential districts was the very picturesque and flamboyant architectural treatment of façades which are easily recognizable by their sawtooth silhouettes. Taken separately, they are often insignificant, heavy, even absurd, and they sometimes display the most atrocious bad taste. Taken as a whole, their very tight texture tends to create an impression of exuberant profusion illustrating the wild optimism characteristic of the Victorian age, an era that was lenient towards those on whom fortune bestowed her graces. Yet, there was a purpose in the midst of all that variety, all that "decorative libido," to use Melvin Charney's picturesque expression;[13] the intention was to decorate the streets, to convert those traffic corridors into a well-identified social environment. Unlike the façades of streets in industrial districts, those of opulent streets were not transparent but resolutely opaque, very ornate screens, and they drew attention from what was going on behind them. From an architectural point of view, these façades were extravagant, and the manner in which they tried in every way to catch the eye is greatly responsible for the disrepute in which Victorian architecture is held. Yet, when we consider the city's plan and its communication system, these streets without an end and these corridors leading nowhere except to other corridors do retain a unique character and assume a role which is not only physical but also cultural and social. (Plates 66 to 69.)

This precious quality of the Victorian street also prevails in the less privileged and more densely populated areas which developed in the early twentieth century on the second terrace, east of St. Lawrence Boulevard—itself a typical offspring of the Victorian age—or in municipalities such as Verdun. Main arteries such as Saint-Denis or Saint-Hubert, or some of the more select avenues such as Cherrier and Laval, may seem somewhat pretentious but the other streets, distinctly characterized by their heavy density and accented by outside stairs, present a physical and social environment that we have only recently started to appreciate. All of Plateau Mont-Royal, which was developed mainly after Queen Victoria's death, is a good example of this specifically Victorian legacy: the streets as an anonymous service corridor from which outside stairs lead directly to dwelling units. The latter enjoy total privacy: they hide behind stone or brick walls, behind the parapets of balconies, behind stair string-boards which through texture and repetition provide a naive but somehow peaceful architectural decor. Façades lending themselves to the character of the streets and architecture for the sake of the passer-by remain constant features of the Victorian environment, as we pointed out earlier in our study of commercial buildings. Those who still need convincing should take a look at the residences located from 3902 to 3928 on Berri Street.

The Square as a Legacy
As a positive contribution of the Victorian heritage the square is just as much a distinctive feature of the heart of our metropolis as the street just described. It is hard to imagine Montreal without Dominion or Saint-Louis Squares. Unfortunately, many such spaces have disappeared today: there were at least twenty of them at the turn of the century and some of those which have survived are but a shadow of what they used to be, three-quarters of a century ago. We specially deplore the loss of Western Square created in 1870, and of Dufferin Square (1871), not merely because they were squares but because their absence today deprives the downtown area of a potential polarization of activities, and certainly of contrasting elements and a freshness and diversity it is now so painfully lacking. Some older squares, such as Richmond (1844) or Viger (built in the same year), are like green oases; they offer a welcome break in an urban setting which is getting more crowded, more stifling, and more dreary as it ages. It is also regrettable that the old respectable gardens, such as Victoria and Phillips Squares, which used to be centres of attraction because of the good landscaping that made them comparable to the most beautiful Georgian squares in London and Dublin, have now been converted: the former into a dull patch of sand used as a doormat for Place Victoria, and the latter into a pedestal for the huge pretentious monument commemorating the reign of King Edward VII the Peacemaker. This statue was unveiled in September 1914. As if it were not enough to crush such a small garden under the weight of such a heavy king, the magnificent elms which embellished the square were shamelessly felled to clear the view.[14]

Today we believe that squares are essential to the life and image of the city; they are necessary to polarize activities, to relate the people to the environment, to rest the eye, and to grace our monotonous urban structure with colour and fresh air; yet, most of our squares were born by accident and those that we now hail as the jewels of the metropolis were seldom the result of a deliberate decision, an express desire, or, even less, of planning. This raises an in-

66.   Left: *The "show street": Laval Avenue, north of Sherbrooke Street*

67.   **Right**: *The "show street": de Lorimier Avenue, south of Mont-Royal Avenue*

68. *Aerial view of Montreal in 1889*

69. *Aerial view of Montreal around 1920*

teresting but ominous point about the importance of the time factor
in the shaping of a town. How many decisions do we make today
without foreseeing their consequences for the city in the year 2100?
For how many omissions will the citizens of the future blame us?
Who can tell whether apparently unattractive sites, still vacant today but earmarked for development, will not become tomorrow's
havens, objects for the admiration of future generations of urban
dwellers? The history of Montreal squares brutally forces these
questions upon us.

Let us analyse the example of Dominion Square. Had it not been a
cemetery—in fact, the Catholic cemetery for the victims of the
1832 cholera outbreak—and were it not for the campaign launched
in 1869 by a health association for its conversion into a park following expropriation by the city, the most popular of our squares might
never have come into being. Its existence, incidentally, was on the
verge of being ruled out before it even started, for the whole cemetery had already been parcelled out into building plots which were
on sale. In fact, building, had been completed on some of the already
sold lots: those parts of the cemetery originally extending west as
far as Stanley Street and eastward onto what was to become the site
of the new St. James Cathedral.[15]

Dufferin Square, located on the south side of Dorchester Boulevard between Jeanne-Mance and Saint-Urbain, and unfortunately
sacrificed to the proposed Complexe Guy-Favreau, was created in
the same manner. From about 1799 to 1847, it was the site of a Protestant cemetery which was expropriated in 1871 at a cost of $20,000
and converted into a square that subsequent generations did not see
fit to preserve.[16] Papineau Square, in the east end of the town, was
also originally a cemetery; today its condition leaves much to be
desired.

Some of the most important squares owe their existence to the
generosity of a few landowners. This is so with Viger Square, the
greater part of which was presented to the city in 1844 by P. Lacroix
and by Jacques Viger, the first mayor of the municipality of Montreal. Other parcels of surrounding land were later purchased by the
city and added to the original nucleus to become the quadrangle that
we know today. Viger Square's main attraction is the local flavour it
adds to an otherwise dull part of the city.[17] Beaver Hall and Phillips
Squares also owe their existence to the generosity of another patron
of the arts, Mr. Alfred Phillips, who presented them to the town in
1842. It should also be noted that a number of these expanses also
came into being as a result of the disappearance of some original settlements: the land thus vacated was wisely preserved.[18] This is how

one of the most beautiful squares in Montreal, Saint-Louis, was created. Its magnificent site was first purchased in 1848 from the Belisle Estate for the reasonable amount of $15,000. A water reservoir was planned for the spot, to serve a community which, at the time, did not extend very far below the Sherbrooke Terrace. In 1878 the plans for a reservoir were discarded and the site was converted into a public garden.

Saint-Louis and Dominion Squares deserve special mention for they are marvellous illustrations of the Victorian urban legacy. Saint-Louis Square is a typical residential square of the romantic days; its general unity of style is reminiscent of the Georgian version but its lavish ornamentation sets it apart. In spite of the unavoidable changes and deterioration it has suffered in the course of the years, the façades surrounding it still vibrate under the ornamental profusion of their architectural details: outside staircases, heavily arched porches, turrets of every kind, protruding dormer windows, bulging cornices. Whether on a sunny day or in the rain, in the morning or in the evening, one can almost breathe the floating fragrances of the past. The place is surrounded by a halo of antiquity which makes it one of the most interesting remains of the romantic urban architecture of the past century, wonderfully softened by its crown of trees. (Plate 70.)

Dominion Square is even more Victorian, for it does not show even a hint of Georgian formality. Like Trafalgar Square in London, it is surrounded by an impressive array of public buildings of various styles; here, however, they are at least related to each other by the green space which they face. Reflecting the taste of those days, it appears like an endearing city-size "bric-à-brac." (Plates 46, 48, 71.) Around this square is found the largest concentration of notable public, religious, and commercial buildings that Victorian architecture ever produced in Montreal. All of them, without exception, have been either referred to or analysed in the previous chapters. St. James (Mary Queen of the World) Cathedral, for instance, is a crystallization of the neo-Baroque trend introduced by Bishop Bourget and is perhaps the only copy in the world of the Basilica of St. Peter's in Rome. Windsor Station is unquestionably the most interesting monument in the square and is also the one in Canada which best reflects the architectural vision of Henry Hobson Richardson. The very beautiful St. George's Church is one of the finest examples of neo-Gothic structures in Montreal or in Canada. The initial Windsor Hotel reflected the cosmopolitanism of Paris in the days of the Second Empire. The Dominion Square and Sun Life Buildings are two commercial edifices which are typically "Beaux-Arts" in their appearance. Today, Dominion Square has lost some of its glamour: the original part of the Windsor Hotel has been demolished and the neighbouring skyscrapers have not only considerably disparaged the cathedral's pride and dwarfed Windsor Station's scale but also disrupted the feeling of spatial unity around the square. In spite of this change and a somewhat constrictive landscaping, the square remains the landmark it has been for a century; as a centre of attraction for pedestrian and vehicular traffic it is a place that generates activities, and is one of the most authentic, magnetic, and magnificent environments in Montreal. Let us recall the impression of a visitor disembarking for the first time at Windsor Station in 1920: "From the moment when first we emerged from the Windsor station and walked up to see the moonlight on the snow in Dominion Square and shining on the dome of St. James Cathedral, we began to be aware of an essence of place unlike any we had ever experienced before."[19]

The Park as a Legacy
The urban park is another legacy of the Victorian era, in Montreal as well as in many other nineteenth-century towns. We must remember that pre-industrial cities had no parks for the simple reason they did not need them; right beyond the ramparts, within fifteen to twenty minutes' walking distance, one could find the countryside in all its beauty and durability. A hundred years later, this happy balance was destroyed. Urban development started to encroach on the natural environment at a frantic pace. Nature had retreated from most citizens; it was no longer accessible by foot, on horseback, or even by tramway. It is at this point that urban parks appeared, in Montreal as elsewhere, created at the urging of philanthropists and social reformers who saw in them an antidote to the aggressive building trends and as a kind of health service, just as essential as aqueducts or sewer sytems. We are not concerned here with the small parks that one finds almost everywhere inserted in our grid of streets; these are residual rural plots that have escaped the urban tide by accident or by stipulations made in a will. We are referring to the large natural park which constitutes a green oasis and is important not only for its romantic and picturesque landscape but also for its function as a soothing place of rest and leisure. At the turn of the century, there were three such parks in Montreal: Mount Royal, Lafontaine, and St. Helen's Island.

The idea of a natural park originated with the English gardens, a great artistic innovation of the eighteenth century apparently initiated by William Kent (1684–1748). Then, around 1800, before any-

70.   *Saint-Louis Square in 1974*

71.   *Dominion Square in 1974*

thing of the kind appeared in America, the Crown, inspired by the writings and the work of Capability Brown, Claudius London, Sir Uvedale Price, Repton, Knight, and a few others, presented the town of London with Regent's Park.[20] It was, indeed, a magnificent and picturesque public ground, with a shape and landscape quite characteristic of the English park. To describe it briefly, the landscaping of this area, as that of English gardens in general, features a large undulating lawn spreading over a vast expanse interspersed with pathways that follow the curves of its natural topography and with trees and bushes which are left to grow in their natural condition.

Without wanting in any way to dispute the genius of Frederick Law Olmsted, we may take for granted that the concept of the natural park was brought to America from England and that Olmsted himself was subject to the English influence, of which he was undeniably the best exponent. His most personal contribution, according to Mumford, was to introduce to America the concept of a "creative landscape" and thus to help the town regain that part of nature it had lost in the course of its evolution.[21]

Montreal's British community, predominant at the time, was rich, powerful, and romantic. Since it was even more concerned than the British themselves with the achievements and the legacy of the mother country, one would be surprised if this group had not wished to provide the town with parks of that kind. Yet, the idea of the picturesque park was slow to evolve and, although the concept itself was imported from England, in actual fact it was the influence of the United States which was to prevail.

The English park aims at providing a natural and romantic setting and a sense of the picturesque as seen through the eyes and emotions of a painter. In America this new concept did not at first materialize into large urban parks but rather into semi-rural cemeteries which were to be found in most larger towns. The landscaping of these cemeteries exerted a predominant influence on the growing trend towards large public parks in urban areas; as well as on the actual design of these parks and even on the plans for the development of certain suburbs.[22] This is true of Montreal as well as of the large American cities. One might argue that long before the romantic cemeteries were ever designed, Montreal had had its large estates such as those of McTavish and McGill. These were private properties and, though they physically resembled parks, they were created mainly to fulfil the need of the new upper middle class to be identified with the old symbols of aristocracy. These estates had little influence on the conception and planning of parks as a social facility destined for the benefit of the urban masses. Until the second half of the nineteenth century, there was no park in the present sense of the word either in the United States or in Canada.

The first large American cemetery, Mount Auburn, was developed in Cambridge, Massachusetts, from 1831 onwards. It had all the characteristics of the romantic layout, including natural ponds, undulating lawns, meandering paths, and clusters of trees and bushes planted at visually strategic places. Its influence was considerable: a short time later, Laurel Hill Cemetery in Philadelphia was created (1836), followed by Greenwood in New York (1838). Laurel Hill in Philadelphia, incidentally preceded by two decades the development, in 1855, of Fairmount Park, probably the first as well as one of the largest public parks in the United States. Greenwood in New York also preceded by several years famed Central Park.[23] In Montreal a similar situation prevailed: the big Protestant cemetery (1852) (plate 72) and the Catholic cemetery of Notre-Dame-des-Neiges (1855) were built on the mountain some two decades before Mount Royal Park.

We can easily understand why a society bent on "laissez faire" and individual promotion would not have been particularly inclined to provide their towns with large natural parks for the welfare of the common man. Yet, this same society would spend enormous amounts of money and spare no effort to improve its cemeteries which, in fact, became the first romantic parks in America, as well as major tourist attractions. Pamphlets published in Montreal at the time invited tourists to visit the Catholic and Protestant cemeteries on Mount Royal and described them as parks of the utmost interest. On the other hand, members of the clergy and devotees condemned this practice and urged the visitors to refrain from considering these places as tourist attractions, a fact which leads us to believe that the cemeteries were indeed attractive. In an era so full of great expectations, death may have appeared as the only unavoidable defeat; the natural reaction was to shut one's eyes and to camouflage reality. The idea must have gained popularity, for the records tell us that entertainment was frequent in those cemeteries, ranging from hunting parties to picnics.

It is interesting to note the way in which the society of that time perpetuated in its cemeteries the same distinction between social classes that prevailed in the world of the living. In a place where all should be equal to face common decay, we find the same social hierarchy, based on worldly possessions: for the poor, the common grave; for the rich, marble tombs. The superb landscaping of this realm of death made it the most romantic and picturesque place in Montreal, especially on the Protestant side. Yet, in spite of this, the city of the living with its patterns of settlement bears upon the city of the dead: the "haves" are not so crammed and they enjoy more greenery than the "have-nots" who seem to be regimented by an orthogonal grid of paths! Robert Furneaux Jordan suggested that the Victorian funeral architecture of Highgate and Brompton cemeteries in London is a world in itself and well worth a study.[24] We might discover that the necropolis is the reflection of the metropolis.

In spite of the fascinating aspects of the cemeteries on the hill and of the important role they played in awakening the people's interest in romantic landscaping and in emphasizing the need for public parks, the fact remains that they unfortunately took up the major part of the site which was unique and had all the necessary potential for the building of a large natural park. In 1852 the cemetery for the various Protestant denominations replaced the one on Dorchester which had grown too small (it was later to become Dufferin Square). This new setting now covers over 100 hectares. The Notre-Dame-des-Neiges cemetery of the Catholic community expanded even further. It started with a purchase of 115 arpents at the time of its inauguration in 1855; it was then considerably enlarged, first in 1865, then in 1872, again in 1907 and in 1909. By 1914 it covered more than four hundred arpents.[25]

Our southern neighbours exerted an even stronger influence on the creation of Montreal's public parks than on the layout of its romantic cemeteries. When the city authorities decided to build on Mount Royal a large natural park copied after Central Park in New York, they hired the most eminent landscape architect of the time to take on the task: Frederick Law Olmsted (1822–1903), an American who may rightly be considered the father of that specialty on this continent. Although his fame remains linked with the concept and completion of Central Park, he was also directly involved in the planning and development of the large urban parks of most of the big American cities, including Brooklyn, San Francisco, Albany, Chicago, Philadelphia, Detroit, Buffalo, Boston, Washington, Louisville, and Milwaukee. He also provided designs for regional parks, university campuses, urban communities, and new towns. He managed to complete this considerable task in forty years of active life, crowning his achievements with a remarkable master plan for the Chicago World Exhibition in 1893.[26]

He worked on Mount Royal Park from 1873 to about 1881 and produced a full-scale master plan, complete with all pertinent recommendations. It reflects all the great qualities which have made a masterpiece of Central Park, even though Olmsted had to work under much worse physical, political, and economic conditions in

72.   *Protestant cemetery*

Montreal. He displayed an innate sense of *genius loci* when he suggested to the Park Commissioners that the best way to use the potential of the site was to improve on nature itself: "All that you have seen and admired of the old work of nature must be considered as simply suggestive of what that is practicable, suitable, and harmonious with your purposes of large popular use."[27] His scrupulous respect for the natural topography of the place, and the way he conceived the project as a whole, at the same time keeping in mind the details, resulted in a very simple arrangement enhancing nature and providing splendid views while preserving privacy. This caused a visitor to say that "To walk in these woods of a snowy afternoon, alone, curtained from the seethe and rumble of the streets below, is to believe illusion. It is impossible that escape from the million could be so easy."[28]

The visionary approach of the park's developers and of its architect harboured some illusions as well. Olmsted explained this when he wrote the following:

> With a little reflection it will be apparent that the property could not have been justly purchased with regard only for the profit to be got from it by a few thousands of the generation ordering it; and that I was bound in suggesting a plan, to have in view the interests of those to inherit it as well as yours; . . . and also to remember that, if civilization is not to move backward, they [these inheritors] are to be much more alive than we are to certain qualities of value in the property which are to be saved or lost to them.[29]

Keeping in mind that Montreal's population in the 1870s numbered a scant 110,000 inhabitants and that the city had hardly reached the slopes of the mountain, one must admit that it took both courage and foresight to expropriate some 182 hectares of land at the cost of one million dollars (an astronomical sum at the time) and to hire the most renowned landscape architect of North America to plan it. (Plate 73.)

Nevertheless, the fact remains that by the scale of today's metropolis, Mount Royal is small. Even at its planning stage, compared with the fashionable romantic parks of the great capitals, Mount Royal, which covered barely 14 percent of the mountain's surface, was one of the smallest, if not the smallest, among them. A few comparisons would make this clear: the Bois de Boulogne and the Bois de Vincennes in Paris, the Prater in Vienna, and Fairmount Park in Philadelphia, each contain more than 810 hectares; Hyde Park in

London, Stanley Park in Vancouver, Belle Isle Park in Detroit, the Golden Gate Park in San Francisco, and Forest Park in St. Louis total over 405 hectares each; and Central Park in New York with its 340 hectares, one of the smallest in comparison with those just cited, covers about twice the surface of Mount Royal Park. Even more revealing, perhaps, is the fact that in 1912 all the parks in Montreal totalled only 326 hectares, an area still smaller than that of Central Park.[30] Moreover, during the past few years, the terrain of Mount Royal Park has constantly been encroached on to make room for projects such as Camillien Houde Driveway or the Pine–Park Avenue intersection. Such a park no longer reflects the vision of a great central pleasure ground contemplated by the fathers of the city a hundred years ago. The present rate of growth and the dwindling of the green-space potential might well turn Olmsted's warning into a prophecy:

> If it [Mount Royal Park] is to be cut up with roads and walks, spotted with shelters, and streaked with staircases; if it is to be strewn with lunch papers, beer bottles, sardine cans and paper collars; and if thousands of people are to seek their recreation upon it unrestrainedly, each according to his special tastes, it is likely to lose whatever of natural charm you first saw in it.[31]

Unlike Mount Royal Park, Lafontaine Park came into being almost by accident, thanks to its first use which allowed the land to be preserved in its natural state; this was also the situation with many other places of public interest which are the pride of Montreal today. In October 1845, at a time when the pressures of urban development had not yet reached the heights of the Sherbrooke Terrace, the colonial government purchased the farm belonging to Mr. James Logan, in order to use it as a military training ground. It was not until 1888 that the federal government, subject to certain terms and conditions, and for a symbolic rent of one dollar per year, handed the land over to the municipality for the purpose of developing a park.

The landscaping of this area, with its two different styles, is a fair reflection of the cultural duality of Montreal. There is the natural and picturesque arrangement in the manner of the English gardens, focused on a pond that follows the channel of a former brook. Then, east of Calixa-Lavallée Avenue, there is a "parc à la française," with linear alleys, smooth, flat lawns cut into geometric designs and carefully framed by beautiful trees lined up in rows. The latter arrangement was allegedly designed by a French town-planner.[32]

It is not so much for its landscaping arrangements, however, that

73. *Mount Royal Park. Frederick Law Olmsted, landscape architect, 1873–81*

Lafontaine Park is remarkable, but rather for its variety and because of the contrasting effects it provides against a built-up environment which happens to be particularly dense and uniform. Unfortunately, here, as in Mount Royal Park, this precious quality is being eroded year after year by various kinds of undoubtedly very useful buildings which are nevertheless gradually undermining the primary character of both parks. Surely, it is a good thing to see them used as well as looked at, but it would be much wiser to choose functions compatible with their specific character (such as riding on Mount Royal Park and rowing in Lafontaine Park), instead of considering every bit of green space as a site available for building facilities for any kind of sport or educational activities. These open areas constitute perhaps the most accessible and the most precious heritage of an idealism of the previous century and we should try to preserve them in their pristine condition by directing the pressure exerted by other kinds of activities towards different open spaces that do not fall into the same category.

Strangely enough, the retrieval of St. Helen's Island as a public park followed the same pattern as that of Lafontaine Park. Once the property of the Barons of Longueuil, the island was purchased in 1818 by the British government in order to set up a military base to protect Montreal, a fact which accounts for the military structures that are still found in that area. Around 1870, the island was handed over to the federal government which authorized the municipality of Montreal to convert the southeast part of it into a public park; the latter was inaugurated in 1874, to the general satisfaction of the public. In 1907 the island was no longer of any military interest and the city was able to purchase it for the fairly reasonable price of $200,000. Following the construction in 1930 of the Jacques-Cartier Bridge, which at last provided easy access to St. Helen's Island, the municipality decided to turn the whole island into a park and hired landscape architect Frederick G. Todd. The work dragged on; it was interrupted by the war, then resumed, and finally completed in 1953, exactly eighty years after the island had first been opened to the public. The result lacked neither quality nor variety; it enhanced the unique location of the island and its romantic charm. This was to be short-lived, for the destiny of St. Helen's Island was to take a new turn after it was selected to become the cornerstone of the 1967 World Fair. We shall return to this in chapter 13.[33]

In brief, as we have learned from the previous chapters, the Victorian era was a boon for our city. The population explosion and urbanization, technical and economic progress, the harbour, the railways and tramways, the industrial areas of Sainte-Anne, Saint-

Henri, and Hochelaga, the Square Mile, the first skyscrapers, and the electric light, all belong to the Victorian era. Again, the monuments we most appreciate, Notre-Dame, Christ Church, Bonsecours Market, the Bank of Montreal, and the City Hall, are Victorian. So are the urban, industrial, commercial, and domestic landscapes that we most often encounter. Most of the problems facing the metropolis today, from downtown congestion to decay in the overpopulated areas, find their roots in the era of "laissez faire." To characterize this age is therefore no easy task, all the more so since it is still prevailing in a certain way, and especially in the attitude of our governing bodies. Yet whichever way we assess that period, we cannot ignore the fact that it was largely responsible for what has become Montreal today. Perhaps we should not pass too harsh a judgement on this era. Although it is true that with the 1850s came the realization that Montreal was in need of large public projects that would combine aesthetics and efficiency if it was to become a city in the full sense of the word, it is equally true that it took but a few decades to see cemeteries, squares, and public parks bring a sophisticated if only partial answer to the objective of the Victorian era.[34]

Part IV

MONTREAL IN THE TWENTIETH CENTURY

Quelle est cette ville
Grandissant au rythme des pulsations électro-
  niques
Montréal qui s'étend comme un vol d'insectes
A la recherche de l'oiseau d'Amérique
Ville fleuve au lit indolent
Océanique enfance des banlieues
Ville parc aux balançoires
Tendues d'enfants libres
Montréal île laissée là ou s'achève la course aux
  terres neuves
Montréal investie comme la porte cochère
D'une froide Amérique
Montréal inlassable
Bâtie à coups de bourse
Sans urbaniste sans architecte
Minerai brut coulé sur le sable
Des fonderies de grands villages
Montréal la gaillarde
Sans robe ni bijou
Etalant sa jeune nudité
Sous le néon des auréoles
Montréal Acropole
D'un prince fou semeur de briques et
  d'aluminium

MICHEL RÉGNIER [1]

12

The Metropolis

It is, indeed, neither city nor country. . . . No longer can it be identified from the outside by its silhouette, clearly set off from the surrounding fields. No longer can it be comprehended from the inside as a system of clearly defined spaces of plazas and streets. It appears as chaos.
HANS BLUMENFELD[2]

A New Reality

In many respects, Montreal today is no longer the Victorian city we have analysed in the previous chapters. It has gradually dissolved into an ever-growing area and has become a metropolis. The present chapter attempts to pinpoint these changes and find out their causes. A bold ambition indeed for a few pages! We shall therefore deal only with aspects that are most likely to reveal the characteristics of the present evolution of Montreal.

During the twentieth century we can witness, in Quebec as well as almost anywhere else, a marked acceleration in the trend towards urbanization. In 1901, 36.1 percent of the population in the province of Quebec lived in the city; in 1971, this percentage had more than doubled, reaching 80.6 percent; according to some projections, in the year 2000 it is expected to be around 90 or 95 percent.[3] Most of the increase has been absorbed by Montreal and the surrounding region: in 1941, 48.6 percent of the total population of Quebec was living in the Greater Montreal area; in 1961, this had risen to 52.4

percent. As for the city itself, we note that in 1901 it numbered 267,730 citizens. In 1971, the latter figure had risen to over one million (1,214,352) as a consequence of demographic growth, the various migrations, as well as the extension of the political and official boundaries resulting from annexations. The urban acceleration has been even more spectacular in the Montreal area, and by this we mean all the territory which the Montreal City Planning Department regards as revolving around the hub of the city's economic, social, and cultural activities. Within the span of two decades, from 1941 to 1961, the population of the area increased by almost 70 percent, jumping from 1,618,000 to 2,757,000 (figure 17). At this rate, a figure of 7,000,000 was once forecast for Greater Montreal before the end of the century.[4]

Trade and communications constitute the true boundaries of this vast area. Its actual borders seem to vary constantly, but the reach of the metropolitan radio and television stations or of the written press seems to provide a good measure of the district, as do also the perimeter within which wholesalers distribute perishable goods, the extent of bus and telephone services, and the maximum distance suburban dwellers are prepared to commute every day. At present, the area covers a surface of about 881,830 hectares, with a 48-kilometre radius starting from Dominion Square at the centre and extending, at the periphery, to municipalities as far away as Saint-Jérôme in the north, Saint-Hyacinthe in the east, Saint-Jean and Iberville in the south, and Valleyfield in the west.[5]

In 1961 the Montreal City Planning Department identified in the heart of the area a more densely populated sector commonly known as Metropolitan Montreal: the economic driving force of the whole region. It is an entity encompassing at the present time the islands of Montreal, Jésus, Bizard, and Perrot; some territory from the counties of Vaudreuil (municipality of Dorion), Deux-Montagnes (municipalities of Saint-Eustache, Deux-Montagnes), Terrebonne (municipalities of Sainte-Thérèse and Rosemère), l'Assomption (municipality of Repentigny), Châteauguay, and the major part of the counties of Laprairie and Chambly. This zone is a world in itself, a social, economic, cultural, and spatial reality transcending the political and official boundaries of its municipalities, whether they be Laval, Mount Royal, Pierrefonds, Lasalle, or Longueuil. Because of the incredibly rapid growth of its population and the latter's distribution over an increasingly large territory, Montreal today emerges as a new reality, a metropolis.[6]

The word "metropolis" in the present instance has obviously nothing to do with Greater Montreal's claim to being the most pop-

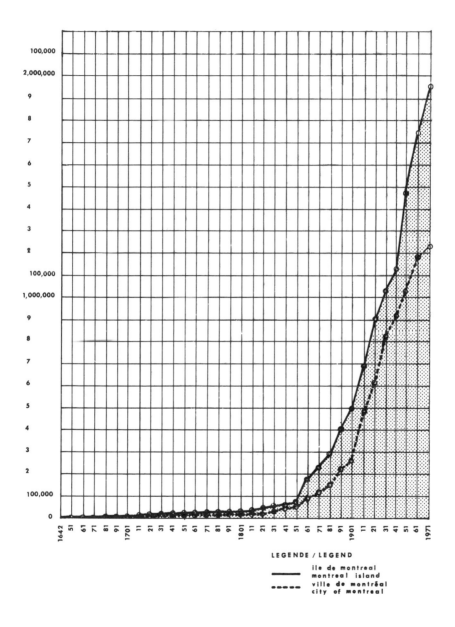

Fig. 17   Population growth on the island and in the city of Montreal

ulated city in Canada in 1974. Rather, it applies to a change in the
very essence of the Montreal area. It means that Montreal has
reached yet another level in its development, a stage that Blumenfeld and Gottmann, together with many other knowledgeable experts, do not hesitate to consider as revolutionary.

Indeed, the metropolis is not simply a more impressive or a more
complicated version of the traditional industrial city, for the well-
defined settlement patterns of the Victorian city and its clear-cut
limits have been replaced by totally different patterns and by a characteristic absence of limitations in general. The idea, for instance, of
developing densely populated residential areas such as those of
Plateau Mont-Royal, or of setting up retail business along traffic-
ways such as Sainte-Catherine, Mont-Royal, or Saint-Hubert Streets,
is now a thing of the past. The fringe of the present urban area presents quite a different picture: its fabric is very loose and the population ratio very low, the settlement pattern is uniform, and services
are concentrated in impersonal centres which are poorly, if at all, integrated into the urban mesh. What has happened?

The nineteenth-century industrial city was the product of technical and economic revolutions which had fostered the telegraph, the
locomotive, the steamboat, and mass production. This contributed
to increased inter-city mobility and led to the concentration of all
activities in privileged centres like Montreal. Yet, because it lacked
adequate means of urban transport and communication, nineteenth-century Montreal still retained its own internal boundaries,
and the lack of accessibility and mobility influenced the structure of
the city. This explains why the first industrial areas in Montreal,
such as Sainte-Anne, Saint-Henri, Hochelaga, and others, developed
along natural or artificial inter-city thoroughfares, and also why
the work force lived in the immediate vicinity of industries and
manufactures.

In the twentieth century, however, telephone, radio, and television made communications instantaneous. The tramway, followed
by the bus and the subway, increased the mobility of the citizens.
In the large cities of North America, elevators, which carry more
people daily than any other means of transport, have replaced the
staircase and its inherent limitations. Lastly, versatile trucks and au-
tomobiles have become the prime means of individual and commercial conveyance. The achievements of modern technology have
liberated the town from its ancestral limitations by transforming
and increasing communications and the intra-urban mobility of
people and goods.

As town planner Hans Blumenfeld has demonstrated, the creation of the metropolis is the result of the interaction of two major forces: a centripetal inter-city pulse which tends to concentrate economic activities and population in the Montreal area, and a centrifugal intra-urban pressure which tends to redistribute the population towards the suburbs within the same area.[7] We shall consider the effects of the latter force in the following pages; but first, let us take a look at Montreal today as a centre of attraction.

Although at the national level it has now come to share its metropolitan prerogatives with Toronto, which has managed to take over the economic leadership, at the provincial level Montreal remains an unchallenged giant. Without indulging in too many statistics, let us simply remember that from 1941 to 1961 the rate of population increase in Greater Montreal rose proportionately faster than that in the province of Quebec or even in Canada.[8] As in the nineteenth century, it is obvious that such a considerable increase cannot be attributed to the birthrate alone and that immigration, and notably migration from the countryside, must have played an important role. In 1971, the number of rural migrants arriving daily in the metropolis was estimated at about one hundred.[9]

Several factors have contributed to maintaining the dynamism of the metropolis. The creation of the St. Lawrence Seaway (1954–59) opened the way to the huge commercial markets of Chicago, Detroit, Toronto, Buffalo, and others, confirming the traditional position of Montreal as a centre for transshipping and distributing freight. At the beginning of the century, about 1000 ships a year, totalling a few million tons, entered our port; in 1965 the National Harbours Board quoted 6,318 arrivals for a total of 21,646,140 tons.[10] In a similar fashion, the development of commercial aviation has contributed to Montreal's position as a centre of attraction. The city is the world capital of aviation, having been selected as the headquarters of the International Civil Aviation Organization and the International Air Transport Association. With the new airport at Mirabel, the city is provided with one of the most impressive such facilities in the world. Furthermore, the development of a modern road network undertaken in the past few years is an incentive to the concentration of industries in our area. The availability of inexpensive and abundant hydroelectric power and the presence of a large and willing labour force ready to adjust to new techniques are conducive to the introduction of more elaborate production systems.

A New Pattern of Industrial Settlement
In the Victorian city, as we already know, industries followed a very simple pattern of settlement. Those involved in processing raw ma-

terials, such as metalwork industries, sugar refineries, flour mills, and textile mills, settled along the port, the Lachine Canal, and the railways. The secondary industries, such as tanneries, textile plants, and tobacco factories, were less dependent on heavy transport and thus established themselves where both labour and a market were available. As for the service industries, as yet little developed, they were confined to the Coteau Saint-Louis with a few extensions in the direction of the main railway stations.

With the improvement of intra-urban means of communication and transport, and with the acquisition of new sources of energy, namely petrol and electricity, this pattern of industrial settlement has now become more complex. Although certain industries of the primary group—the petrol refineries of Montreal East, for example—remain dependent on the railways and the port, others (especially in the secondary sector) avail themselves of the new means of communication and sources of energy to locate wherever they have a better chance of maximizing their efficiency and their profits. Nowadays, their pattern of settlement is influenced by various factors: the availability of space required by modern production methods (in view of foreseeable expansion), the wish to avoid congestion and to escape the taxes levied in the central urban zones, the need to minimize transport costs and to be closer to the customers, to available manpower, and to complementary industries, or, lastly, the existence of private or municipal industrial parks, adequately served by the new intra-urban communication network.[11]

Since World War II these industries as a whole show a definite trend towards settling along the main thoroughfares of the island and region, such as the Laurentian autoroute, the Trans-Canada Highway, the Metropolitan Boulevard, Côte-de-Liesse Road, or the Montreal–Toronto Road. Besides, the road often complements the other means of transport: witness the Côte-de-Liesse sector, which is about to become one of the main industrial zones of the metropolis thanks to its position near Dorval airport and to the railway and highway networks.[12]

An interesting aspect of the pattern of industrial settlement is the recurrence of the traditional axial trends engraved in the geography of the Montreal territory. Here again, the island's old vocation as a key to the West is reasserted through this new communication network: for instance, the Trans-Canada Highway and the Metropolitan Boulevard. Moreover, as already demonstrated, the layout of this modern infrastructure of expressways often exactly, or almost exactly, duplicates that of the old king's ways built on the côtes at the very beginning of the colonial settlement. Such is the position, for instance, of the major part of the Trans-Canada Highway, the Metropolitan Boulevard, and Côte-de-Liesse Road.

In spite of the essential part it played in the development of Greater Montreal, we must remember that the processing industry accounts for only about one-third of the labour force today. From 1940 onwards, it would be surpassed by the service industry which includes public and private administration, transport and communications, banking, financial, and commercial activities, hotels, education, research, culture, and recreation. A glance at the Central Business District would demonstrate the importance for Montreal of this tertiary sector and its impact on the urban fabric. Its boundaries, as set by the Montreal City Planning Department, are Pine Avenue to the north, Saint-Denis Street to the east, the river and Lachine Canal to the south, and Guy Street to the west. This very large territory, of some 535 hectares, is the most important in the metropolis because of the quality, the quantity, and the variety of businesses established within its boundaries. It sets the tone for the whole Montreal area.[13]

The district grew gradually, horizontally as well as vertically. At the end of the Victorian era, the financial and commercial business sector was still confined to the old Coteau Saint-Louis and was mainly centred on Notre-Dame and St. James Streets. It was to assume a new dimension with the construction of the large railway stations of Viger, Bonaventure, and Windsor, which, by attracting hotels and other related activities, gave it a new start. Around the same time, in 1892, Birks and Morgan and other dynamic merchants moved their premises to Sainte-Catherine Street, which, by 1910, had become the main commercial thoroughfare in town; until then it had been almost exclusively residential. The business district was split into two sections: the financial transactions remained centred on St. James Street, whereas commercial firms flocked to Sainte-Catherine Street.

Today, the most striking feature of this area is its heavy concentration of skyscrapers; it is perhaps the most spectacular development in Montreal in the twentieth century. The impact of those tall buildings on the image and the identity of our metropolis was probably just as significant as the impact of industry on the Victorian city. The figures indicating the growth in floor space available in the business area for the service industry speak for themselves: the surface in office buildings increased by 77 percent between 1949 and 1962, leaping from 1.05 to 1.88 million square metres. Floor space for administrative and government functions expanded by 31 percent, rising from 0.33 to 0.44 million square metres. For the same

period, hotels added about 0.18 million square metres to an estimated 0.25 million square metres, for an augmentation of 53 percent. Cultural and recreational activities show a similar increase of
32 percent.[14]

The concentration of all these functions is the result of a combination of several factors. Because such activities cater to a sizeable
regional, national, and even international market, they have to be
grouped in a place of maximum accessibility like the downtown
area. Factors like prestige, complementarity, and the fact that each
business benefits directly or indirectly from the presence of others
also come into play. For certain functions, such as administration or
finances, centralization is a prerequisite for optimum operating conditions. In this respect, what location could be better than the heart
of downtown, which reaches out to every part of the metropolis?
Efficiency demands centralization and the concentration of business
activities; this latter aspect is obviously reflected in the size of the
downtown buildings.

This double feature of concentration and centralization is certainly not unique to Montreal; it is found in Toronto, Chicago, and
New York as well. What is typical of Montreal, however, is the fact
that these functions tend to gather downtown around the plazas and
public squares inherited from the past centuries. This trend is by no
means recent. The large railway stations, Viger and Windsor, date
back to the end of the previous century when they were built on
Viger and Dominion Squares respectively. The first tall building
erected in Montreal (a skyscraper in those days), the New York Life
Insurance Company, which today houses the main branch of the Société de Fiducie du Québec, was put up in 1887 on the old Place
d'Armes. It was to be matched some decades later by the Aldred
Building, bordering on the same square. Meanwhile, the Windsor
Hotel, a prestigious building for its time, was being constructed on
the west side of Dominion Square. It was soon to be followed, along
the same green rectangle, by the two largest commercial edifices of
the beginning of the century: the Sun Life and the Dominion Square
Buildings.

Since the economic boom of the fifties, these public squares have
become more and more attractive as places of prestige, with the result that downtown business is now heavily concentrated around
them. As a matter of fact, functions concentrated in the Central
Business District, and indicating a floor-space index of 4.0 and over,
are mainly located around those squares.[15] Without making an exhaustive list of such skyscrapers, let us mention the Bank of Mon-

treal and the Banque Canadienne Nationale Buildings on Place d'Armes, the Court House at the edge of the Champ-de-Mars, the Stock Exchange Tower on Victoria Square, and on the periphery of Dominion Square, the Place du Canada, the Laurentian Hotel (demolished in 1978), and the Canadian Imperial Bank of Commerce.

It is evident that not all business functions can be located around such prestigious sites. As we shall find out in the next chapter, the acquisition of building rights above the former railway installations in the downtown area have had some influence on the latter's renovation. The widening (in 1955) of Dorchester, formerly a residential street, changed it into a traffic boulevard; it was a determining factor in the development of this new commercial canyon with its tall landmarks such as the Hydro-Québec Building, CIL House, the Queen Elizabeth Hotel, and others. Thus, we may consider the regrouping of those great promoters of activities around the public squares of our past as a specific pattern of the Montreal downtown area.

A New Residential Pattern
The changes in the pattern of industrial implantation in the course of the twentieth century are paralleled by similar transformations in the type of dwellings and in their pattern of settlement. In the nineteenth century, the rich used to build their houses wherever they pleased whereas the working class tended to congregate in areas close to employment opportunities. Railways and waterways had contributed to some extent towards the structure of the new urban satellites such as Lachine or Hochelaga–Maisonneuve. However, the development of an intra-urban mass-transport system, the steady growth of the population, fluctuating foreign immigration, and the uninterrupted flow of rural migration would soon generate residential areas which became the working-class suburbs of the time. The population of the latter, which were distributed as a crescent around a buffer zone of poverty that surrounded the old city, increased to a high density as a result of the limitations of mass transport, whether horse-drawn or electric-driven. Our analysis, in this connection, of the built-up areas of Plateau Mont-Royal with their typical dwellings leads us to believe that they are truly representative of the patterns of residential settlement prevailing at the end of the previous century.

It is obvious that radical changes have taken place when we compare the previous century's housing to today's downtown residential towers and suburban detached family units. These shifts may be attributed to the improvements in intra-urban and inter-urban means of transport and communications, to the subway, the bus, the telephone, the radio, the television, and, above all, to the automobile and a modern network of roads. Within the span of two decades, from 1951 to 1971, the percentage of households owning a car in the metropolitan area has more than doubled, from 27.8 to 68.1 percent. This revolution in communications was undeniably of prime importance, but it shares with other factors the responsibility for changes in the types of dwellings and in the patterns of settlement.[16]

Thus, the gradual changes in the structure of the family constitute the factor which most contributed to alter the Victorian type of dwelling. Indeed, in the course of the last decades, the family cell has considerably shrunk, in the sense that the number of people living under the same roof has continually decreased. Several causes account for this trend, among which falling birthrates and the erosion of family traditions are the most commonly mentioned. However, the overall rise of income levels and social benefits also contributed to the fragmentation of the old monolithic family structure. Thus, early marriages became more frequent. In Canada, in 1941, the percentage of married individuals over the age of 15 was 57 percent; in 1961, it had risen to 66 percent. The same factor resulted in the gradual decrease of the "three-generation" or "double" family living under the same roof. Their number was almost halved in Montreal, between 1951 and 1961. Another element which is also related to the increase in incomes and social benefits is the growing number of non-family households made up of individuals residing alone, whether young or old: unmarrieds, widows, or divorcees who have decided to live on their own.[17]

As a consequence of the growing number of small households there was an added need for small, compact, and well-equipped units for occupants who would normally be busy working elsewhere and would thus be unable to spend much time on maintenance. These units are generally located in the city, near the city centre, or along main roadways providing fast access to downtown. Indeed, young people or adults without dependents do not feel the urge to live in spacious suburbs as much as the need for easy access to work, not to mention the fascination exerted by the downtown area. In fact, from 1951 to 1961, the increase in the number of non-family households in the municipality of Montreal alone was three times that of their corresponding growth in the rest of the metropolitan area. Furthermore, in 1961, almost 25 percent of the town's population was made up of individuals who were living independently from their family.[18] Of course, lone individuals are not the only ones who live by choice in densely urbanized surroundings; this tendency is partly shared by small families of two or three. However, as the size of the family grows this trend decreases, as we shall see later.

The demand for small housing units resulted in a gradual transformation of the large homes inherited from the Victorian era. The remodelling of large units into several compact ones is now common practice, especially in the urban-core sectors which are desirable because of their easy access to the downtown area, the charm of their surroundings, and the quality of their traditional buildings; these advantages offset somewhat the parallel pressure of property taxes. Of the large residences built along the old Square Mile or in its neighbourhood, very few have escaped these renovations.[19] Here, we need no statistics: the facts speak for themselves. Those dwellings are unfortunately but not unexpectedly deteriorating rapidly because of an increase in the density of population and a lack of interest in the old homes on the part of tenants and landlords alike.

This is only one aspect of the situation. The thrust of the residential towers is, visually, even more dramatic. Real estate corporations and speculators prefer investing in modern high-rise apartments rather than converting traditional residences because the value of the land on which the latter are built is often much greater than the potential dollar value of the old structures. In the better urban sectors, the price of land per square foot is often higher than the gross cost of equivalent floor space for traditional construction. On the other hand, the use of new building techniques (steel and concrete), of new heating and ventilation systems, and of powerful electric elevators have made the construction of high buildings possible, thus bringing down the value of land per square foot to 10 to 50 percent of the price of the gross floor space of these high-rises.[20]

It is interesting to note the permanent influence of the older structures and former patterns of settlement on the establishment of the new residential towers. For instance, Sherbrooke Street, which had been the most fashionable street of the last century (towards the west end in particular), has attracted a great many of these high-rises. The oldest among these are Le Château, the Linton, the Acadian, whereas Cantlie House, Le Cartier, and Port-Royal are some of the most recent. Côte-des-Neiges Road is another characteristic artery; built at the beginning of the colony (1698) as a link to the fortified Ville-Marie, it has been adorned during the last fifty years with many of these towers: the most architecturally successful are probably the Rockhill Apartments completed towards the end of the sixties.

The selected abode of the wealthy Victorians, the old Square Mile, was not spared the invasion of the high-rises either. The exceptional qualities of this hillside location and its proximity to the main traffic arteries, to the subway, and, better still, to the downtown area with its active life and entertainment have attracted a clientele interested in living right in the heart of the city; this eventually induced the municipal authorities to pass zoning regulation No. 2812, promoting housing—unavoidably high-profit lodgings—and banning any other function. As a result traditional streets such as Hutchison and Durocher, remarkable for their picturesque surroundings, are losing their scale and character. This erosion can only grow worse, especially if more projects like Cité Concordia materialize.

Parks are another urban element inherited from the previous centuries that now attract residential high-rises. Lafontaine Park, which will soon be almost surrounded by such towers, is a good example.

The development of high-rises as a favoured type of housing, resulting from drastic changes in the family structure, and their concentration in certain appropriate sectors of the town constitute one of the two basic aspects of residential settlement in the metropolis. Opposing this centripetal force, a centrifugal pull tends to channel a considerable number of families towards the detached single-family units in the suburbs.

Consider the following data: in 1941 two-thirds of the population of the Montreal region was still living within a 6.5-kilometre radius of the centre. By 1961 the same population would be spread over a 13-kilometre radius. The expansion follows a pattern of concentric zones gradually encroaching on the surrounding countryside. Between 1941 and 1951 the highest rate of increase was found in areas located 6.5 to 10 kilometres from the centre, where the population more than doubled. In the course of the following decade, the increase was felt mainly in sectors extending 8 to 30.5 kilometres from the centre and where the population grew by some 146 percent.[21]

Unfortunately, it is the large rural plain of Montreal, an area with the best farming land in the province, which is bearing the brunt of the steady progression of construction. In 1941 a Montreal citizen could still enjoy all the low-density characteristics of country living at the limits of a 14.5-kilometre radius from the centre. A mere twenty years later, he had to travel up to 40 kilometres to find the same rural environment.[22] This is due not just to the increase in the urban population; it also reflects a more liberal use of the land which is the direct result of speculation. In 1964 it took twice as many hectares (39) of land to absorb a population increase of 1000, compared with 20 hectares in 1952.[23] Such low-density expansion gradually contributed to bringing down the average population concentration in the metropolitan zone and on Montreal Island in the present century, in spite of the increasing convergence of small households and families to urban high-density residential towers. This fact is demonstrated by the following figures: for the total metropolitan area, the population density fell from 79 residents per hectare in 1907 to 69 in 1961. A similar downward trend applies to the island of Montreal: 82 residents per hectare in 1907 and only 69 in 1961.[24]

This flow towards the outskirts and the gradual decrease in density are due mainly to the settlement in the suburbs of middle- and large-sized families. For many years now, statistics indicate that the larger the size of the households, the more they tend to move away from the centre of town towards the periphery.[25] One last figure: in 1961 residents under the age of 20 accounted for almost half of the population of the metropolitan area outside the boundaries of the municipality of Montreal.[26]

Middle- and large-sized families are said to be attracted to the suburbs because the latter provide a better environment for the children's education. However, there is a more basic reason: these peripheral sectors are now easily accessible by cars and other means of rapid transit which have improved the mobility of people and goods and reduced distances. Again, these reasons should be assessed in relation to other factors which have encouraged the exodus towards the urban outskirts.

Undeniably, the gradual improvement in the standard of living of the middle class has enabled it to enjoy private ownership, which usually takes the form of a standard detached family unit on a lot 15 to 18 metres by 27 or 40 metres. Indeed, large-sized families that do not normally follow this migration pattern are usually forced by low income to remain in older areas, the only places where adequate housing is available at a low cost.[27] On the other hand, for the average-income families, privacy and space around the house for the children are cheaper on the metropolitan periphery than in the town itself where density is higher and land more expensive. Real estate firms and speculators have been taking advantage of this situation and, through extensive use of the press, radio, and television, have managed to create and maintain the myth of the suburb and the suburbanite. One might suppose that, as time passes, the benefits of living in the suburbs would dwindle to the point of often being cancelled out by the cost of commuting and by the absence of adequate social and cultural facilities. True as this may be, the image of private lawns, garden parties, schools set in parks, and neat and functional shopping centres is deeply rooted and cultivated in the consumer's mind. Publicity and speculation are joint partners in this venture and it would be an error to ignore them as factors in the migration of families towards the periphery.

Among other agents which have influenced this migration, we should mention the gradual decrease in the amount of time spent in productive work. The periods that a suburbanite is now able to devote to enjoying and maintaining his residential environment justify his investment and make up for the hours wasted in commuting. Tunnard and Reed point out that, in the United States, life in the suburbs remained the privilege of the rich until about 1930, that is, until the forty-hour week became a universal practice and replaced the sixty-hour week still generally enforced in the first decades of the twentieth century.[28]

At first sight, the peripheral expansion in the metropolitan zone of the detached unit does not seem to follow any definite plan or structure; it appears to have been ruled only by the speculators' and contractors' interests. However, a closer scrutiny shows that the areas of concentration as well as the axial parameters were determined by the initial network of towns and villages as well as by their web of communications. The simple fact, for instance, that there was a belt road surrounding Montreal Island and connecting the older settlements has obviously contributed, from World War II onwards, to extending the suburban expansion around the island's periphery even before the centre was fully settled.

Once better communications were effected with the centre of Montreal, new suburban residential settlements, which so far had depended on the services of already established communities, began to develop at an incredible pace. The many bridges connecting the island to the mainland played a definite role in the expansion of budding communities such as Chomedey, Laval-des-Rapides, Pont-Viau, Duvernay, and the great Laurentian axial way (Vimont, Sainte-Thérèse, Saint-Jérôme, etc.), as well as Longueuil, Saint-Lambert, Saint-Bruno, Brossard, and others on the south shore. The latter only started prospering after the inauguration of Harbour Bridge (Jacques-Cartier Bridge) in May 1930. Today, with a subway station as its bridgehead, Longueuil has become practically a suburb of downtown Montreal.

Even though it was guided by existing structures, this kind of uncontrolled expansion had one negative result: it disrupted once and for all the balance achieved on the island and in the metropolitan area between the "tight" and the "spread-out" patterns of habitation. The process of erosion and growing uniformity, which began with the industrial era, has now reached its logical conclusion: an amorphous urban magma, devoid of any structure or identity, is now threatening to engulf whatever is left of the rural space and natural landscapes. A dissolving tide which has already destroyed the charm of the old island villages, such as Pointe-aux-Trembles, Sault-au-Récollet, Sainte-Geneviève, Sainte-Anne-de-Bellevue, Pointe-Claire, and Saint-Laurent, is now undermining the identity of still more distant communities, including Saint-Eustache, Boucherville, and Laprairie. This is the price we have to pay for real estate speculation, a fact we are only too inclined to forget. (Figures 18 to 27.)

Attempts at Planning
Considering the powerful and contradictory trends, whether centripetal or centrifugal, which are now shaping our urban world, we wonder if urban planning played any part in the development of our modern metropolis. Although scientific city planning is a product of the twentieth century, it seems to have reached Canada somewhat later than other countries. As a matter of fact, it did not play any major role in Montreal. A few preliminary attempts at drafting guidelines never really resulted in any compulsory plan. A short analysis of these attempts, nevertheless, might throw some light on the matter.

There are, in the course of Montreal's history, some local developments which were indeed planned and which demonstrate at least some concern for organization. Dollier de Casson, for instance, had drafted a kind of master plan for the city on Coteau Saint-Louis. Similarly, the commissioners charged with pulling down the eighteenth-century fortifications produced a plan for the renovation of the sectors concerned. We shall see, in the following chapter, that the most spectacular development achieved in Montreal in the twentieth century, the creation of a new downtown centre (beginning with Place Ville-Marie), was the result of first-rate planning. Let us consider, for the time being, the Town of Mount Royal, the "Cité-jardin," and the new Nuns' Island project, all the result of advance planning.

The origin of the Town of Mount Royal may be traced to a large real estate deal which took place in 1911. In that year, two high-ranking officials of the Canadian Northern Railway, Sir William Mackenzie and Sir Donald Mann, who wanted to be assured of station and terminal facilities in Montreal for their railway, made a substantial purchase of property in the city. It included the land on which Place Ville-Marie, Central Station, and Place Bonaventure stand today, as well as 2,307 hectares of rural acreage to the northwest of Mount Royal. They intended to dig a tunnel through the

mountain to bring the railway directly into the heart of the city and
to build a pilot city on the other side of the hill. This project en-
tailed, of course, very large profits based on the increased value of
land, which was now accessible, and on a steady flow of railway customers. The 5-kilometre-long tunnel, together with a blueprint for
the new suburb, was completed in October 1918.[29]

The layout, which drew its inspiration from various sources,
shows the influence of Ebenezer Howard, the father of the garden-
city concept. The star-shaped intersection of the long boulevards in
the heart of the town is reminiscent of the Paris avenues designed
during the Second Empire. The diminutive station standing right in
the middle of the intersection, however, ruins this ambitious perspective and deprives the plan of its original intent. The layout of
the residential area, with its curved and circular streets, is the direct
offspring of the romantic designs which were first created for cemeteries and public parks and finally became a model for architects engaged in the planning of residential suburbs. Other municipalities
like Hampstead and Saint-Michel were to follow the lead, though
not quite so successfully or on such a large scale.

Today, the Town of Mount Royal is looked upon by some people

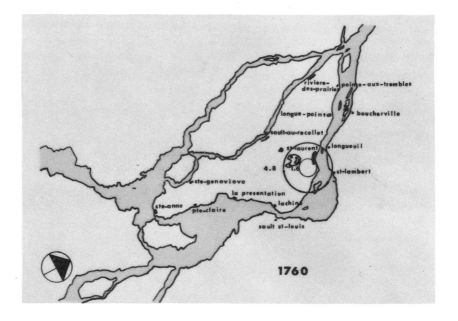

Fig.18　Urban growth, 1760

as a mere enclave of the privileged few; its landscape has lost some of its original spark, and the pioneer role it once played as a model for residential planning is now mostly forgotten. The Cité-jardin has also been forgotten, although the principles on which its planning rests go far beyond those involved in the Town of Mount Royal. The plans were drawn up in the early forties by Auguste Gosselin and Father Jean d'Auteuil Richard, S.J., both laymen in that particular field. Their purpose, based on moral, social, and economic grounds, was to provide working-class people with a healthier environment than the kind of surroundings they usually had to live in. This development (to the northeast of Maisonneuve Park) was plagued all along with all sorts of frustrations. Only one-fourth of the original plan was ever completed. However, it came very close to matching the qualities that have contributed to the fame of Radburn (New Jersey), by Clarence S. Stein and Henry Wright, which is a masterpiece of community planning. Like Radburn, Cité-jardin aimed at limiting motor traffic to a minimum, and at enforcing a practical segregation between the flow of pedestrians and the traffic of vehicles. It was designed to leave as much space as possible for playgrounds and parks which would be open to the public. All streets

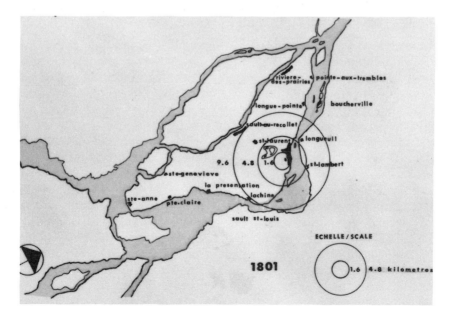

Fig.19   Urban growth, 1801

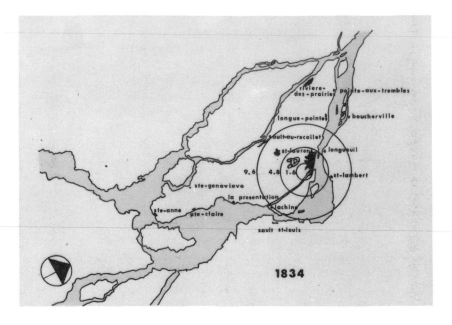

Fig.20   Urban growth, 1834

were dead-end, and there were no sidewalks. Pedestrians could opt
for a parallel network of roads traced after a simple and flexible pattern. In the opinion of Paul Ritter, author of the well-known book
Planning for Man and Motor, Cité-jardin "works as well, or better,
than any other traffic-segregated scheme I have seen in any country."[30] This is indeed flattering, but considering what is at present achieved in our suburbs, whether Ville d'Anjou, Saint-Léonard,
Ville de Laval, or the South Shore, it is clear that the lesson of Cité-
jardin has been totally ignored, almost as if it had never even been
acknowledged.

The only residential planning that might rival Cité-jardin is the
development of Nuns' Island, a 405-hectare reserve on the St. Lawrence River to which access was provided when the Champlain
Bridge was built in 1962. Designed to accommodate a potential
50,000 residents, it is based on the well-known concept of articulated neighbouring units: there are three main residential communities, clustered around a small town centre. The master plan, designed by Johnson, Johnson & Roy of Michigan, is good. It takes into
account the visual potential of the site and provides for an integrated traffic network which applies the principle of pedes-

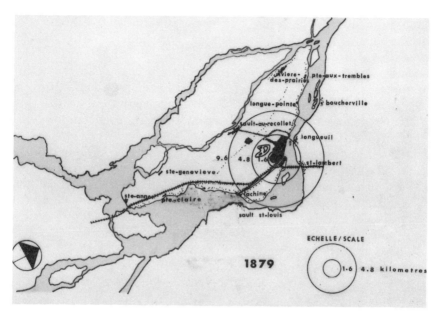

Fig.21   Urban growth, 1879

trian–vehicle segregation. However, it is not in any way specific to our Canadian environment, for it has already been successfully applied to the new postwar cities of England, such as Stevenage, now thirty years old. Moreover, it will take a few more decades before it is permeated with an authentic life of its own.[31]

The first attempt at any overall planning for Montreal was a tentative master plan drafted in 1944. It was the outcome of long and considerable efforts to prepare the ground and educate the public, going as far back as 1909 when the City Improvement League was founded to promote the idea of a master plan that would control the growth of Greater Montreal. In 1921 an amendment to the city's charter set up a planning commission with a mandate to make suggestions and recommendations for the improvement of the city. Committees and commissions followed one another, but it was not until May 1941 that the Montreal City Planning Department was established on a permanent basis, as were the Departments of Health, Public Works, and Finances. Its purpose was twofold: it was to prepare a master plan that would provide for the orderly development of the city as a whole, while at the same time controlling settlement patterns and other related activities.[32]

Strangely enough, the 1944 blueprint suffers from a lack of any regional perspective. The same applies to the solution it proposed for land use and traffic patterns. The proposed traffic network, for one, seemed aimed at relieving the existing thoroughfares rather than at providing a structural framework. It resulted in confusion as to the specific functions and character of the various arteries. In some instances, heavy traffic was diverted to areas and municipalities of a highly residential character. Although conceived in the forties, this plan does not seem to have foreseen the importance of motor vehicle transport, thanks to the internal combustion engine. The industrial zoning it proposed was merely an extension of the existing industrial areas, which were all connected to waterways or railways. On the other hand, the mass-transit network was well integrated. The initial plan suggested for a subway, as well as for its potential extension, was very close to our present route, adopted two decades later, and to the additional lines contemplated for the future.

There are other suggestions worth mentioning in that preliminary draft. One was the idea of reclaiming the island's shores to convert them into parkways. Had it been achieved, even on a very limited scale, it would have been a positive and particularly welcome

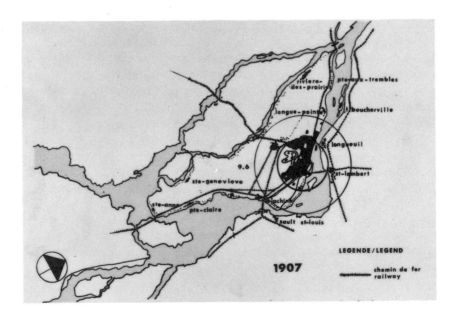

Fig.22 *Urban growth, 1907*

contribution today, since this project seems less and less probable as the years go by. The same remark applies to the proposal for building similar parkways along administrative boundaries of the city core. The latter suggestion perhaps was not very realistic, and the pressures of development probably would have made the completion of such a network impossible. Nevertheless, the slightest green space that such a policy might have preserved would have been a welcome contribution to an area which needs them so badly today.

To conclude the present analysis, we must concede that, in spite of its good points, the master plan remained a prisoner of the traditional image of Montreal, that of an industrial town, structured in the days when its survival depended on steam and water. Our present metropolis has now outlived that state. However, the planners do have a valid excuse: in the early forties, the growth rate was very low in Montreal, following several decades of economic stagnation resulting from two world wars and from the great depression. This may well have influenced their vision of the future.[33] (Plate 74.)

A more realistic and flexible approach was later to be provided by the municipal town planners and technicians who, in August 1967, submitted a new draft called "Horizon 2000." It was based on the

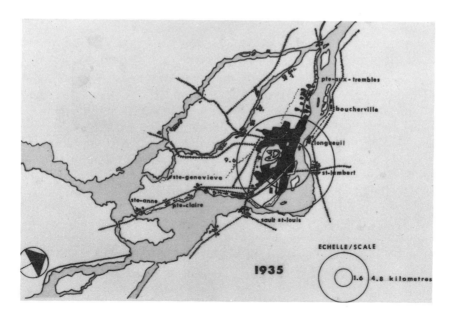

Fig.23   Urban growth, 1935

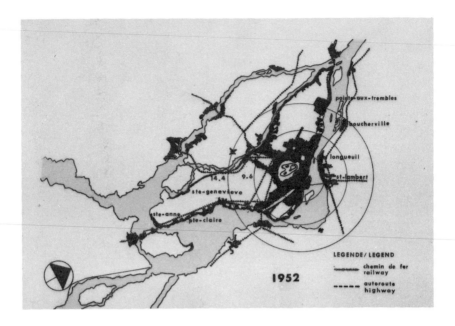

Fig.24   Urban growth, 1952

premise that the urban reality of Montreal is a demographic, economic, social, cultural, and spatial reality that goes far beyond the
artificial boundaries which put its municipalities into a political
and legal straitjacket. The new draft tried to take into account the
fact that by the time we reached the year 2000, Greater Montreal
would be housing about seven million people, with an approximate
per capita income of $3,300, and with some 3,200,000 cars. Its pur-
pose was to provide the citizens of the future with an organized
framework that would enable them to live, work, move around, and
enjoy leisure under the best available conditions which can only be
achieved by respecting the physical characteristics of the site, its resources and opportunities, its existing activities, its historical and
geographical values, and also its economic ties with the rest of the
world.

To achieve this purpose, the draft suggested a regional structure of
development, oriented along two axial lines. The first one would be
an axis of economic growth determined by the river; it would cover
all the economic activities likely to benefit from the presence of the
river, such as port operations, industries depending on water transport or needing large quantities of water. This shaft would even-

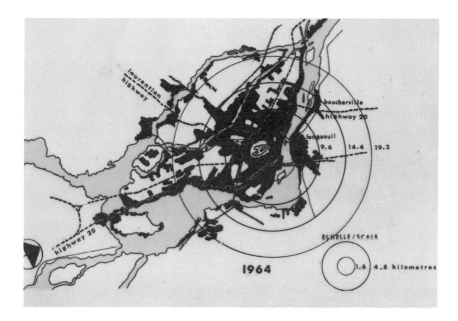

Fig.25 Urban growth, 1964

tually extend from Valleyfield all the way to Sorel–Tracy. Perpendicular to this "heavy" axis would be a "light" one of demographic growth with light industries and tertiary services. It would extend on both sides towards such important recreation areas as the Laurentians and the Eastern Townships. At the intersection of the two axes, the City of Montreal proper, surrounded by a dozen municipalities, would become the heart and motor of the whole area.

As a matter of fact, this draft respects all the present development trends. One new idea it incorporates consists of adding many urban cells to the existing regional skeleton. They would consist of large concentrations of population polarized around centres providing the social animation and services needed for the economic, social, and cultural demands of life. Such functional units would be partly self-sufficient and would gravitate around their central hub of exchange; they would act as catalysts for populations now scattered without any order or coherence throughout nondescript suburbs. Such a structure, supported by an appropriate policy, would also help to reclaim land suitable for farming or recreation. Beyond these urban units, satellite towns such as Valleyfield, Saint-Jean, Saint-Hyacinthe, Sorel, Joliette, Saint-Jérôme, and Lachute would play a similar role for the peripheral populations. It has already been forecast that within the next twenty-five years each of these satellite towns will be catering to the needs of 150,000 to 300,000 people.

Communications with and within that large metropolis, spread as a galaxy, would be provided through both public and private transport networks; each system would preserve its own speed and specific characteristics but all of them would complement each other for an overall more efficient use. The emphasis, however, would be on public transport. Thus, the main regional centre would gradually be equipped with a complex subway network that would cover 160 kilometres by the year 2000. As for the urban cells, they would be linked to each other as well as to the central core by an appropriate network of highways supplemented by a regional service of express buses (two main lines: Sainte-Adèle to Saint-Hyacinthe; Rigaud to Joliette) and commuter trains.[34]

Thus, far from trying to slow down the growth of the metropolis—which was already foreseeable in the long run—the pilot plan attempts rather to provide for a framework ensuring a regional balance between the heart of the city and its satellites. It is also a very flexible plan. It implicitly acknowledges that, although people have

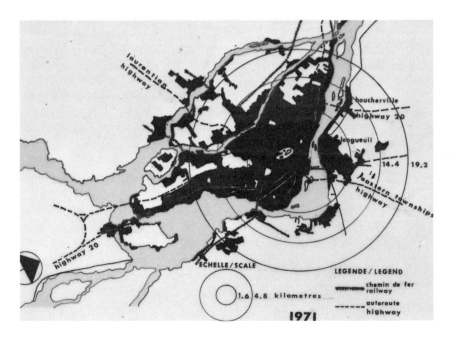

Fig.26   Urban growth, 1971

to earn a living, they have the right to live as they please and to choose the place where they wish to reside and the means of transport they want to use. The draft, therefore, constitutes a mere guideline; it simply tries to inventory the interactions of the varied urban activities and to regulate them so that they complement each other instead of being competitive. And although it is respectful of existing trends, it emphasizes the physical features which are specific to our metropolis.

Whereas the planners of the draft may be commended for their vision, their project cannot be implemented unless two basic conditions are met (the same may be said of other similar plans, including Stockholm's). First of all, the numerous administrative boundaries which fragment this large area into hundreds of autonomous elements should no longer be allowed to jeopardize truly regional planning. A first step was taken in that direction in 1970, when the Montreal Urban Community was established and was granted jurisdiction over the whole of Montreal Island. It is responsible, among other things, for land assessment, integration of public utilities, and for the drafting of a pilot renovation plan. Yet, it is once more to be feared that its field of jurisdiction is not going to encompass the

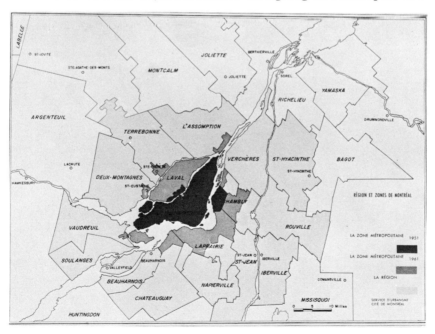

Fig.27   Region and zones of Montreal

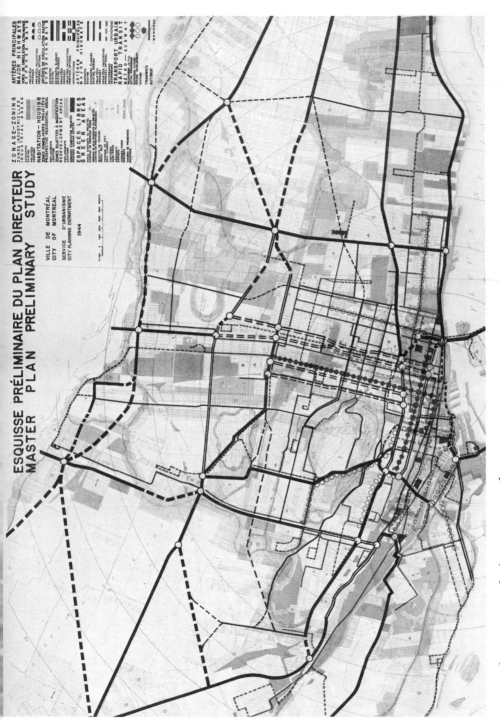

Title block:
ESQUISSE PRÉLIMINAIRE DU PLAN DIRECTEUR
MASTER PLAN PRELIMINARY STUDY

VILLE DE MONTRÉAL
CITY OF MONTREAL

SERVICE D'URBANISME
CITY PLANNING DEPARTMENT

1944

Legend:
ARTÈRES PRINCIPALES
MAJOR HIGHWAYS

ZONAGE-ZONING
ZONES INDUSTRIELLES
INDUSTRIAL AREAS

HABITATION - HOUSING

ESPACES LIBRES
OPEN AREAS

TRANSPORT URBAIN
RAPID TRANSIT

Caption:
74. Preliminary study for a master plan, 1944

ESQUISSE PRÉLIMINAIRE DU PLAN DIRECTEUR
MASTER PLAN PRELIMINARY STUDY

VILLE DE MONTRÉAL
CITY OF MONTREAL

SERVICE D'URBANISME
CITY PLANNING DEPARTMENT

1944

ARTÈRES PRINCIPALES
MAJOR HIGHWAYS

ZONAGE-ZONING
ZONES INDUSTRIELLES
INDUSTRIAL AREAS

HABITATION - HOUSING

ESPACES LIBRES
OPEN AREAS

TRANSPORT URBAIN
RAPID TRANSIT

74. *Preliminary study for a master plan, 1944*

whole economic and social reality of the metropolitan area. Secondly, something should be done to curb the nefarious practices of the real estate speculators who now control most of the Greater Montreal area, for they are primarily responsible for the unrestrained and ugly developments with all their accompanying social costs. All in all, if Horizon 2000, as originally intended, has contributed to arousing among the people and the leaders a form of regional awareness, as well as the desire to preside over the future development of the metropolis, it will not have been conceived in vain.

Liberation: A Challenge

As may be gathered from the foregoing, today's Montreal is indeed very different from what it was in the nineteenth century. The image of the Victorian city as a relatively coherent entity made up of municipalities, industrial and residential districts, each with its own individuality—such as Saint-Henri or the Square Mile—is rapidly fading. So is the concept of the "two cities" or "two solitudes," one French, the other English, separated by their standard of living, their language, their social milieu, and their environment. Today, we see a fragmented metropolis pulling towards the undefined fringe of its own perimeter which is gradually but steadily eroding the rural countryside. It is hard to detect any kind of physical or social framework on the periphery; even the linguistic dividing line no longer follows the pattern of the previous century. The only remaining boundaries are those that vaguely separate the various social classes. In fact, the built-up expanses are no longer a city, in the real sense of the word, but an urbanized area seemingly devoid of any spirit or identity except for a few square miles at the centre of the city and in its immediate neighbourhood which have retained some of their traditional aspects.

The blame lies with the economic and technical revolution, itself an offspring of the industrial revolution, which submerged the traditional city in this urbanized ocean. It has changed the relationship between man and his resources and environment; it has fostered a gradual secularization of society and has upset the patterns of settlement and the type of social organization identified with the concept of a traditional city. The technopolis is in the process of replacing the industrial city of the nineteenth century, just as the latter once replaced the merchant town of the eighteenth century. Between these different types of cities lies more than a simple evolution. There were two eras and two revolutions. To discuss the present metropolis in terms of an industrial city is to deeply misunderstand its true essence, even though in Montreal—as well as in any other metropolis—the process of postindustrial conversion has not been completed. It is happening right now. We do not as yet know what the end result of these changes will be, when the city will have crystallized in its new stage of evolution. We may, at best, venture a few thoughts on the impetus which has caused the explosion of the traditional city.

The overall effect underlying this force is one of liberation which, indeed, is the most significant aspect of this economic and technical revolution: man has been liberated from a number of physical and spiritual limitations and constraints. Railways, roads, efficient and flexible private or public transport as well as electronic communications have allowed industries to ignore the confines of their actual physical environment. By the same token, most citizens are no longer bound to reside close to their place of work and can select a residence in the area of their choice, something which their grandparents never could have dreamed of. Today, within a radius of fifty kilometres—even this figure is temporary—the constraints of distance no longer exist. Another kind of liberation has taken place at the sociocultural level: the mastery man has acquired over the physical world is now paralleled by his control over his own human destiny and by his repudiation of the myths of the past. As Harvey Cox brilliantly explained in *The Secular City*, the technopolis has generated a new kind of man, the "secularized" man. Liberated from religious taboos and from obsolete cultural concepts, his interests are focused on the tangible world and he is now ready to ensure that all the promises this world holds for him are fulfilled.[35] In Quebec, perhaps more than elsewhere, the deep transformation thus undergone by society was so acutely felt that it has quite appropriately been called the Quiet Revolution. This awareness of new values by the people of Quebec is particularly striking since Quebec's society, as we have tried to demonstrate in chapter 3, had until quite recently maintained an almost medieval system of values which, as André Saumier points out, was "all the more structured and grand that it was more isolated from the real world of urban and industrial revolution."[36]

However, this liberating force carries seeds of danger within itself. The "City efficient," as it has been termed, with its emphasis on efficiency, production, concentration, and centralization of the organs governing its economic life, is entirely focused on the profitability of invested capital, often at the expense of basic human values. The jeopardy is all the more serious now that industry is dependent on highly developed machinery. We are learning at our own expense that both production and the city which supports it have but little respect for the biological, physiological, and psychological needs of human beings. Pollution in all its forms is a consequence of this system and threatens the very life of the individual, not to mention the heavy menace it constitutes for the quality of life in an urban environment. For example, few large cities benefit from as many natural amenities as Montreal, such as the large fresh water basins around the city. Yet, because of pollution, those lakes and rivers are already almost unfit for consumption or for educational or recreational purposes.

In many respects this so-called liberation is a delusion: urban man is in many ways more of a slave than he ever was before. Investment profits, real estate speculation, and good old "laissez faire" are all forms of slavery in their own right, but are not new. What is new and threatening, though, is the scale on which they operate. They feed on the freedom obtained through liberation, and to achieve their goals they rely on the powerful weapons of modern technology, among which the means of communication and the information media figure prominently. As the authors of Technical Bulletin No. 5 of the Montreal City Planning Department point out, the development of the metropolis is neither oriented nor controlled, but rather scattered according to the whim and interests of speculators, developers, and contractors. Between 1961 and 1964 there were more than five hundred building sites or development starts for the metropolitan area alone, all of which were totally unrelated to one another, without any functional or formal correlation with the existing urban fabric.[37] Thus the urban area, which claims to be a functional entity, becomes less so every day. This is achieved at the expense of the city itself, of the countryside which is too readily sacrificed to the development frenzy, and, lastly, of the citizens themselves who eventually have to bear the economic and social costs as well as suffer the loss in the quality of life. Moreover, these burdens rise with each passing day. Indeed, the combination of vested interests and unworkable structures will eventually constitute a major obstacle in the way of rational development of the future metropolis.

The same comment applies to the social and cultural changes generated by the Quiet Revolution. Although very promising in terms of benefits, they leave some rather alarming gaps unfilled. Thus, except for the attachment that people have for their neighbourhood as a living environment, nothing very consistent thus far seems to have replaced the parish as a base for social organization. Also, the repudiation of some values of the past has not ipso facto generated a new set. This vacuum is often poorly filled by false ideals such as the importance attached to one's standard of living or social status, or the veneration linked to certain superficial cultural fashions, mostly imported from the United States. There is a danger of falling into sterile social and cultural conformity, with no room for creativity or originality; unfortunately, life in our suburbs all too often reflects this fact.

Modern architecture as it appeared in Montreal, with a few exceptions, began around 1930; it too reflected deep changes. Like the technopolis which strived to offer functional solutions to the needs of the metropolis which had by now been liberated from its old physical and sociocultural constraints, modern architecture made a dramatic break with the past in an attempt to offer its own answers to the new needs. Not only were the latter different from those of the previous era, they were conditioned by a new scale imposed by the large concentrations of people in the urban centres.

The technological revolution produced new materials and new construction methods as well as new devices, such as the elevator and mechanical ventilation, thereby liberating architecture from its former limitations and converting it into a rational form of art based on abstract principles and scientific rules applicable under any conditions and anywhere. Its current appellations illustrate this change of direction: international architecture, functional architecture, abstract architecture, and so on.

The aim of modern architecture is to provide the functional spaces required by specific architectural programs and to preserve only the forms required by the functions, instead of borrowing, like Victorian designs, from a legacy of established forms inherited from previous styles. It therefore rejects anything Victorian. On the other hand, we must admit that modern architecture partly was born from the Victorian, which had been characterized by a conflict between the product of a machine and that of an imagination in quest of sensitive stimulations, between the very precise art of the engineer and the loose inspiration of the artist. The machine was to win.

With the twentieth century, we have entered an age of logic and abstraction; it was not a mere passage from one century to another. Queen Victoria's death in 1901 meant more than the end of a long reign: a whole epoch died with her. The new era had rejected the romantic ideals and proposed another set of values which sometimes opposed the former. Thus, in the field of planning and architecture, the romantic city has been replaced by the rational city, symbolic and Picturesque architecture by a functional and abstract architecture. Therein lies all the difference between the Sun Life Building and CIL House, between Viger Station and Dorval Airport.

The supremacy of technology has replaced the predominance of culture.

Yet, if the Corinthian columns, the Italian arches, and the Gothic pinnacles seem to have disappeared forever from the plans and work of the architects, the latter as well as the town planner have yet to grasp fully the implications of this totally new world. Even though town planning and architecture in Montreal have made considerable progress, and in spite of some modern feats such as Place Ville-Marie and Place Bonaventure which have given our city a lead in urban design, the Victorian phenomenon remains a latent fact. Just as in Victorian times, many huge modern buildings have been simply compressed within a network of streets designed to answer the needs of the small eighteenth-century town. Fifty years of progress separate the Aldred Building from the Banque Canadienne Nationale on Place d'Armes, and, architecturally speaking, the latter structure does indeed reflect the advances made. When it comes to its location and integration within the urban fabric, however, it faithfully repeats the mistakes of the former. The same criticism applies to the tragic parade of modern apartment towers which have been grafted onto the old residential avenues. Streets like Saint-Mathieu and Lincoln are on the verge of duplicating the Wall Streets of the previous century.

However, the permanence of the Victorian influence is most obvious and most puzzling in our new suburbs, even when they have been subjected to a certain degree of planning. Vague romantic concepts inherited from the previous century affect the road network in the most superficial manner: there, planning sometimes consists of a mere curve in the road. All at once, streets have lost their density of habitation, their picturesque decor, and their quality as a social environment; in brief, they have lost all the qualities which were so characteristic of the true Victorian avenues, without bringing any satisfactory solution to the problems of motorized traffic or to the needs of pedestrian safety. Here again, a degenerate form of Victorian culture, clinging to its small cottages, displays all the pretensions of the new small-time parvenus, without being able to express any of their ideals. These aspects will be dealt with in the next chapter.

13

The New Core of the City

Montreal is about to become the first 20th century city in North America
PETER BLAKE [1]

Fifty Years of Gestation

Twentieth-century architecture in Montreal presents many aspects which merit our attention. We could attempt to retrace the evolution, on the whole rather disappointing, of apartment-building architecture, starting with a survey of the amazing concrete structures of the twenties such as the building looking onto Christin and Savignac Streets (near Sanguinet) or the rather amazing multifunctional building at 2 Sherbrooke West (corner of St. Lawrence), with its Art Nouveau flavour, all the way to a discussion of the icy qualities of a complex like Westmount Square or the delirious plasticity of Habitat 67. We could also discuss some of the structures which were famous at the time of their inauguration but whose style was unable to withstand the passage of time; an example is the main building of the Université de Montréal designed in 1925 by Ernest Cormier, which according to Alan Gowans is but a conventional design adorned with some modern clichés.[2] Again, it might be enjoyable to visit the many churches and sanctuaries which, after World War II, have illustrated, with occasional hints at the Baroque, the carefree mood of a religious regime already on its wane. The name of Roger D'Astous, a Montreal architect, is associated with several of these constructions; they offer a rather strange and naïve mixture of magazine pictures combined with a genius for innovation. All these efforts, however, would only lead to the selection of a list of buildings, a sort of catalogue from which the city and its reality would disappear. We feel much more inclined, as we cast a final glance at Montreal and its architecture, to emphasize those achievements directly and physically related to the city, its life and development, such as the new downtown area and the subway.

This new part of the city centre, which started with the Place Ville-Marie project, is of particular interest, for it is the town planners' dream come true. It is now well on the way to fulfilling their long-cherished vision of a metropolis with a multipurpose, multi-level core. Although its scattered towers have certainly contributed to altering the traditional silhouette of the Victorian city, its most distinctive feature, by far, is its intricate infrastructure: an underground network of subways and highways, 10 kilometres of shopping galleries, malls, and car-parks, as well as train and motor-vehicle services.

In the opinion of many experts, thanks to its new core, Montreal is at the forefront of urban design.[3] Montrealers are generally unaware of this reality and even less conscious of the many factors which made the existence of such a centre possible. The postwar economic boom certainly played an important role but it cannot account for the quality which characterizes this development. Not only were the opportunities available but there were also talented and determined men ready to take advantage of them.

The starting point of this achievement, according to Vincent Ponte,[4] was the existence right in the middle of the downtown area of three adjacent blocks totalling about 9 hectares of land belonging to one owner.[5] As mentioned in the previous chapter, the purchase of this valuable terrain was completed in 1911, when two senior officials of the Canadian Northern Railway decided to boost its operations by building a large terminal in Montreal. A 5-kilometre-long tunnel through the mountain provided access to the site, ending south of the Beaver Hall Ridge in an open trench that disfigured downtown Montreal for almost half a century, despite an attempt made as early as 1913 to exploit the aerial rights for development.

A few years later, in 1923, an important event took place which had a determining effect on downtown development: the Canadian National Railways was incorporated as a crown corporation, bringing under it various companies such as the Grand Trunk, the Pacific Grand Trunk, the Northern Canadian, in fact almost every railway in the country with the exception of the Canadian Pacific.

The merger compelled the officials of the Canadian National to rationalize the operations of the various lines. In Montreal, this called for the phasing out of certain passenger stations, including Moreau and Bonaventure, and combining them into one single central station, while at the same time the various offices formerly situated in about fifteen buildings scattered around the city would be brought together under one roof.

Such was the picture when, in 1929, a new plan was put forward for the development of the site. Inspired by the Rockefeller Center in New York and drafted by Hugh G. Jones, it provided for several office buildings and appropriate space for retail business in addition to the new Central Station. The proposed renovation with its broad central perspective was classical in design and decidedly conservative in its architectural components. The project, however, was cut short because of the great depression and World War II, except for Central Station which was constructed in 1938 as part of an unemployment assistance program of the federal government.[6]

The building of the station proved to be an important step for two reasons: first of all, it provided a valuable crossroad of communications for an area which already contained Windsor Station and the Bell Telephone and Communications Buildings. Furthermore, it turned out to be the first important architectural building in Montreal without any façade, a sort of huge, multipurpose envelope.[7] This kind of "celebration" architecture, as architect Ray Affleck called it, would later influence other structures, such as Place Bonaventure.

After the war, Jacques Greber, the famous French town planner— to whom, incidentally, we owe a master plan for the national capital—was called upon to discuss the renovation of the site for the CN properties. One of his suggestions deserves special mention: the idea to reserve enough free space on the northern side of the site to provide for a public plaza. Since Montreal was the only city with a downtown area wedged between a mountain and a river, Greber assumed that a plaza of this kind would give the final touch to a long vista joining the mountain and the beautiful McGill campus on one end to the downtown area on the other. This suggestion was followed up by municipal authorities, who then compensated the CN by widening the surrounding streets in order to absorb the increased traffic that such a major complex would create.[8]

In the meantime, new renovation plans had been prepared under the direction of the architect G. F. Drummond. Some of them materialized on that part of the site partly occupied by Central Station. They account for the existence of the original International Civil Aviation Organization (ICAO) Building, the Terminal Building, the

Queen Elizabeth Hotel, and the CN Station. None of them deserves special mention from an architectural point of view. There was no follow-up on these or later suggestions concerning the area north of the latter sector. When William Zeckendorf was asked in 1955 to develop the site, he found it in exactly the same condition as in 1918: a deep open trench for the rails that were swallowed up on their way through Mount Royal.[9]

Zeckendorf, whose energetic drive in this matter was to give a start to the renovation of downtown Montreal, very wisely commissioned I. M. Pei and Associates to submit a master plan for the development of all the land owned by the CN on the site. The design was accepted by CN in 1954, thus giving it, by means of a ninety-nine-year lease, the necessary rights and privileges to develop the northern part of the site.

This plan deserves our attention for it is based on a set of principles aimed at making the renovation of the heart of the metropolis a lasting achievement. First, it assumes that a development of this size will generate a tremendous flow of activities. Today, for example, an estimated 15,000 people work in the Ville-Marie complex alone, and some 60,000 to 100,000 individuals pass through it daily, not to mention hundreds of trucks stopping for deliveries. In an era when the emphasis is on cooperation and interdependence in activities and on concentration and centralization of enterprises, a complex of this kind is also a powerful hub of attraction. No wonder that commercial buildings such as CIL Tower, the Canadian Imperial Bank of Commerce, and the Stock Exchange were located in the immediate vicinity of Place Ville-Marie. To absorb the prevailing pressures, Pei proposed a peripheral highway aimed at diverting the through traffic. The original plan for this boulevard was not realized as expected, but the network of urban highways later constructed, and especially the subway, nevertheless have helped to relieve the congestion inherent in a downtown area wedged between the river and Mount Royal.

The second renovation principle is characteristic of the plan: it calls for a complete segregation between the various types of traffic throughout the site (and eventually on the adjacent plots as well). This segregation applies not only to horizontal traffic, such as traditional streets and sidewalks, but also to vertical: indeed it provides specific levels for specific types of movement. There are, for instance, in both Place Ville-Marie and Place Bonaventure, separate levels for trains, motor vehicles, and parking lots as well as pedestrian passageways.

A third aspect of this plan is its departure from the traditional de-

velopment design that considers land as a mere site on which to
erect a building to house the headquarters of a dominant function.
This concept has generated cities where the core is fragmented into
a series of specialized units. The new downtown area of Montreal is
unique because of the multiplicity and the variety of its closely in-
terrelated functions. Place Ville-Marie and Place Bonaventure both
show a remarkable concentration of many activities under the same
roof: tertiary services, retail businesses, hotels, industrial concerns,
culture, recreation, and others.[10] The example set here was soon followed by Place Victoria, Place du Canada, and the Alexis Nihon
Plaza.

Finally, this plan is a deliberate contribution to the idea of re-
organizing the city along visual lines. Most decisive in this respect
was the suggestion made by Greber, and carried out by the planners,
which was to design a vast urban perspective linking Mount Royal
to Place Ville-Marie. While this proposal, inspired by the traditions
of the Beaux-Arts, can hardly be considered as an innovation in the
field of urban renovation, one cannot but agree with Henri Cobb
that the plaza of Place Ville-Marie provides a truly dramatic setting
for a visual confrontation between Mount Royal and the city.[11]

The Downtown Giants
Let us now take a look at the Place Ville-Marie complex itself. It
owes its existence to the intuition of the promoter, Zeckendorf, who
realized that there was a market in Montreal for office buildings offering a minimum of 1,860 square metres of floor space on every
storey. Zeckendorf felt—and subsequent events proved him right—
that a standard renting space of this size would best answer the
needs of the large modern corporations which had always showed a
marked preference for prestige buildings.[12]

The cruciform tower of the Ville-Marie complex offers 3,530
square metres per floor. In fact, the shape of the tower was dictated
by these exceptional dimensions. Indeed, in all buildings of this
type, where the site itself is not a limiting factor, it is usually the
need for standardized floor space free of any obstacle and adequately
lit with natural light which prevails. Considering the overall area of
the typical floor, it was obvious from the start that the traditional
square or rectangular shape would not be able to provide sufficient
natural lighting. The obstacle was overcome by splitting the floor
area into four rectangles of equal dimensions articulated around a
central service core.[13]

Although internally functional, this cruciform tower may appear
somewhat heavy on the outside, especially when viewed from a cer-

tain angle or in the absence of the sunshine which usually enhances its volumes. The feeling of heaviness it conveys is further accentuated by its aluminum curtain-wall, visually neutral and too uniform.

Although the cruciform shape was accepted without question from the start, the design of the complex itself was to undergo considerable changes in the course of its construction. All in all, these alterations were for the better, especially the addition at the base of the tower of four powerful overhanging quadrants. These huge blocks, entirely blind on the outside, but lit through the roof by skylights, were added to comply with the requirements of the first and most important tenant, the Royal Bank of Canada. These masses provide a better link between the tower and the plaza than was originally planned for. Similarly, the design of the IBM and Esso Buildings, built on two sides of the plaza, was altered to integrate them better into the overall layout of the plaza.

On the other hand, some of the original drafts did not materialize, much to the detriment of the whole complex. For instance, the architects had proposed that a ramp provide direct access from the plaza to Sainte-Catherine Street, the main commercial artery of the metropolis. This suggestion was in keeping with the broader plans aimed at redeveloping McGill College Avenue and converting it into a long perspective linking Place Ville-Marie to the mountain. So far, the unwillingness of neighbouring owners has jeopardized the prospect of establishing such a passage which would have allowed pedestrians to commute between the plaza and Sainte-Catherine Street. As matters now stand, McGill College Avenue comes to a pitiful end at the entrance to Place Ville-Marie's parking lot.

The plaza itself is not without flaws. Even though it is itself a viable space, dramatized by the cruciform tower and handsomely framed by the IBM and Esso Buildings—though rather poorly by the monotonous façade of the Queen Elizabeth Hotel—it does not seem especially inviting and is only sporadically used. One cannot help wondering why.

First of all, it is physically and visually far too insular. Dorchester Boulevard, on which it borders on one side, is essentially a thoroughfare and does not attract pedestrians. On the opposite side, the base of the plaza stands far above Sainte-Catherine Street and, viewed from the latter's level, it does not look like a public square. Moreover, subjected to the effects of microclimate, it is plagued at all times by violent and often icy winds. Furthermore, the covering on the walls of the tower and the surrounding buildings does nothing to create a feeling of warmth.

The plaza's greatest drawback as a centre of attraction lies in the fact that, compared with the shopping galleries it covers, it is most uninteresting. Is it a public plaza or the roof of a commercial centre? This dual function is awkward because of the particular success enjoyed by the gallery which is more easily and more directly accessible to pedestrians.

Running above two levels respectively assigned to parking (1,500 cars) and to services, and extending at the end to the level of the CN railway tracks, the galleries are the end-product of good design, pleasant proportions, and first-class materials. From a strictly commercial point of view, they constitute an adequate answer to the competition generated by the large suburban shopping centres by offering, right in the centre of town, almost the same selection of goods, the same separation between pedestrians and motor vehicles, and the same convenience for the customers. However, it is still patterned after a conservative concept, duplicating underground both the street between two rows of shops and the orthogonal grid prevailing almost everywhere above the ground.

Strictly speaking, had Place Ville-Marie been limited to its cruciform tower and its plaza, it would not have been a very striking achievement, despite some details of construction and engineering worth noting. The main features which account for its originality are the variety and the complementary nature of its functions, and the climate-protected passages with different alleys of traffic segregated from each other according to the respective nature of their functions. (Plates 75 and 76.)

Between the time when the Place Ville-Marie project was launched and the day it was inaugurated, two important commercial towers were completed in its vicinity: the Canadian Industries Limited Building (CIL House) and the Canadian Imperial Bank of Commerce Building. It was not so much because Dorchester Boulevard was widened in the early fifties that these buildings were located on its edges, but rather because Place Ville-Marie was growing into a hub of attraction. In the minds of the planners, the enlargement of the boulevard was intended to channel the downtown development towards the east, but Place Ville-Marie brought this trend to a standstill.

Considered from a technical point of view, CIL House is close to perfection; inundated with daylight, it has a standard floor surface totalling about 1,860 square metres, an ideal size for renting purposes. Its volume, housing some thirty-four floors, does not lack elegance; its architectural features are a tribute to all the precepts of the modern school of architecture. It was designed by Greenspoon, Freedlander, and Dunne, but consulting architects Skidmore,

75. *The giants of the city centre*

76. *Central Station and Place Ville-Marie buildings*

Owings, and Merrill undoubtedly had a determining influence, for the latter firm is among the most committed to modern trends on the American continent and is well known for its ability to make the best possible use of all the modern techniques at its disposal.[14]

As for the way it blends with the urban fabric, CIL House unfortunately remains an isolated block; it conveys the impression of having been forced into the grid of the existing streets, a feeling that the building's mini-plazas do not help to relieve. Incidentally, the existence of such plazas is only due to a municipal regulation which allows the floor space to be increased for that part of a building located above the average ground level, in direct proportion to the space left at the ground level for public use in the form of a plaza or other structure.[15]

In the absence of any detailed plan for the remodelling of the downtown district, a regulation like Amendment 2887 (adopted on 9 September 1963) was a lesser evil. Its essential purpose was to avoid any repetition of dark, corridor-like streets such as New York's Wall Street and St. James Street in Montreal. This enactment, however, was more the result of a defensive reaction than the outcome of a creative impulse: public squares derived from regulations of that kind are often insignificant and poorly integrated. They look more like perrons or parvis than real plazas.

This is particularly true of the Canadian Imperial Bank of Commerce Building, located at the northwest corner of Peel and Dorchester. Its recessed position with respect to both avenues is ridiculous; only the presence of Dominion Square compensates for this drawback. The edifice is a 189-metre-high skyscraper erected on the site of the early Windsor Hotel, the oldest part of which was pulled down to make room for its construction. It has a comparatively narrow base—42.7 by 30.5 metres—which enhances its tall and slender aspect. Critic Peter Collins has compared its proportions to those of the campanile of Piazza San Marco in Venice.[16] Designed by the architect Peter Dickinson, it certainly does not lack elegance, but of all the large modern office buildings in the city it is perhaps the least fit for business. Its renting floor surface lags far behind the optimum 1,860 square metres achieved in CIL House: it ranges from 1,161 square metres on the lower floors to some 1,282 square metres on the upper levels.[17]

The Stock Exchange Tower on Victoria Square is another very elegant building. A number of architects contend that it may be listed among the most beautiful towers in the world. Bordering on Victoria Square, it creates a marvellous physical link between the old-time business centre of St. James Street and the new commercial centre launched at the same time as Place Ville-Marie. The developers' purpose was to instil new life into the old financial district and to save it from obsolescence through an architectural program aimed at boosting business by providing it with the best network of communications and services available.[18]

This architectural program resembles that of Place Ville-Marie: two underground floors for parking and services, above which is a double deck of shopping galleries and direct connection to the Victoria subway station. A lower extension of the edifice (five storeys), catering mainly to Stock Exchange activities, acts as a hinge between the base and the forty-seven-floor tower. It was designed to accommodate a potential expansion towards the west and as a base for a second tower similar to the first. The whole centre will eventually be connected, through an underground pedestrian network, to all the other key points of the city centre: Place Bonaventure, Place Ville-Marie, Central Station, and others.

At the time the Stock Exchange complex was first proposed to Montreal, the project drafted by the Italian architect Moretti and by the world-famous engineer Nervi was much more ambitious. It included three huge towers placed diagonally across a low base. This plan, however, presented some drawbacks: besides obstructing the view of Mount Royal, it multiplied the costs of vertical services and communication centres at the expense of renting space. It was therefore altered for the better: only two towers would be built, one at a time. What we now admire is only the first phase of this development.

The foremost quality of the tower lies in its beauty. It rises forcefully from the ground, strongly supported by four tall columns erected at the corners and harmoniously rounded out with panels of precast concrete. The tower itself is divided into three equal and similar blocks separated by levels housing machinery (5th, 19th, and 32nd floors), providing interesting points for partly visible concrete diagonal braces. Its surface is lined with a smooth curtain-wall made of anodized aluminum with an antique-bronze hue, offering a pleasant contrast with the stark white colour of the four columns. This tower represents an exceptional marriage between function and form, between engineering and architecture. Here an indescribable spark of genius emerges from the union between techniques and aesthetics. This is dynamic architecture, evolving along a logical, descriptive process. Moreover, all this was achieved while assuring an optimal 1,672 square metres of renting space per floor, flooded everywhere with natural light.

Place Victoria once more bears witness to the European influence which never ceased to prevail in the architectural tradition of Montreal, whereas CIL House is closer to the American influence, another pillar of our history. One is cool, classical, and formal, and an outstanding technical success, demonstrating the mastery attained in the field by the nation which developed the techniques of sky-scraper construction. The other is a remarkable achievement—it is the highest concrete building in the world—whose appeal lies chiefly in its architectural lyricism.

Unfortunately, in this particular respect Place Victoria has had a questionable impact on the environment of the city's centre. It has indeed deprived old Victoria Square of its very essence: a meaningful space drawing all the peripheral components into a single urban cell; now it no longer looks like a city square, but rather like a lobby leading to the tower. This was unavoidable, for the Stock Exchange is not built on the same scale as the Victorian city and cannot be integrated into its environment of squares and narrow streets. The tower now belongs to a different milieu, that of the other sky-scrapers, built on the scale of the Greater Montreal region. This is a somewhat frustrating aspect of the new downtown Montreal: at the top level of the towers we perceive a new pattern which is neither on the same scale nor of the same period as that at the base where all these buildings are crammed within an urban configuration which developed during the previous centuries.[19]

The Place Victoria complex, at least the part rising above the ground, remains essentially a powerfully conceived three-dimensional structure. By contrast, Place Bonaventure, one of the most original edifices of this new downtown area, appears as a huge wrapper or, to borrow a phrase from Eiler Rasmussen, as an architecture of cavities.[20] Here the peripheral walls are not so much façades as climatic barriers delineating multi-level spaces where various functions and activities are intertwined. For Ray Affleck, the chief architect of this project for the Montreal firm of Affleck, Dimakopoulos, Lebensold, and Sise, it represents what he calls "celebration architecture," which is inward-looking like that of a cathedral.[21]

Place Bonaventure was erected on the last plot of CN land south of Central Station and had been included in the renovation plan of I. M. Pei. Because of its lack of façades, it is closer in spirit to the station than to the Ville-Marie complex. Yet, the developers of the Concordia Company had first envisaged a more traditional building, such as the Stock Exchange, with a low volume, housing a shopping centre and a large exhibition hall, which would have been used as a base for a high tower accommodating hotel services. The architects, however, suggested a different approach: namely a single wide and massive block covering the 2.4 hectares of the site, the roof of which would serve as an artificial ground for the development of hotel units.

Fortunately, the latter choice was to prevail, for a rather particular reason: in order to realize this plan of development, architects, developers, and contractors for once did not assume their usual role, which is to work in a linear sequence of action. Rather, they were united in a single plan of decision-making and action so that they all participated, simultaneously and with unity, in the creation of the complex. According to Ray Affleck, it was a successful approach; it demonstrated that creative ideas are not all confined within the traditional limits of the professional disciplines.[22]

In essence, Place Bonaventure is therefore a multifunctional building (shopping centre, exhibition hall, auction rooms, international business centre, hotel, and assorted services) linked, as in a living body, to various kinds of circulation (metro, pedestrian, motor-vehicle). Here a very complex network for pedestrian traffic plays a particularly significant role. Far from attempting to impose a pattern of traffic on pedestrians, the architects devised their plans after a simulated model of the users' activities and this blueprint became the prime generator of the whole design. And architectural skills were put to good use in the layout of a number of centres of activities spread throughout the overall plan.

One of the most difficult problems arising from such kinetic architecture was that of links and communications between the various functions of the complex. This difficulty was never resolved in any satisfactory way, with the result that people unfamiliar with the place are sometimes utterly confused. Although Place Bonaventure is definitely original in that all these functions are integrated as a whole rather than scattered towards isolated individual units, it still has to make this new architectural concept "legible" and coherent in a total experience.

Leaving aside the functional aspects and turning to the spaces thus created, it is obvious that some of the latter have achieved a rare quality. The big Concordia exhibition hall, for instance, is impressive with its sombre and stark majesty. Some thirty feet high, its huge columns and their structural capitals are reminiscent of the grandeur of the hypostyle hall in an Egyptian temple. Equally remarkable is the location of the hotel whose four hundred rooms are distributed on several floors around an inner courtyard which houses all services in its centre. Efforts have been made to preserve the privacy and independent aspect of those various units, and it has been so successful that were it not for the surrounding downtown skyscrapers one could imagine oneself anywhere except in the heart of the metropolis.

Seen from the exterior, and in spite of attempts to articulate its surfaces, Place Bonaventure appears as a massive cube impregnated by the influence of Paul Rudolph. Its designers are the first to agree that the problem of the outside walls has not been resolved.[23] We are led to wonder whether walls were at all necessary for that type of architecture. A thin sheet of glass covering this centre of activities, in the fashion of a geodesic dome, for example, would have given true meaning to outer walls which after all serve no other purpose than that of a climatic and environmental barrier.

The structures we have just analysed—Place Ville-Marie, CIL House, the Canadian Imperial Bank of Commerce Tower, the Stock Exchange complex, the Place Bonaventure—are among the most interesting buildings constructed in downtown Montreal from the middle of the twentieth century onwards. There are others, of course, such as Place du Canada, Alexis Nihon Plaza, or, going eastwards, Place des Arts whose main concert hall is of a classical, somewhat superficial design; or again the tower of the Banque Canadienne Nationale on Place d'Armes, a rather ordinary building poorly integrated into its urban context. If any of these complexes deserves mention it would be Place du Canada, not so much for its actual merits but for those it could have had. Indeed its Château Champlain tower seems to be the only skyscraper to have escaped the standardized design of modern buildings of this type. It is the first significant edifice to be designed by francophone Quebecers, the architects D'Astous and the late Pothier. Its architectural features remind one of the shapes favoured by the great American architect Frank Lloyd Wright; this is not surprising since Roger D'Astous was one of Wright's students and attended his famous school in Wisconsin. However, even though the Master had many disciples and many imitators, he alone had the genius. This is painfully apparent in the Château Champlain.

Criticisms and Future Guidelines
We should now attempt to learn something from the partial reconstruction of downtown Montreal. It demonstrates, for instance, that there is room for bold ventures, especially in a field where the creation of equipment often promotes the creation of functions. Had it not been for the CN officials' idea of an integrated development of their land in the downtown area, or for Zeckendorf's determination and willingness to accept costly risks, or for the imagination displayed by the town planners and the architects of the Pei firm, one

can assume that the renovation of the downtown area would have taken an entirely different and probably less satisfactory turn, if it ever took place at all. In spite of the complex conjunctions that usually surround such renovations, the impulse created by this new downtown area demonstrates that it really is possible to intervene in the process of urban development. Nowhere is this more obvious than in the axial change that took place in the course of the redevelopment of downtown Montreal which, until then, had always followed the east–west axis of St. James, Dorchester, or Sainte-Catherine Street. Now, through conscious and deliberate action, this axis would henceforth be oriented in a south–north direction from Place Bonaventure to the McGill campus.

Another fact demonstrated here is that capitalism is apparently not incompatible with good renovation. Traditionally, capitalists have always sought rapid and maximum profitability of urban spaces at the expense of continuity in the city, of the community's welfare, and even of their own interests. The renovation of downtown Montreal helped the developers to realize that if their investments were to be profitable in the long run, planning and management should be such as to ensure the future social and economic viability of their projects.[24] It is quite certain, for instance, that the new downtown hub would have slowly withered away were it not for the parallel solutions found for access and communication. It is equally certain that if this central zone had not provided, at the retail level, for a regrouping of the various functions and a network for pedestrians ensuring climatic protection, comfort, safety, as well as an architectural framework with visual and acoustic qualities, it could not have survived the competition of the suburban shopping centres. The latter have demonstrated that these features of good planning and management have now become an economic factor of prime importance.[25] The downtown Montreal network seems to be fairly well planned in this respect; it provides a larger surface and greater capacity than Rockefeller Center in New York and its quality surpasses that of Penn Center in Philadelphia.

However, there is no reason to be carried away by this achievement. Remarkable as it may be, it is in no way revolutionary. The concept, for instance, of a controlled-climate shopping gallery isolating pedestrians from vehicle traffic is by no means recent. It is present in the Galleria Vittorio Emmanuele in Milan, built in 1865–67, or, better still, in the famous Chester Rows in England which, as far back as the Middle Ages, contained covered shopping galleries on two levels; in the fifteenth century, Leonardo da Vinci was already advocating vertical segregation of all kinds of urban traffic. The same concept was later to be realized in London by the Adams brothers in the Adelphi residential complex (1768–74), where they devised an artificial foundation—allowing separate traffic on different levels—which compares favourably with the construction of our most modern centres.[26]

In fact, the originality of the urban development of downtown Montreal lay not so much in the concept of a multi-level city core—an idea that had haunted architects and town planners for several generations—but in the fact that it had at last materialized in a tangible, major achievement. And this because of one particular reason that we should stress once again by quoting the town planner Vincent Ponte: "What has really made Montreal's urban miracle possible is the presence of large reservoirs of downtown real estate, held in single ownership, often by railroads or other corporate entities. These break the shackles of lot-by-lot piecemeal development. They have enabled the entire core to be redeveloped as a unit."[27]

This is quite true. In fact, for the whole project the failure to link the Ville-Marie Plaza to Sainte-Catherine Street was the only setback the architects and planners suffered. Here, as in more conservative achievements, they were unable to overcome the obstacle of vested interests or to save the legal problems arising from the rights to build over public thoroughfares or private property. So they simply bypassed the obstacle by burying the essential human activities underground. Our proud master, the automobile, which is but an accessory to human activities, managed to remain above the natural ground and carried on as the ungrateful user of sun and air.

For those who reject this kind of criticism and insist, with Pelletier and Beauregard, that this achievement constitutes one "of the most remarkable feats of adjustment to geography,"[28] we would like to make the following comment: although it may be true that the natural topography of the site was aptly used to integrate the various services, it is ludicrous to think that our climate is so miserable that we should be compelled to live permanently underground. After all, we do enjoy six months of very mild temperatures, with many days of sunshine. Even though the hardships of winter certainly justify the principle of carrying on business underground, one should assume that the pleasant weather in the warm season would favour doing so in the open air. The new downtown facilities do not permit such a choice. Yet, a structure erected in the previous century, the Galleria Vittoria Emmanuele in Milan, ensures as good a protection against bad weather and other inconvenience as that provided by the shopping galleries of Place Ville-Marie and Victoria Square while at the same time dispensing abundant daylight and fresh air.

Architect Affleck[29] and other experts contend that it is inaccurate, in the present instance, to talk about underground networks since the ground level of these buildings is artificial. This is perfectly true but, to all intents and purposes, these galleries and networks are concealed, whether truly underground or under an artificial surface. In fact, there is no more visual link at the original ground level between Place Ville-Marie, Central Station, and Place Bonaventure than there ever was between earlier structures such as the stores of Morgan's or Birks. Unless informed beforehand, no one walking on the street could even suspect what is going on below the street level. In fact, seen from the outside, each of these new complexes retains its traditional character and its insularity because each remains enslaved to entrenched rights and to vested interests.

Ideally, since they all participate in the same main functions, complexes of this kind should be gathered around a common identifiable nucleus at the true soil level, thus providing a visual as well as a physical relationship between the different components. This would have been a truly new vision of urban development, one liberated from the constraints inherited from the past centuries. The city centre would have benefited from a real "place," a specific urban space, physically and visually related to its different components. For none of the present structures, except perhaps the Ville-Marie Plaza, with its somewhat ambiguous role, could be properly called a "place"; furthermore, by consistently applying this French word to complexes which are nothing of the kind, we run the risk of depriving of their meaning and character the true public "squares" of Montreal, such as Place Jacques-Cartier, Place d'Armes, Victoria Square, Phillips Square, Dominion Square, and others.[30] We shall again refer to this subject in the conclusion of this book.

The Subway
We would be remiss if we ended this analysis of twentieth-century Montreal without a few words about the subway and the 1967 World Exhibition, for both these achievements show a great deal of originality and vitality and have significantly contributed to Montreal's long and proud architectural tradition. We shall first consider the subway.

The first network composed of three lines totalling 22.5 kilometres and twenty-six stations became operational in October 1966. The idea of building a subway in Montreal dates as far back as 1910; the preliminary report on the 1944 master plan recommended a network very similar to what we have today. The vigorous campaign conducted by Mayor Drapeau, claiming Montreal could not survive as a metropolis without a subway, was certainly a decisive factor.[31] Going ahead, however, was out of the question unless the existence of certain basic conditions justified the venture, including a sufficient density of population and a reasonable concentration of activities.

These conditions were achieved only in the second half of the twentieth century. In 1961 the population of the administrative territory of Montreal was over the million mark with an average of 7,700 residents per square kilometre. It was further complemented by a population of two million residents in the metro area. At the same time, as we have just read, there had been a parallel increase of activities downtown. A subway therefore became possible and its present popularity—more than 125 million passengers yearly—is ample proof that its time had come.[32]

The Montreal subway, which was a local achievement, is interesting in many respects. First of all, it was not conceived, as were many others throughout the world, as an autonomous transportation service, built underground to provide protection against the weather and to ensure a higher degree of efficiency. Rather, it was envisaged as a direct extension of the total traffic pattern, a concept which accounts for some of its most important features.

The two main lines of the network are not situated exactly under the great axial lines of the town, along which activities are generally concentrated, Saint-Denis and Saint-Hubert Streets (north–south) and Sainte-Catherine and St. James Streets (east–west), but slightly outside these axes. Taking advantage of the long, narrow blocks, of the grid of streets, the north–south line runs under a secondary street, Berri–Lajeunesse; it is therefore half way between two important arteries, Saint-Denis and Saint-Hubert Streets. The two east–west lines follow a similar pattern. One is located under de Maisonneuve Boulevard which is half way (for the main part of its course) between Sherbrooke and Sainte-Catherine. The other, which is the extension of the north–south line, runs between Vitré and Saint-Antoine (Craig) Streets and is therefore able to serve both Dorchester and St. James Streets. In the two situations, these lines have significantly contributed to the redevelopment of de Maisonneuve Boulevard and of the Vitré–Saint-Antoine valley.[33]

In addition to facilitating building operations while the subway was under construction, without disturbing the intensive business activities of the commercial streets, these locations also allowed for a better functional and formal integration of the underground transport system into the urban fabric. For instance, access to the stations is provided by way of large halls instead of being compressed along sidewalks, as in most subways. Also, the presence of residual land around those accesses suggests the possibility of urban re-development which could include these volumes. The aerial rights above the Guy and Atwater Stations have already been developed in this manner. The spaces thus redistributed away from the heavy traffic of the axial lines provide room for bus terminals which help to integrate surface transport services with the underground system. Outside the city centre most buses stop at the subway stations, which are thus becoming the converging points of all public transport.[34]

Another aspect of the Montreal subway worth mentioning is the active involvement of its architects. This was something new in the sense that the architects from the public service and those from the private sector were brought under the same leadership. They did not just turn up at the end of the project to put the final touch to structures which had been dictated by strictly technical imperatives; they were included right from the start, when the program for the stations was first formulated. The results of their association speak for themselves: contrary to most subways around the world, whether Toronto's or Stockholm's, the manner in which both traffic and space are organized in the Montreal underground goes far beyond a mere concern for functional efficiency. At the present time, the only other subway involving the active participation of its architects is that in Moscow.

The single tunnel system with a platform on each side, selected for the Montreal subway, required mezzanines or foot bridges leading to each platform from a single hall. In the opinion of Hans Blumenfeld, this kind of device is ordinarily less satisfying, from the point of view of space distribution and traffic identification, than the principle of one central platform giving access on each side to the subway trains.[35] In Montreal, thanks to their active involvement, the architects have in most instances succeeded in limiting such inconveniences. They have organized mezzanines and foot bridges so as to provide passengers with a feeling of space which enables them to remain aware of their position in relation to the various lines of traffic. We find a good example of this in the Berri-de-Montigny Station designed by the architects Longpré and Marchand. Berri-de-Montigny is the central transfer point for the three subway lines; it is spatially distributed over three main levels which are functionally and visually interconnected.

Despite the similarity of approach toward spatial organization common to most stations and the unavoidable standardization of traffic patterns and of a certain part of the equipment, the stations display a great deal of variety with respect to volume, the choice of materials and colour, and the type of lighting. The combination of these features relieves passengers of the monotonous feeling that tunnels often generate in transport of this kind. On the contrary, commuters participate in a rather unusual spatial and emotional experience, as the trip rolls on to the beat and rhythm of changing images and impressions. The Montreal subway stations are identifiable by their volumes, shape, materials, and colours before they are even recognized by their name.

It does not follow that they are all of equal architectural value. Some, like Sherbrooke or Beaudry, lack imagination in the distribution of volume as well as in the choice of materials. Others, like Henri-Bourassa, convey a cold feeling because of the predominant use of an unattractive covering material. Still others, including Crémazie, display a disconcerting patchwork of odd materials. The stations just described have all been designed by architects from the Department of Public Works. This does not mean, however, that they are all mediocre.[36] The station on St. Helen's Island, for instance, completed by the young architect Dumontier, is particularly striking because of the impression of strength and unity it conveys; this is partly due to the clever use of unfinished concrete. At any rate, and without wishing to be ironical, we may suggest that the few somewhat naïve stations contribute to a better appreciation of those which manage to create a true architectural mood. Among the latter, we should mention Beaubien, Mont-Royal, Peel, and Bonaventure.

Beaubien Station is remarkable in that its architect, Roger D'Astous, has obviously tried to avoid the feeling of confusion and claustrophobia usually prevailing in underground stations. The pedestrian traffic, for instance, follows one sole axis from the urban sidewalks to the platforms. The latter are perpendicular to and perfectly visible from this axis which straddles them as a mezzanine. To avoid the feeling of claustrophobia, the volume of the station expands as one progresses inside, and natural daylight is dramatically supplied through a skylight to twelve metres below the ground level. Apart from such features, the station displays the obvious predilection of Roger D'Astous for shapes inspired by Frank Lloyd Wright.[37]

Peel Station, on the other hand, is equally remarkable even though it is located in a low and narrow space; this was a handicap for a station which was bound to absorb the large and sudden influx of crowds during the rush hours because of its location near the heart of downtown. The crushing feeling was cleverly avoided by the architects who designed a sunken-panel ceiling, with high and low volumes alternating. As for the feeling of narrowness, it was remedied by adding rhythm to the inside volumes through a series of twin columns. The mezzanine leading to the platforms follows the axis of the tracks; it consists of one large but thin slab. Architects Papineau, Gérin-Lajoie, and Leblanc designed this station which bears witness to the structural sense and care for details that characterize the work of this firm, which also designed the Quebec Pavilion at the Montreal World Fair.

Designed by Victor Prus, a talented architect from Montreal, Mont-Royal and Bonaventure Stations are like extensions of the urban scene above. To achieve this purpose he relied on two main devices: first, he used brick, concrete, tiles, and so forth, in keeping with the building materials used above ground. The second consisted of leading the passengers through a sequence of spatial experiences commonly found in the city and closer to the city's scale than to that of a building. In this respect, Bonaventure Station is more captivating, in our view, than that of Mont-Royal. It is an important stop since it constitutes a converging point for the underground passages leading pedestrians from Windsor Station, Central Station, Place Bonaventure, Place du Canada, and, in the future, Chaboillez Square. It is a true urban crossroad set in a fascinating volume created by a sequence of groin vaults.[38] (Plate 77.)

In conclusion, we should elaborate on a few technical features of our subway which show the creative way in which it has been adapted to conditions existing in Montreal. The cars, designed by Jacques Guillon, depart from the standards commonly applied in North America. The usual car, 22.9 metres long by 3 metres wide, has been replaced by a smaller one 17.4 metres long by 2.5 metres wide which has several advantages: with four doors on each side, the short length helps to reduce parallel circulation of passengers inside. This in turn accelerates entry and exit. The overall capacity of the train, with its 152.4-metre length, is as large as that of other North American systems because it is made up of nine cars instead of six. There is also an economic advantage to the narrower cars: both tracks may be laid in one, single-span, 7-metre-wide tunnel.

These cars possess another important characteristic: they are equipped with rubber tires. This French innovation, introduced to Montreal by the consultants of the Régie Autonome des Transports Parisiens, presents many advantages compared with the metal-wheel equipment used elsewhere on this continent. Besides ensuring smooth and relatively noiseless transport, the rubber tires provide for faster acceleration and deceleration, thus reducing the

77.   *Bonaventure metro station. Victor Prus, architect*

minimum safe distance required between trains. The most important advantage of the rubber-tire wheels combined with small cars is to permit greater flexibility in track design, either horizontally (because of the short radius of the curves), or vertically (because of possible gradients up to 6 percent). In Montreal this feature allowed the tunnel to be built for the major part right in the rock and to cross under the St. Lawrence River with a minimum of difficulty.[39]

Man and His World
One could not think of a better conclusion to this volume than a visit to the International Exposition which took place in Montreal in the summer of 1967 and which has since reopened its doors every summer under the name of Man and His World (Terre des Hommes). We need not describe it here: the public in general, whether in Montreal or abroad, is sufficiently acquainted with it. Nor do we have to elaborate on the interest it has created. It has met with astounding success, attracting some 50 million visitors in 1967, and hundreds of newspaper and magazine articles praised its attractive and interesting aspects.

Yet, we must emphasize that the success of the exhibition was in large measure due to the quality of its planning, the principles of which also apply to the city itself. This is all the more interesting in that exhibitions in the past have often exerted a definite influence on urban architecture and development or have at least anticipated important developments in these fields.

The famous Crystal Palace, for instance, created for the first such exposition, that of London in 1851, heralded for the first time large-scale pre-fabrication in the building industry. The same can be said of the Galerie des Machines, by Contamin, and of the Eiffel Tower, the two most impressive structures of the Paris World Fair in 1889. The Stockholm Exhibition of 1930 was also a turning point in the evolution of modern architecture.

From the urban point of view, the most influential of the world fairs in North America was probably the Chicago Exhibition in 1893. Designed by Frederick Law Olmsted, the great landscape architect, and by Daniel Hudson Burnham, it was truly, as Hitchcock called it, "a great 'White City,' the most complete new urbanistic concept to be realized since the replanning of Paris and Vienna in the third quarter of the century."[40] Essentially Academic or Beaux-Arts in style, it was characterized by the symmetrical grouping of large classical buildings, complete with dome and antique-style columns, surrounding a formal courtyard. The architect Sullivan has rightly criticized this kind of architecture on the grounds that it was based on fiction and on a lie, that it borrowed its inspiration from Greco-Roman buildings, at a time when he himself and others, such as William Le Baron Jenney, were producing masterpieces of commercial architecture, worthy precursors of today's designs. Yet one cannot totally assess the influence of the Chicago Exhibition from such a negative point of view, for it generated in the American public, from every walk of life, both interest in and a taste for civic order and the beauty of these displays. Considered from this angle, it can be said that the Chicago Exhibition gave a new impulse to urban planning in the United States and this brought about some happy results in a number of cities. We may even probably assume that the big axial thoroughfares basic to the very structure of the Town of Mount Royal are reminiscent of its influence.[41]

We can only welcome the prospect of witnessing some day the impact of Expo 67 on the development of Montreal and other towns. Its master plan was even better than the design of its most successful pavilions—which merely illustrated some already well-known trends—and possessed undeniable qualities with promising features for the improvement of the urban environment.

To understand the essence of this master plan, we should remember that the site selected for Expo 67, as dramatic as it appeared, constituted an enormous challenge: how was unity to be achieved, on such a large scale, among four different sites (the Mackay Jetty, St. Helen's Island, Notre-Dame Island, and La Ronde) separated by the arms of the river?[42] Providing an overall structure that would be rigid enough to ensure the necessary functional and visual order, but also flexible enough to allow for all the desirable variety, is another problem common to any exhibition of that scale.

The adherence to two basic concepts provided a reasonable measure of success in this respect. First, unity was achieved through a hierarchy of transport networks, each with its own particular scale and speed, and designed to enable the visitor to get acquainted with the site as a whole, without missing its details. The second basic concept was to achieve unity by grouping around a central theme a certain number of subthemes corresponding to the main sectors of the exhibition. The focus of each of these areas was therefore to be a pavilion illustrating a special aspect of the general theme, and serving also as a transfer point for the various transport networks.[43]

The basic system, or framework, on which the graded series was to be grafted was the Expo-Express, a railway train with a capacity of 30,000 passengers per hour. It ran on an elevated track from Place d'Accueil (Pointe Saint-Charles) right into the heart of each sector of the exhibition—St. Helen's Island, Notre-Dame Island, and La

Ronde—thus providing a physical link as well as visual continuity between the four sites. It seems to have achieved both aims. Not only did it transport visitors efficiently but, as subsequent polls demonstrated, those who used the Expo-Express were better able to picture the grounds than were other visitors.[44] Elevated stations located close to each of the theme pavilions and bedecked with brightly coloured materials also helped to illustrate the basic visual concept of the system.

There was only one weakness in the Expo-Express network: it did not provide any direct connection with the Montreal subway station on St. Helen's Island. The lack of such a connection used to confuse the visitors who came to Expo by subway.

A second network, the minirail, was integrated into the first and played an important role in encouraging closer contact with the environment of each of the exhibition areas. Slower and more flexible than the Expo-Express, the minirail, with its small open carriages, winding along on its tracks well above the ground, allowed the visitors to get a more detailed look at the general picture already perceived from the Expo-Express circuit. It was also a stimulating spatial experience: most of those who took a trip on the Notre-Dame minirail agree that it left them with the most memorable impression they could hope to retain of their visit to Expo 67.

The other transport subsystems did not, however, achieve a comparable success. It had been suggested at an early stage that boats sailing on the many waterways of Notre-Dame Island might be an attractive means of transport. Unfortunately, the visitors seem to have deliberately ignored this system, possibly because the view of Expo from below was less interesting than that from above. Whereas the Expo-Express and the minirail maintained a strict segregation between circulations of different scales and speed, there was no such separation on the surface paths leading directly to the pavilions. Every kind of vehicle, whether motorized or manual (including pedicabs), was allowed side by side with pedestrians, which disturbed the latter, even though they were not always aware of it. (Plate 78.)

The hierarchy established for traffic movements certainly made for a high degree of synthesis among the various elements of a plan conceived as an operational and dynamic unit. On the other hand, the idea of theme pavilions for each sector of the exhibition, which was meant to emphasize the unity of the whole, was not, in our opinion, a complete success. The theme pavilion of Notre-Dame Island (Man at Work), for instance, seemed somewhat lost in the midst of impressive large-scale structures, whereas its counterpart on St. Helen's Island (Man and His Universe) was truly a focal point, well related to the neighbouring structures. One wonders how many people actually realized that both pavilions were part of a unifying device. To provide truly conceptual and visual links between the various sites of the exhibition, such structures should have been more conspicuous in the general landscape of Expo.

Among the other features of the master plan, the general layout, which was distinctly urban, should be mentioned. It was characterized by the closely knit structure of the built-up areas. This helped to enhance the scale of the plazas, the recesses, and other open spaces and to emphasize the contrast with the natural environment, namely, the river and the parks on Notre-Dame and St. Helen's Islands. The distribution of the pavilions according to their respective appeal to the public (U.S.A., U.S.S.R., Canada), so as to channel the crowds towards areas of lesser interest, enabled the planners to maintain a general balance based on the geometrical (though by no means rectilinear) pattern of the ground and water thoroughfares. And finally, everyone agrees that the different service equipment—from snack bars to telephone booths and campsites— were well designed, well built, and well integrated with the general surroundings.[45]

This integrated development conferred on the different areas a certain overall unity and clarity and an orderly and harmonious balance combined with great diversity. This illustrates once more a principle of urban development which has unfortunately disappeared from the cities of today: that the whole should be more significant than the sum of its parts and components. Is this principle still applicable to our cities? The question remains unanswered. Here the planners were presented with a virgin site, with three-quarters of it built from scratch and free from any previous structure or any vested interests; moreover, they were granted an unrestricted budget combined with more control over the actual development of the plan than usual. These are factors which contributed to the image of Man and His World as the prefiguration of a dream city rather than of a workable town.

As for the architecture of the various components of Expo, it was not revolutionary, nor was its overall plan, whose principles and concepts had been known for a very long time. Indeed, we have only to think of Venice, that masterpiece of organization. Yet, the principal merit of Montreal's exhibition was to have superbly illustrated, through its best pavilions, certain already well-known trends. The best example of such tendencies is the principle of the building as an "envelope" which was demonstrated in the structures erected by the United States, Germany, Ontario, and Quebec, as well as in the

78. *Expo 67: a hierarchy of transport systems*

theme pavilions. The idea, essentially, is that of a climatic barrier surrounding the various functions distributed over several levels and served by a network of services and circulation.

The American pavilion, a huge geodesic dome designed by Buckminster Fuller, was the most straightforward example of this idea of a climatic envelope, for it was completely isolated from the three-dimensional traffic and service network. A remarkable feat, indeed, but already practically achieved a century before with the Crystal Palace in London and the Galerie des Machines in Paris. Considering its 76.2-metre diameter and 1,900,000 cubic-metre volume, covered with an acrylic envelope, one hesitates to refer to it as a building; the American dome could have easily sheltered the whole town centre of a small community. It is for this type of use that its prospects seem the most promising.

Unlike the American geodesic dome, the climatic envelope of the theme pavilions did not bring all the various functions together under the same cover, but dealt in a highly flexible manner with the individuality of functional spaces and their service networks. The design of the theme buildings was based on the universal cell of the truncated tetrahedron, which proved to be the most practical geometric form because of the great flexibility of patterns made possible by the juxtaposition of modules. Yet, aesthetically speaking, the pavilions were disappointing. For a variety of reasons, among which was the complete failure to standardize and prefabricate the structural components, they looked particularly heavy and lacked elegance. Their design seemed unable to bring a satisfactory solution to the problem of environmental and climatic protection. Incidentally, the architects responsible for the pavilions were the same ones who designed the Place Bonaventure Shopping Centre. In neither one did they seem to succeed in doing away entirely with the traditional concept of façades.[46]

The German pavilion appeared much more satisfactory, and was also the best individual architectural achievement of the whole exhibition. Completed by Frei Otto and Rolf Gutbrod, it won the enthusiastic approval of the critics, who hailed it as a major architectural innovation which would assume a leading role in the city of tomorrow. Here, as with the Ontario pavilion, there was no compromise: it was just a roof, or rather a tent, without any reference whatever to articulated buildings; it was a bare shelter from which the very notions of façades and doors had been eliminated. It was reminiscent of the large circus tent under which spectators may move about freely amid displays and exhibits. It relied on sound construction principles, resorting to poles to hold a net of tight steel cables which supported a plastic sheet. It was light, inexpensive, easy to assemble and to dismantle, and possessed a profound lyricism which, at night, had a magical fairy-tale quality.

The Quebec pavilion was also an outstanding architectural success at night, and in a way it was also an envelope, though a rather formal one. It was the joint achievement of Quebec architects Papineau, Gérin-Lajoie, and Leblanc, and displayed the simplicity and the concern for quality and detail that have made the fame of a Mies Van der Rohe. Ada Louise Huxtable, the *New York Times* critic of architecture, referred to it as the "Barcelona Pavilion of Expo 67."[47] And in the opinion of Peter Blake, it had a style and a dignity that made it more akin to a town hall or a museum than to a pavilion in a fair.[48] Like most buildings, impregnated with formal dignity and solemnity, it may well age faster than its German and Ontario counterparts.

CONCLUSION

The history of the evolution of Montreal described in the previous chapters may be divided into three different stages: pre-industrial, industrial, and metropolitan. Each of these periods has generated a characteristic type of human community and of architecture.

During the pre-industrial stage, the European settlers were too concerned with adjusting to the environment of the new continent to try to control it. This is reflected in the patterns of settlement (the côte and the rang, or range) and in popular architecture. This dependency on environmental forces arose from the fact that man had achieved only a limited mastery of energy; he was confined to the control of live energy (men, animals) and to the use of rather primitive means of converting inanimate forces: windmills and water mills. Consequently, and for historical reasons which it is not our purpose to discuss here, the main economic activities were directly related to the environmental resources which seemed the easiest to exploit: farming and the fur trade.

During this period, Montreal Island was essentially a rural territory, a true "ecological" human environment, physically structured by the subdivisions of the côte, socially organized by the parish, economically and politically integrated into the seigneurial system. Villages and hamlets, like Pointe-Claire and Pointe-aux-Trembles, were built at strategic points. The most important concentration of dwellings was centred in the town of Montreal. However, since it closely depended for its subsistence on the food surplus of its hinterland, its growth, partly guided by the development scheme of the Sulpician Dollier de Casson, was rather slow: two centuries after its foundation (1842), the town's population had scarcely reached the

40,000 mark. Thus, a stable balance prevailed between clustered and scattered dwellings.

The Market Place was the focal point of the small town and reflected the latter's dependence on the rural community. It was an indispensable meeting place where farmers, city dwellers, craftsmen, and tradesmen exchanged their goods. Its functions were complemented by Place d'Armes, the social core of the community, bounded by the parish church and the seigneurs' residence (the old Seminary of Saint-Sulpice). Until the end of the pre-industrial period, the public square was to remain a characteristic urban feature, as the subsequent planning and construction of Place Jacques-Cartier and Victoria Square tend to show.

During the second stage of development, the mastery over inanimate energy, through mechanical converters, and the subsequent economic revolutions completely upset the patterns of production and of settlement of the land. The steamship, railway, and telegraph polarized economic activities towards Montreal and emphasized its privileged geographic position. On the human level, foreign immigration from different countries came as a forecast of the cosmopolitan nature of the city. Parallel to these trends, the mechanization of the means of production, the division and specialization of labour required more manpower and appropriate production workshops, thus dissociating for the first time the place of work from the residence. This signalled the onset of urban development by attracting rural people to the town. It had taken two centuries for the urban population to reach the 40,000 mark: fifty years later, the figure greatly exceeded 200,000 (219,616 persons in 1891). In turn, the availability of an undemanding and abundant labour force stimulated industrialization which, because of the workers' lack of training and education, was mainly focused on the production of non-durable consumer goods. The concentration of labour in these industries where wages and technology were equally low would be reflected in the poverty prevailing in the working-class sectors, "the City below the Hill."

From now on, the population would be distributed according to employment opportunities. Industries dependent on raw materials and heavy transport would settle near the port, the Lachine Canal, and the railways which complemented the waterways. Thus, the first industrial municipalities and sectors were created: Sainte-Anne, Saint-Henri, Sainte-Cunégonde, Hochelaga–Maisonneuve, and others. Industries which depended on both the availability of labour and the proximity of a market, such as the manufacture of clothing, would tend to follow the demographic thrust, which was predominant along the axis of St. Lawrence Boulevard. Under Bishop Bourget's influence the old parish, which used to cover the whole city, was fragmented into as many independent units as were deemed necessary to answer the social and spiritual needs of the newly implanted populations.

With the introduction of the first public transport, starting with animal traction and followed by electricity-driven cars, a high-density residential belt developed on the periphery of the first residential areas of the industrial era. The Plateau Mont-Royal and Verdun districts belong to this loop, and their houses with outside stairs providing access to apartments built one on top of the other are typical of the period. Only those who enjoyed greater mobility, the rich (mostly British) who controlled trade and industry could afford the best locations, especially on the slopes of Mount Royal: Westmount, the Square Mile, Outremont. The architecture of their mansions bears witness to their excessive wealth. Here lies the origin of the "two solitudes" of a city divided between anglophones and francophones, between the rich and the poor, between Westmount and Saint-Henri.

At this time, the city centre was turned into a warehouse (as witnessed by the presence of grain elevators) and into an administrative and distribution centre for industrial production. Land in the city core became a commodity and since commercial buildings were in high demand—of rather astounding architecture at the beginning—they replaced on Coteau Saint-Louis the residential and social functions inherited from the previous centuries and invaded almost every available space, private or public, stopping short only of the streets.

All in all, the street seems to have been the main feature of the industrial era in Montreal, the physical link between the city centre, its industries, and the living quarters, or, in other words, between the place of management and production and the residence of both producers and consumers. In an urban area forcefully striving to earn its daily bread and to achieve economic growth, could one think of a more appropriate communication network than that provided by the orthogonal grid already implanted in the land by the former occupants under the côte system? At a time when the dynamics of concurrent forces were a substitute for planning, the layout of streets was taken for granted because it comprised the simplest form for ensuring proper communications and for maximizing the profits made by the land speculators and by the builders of row houses. Even the square, which used to be the dealers' favourite meeting place, was replaced by the shopping street, for business was now benefiting from the dynamics of communications. Sainte-Catherine, Ontario, Mont-Royal, St. Lawrence, and Saint-Hubert Streets bear witness to this new trend.

Although we must generally deplore the effect caused by the techno-economic drive in the working-class environment, the sectors inhabited by the well-to-do remained more tranquil. The solace which the Victorian upper class used to seek in the past, and in nature, to offset its cultural insecurity and to justify its philosophy of "laissez faire," is reflected in urban architecture and design. The Victorian street was a place where daily business and recreation activities were conducted at a slower and more relaxed pace than they are today. It presented an exuberant decor, mainly due to the emphasis laid on façades by the architecture of the time. The town itself was embellished with squares, churchyards, and romantic parks, among which Dominion Square, the Protestant cemetery, and Mount Royal Park are worth mentioning for the exceptional quality of their layout.

In the present stage of development, other deep changes are taking place. They may be traced to the real revolution which occurred in the fields of intra-urban transport and communications: telephone, radio, television, and internal combustion engines (cars, trucks, etc.) which replaced the messenger, the horse, and the streetcar. The mastery over machinery and electronics would now affect the economy and launch a powerful centrifugal trend scattering the city towards the outskirts and counterbalancing the centripetal trend that had prevailed all through the industrial period. The city now tends to expand its limits as far as the new means of communication allow; the railway is no longer the backbone of all transport; it is being superseded by the much more versatile road; the densely populated industrial sectors are being replaced by the suburbs, and the commercial street by the shopping centre. Can we still speak of a city in the traditional sense of the word? Are we not rather dealing with a large urbanized area which seems to rely for its density on its downtown core with its large business complexes (Place Ville-Marie, Place Bonaventure, Victoria Square) which epitomize the mastery over technical skills and the predominance of the service industry?

Around the downtown area and along the axial express roads that lead to it, residential towers are gradually appearing in answer to the needs of small families and households attracted by the prospects of employment opportunities in the downtown area. On the outskirts of the city the situation is exactly the opposite: single-family units prevail; they appeal to large families with a reasonable income. The others, the disadvantaged, have found refuge in the dilapidated sectors surviving from the last century, for only there can they find adequate accommodation at a reasonable price. It is a greedy fringe that is blindly swallowing up land that could be developed more profitably and more practically, and used for different purposes, such as farming or leisure activities. Initiated by land speculation which is very often encouraged by governments and backed by advertising, this growing wave of low-grade cottages appears to be totally unstructured; it is wiping out the landscape and submerging or threatening the identity of the former villages of the island and the plain. In short, Montreal can no longer be perceived or regarded as an entity; its reality is now immersed in a maze of forms and landscapes, with no relationship to each other, whether conceptual, structural, or visual; they are held together only by hidden economic ties.

Each stage of this evolution has imprinted its mark on the developing city, shaped its environment and architecture, and contributed to its image and identity. But we should not be misled; for these rungs have only been isolated for the purpose of our study. Since a city is a dynamic phenomenon, the characteristics of each of these periods are intermingled in reality; the traits and physical features inherited from a given period have mostly served as a blueprint for the following age.

This can be demonstrated on a large scale as well as on a small one. The rural division of the land has led to the standard grid of streets with its very rigid milieu, where even contrasting features such as parks or monuments are subject to the same strict pattern, in spite of their social and cultural pretensions. Similarly, traces of the king's ways of the old côtes may be found on main axial roads: the Metropolitan Boulevard, Côte-de-Liesse Road, Côte-des-Neiges Road, and others. Likewise, the villages of the island and the plain, which today are being engulfed by suburbs, are deeply rooted in the organized network imposed long ago on settlements during troubled times. On a smaller scale, we could quote dozens of examples, but will note just a few. Place d'Armes, for instance, which was a typical urban component of the pre-industrial days, was endowed during the industrial period with its most characteristic monuments, the second Notre-Dame Church and the Bank of Montreal, but lost its primary role as the focal point of the town; it became instead a leisure site, like the Georgian square. It was once more to forfeit its character in the twentieth century and also, unfortunately, its scale when it became host to the Aldred and the Banque Canadienne Nationale skyscrapers. Dominion Square, originally a peaceful cemetery on the outskirts of the built-up area, was to assume an entirely different significance when its prestige began to attract such centres of activities as Windsor Station, followed by a series of remarkable Victorian buildings which made it something quite unique in urban North America. By and large, in the course of the modern era, most of the downtown squares seem to have played this new role of attracting the big complexes and the hubs of circulation. Along the same lines we could also mention Saint-Louis Square which began as the site of a reservoir, or Lafontaine Park and St. Helen's Island which were originally military grounds. Thus the "dynamic perenniality" of structures implanted in the ground at various times appears to be a basic feature in the development of our city, without which it would be hard to explain how it acquired its present image and personality.

So far, we have only dealt with the material organization of structures and the physical environment. All this would scarcely be of interest were it not immersed in a rich human life with all its ethnic variety, from the indigenous Quebecers—two-thirds of them coming from a rural background—to the immigrants originating in every European and Asian country. It is a life enriched with varied social and cultural characteristics that are reflected in the mentality and behaviour of all the ethnic districts of the city, whether Jewish or Italian, as well as in some of the streets, from St. Lawrence Boulevard to Park Avenue, or even in the service areas, from Jean-Talon Market to exotic restaurants. That life seems to be in a permanent state of flux: the Irish cluster around St. Patrick's Church was to give way to Chinatown, whereas Park Avenue was in succession British, Jewish, and now Greek. It is by no means easy to pinpoint the characteristics of a multiform life in a state of flux innervating an environment in the making. We can only conclude that our urban habitat is rich in forms, expressions, life, and spirit.

From the study of this life and these physical features, how can we now assess man's intervention in the management of his environment and his habitat? What guidelines may we draw for the future, bearing in mind that wisdom is not acquired from the listing of historical facts but from their interpretation? At this point some clarification is necessary. It is indeed generally assumed that Montreal, like most North American cities, is the outcome of a set of uncontrolled forces, of the so-called American dynamism, and that the influence of planned action is practically negligible. This assumption is partly true, but it should be weighed by facts. For American cities, studies such as the ones by Reps (*The Making of Urban America*) or by Tunnard and Reed (*American Skyline*) tend to present the matter in a more balanced perspective. As for Montreal, the preceding pages lead us to the conclusion that human intervention played a certain part in its development.

On the one hand, the whole system of settlement of the territory of Quebec and the island of Montreal, based on the rang and on the côte (a territorial unit closely integrated with the political and economic system of the seigneury and strongly structured by the parish), generated an "ecological" environment of a rare quality and homogeneity. Even now, Quebec is seeking—as if it were some paradise lost—a form of political, economic, social, and cultural unity as satisfying as that which it enjoyed under the old regime, the very kind of oneness that the conquest and the subsequent industrialization had dismantled. On the other hand, all the sectional plans of development have had an undeniable impact on the destiny, the social and cultural composition, the practical organization, and the physical environment of our metropolis. We need only remember the plans of Dollier de Casson, of the commissioners in charge of tearing down the fortifications of the old citadel, of the large cemeteries, Mount Royal Park, the Cité-jardin, Nuns' Island, of Pei for the new downtown area, and of the subway. We should also think of all the deliberate efforts made to improve navigation on the river, to build canals (Lachine Canal, for one), and to convert Montreal into a national port and a hub for the railway network.

Whether we consider the architecture and the environment of Montreal, depending on periods and circumstances, as the reflection of a natural dynamism or as the result of the intervention of man, one conclusion must be drawn: the results were authentic and valid, in so far as they reflected a balance between the prevailing forces and influences, such as geography, climate, economics, and culture.

Thus it appears that the pattern of settlement based on the côte-cum-parish-cum-seigneury was a remarkable answer to the overall circumstances arising from the colonization of a new continent. Indeed, the territorial unit known as a côte (as well as the range) prevailed over the more contemporary concept advocated by the ruling class, that is, the star-shaped villages of Intendant Jean Talon. The latter concept proved to be a cultural import totally alien to the living conditions prevailing here. Similarly, the gradual adaptation of the Quebec house to the environmental conditions and the living habits adopted therein resulted in a much more authentic architecture than the attempts of a Chaussegros de Lery to build in New France Baroque châteaux, copied from those of the European homeland.

The dichotomy between the adaptation to the basic circumstances of the environment, which is the hallmark of popular architecture, and the prevalence of "culture" which pervades official and academic planning was not characteristic of the French regime only. It was perpetuated throughout the history of Montreal. Thus, for instance, during the Victorian era all the so-called historical, eclectic, or Picturesque styles were imported images to which academic architecture held fast at the expense of the deeper roots of our reality. Was any style, therefore, ever more alien to our geography, to our vast northern expanses, than the Baroque or the neo-Baroque? Was there ever a better example of cultural (and spiritual) colonization than the reduced-scale reproduction of St. Peter's Basilica, planted like a conversation-piece on the threshold of Dominion Square? Was there ever any style less attuned to our climate than that of the French Second Empire or the Picturesque which participated in an orgy of stone, brick, wood, iron, and sheet-metal? Is it not revealing to discover that the only authentic architecture of that period—and the previous one, for that matter—remains an architecture that makes no pretense of being one, an architecture without an architect, which escapes all entrenched cultural traditions or institutionalized systems? We are obviously not thinking here of Christ Church Cathedral or Mount Stephen House, but of the industrial-sector house, with its corridors and outside staircases, of commercial architecture with its open, well-lighted plan and its stone skeleton façades, and of the grain elevators, those huge machines that have no pretension apart from being functional.

Many people, mainly because of sentimental ties, are willing to acknowledge the true architectural value of the domestic colonial buildings inspired by the old French models. Yet they adamantly deny it to typical houses such as those built in Plateau Mont-Royal or Verdun. Should one label "architecture" these shabby houses whose outside additions of balconies, galleries, staircases, and sheds are really an eye-sore? Why not? Mount Stephen House (and others of its kind), with its large, high-ceilinged, well-lighted rooms, its opulent appearance, and its orderly surfaces, undoubtedly conforms more to our usual idea of architecture. But architecture is not an image; it should be a complete answer to the needs of a given situation. Without condoning poorly lit rooms or suicidal staircases, we have to admit that these typical houses, because of their inside plan and outside complements, their ingenious contrivances so well adapted to the requirements of our climate and to our building materials, and their reasonable price made possible by prefabrication and standardization, have provided an appropriate answer to the need for accommodating in a minimum time thousands of rural migrants, particularly those who were disadvantaged.

It does not follow that we should reject, as a whole, the academic architecture we have inherited and abandon it to oblivion and to the mercy of the speculators. Some old buildings lack neither charm nor character. For instance, although Victor Bourgeau, like most of his contemporaries, indulged in the historical style, his churches show a distinctive, personal touch, a blend of simplicity and vigour. And the city would certainly be the poorer were it to lose such monuments as Notre-Dame Church, Bonsecours Market, Windsor Station, the National Library, and other similar buildings. This architecture, in addition to being interesting in itself, is a strong reminder of the past. This is one of the essential conditions for humanizing a city; like man, it, too, must possess a memory. We must also concede that, since it developed in an urban environment, this architecture has acquired another dimension by contributing to city landscapes and to their identity. In this respect, most of the buildings in Old Montreal, regardless of their style and architectural value, are an integral part of the character of the streets. Similarly, most of our large churches and cathedrals, whether neo-Gothic or Baroque, whether worthy of the historians' attention or not, seem to be irreplaceable as landmarks dominating the city with their tall silhouettes.

Coming back to the present time, we need not look very far to find proof of social and cultural colonialism, both at the core of the city and on its outskirts. It is reflected, as a mirror, in all our suburbs: the mentality, the way of living, the styles, all are imported from the United States. The "Colonial" models of New England, the Texan "ranches," and the Californian "cottages" or "Spanish Colonial" houses are shamelessly copied and reproduced on a smaller scale to fit the budget of the average consumer. These dwellings are crowded together in developments where the curve of the streets is a substitute for any planning effort. They are often grafted to existing villages or developments, depriving the latter of their substance and destroying their homogeneity. Even the claims made by advertising cannot conceal the ridiculous features of these houses, the real motivation of their developers and contractors, and the lack of concern of the government authorities who encourage them.

Downtown, except for certain complexes such as the Alexis Nihon Plaza, Place Bonaventure, or Château Champlain whose tower blends in well with the predominant forms of Dominion Square's environment, the new constructions also display the same nondescript architecture. Though in most instances it claims allegiance to the modern international style, it seems to become a prisoner just as the Victorian which it had once sought to liberate. Relying on the scientific approach, obeying strict canons, banning every ornament, and exhausting technology to its limit, it represents the quintessence of the drawing board and generates the kind of stereotyped forms that are found all around the world, from Timbuktu to Toronto. In spite of all its contradictions, the 1967 World Exhibition had one good point: it brought colour, imagination, and an ephemeral quality to an urban landscape which was gradually assuming a pomp and formality best illustrated by the heavy and austere new Court House. We have reason to believe that there is a reaction brewing against the dictatorship of this international modern style. Will it lead to an architecture better able to express the true identity of the community? Or do we have to fear the opposite excess as so often happened in the course of the history of architecture?

In Montreal as elsewhere, modern town planning seems to be heading towards a dead end. The fact that cities are deteriorating despite a half-century of scientific urban renewal seems like a paradox. Was it not in the very name of town planning that a highway was built right in the heart of the city, marring landscapes, slashing into residential areas, increasing pollution, and adding to the traffic problems of the downtown area? Is it not in the name of town planning that retail shopping centres are proliferating downtown? Pleasant and comfortable as they may be, they appeal only to the wealthier classes and contribute to the deterioration of another commercial centre, that of Sainte-Catherine Street, for which nothing has been done. Is this not one way to plan and program the downfall of the traditional city? Again, is it not in the name of town planning that huge office and residential towers are allowed to rise downtown as well as on the outskirts? They artificially raise the value of the land to such an extent that other less profitable buildings, in spite of their potential usefulness, are condemned to disappear, leaving behind them gigantic gaping holes that mar the beauty of the city.

The main danger of modern urban renewal is that it is all too often a slave to an all-powerful technology and an economic system which seem only concerned with their own growth. Pollution, in all its aspects, was the result of blind technical and economic development and may well be the first link in a series of catastrophes, unless the goals of our system are re-assessed and become more concerned with people. Above all, we should not deceive ourselves: for the first time in its history, Montreal is at a critical crossroad. We have inherited one of the most remarkable cities in North America but its uniqueness, its quality of life, and its environment are henceforth menaced. The corrosive effect of this socially and economically costly dismantlement, the accelerated aging of a large part of its urban fabric, the impact of automobile traffic, the ravages of increasing land value generated by the gigantic size of modern complexes, the gradual disappearance of trees, green spaces, and monuments of historical or architectural interest, and a municipal policy entirely inspired by the kind of grandeur which prevailed in Vienna just before the fall of the empire, all have launched Montreal on a very dangerous descent. At the bottom there lies nothing but inexorable physical and moral degradation, decrepitude, ugliness, and the disgust and intolerance of its citizens. The threat should be taken seriously, for other cities in the world have already reached such an advanced stage of decay.

We may well wonder why there should be this sudden vortex after three centuries of unthreatened development. In our view—and this is something we have not yet fully come to realize—it happened because both the mechanical and electronic transformers of energy have become too powerful. They now provide unlimited opportunities in terms of investment profits together with extraordinary prospects for rechannelling these gains. This is being achieved by conditioning all human activities through the information media, especially radio and television. Technological revolutions, the history of our city tells us, followed by economic upheavals, are the factors which have truly governed the activities of man, and, consequently, changed the form and structure of our city. We must therefore be master of our technology and of our economy if we want to organize and control our urban environment. The conversion of energy in itself is neither good nor bad: it is a mere tool. Whether it is left in the hands of a blind and anonymous techno-economic system or put at the service of an authentic urban society dedicated to the quality of life should mean the difference between decay or fulfilment for the city. It cannot be achieved without a parallel flowering of the citizens themselves, who must be liberated and made more aware so that the weight of their knowledge and participation may become a factor in town planning. The city and its architecture represent too complex a phenomenon, too pervaded with the dynamics of life for it to be entrusted to specialists alone.

In order to become creative, awareness and participation must be rooted in the deep reality of our environment. Among other things, citizens must comprehend that it is economically unsound to entrust the development of the metropolis solely to the interests of the developers and speculators; it is also a folly, for instance, to waste the best farming land in the province to provide space for the development of housing units which already contain the seeds of the greatest problems facing future generations. The way our city has evolved clearly demonstrates that the vested interests and the structures implanted in the soil are terribly permanent: will it be any different the day we have to face the tide of uncontrolled building? Now that the age of leisure is at hand, and Montreal is one of the few cities in the world endowed with enough natural resources to satisfy its needs, it is economically unsound, as well as anti-social, to sacrifice those resources on the altar of an individualistic, liberal economy, to allow rivers to be polluted, to deface the landscape, to erode the sites for leisure, in brief, to destroy for future centuries the huge potential our region holds for the quality of life. Our collective future is at stake and at this stage the solution is of a political nature, and planning must become a regional matter. A pilot plan such as Horizon 2000 is already a first step in the right direction. Projects of this kind, however, tend to be illusory if they are not accompanied by appropriate legislation and proper enforcement mechanisms.

At a different level, citizens must come to realize that it is up to them to remodel their urban environment in order to answer their daily needs and aspirations. This kind of action, for lack of a better word, may be described as opportunity planning. It does not require any more legislation or mechanisms than those already available to our society. From the parks created out of former quarries or military grounds, from the squares which have contributed to the remodelling of a modern city centre, all the way to the restoration of Old Montreal, the evolution of our city reminds us that many components which have contributed to the identity, character, comfort, and quality of life in our environment were indeed acquired through voluntary or accidental renovations of the environment. The opportunities are ample: there are old sectors to restore, obsolete industrial zones to convert, public easements to open up, properties belonging to parishes, religious entities, or corporate bodies to reclaim and to recycle in the best interest of the community. At such a level, imagination and good will are the best tools for planning.

Let us say finally that this civic awareness traces its inspiration to the earliest tradition. In the course of its history, Montreal has always found groups or individuals who had a deep love for their city and who were willing to improve and embellish it. We may question their achievements, but as long as their spirit of love for the city remains, Montreal shall survive through defeats and victories, through ugliness and beauty, alive with hope.

PILOGUE

It is symbolic that the first edition of *Montréal en Evolution* ended with a description of Man and His World. The 1967 universal exposition was, in a way, an extraordinary manifestation of confidence in the future by a small society which, since the Quiet Revolution, has been trying to catch up to the American giant.

Carried out under artificially idealized circumstances, Man and His World presented almost perfect planning and management without equal. It constituted the apotheosis of an avant-garde technology that growing prosperity had made more and more accessible to city dwellers. By putting Montreal on the world map, it gave the Quebec population (which had not yet taken its own culture for granted) the illusion that henceforth it could place itself on the roster of international cultures by a presentation worthy of a western Indian "potlatch." Finally, Expo seemed to foreshadow good fortune for a metropolis destined to have seven million inhabitants by the year 2000.

Unfortunately, Man and His World was neither a beginning nor an ending, but only a spectacle for the moment, magnificent but without any future. Far from heralding an exceptional future, it masked the rapidly evolving reality of approaching decline. The flow of events confirmed this: economic recession (or rather stagflation), unemployment, social problems, the "October crisis," the collapse of liberal reformists, the national identity crisis, the return of uncertainty and conservatism. The 1976 Olympic Games, by increasing public indebtedness in a catastrophic manner, did nothing to improve the picture. This situation, however, was not restricted to Quebec, or even to Canada. In 1958 John Kenneth Galbraith con-

fidently published *The Affluent Society*; twenty years later he wrote
The Age of Uncertainty.

Using 1976 census data, we can predict that the Montreal metropolitan region will not attain the seven million population figure
forecast for the year 2000. From 1971 to 1976, the city of Montreal
itself lost 11 percent of its population, dropping from 1,214,352 to
1,080,546. The city therefore had fewer people in 1976 than it did at
the end of the 1950s. On the whole, this decrease would not have
been serious had there been a parallel increase of population in the
Montreal Urban Community or in the surrounding area. Such an increase did not occur, though, because the MUC lost 4.6 percent of
its inhabitants, going from 1,959,143 to 1,869,641; whereas the metropolitan region gained only 2.6 percent, rising from 2,743,208 to
2,814,070.[1]

This problem was not exclusive to Montreal. Recent data reflect
the same tendency, whether in Canada, the United States, or Europe: in the Western world the birthrate has declined regularly since
the late 1960s. From 1971 to 1976 the growth rate in Toronto and
Vancouver, just as in Montreal, had dropped substantially, and was
even more marked in most of the great cities. In the majority of European capitals, as in large American cities, the population will
henceforth remain stable or, in certain instances, decline.

This new circumstance is explained in the conclusion to a recent
atlas of large American cities: "Three decades of almost constant
growth and expansion produced the widespread impression that
continued metropolitan growth was inevitable. But history and
common sense suggest that this is naïve. The late 1960's and early
1970's were especially turbulent and traumatic as civil disorders
erupted in metropolitan areas, a deep recession dashed unrealistic
expectations for unlimited prosperity, and energy shortages raised
the price of mobility."[2]

With the urbanist Hans Blumenfeld, one might suppose it is too
soon to conclude that there is a countercurrent to metropolitan
growth. For large cities, it would seem that we are dealing with a
"slowing down that could be attributable in part to the falling off of
national population growth, to the drop in the business cycle, and to
a more equal distribution of services among large and small centres."[3] Or perhaps this drop is due to a metropolitan expansion that
from now on, at least in part, will extend beyond the boundaries of
the census zones.

No doubt all these factors, in varying degrees, have played a role
in the slowing down of demographic growth in the Montreal region;
they are in addition to a particular local circumstance that inten-
sifies their effect. It is obvious that the pole of Canadian economic

development is being displaced toward the centre of the country, particularly to Toronto. Montreal thus sees its historic leadership role challenged in several fields and reduced more to the level of Quebec, which is itself in the process of redefinition. If the rates of birth, immigration, and internal migration remain at the present level, the 1981 census will indicate a net loss of population in the metropolitan region.

This new phenomenon must be taken into account in the future planning and development of the metropolis. The challenge will no longer be, as we believed a decade ago, in arranging to accommodate the largest number of inhabitants possible in the urban agglomeration, but rather to know how best to develop the city to handle zero population growth.

Before going into this issue, however, let us make a brief inventory of the most striking additions to Montreal architecture in the last few years; it will be noted that they belong to the aforementioned approach, that of catching up at any price. In their own way, they add to the idea of the triumphant city, the showplace city forecast by Man and His World. We will be concerned here with Cité Concordia, Complexe Desjardins, and the Olympic installations.

Recent Projects of the Catch-up Period
Cité Concordia is the first large structure in the centre of the city to include such a wide range of uses. It occupies an area bounded by Pine Avenue, Hutchison, Jeanne-Mance, and Milton Streets; Park Avenue serves as a central axis and access route. The name Milton-Park has been applied to this sector.

The project has three 30-storey towers, containing a total of 1,352 apartments; the general appearance is of giant stairs. Each tower has a public garden at street level and a series of private terraces. Two of the structures are located south of Prince Arthur Street, on either side of Park Avenue. The third is on the west side of Park, to the north of Prince Arthur. Facing the latter, on the east side of Park, is the Hotel Loews, in the form of a Z, with 15 storeys and 500 rooms. Immediately to the north of the hotel, completing the project, is a 26-storey office building with a rather unusual form, due to its rounded corners. All these elements are linked by five levels of underground passages. On two of them can be found a promenade of boutiques with 20,440 square metres of shopping space.

If one accepts the inevitability of such office and apartment towers in the city centre, because of the high cost of accessibility, an integration of multiple uses appears to be more interesting than a simplistic alignment of unifunctional buildings such as are found along Dorchester Boulevard or Lincoln Avenue. A Cité Concordia-type grouping permits greater activity and diversity while favouring a spatial organization that increases the comfort of the users and promotes integration into city life. The architects (Eva Vecsei, in association with Dobush, Stewart, Longpré, Marchand, and Goudreau) oriented the buildings of La Cité in such a way as to receive maximum sunlight, and at the same time maintain an urban aspect at street level.[4]

Despite the imposing size of the elements, this objective has been well met. Other than the office tower, which is conventional in spite of its rounded corners, the units are not visually oppressive. The maintenance of an interesting urban scale has been assured by the forms of the buildings themselves and by the gardens and other features at street level. Other merits of this grouping include good workmanship and high quality of material, colours, and textures. The complex has avoided the ostentatious luxury of Westmount Square as well as the poor quality of construction that afflicts many of the high-density projects built since the war.

La Cité thus could be considered a positive contribution to the city, except that it brought about the destruction of 255 residences, the loss of 20 neighbourhood stores, and the disappearance of a viable human community.

In fact, the growth of this project was typical of a certain urban renovation that does more harm than good. This Milton-Park sector, known traditionally as the Quartier Sainte-Famille, was at first the site of row houses, mostly built of Montreal limestone, comfortable and well made, dating from the beginning of the century. Since the war, however, the area lost its bourgeois owners and began to attract a more varied and less moneyed population: students, immigrants, labourers, people happy to find large apartments at a reasonable price and with varied services just at the periphery of downtown. "People simply appreciated the well-preserved, human-scale buildings and the spacious but inexpensive homes they provided. They liked the old trees that lined the streets. They enjoyed the meeting places—the corner grocery stores, the restaurants, the tobacconists and the laundromats."[5]

Even though the Service d'Urbanisme, at that time, considered the area in too good shape physically and socially to be classified as an urban renovation zone, Concordia Estates Ltd. was not hindered in acquiring—by various means and under several names—98 percent of the non-institutional properties in the territory bounded by Sainte-Famille, Milton, and Hutchinson Streets and Pine Avenue. The promotors subsequently evicted the residents and demolished the houses, despite the vigorous opposition of local inhabitants, who had grouped together as the Milton-Park Citizens' Committee.

Unfortunately, the destructive impact of this project is far from ended. Through the concentration of large numbers of services and the considerable increase in land-use density in this area, the whole periphery of Cité Concordia has become a sector of high-development potential. The old Victorian residences, especially on Sainte-Famille Street, risk a rapid demise if drastic protective measures are not taken.

One often thinks that modern redevelopment such as that of Cité Concordia is not possible unless a certain amount of demolition is accepted to create space. In downtown Montreal, however, coherent renewal is not so much a matter of availability of space as of its organization. If an inventory were to be made of the unused terrain, the parking lots, and the public service areas (railroads and autoroutes over which building is possible), it would be evident that there is no lack of space but rather an overabundance. An integrated strategy of redevelopment, based on the conservation of an architectural heritage and a socially well-organized society as well as on the rational use of various available lots, would have permitted the preservation of the local Milton-Park community while building elsewhere a modern complex of the same quality as La Cité.

Complexe Desjardins, in contrast with La Cité whose construction brought about useless demolition, was built on a physically and socially degraded site which had already been designated by the Service d'Urbanisme as a zone for urban renewal. Occupying a block formed by Sainte-Catherine, Saint-Urbain, and Jeanne-Mance Streets and Dorchester Boulevard, it is a complex of structures with a multi-functional character, and houses commercial, socio-cultural, and administrative operations. Making up the ensemble are three towers (27, 35, and 41 storeys) and a 600-room hotel, all of which rest on a large substructure. An open square, deployed on two levels, occupies the centre of this podium. Three underground levels provide various services and a 1,150-car parking area.

This accomplishment constitutes the best symbol yet of recent attempts by French Canadians at catching up to the standard of North America. Conceived and financed by French Canadians, the complex is now the largest architectural ensemble in the metropolis and one of the most imposing in Canada. Covering an area of 3.2 hectares, with a floor-space index of 8.6, and with a total of 391,026 square metres, it surpasses its major rivals: Place Ville-Marie (325,158 square metres) and Place Bonaventure (306,577 square metres). Built in a sector traditionally associated with francophones, the super-complex tends to reserve this part of downtown for this group, and to create a new version of the "two solitudes."

The integrated concept of Place Ville-Marie was pleasing to the citizens and appeared, to the promotors, administrators, and urban planners, to be a project that could lead to the revitalization of the downtown area. It served as a model for Complexe Desjardins which, in fact, filled a major role in the polarization of a new north–south axis of redevelopment. In 1967 the Jean-Claude La-Haye Company presented a development plan which showed this axis as essentially pedestrian, linking the metro station at Place des Arts with that of Place d'Armes. It would serve the following activity-generators: the campus of the Université du Québec à Montréal (at that time destined for the site of the Institut de Technologie), Place des Arts, Complexe Desjardins, and others which now are Complexe Guy-Favreau and eventually the Convention Centre; all of these are equally accessible by east–west vehicular routes.

As far as architecture is concerned, the designers tried to blend the scale of the complex with that of Place des Arts. Thus, the height of the units decreases toward Sainte-Catherine Street, from 40 storeys for the South Tower to 32 for the East, 27 for the North, and 12 for the Hôtel Méridien. Adding to the dynamic spatial composition is the slight off-centring of the units in relation to each other. Despite this juggling of sizes, the complex still gives the appearance of a severe and massive fortress.

Several factors contribute to this effect. First of all, the architectural treatment is conservative: as on other sites the idea of towers over a shopping mall has often been used. Here, however, the designers preferred to build four distinct blocks on the podium rather than one lone tower with a hundred storeys. This is an encouraging sign in that they looked for alternatives to the excessively tall images presented by the World Trade Center in New York or the Sears Tower in Chicago.

Large corporations now demand floor space of at least 1,860 square metres per storey, and this created a problem for the architects: how to design elegant structures on the limited area and heights available. Blouin, Blouin, Guité, and Roy tried to resolve this impasse by using a polygonal form for the towers. From the functional point of view, this doubled the number of corner rooms, which are particularly desirable; on the aesthetic side, the effort was too limited to really cut down the monolithic appearance.

The exterior of the towers is smooth and bare, contributing to their appearance of excessive mass. There are no features to catch the eye so one is obliged to envisage the whole ensemble at once. The Hôtel Méridien, designed by the architects Ouellet and Reeves, is more lively in shape than in texture. In contrast to the buildings at Westmount Square, fortunately, the hotel is easily distinguished from the other units, although its style is not forceful. The uniform grey of this set of buildings also adds to its heavy and oppressive character.

It is the scale, tentacular shape, and texture of the concourse area that make it the most interesting element of Complexe Desjardins. Along with the infrastructure, the concourse is the work of architects Longpré, Marchand, and Goudreau. Three storeys high, it seems to carry through the scale of buildings on Sainte-Catherine Street, permitting a transition between the towers silhouetted against the modern skyline and the more traditional ambience of the built-up area.

On entering the concourse and looking out on this large central plaza, one notes a vastly different and more interesting architecture. With an area of a half-hectare, overlooking which are floors in the form of superimposed mezzanines, the plaza is on a par with the city, its streets, and its traditional public squares. It constitutes a crossroads of pedestrian circulation generated by the metro and the automobile, by service cores, and by commercial activities.

The mall contains two levels, of which the lower is a large open area some 55 metres on each side, with a pedestrian passage under Sainte-Catherine Street linking it to Place des Arts to the north and on to the metro station; in the opposite direction it will connect with Complexe Guy-Favreau through a similar corridor. The upper level is of variable width and irregular shape; it links the Sainte-Catherine Street sidewalk with that of Dorchester Boulevard. Several stairways and escalators permit communication between the two levels.

The mall is linked with the city outside, not only functionally but also visually, because of the immense windowed walls that enclose its two extremities. From the outside one can perceive the entire area and its activities. From the inside one has a magnificent view of Place des Arts in one direction and Old Montreal in the opposite. Only one glaring flaw mars this splendid visual continuity, and that is the system of doors. For whatever reason, the architects fell back on a design more in keeping with an ordinary building than with one which functions, in part, as a public square.

Another quality evidenced by this plaza, despite a flat roof made of waffle-type concrete panels, is the abundance of natural light that enters through skylights and lateral glass walls. This is a definite improvement over previous covered galleries in Montreal. One regrets, however, that the originally planned translucent roof was not constructed. The present solution, in addition to its lack of elegance, does not offer sufficient visual clearance toward the sky or give a feeling of the outdoors. Furthermore, a translucent roof, at night, would have allowed light from the plaza to give a fairylike appearance to the towers.

Well-organized, functional, spacious, and welcoming, the plaza is bordered by more than a hundred businesses, including a dozen restaurants and four cinemas. Because of free activities, space for shows and exhibitions, the area can provide in one spot all the interactions that are part of the dynamics and attraction of the city. Ever since its inauguration in spring 1976, the concourse has been well received by the citizens and, thanks to the excellent schedule of activities, its visitor-use level has been very good.

In conclusion, Complexe Desjardins remains a conservative structure from the exterior, with little appeal and no great elegance. It is redeemed, however, by its vast and dynamic interior space. The latter constitutes the first really modern plaza in the metropolis and, for the moment, marks the culmination in the evolution of a concept that began with Place Ville-Marie—a simple corridor of exclusively commercial boutiques—then was developed further at Place Bonaventure and especially at Alexis Nihon Plaza; the latter was the first to let in natural light, although timidly, and to promote free activities. It is ironic that Complexe Desjardins does not bear the name "Place,"[6] whereas its predecessors, all of which are really complexes, are called Place.

Since 1974 the most spectacular and controversial architecture has been the Olympic installations. The two principal units, the village and the stadium, will be analysed next.

Rarely has a project created so much conflict on the part of the public that its promotor, Mayor Drapeau, was forced to defend it before a parliamentary commission in Quebec. A coalition of more than a hundred community organizations under the name Regroupement pour la Préservation des Espaces verts vigorously protested the use of Viau Park for the Olympic Village. Its opposition was one of principle: in a city short of green spaces, it was unthinkable for the city powers to allow the sacrifice of an open space which was close to the populous sectors of Rosemont, Hochelaga, Maisonneuve, and Mercier, and which had been developed at taxpayers' expense and used as a park for more than twenty years.

Other organizations, including the Comité d'Habitation du Montréal métropolitain, the Service d'Urbanisme et d'Habitation de

Montréal and the Quebec Order of Architects, condemned not only the choice of site but the concept as well. The Comité d'Habitation stated that it was impossible to conceive an Olympic residence within a social housing policy. The Olympic Village called for great density of occupation and special infrastructures, whereas a socially progressive housing policy required low density, an integration into local communities, and a program answering the needs of the neighbourhood. Arguments were raised against the project. First, it was antisocial to squander green spaces belonging in the public domain for the benefit of an already privileged minority. Given the great need for moderately priced housing in Montreal, it was indecent for the municipal administration to create facilities favouring a class that already had a great capacity for consumption and for choice. Finally, it was socially unacceptable to concentrate thousands of people, at high density, on an isolated site that was poorly linked to services of the city.

Despite this articulate and well-organized opposition, the village has been built as originally planned, but at a cost four times higher than forecast (about $100 million). The architectural design consists of two pyramids enclosing apartments in the upper parts, public space in the middle sections, and a 696-car parking garage below ground. Each pyramid contains 490 lodging units, each of which in turn opens onto a balcony on one side and a walkway on the other. Those at the ends of the pyramids are also provided with a terrace. The architects D'Astous and Durand considered the walkways the equivalent of superimposed streets.

Although the structures show much character from the outside—the influence of the Baie des Anges in southern France cannot be denied—and even suggest luxury apartments, the impression changes radically on the inside. The net habitable floor-space of the apartments is only slightly higher than the norm applied to moderately priced housing. Furthermore, the rooms are sombre because the natural light is kept out by the projection of balconies and walkways. In addition, a view over the park surrounding the village is practically impossible from the interior because of the screening effect created by the guard rails. Finally, even though the walkways counteract any claustrophobia resulting from the maze of interior corridors and offer security in case of fire, they are not appropriate in Montreal's winter. One can imagine the inconvenience of repeatedly donning winter wear to go to the pool, the post office, the convenience store, all located in the centre section of the same building.

Because of its architectural treatment, its structural systems (concrete walls 36 cm thick every seven metres), and its restrictive mechanics, this complex can be used only for housing. The committee charged with studying its future pointed out, however, that the village, as far as habitation is concerned, is located too far from the community facilities of neighbouring areas and its population density is too high. From the very onset of the plan, these inconveniences were denounced by thousands of citizens, but that did not stop the municipal administration from planting this large-scale monument in a park.[7]

If Montreal has any building that merits the title of monument it certainly is the Olympic Stadium. It has all the attributes of Beaux-Arts architecture: beauty, clarity of style and function, harmony of the ensemble, which itself is well balanced and rhythmic. Its design is dynamic and vibrant, enclosing spaces by ample movements. The majesty of this structure, particularly from the infield, is impressive.

The stadium has seven storeys, the first at ground level. Its infield serves many purposes and the bleachers (both permanent and temporary) can accommodate 56,549 spectators. Part of this design concept is the pool complex at the base of the mast. The hemispheric shells of the pools enclose six basins. This section contains more than 21,370 square metres of usable floor space on five levels and includes cloakrooms, exercise rooms, and water filtration and treatment services. The permanent bleachers around the pools can seat 3,000 people.

As conceived by the French architect Roger Taillibert, the mast has a fixed shape starting from a tripodal base covering the shells of the pool complex. When finished it will reach a height of 168 metres, thus providing the spatial position and creating the necessary volume for the operation and storage of the movable roof. Although it will have 37 storeys, all with some structural function, only about 28,000 square metres of usable floor space will be available.

The ensemble is splendid already, and will be even more so when the mast is completed. But at what price? Can architecture be justified regardless of cost? Any architectural creation that is not subject to a minimum of financial constraint risks getting out of hand. In comparing the cost of this Olympic Stadium with that of large American stadiums, open or closed, one is justified in asking if there was not too much freedom of expression in this work.

In its actual state of completion, including the parking garages but not counting the investment for the pool complex and the eleven floors already built on the mast, the Montreal stadium has cost nearly $700 million. This is some $650 million more than the average price for large sports enclosures in the United States. At the largest contemporary American stadiums, the investment is in the order of $725 per seat. At the Olympic Stadium, it is $11,500 per seat!

There are several reasons for these excessive costs. Taillibert blamed local backwardness in the technologies of prefabrication, prestressing, and post-tension. However, prefabrication is well known on this continent, and notably in Quebec. Furthermore, the prefabricated and prestressed girders which served to pave the exit corridors of the stadium are standard products of Quebec manufacturers. It would be more exact to say that we were not equipped to prefabricate "feats of strength." For example, the components of the technical ring were two storeys high and weighed 180 tons each: here we find ourselves far afield from everyday problems of prefabrication and manipulation! In his book *Construire l'avenir*, Taillibert himself recognized this fact when he spoke of "structural consoles with 70 metres overhang, made for the first time in the world."[8] Thus, we had no moulds of variable shape or vast experience in post-tension at this scale. It was necessary to build a special factory for prefabrication (Shokbéton, at Saint-Eustache) and to import from France the necessary moulds and technicians. Over and above this cost, the operation delayed by several months the construction of the consoles, which in turn contributed to tighter deadlines and inflated prices.

Even if we grant that the degree of specialization of our prefabrication industry and our labour force, unlike that of France, did not favour such projects, it would be difficult to find excuses for the stadium mast, especially when we learn from *Construire l'avenir* how Taillibert came to propose this design for Montreal. He acknowledges that he was inspired by a system with which he had successfully experimented at the Carnot Pool in Paris, "the pool with a movable roof which later brought to my mind the 'umbrella' roof of the Olympic Stadium."[9] He added several sentences, however, which contain words that should be underlined in the light of present information: "I pushed my research in this way because the form appeared very seductive to me. It was both *economical* and *functional* because it permitted a maximum of sunlight to enter without the necessity of *heavy* and *costly* structures."[10] What can be considered economical, functional, less heavy, and less costly about the Olympic mast, the incredible structure that is equivalent to a forty-storey leaning skyscraper? As for sunlight, not much can be expected when the umbrella is opened: the canvas to be used is opaque!

The error was to believe that a system designed to cover a surface of 2,000 square metres with a 27-metre-high mast could be adapted easily to cap a completely different building whose area to be closed in was ten times larger, in a totally different climate. Further, at the Carnot Pool the mast was consolidated by stays and absorbed the mechanical stresses in a structurally logical way, whereas the Montreal mast had a totally illogical shape. In fact, it harks back to the form of a lever, but the arm least resistant to strain is the one called upon to absorb it all. The consequence was inevitable: to support the weight of the roof, the snow, and the overhang of the building, thousands of tons of concrete had to be poured at the base of the mast as a counterweight.

In normal times, and leaving out the investment for the pool complex, the cost of building such a mast should vary between $60 and $70 million. That is the total cost ($67 million) for the famous Kingdome, in Seattle, with its covered area of 64,752 seats and 2,000 parking places. How can an architect recommend, just to cover a stadium, an "umbrella" whose handle is as expensive as an entire enclosed stadium elsewhere? This is an excessive outlay for the luxury of a mobile roof that will be useful only during the several months of summer. In an era of geodesic domes, inflatable roofs, and suspended membranes over lightweight structures (as used by Frei Otto for Expo 67 and for the Olympic Stadium in Munich), the "umbrella" concept at that scale and price seems a dangerously backward and outmoded solution.

The truth is that Taillibert, protected by a mayor deluded with grandeur, sacrificed all to the god of formal aesthetics. He realized a personal dream, but in doing so disregarded the real needs of a society—its economy, its potential, its know-how—on the site as well as in the work. As a result, the stadium seems an abstraction, more like sculpture than architecture. From the heights of Mount Royal or from the south shore, it appears to be a huge flying saucer, completely alien to the city around it. From close up, it is difficult to appreciate because the scale is out of proportion to the site. This is probably the most disembodied monument in the metropolis and sets before us the whole problem of cultural expression in architecture.[11]

The Future of Montreal

To determine the objectives to follow in planning the future of Montreal, it is important to take into account the present circumstances. One of the most striking of these elements, mentioned earlier, is the population decline. This factor reflects the weakening in the last decade of Montreal's role in most of the economic sectors where formerly it was a leader: transport, finance, research, and manufacturing. We must respond to this stagnation, or else the city risks not having the means to provide the desired amenities.

Parallel to the weakening of these traditional forces of development, Montreal has been subjected to increasing expectations on the part of the population. Since the end of the 1960s volunteer associations and pressure groups have alerted the public to the need to work together for a better environment. They have striven to protect tenants, green spaces, and the city's architectural heritage and to promote bicycling, public transport, and participation in decision-making. This trend in education will very likely continue in one form or another. One can predict that the population will demand a much larger share in actions and projects of this kind, after the reign of the Drapeau administration, and will participate more fully in the development and management of collective spaces and facilities.

In these circumstances, one can hypothesize that the best way to assure Montreal of dynamic development and appropriate management, as well as to encourage the support and participation of popular groups, would be to plan and organize the urban agglomeration as a function of the growth of the quality of life.

But, first of all, how can promotion of the quality of life contribute to the economic dynamics of the metropolis?

With the displacement of the Canadian economic pole towards the centre of the country, Montreal is suffering a decline similar to that which earlier affected—and for analogous reasons—large Atlantic Coast cities, such as Boston and Philadelphia. It is doubtful that Montreal can retain the leadership it held, until World War II, in almost all branches of the Canadian economy. Montreal must henceforth redefine its position, firstly in relation to Quebec, in order to re-establish itself as an important force in Canada.

A recent report from the Office de Planification et de Développement du Québec [12] suggests that Montreal must develop a strong tertiary sector of development and exportation if it is to fulfil its role in Quebec as the only truly urbanized region and the principal economic and cultural centre. It is among economically advanced nations that one finds the most widespread tendency toward specialization. In Montreal the leading industry could well be transport and communications and all the tertiary (sometimes called quaternary) movements, including finances, head offices, research, professional study offices. Development of this third force constitutes an important factor favouring the growth of modern manufacturing companies and in the long term could become the principal agent in transforming the obsolete manufacturing structure of Montreal. It is precisely this crippling weight of old Montreal industries, notably in agriculture and food, textiles, hats, and clothing, that is responsible for the growing slowdown in Montreal's economy in comparison with Toronto's. A dynamic development of the service industries would allow better use of human resources and favour the hiring of competent young people, who are now available because of the considerable efforts toward catching up made by Quebec society since the Quiet Revolution. At the least, this action would go a long way toward making profitable the huge investments of public money in the field of education.

One of the great advantages Montreal has for developing this service industry lies in the quality and diversity of its human resources. In a period when capital and qualified workers are very mobile, Montreal must retain and enrich this resource. In this sense, then, the population decline in the city of Montreal and eventually in the region constitutes a serious warning.

The majority of economists, even the most conservative, agree that the development of the quality of life—as banal as this notion is—is likely to retain qualified people in Montreal and eventually to increase their numbers. Quality of life, however, depends on factors as diverse as health, security, education, employment, income, housing, and leisure. It is also linked to functional and spatial elements related directly to the physical administration of the city. To be significant, therefore, the furthering of health, public security, education, and employment must be translated, in one way or another, into physical organization that will tend to optimize the potential of these functions in themselves and in relation to others.

It goes without saying that the search for an improved quality of life in urban settings constitutes a motivating and sufficiently encompassing objective to promote and stimulate wide public participation—even though the appropriate mechanisms to assure real consultation and participation have yet to be defined. Citizen involvement must be sought out and encouraged, because the satisfaction of complex and often contradictory contemporary needs cannot be fully obtained through the intervention of experts alone. In past instances, notably the Ville-Marie autoroute, the Olympic Village, and the Milton-Park project, the experts and the politicians recognized that if they had paid more attention to the complaints of pressure groups costly errors could have been avoided.

In the fields of planning and management, however, public opinion has been alerted to the problems but rarely to the objectives to be followed and even less to alternative solutions. This is clearly revealed by literature available to the public: *Montreal at the Cross-roads* (1975), *Les vraies propriétaires de Montréal* (1977), and other publications. Furthermore, when Montrealers were asked to take a stand on urban questions, most often these were of a defensive nature: conservation disputes or protection of existing features. There is an urgent need for intellectual input to define objectives and elaborate concepts in order to undertake coherent offensive action.

What should be the objectives, in a large sense, of a long-term offensive in urban planning and management that would promote the quality of life? These are of two orders, and are complementary. First, we must aim at a true urban ecology, that is, we must learn how to satisfy the physiological, psychological, social, economic, and ethnic needs of individuals while at the same time respecting the natural environment and searching for a more just social equity. Second, we must promote an authentic "cultural" expression in Montreal as a whole.

We have nothing to gain by ignoring or rejecting without analysis the emerging Western architectural and urban tendencies and results; but a servile fidelity to modern theories and concepts does not guarantee good management and improvement in the quality of the environment. Most of the architectural realizations and contemporary planning in Montreal, where the rules of the art were followed to the letter, have revealed works with neither character nor soul, unable to take root in the community, sometimes even destroying the quality of life that was sought (for example, almost all recent redevelopment on Sherbrooke, Côte Saint-Luc, Lincoln, and Drummond Streets). This has come about because the concepts are submitted to theoretical norms (notably the primacy of air, sun, greenery in the Athens Charter) before being universally applied, no matter who the user of what his life style. These concepts ignore the cultural dimensions of human communities (cultural used here in the generic sense), and how to integrate geographical, social, economic, and technical dimensions.

In analysing the architectural and urban heritage of Montreal, *Montreal in Evolution* has identified two principal currents of influence. The first, relating to the great cultural movements of the West, left its mark particularly in the development of large parks and romantic squares, and in the exuberance of the eclectic architecture of the Victorian period. The second, more indigenous, also appeared more original. It was evident in the progressive development of a particular savoir faire, drawing its roots from geographic, economic, and social reality, that is, from the "culture" of the country and its inhabitants. Witness the "rang" system, the traditional Quebec house, the urban lodgings of the populated quarters at the turn of the century, the concentration of community services around the church. It is this last wave, duly nourished by the first, that must be revitalized and rehabilitated to bring about solutions better adapted to our future. We are able to identify and characterize Montreal society by this cultural continuity that can be translated into the physical environment and can be reflected in a system of significant values.

ABBREVIATIONS

ABC   *Architecture-Bâtiment-Construction*
BRH   *Bulletin des recherches historiques*
CANJ   *The Canadian Antiquarian and Numismatic Journal*
CESH   *Contributions à l'étude des sciences de l'Homme*
CGQ   *Cahiers de géographie de Québec*
CHAR *Canadian Historical Association Report*
DCB   *Dictionary of Canadian Biography*
JRAIC   *Journal of the Royal Architectural Institute of Canada*
JSAH   *Journal of the Society of Architectural Historians*
MSRC *Mémoires de la Société Royale du Canada*
RAPQ *Rapport de l'archiviste de la Province de Québec*
RGM   *Revue de géographie de Montréal*
RTC   *Revue trimestrielle canadienne*
SHM   Société Historique de Montréal

Sources followed by an asterisk are listed in the bibliography under
the heading General Sources.

OTES

Chapter 1   THE KEY TO THE WEST

1. William Bennett Munro, ed., *Documents Relating to the Seigniorial Tenure in Canada, 1598–1854*, pp. 97–98.
2. Reuben Gold Thwaites, ed., *The Jesuit Relations and Allied Documents: Travels and Explorations of the Jesuit Missionaries in New France, 1610–1791*, 48: 169.
3. Marcel Trudel, "Jacques Cartier," in *DCB*, 1: 165. Extract from the king's order, dated 18 March 1534.
4. *Ibid.*, pp. 165–66.
5. *Ibid.*, p. 167.
6. *Ibid.*, p. 168.
7. Many of these cities were built on the site of old French strongholds controlling strategic points of the St. Lawrence empire: e.g., Fort Frontenac became Kingston, Fort Rouillé became York and then Toronto, Fort Pontchartrain became Detroit.
8. Trudel, "Jacques Cartier," *DCB*, 1: 171.
9. Michel Brunet, Guy Frégault, and Marcel Trudel, *Histoire du Canada par les textes*, pp. 41–42. Original text: "différamment arrousé par le fleuve de St-Laurens et par de belles rivières qui se deschargent dans son lict par ses costez, [qui] a ses communications par ces mêmes rivières avec plusieurs nations sauvages riches en peleteries."
10. Thwaites, *Jesuit Relations*, 22: 205–7.
11. *Ibid.*, 36: 201.
12. Gustave Lanctôt, *Montréal sous Maisonneuve, 1642–1665*, p. 16. Original text: "l'île entre les rapides."
13. Raoul Blanchard, *L'Ouest du Canada français*, 1, *Montréal et sa région*, pp. 173–81.*
14. Gabrielle Roy, *The Tin Flute*, p. 26.
15. Blanchard, *L'Ouest du Canada français*, 1: 58–59.

16. H. P. Biggar, trans., *The Voyages of Jacques Cartier*, p. 168.
17. Blanchard, *L'Ouest du Canada français*, 1: 14–48; see also Montreal, Quebec, City Planning Department, *Physical Characteristics of the Region.*
18. Blanchard, *L'Ouest du Canada français*, 1: 48–59; see also Richmond Wilberforce Longley, *Le climat de Montréal.*
19. Stephen Leacock, ed., *Lahontan's Voyages*, p. 15.
20. Exactly 46,481 hectares, excluding Bizard Island, or 48,749 hectares including this island; 49,282 hectares, or 492.83 square kilometres, including some other islands belonging to some riverside municipalities: Montreal, Quebec, City Planning Department, *Areas of Municipalities*, pp. 3–4.
21. Biggar, *Voyages of Jacques Cartier*, pp. 153–54.
22. Thwaites, *Jesuit Relations*, 48: 167, 169.
23. Joseph Bouchette, *A Topographical Dictionary of the Province of Lower Canada*, see "Montreal."
24. This subject will be dealt with in chapter seven.
25. Munro, *Documents, 1598–1854*, pp. 97–98. Original text: "n'estoit presque qu'une forest de toutes sortes d'arbres très gros particulièrement des pins, érables, bois blancs, ormes, hestres et merisiers et cèdres."
26. H. P. Biggar, ed., *The Works of Samuel de Champlain*, 2: 178.
27. J. Stanfield, *The Pleistocene and Recent Deposits of the Island of Montreal, Canada*, pp. 43–50.
28. Blanchard, *L'Ouest du Canada français*, 1: 38–39, 190–203.
29. Marcel Trudel, "Samuel de Champlain," in *DCB*, 1: 186–99.
30. Laverdière, *Oeuvres de Champlain*, 1: xxiv. Original text: "de s'aller loger dans le fleuve Saint-Laurent, où le commerce et traffic pouvaient faire beaucoup mieux qu'en Acadie."
31. Incidentally, "Quebec" is an Algonquin word meaning "narrowing of the river."
32. Biggar, *The Works of Samuel de Champlain*, 2: 175.
33. *Ibid.*, pp. 175–78.
34. *Ibid.*, p. 178.
35. This refers to the "Messieurs et Dames de la Société de Notre-Dame de Montréal pour la conversion des Sauvages de la Nouvelle-France."
36. SHM, *Les véritables motifs de Messieurs et Dames de la Société de Notre-Dame de Montréal*, p. 14. Original text: "d'y assembler un peuple composé de Français et de Sauvages qui seront convertis pour les rendre sédentaires, les former à cultiver les arts mécaniques de la terre, les unir sous une même discipline, dans les exercices de la vie chrétienne."
37. Letter from the members of the "Société" to Pope Urbain VIII in 1643, quoted in [Etienne-Michel Faillon], *Histoire de la colonie française au Canada*, 1: 398.* Original text: "pour quatre-vingts nations barbares, comme un centre propre à les attirer, à cause des riviéres qui y affluent de toute part."
38. See Lanctôt, *Montréal sous Maisonneuve*, pp. 150–51; John William

Reps, *The Making of Urban America: A History of City Planning in the United States*, pp. 68–71.*

Chapter 2 THE ISLAND COLONY

1. Steen Eiler Rasmussen, *London the Unique City*, p. 16.
2. John Summerson, *Georgian London*, pp. 17–18.
3. *Ibid.*, p. 18.
4. Donald Creighton, *Dominion of the North: A History of Canada*, pp. 110–12.*
5. *Ibid.*, pp. 13–14.
6. Gustave Lanctôt, *Montréal sous Maisonneuve, 1642–1665*, pp. 23–24.
7. This war was not continuous, but interspersed by periods of peace.
8. Marcel Trudel, *Le Régime seigneurial*.
9. Creighton, *Dominion of the North*, pp. 45–46.
10. See the reconstruction from a map drawn by Franquet in 1752, in Marcel Trudel, *An Atlas of New France*, p. 118.
11. "Arrêts & règlements des intendants du Canada," 24 January 1667. Quoted in [Etienne-Michel Faillon], *Histoire de la colonie française en Canada*, 3 : 342–43.* Original text: "Cette manière de donner un pays nouvellement conquis, répond à l'usage autrefois reçu chez les Romains, de distribuer aux gens de guerre les champs des provinces subjuguées, qu'on appelait *praedia militaria*, & la pratique de ces peuples politiques & guerriers peut, à mon sentiment, être judicieusement introduite dans un pays éloigné de mille lieues de son Monarque, qui, à cause de cet éloignement, peut souvent être réduit à la nécessité de se soutenir par ses propres forces." Concerning this "military plan of Talon," see Dorothy A. Heneker, *The Seigniorial Regime in Canada*, pp. 71 ff.; William Bennett Munro, ed., *Documents Relating to the Seigniorial Tenure in Canada, 1598–1854*, pp. xxxv ff.
12. Munro, *Documents, 1598–1854*, p. xxxv.
13. *Ibid.*, p. 116. Original text: "très belle et la plus convenable, et le seul entrepôt entre Montréal, les Trois-Rivières et Chambly."
14. *Ibid.*, p. 111. Original text: "coste pour ce qu'elle contient est une des plus belles et des plus unies du Canada; les habitans y sont les plus aisés du gouvernement."
15. Concerning these concessions by Intendant Talon, see Faillon, *Histoire de la colonie française*, 1 : 346 ff.
16. *Ibid.*, p. 351. Original text: "avec obligation pour eux de s'y établir, de les faire cultiver & d'y attirer des colons, principalement les soldats licenciés qu'ils avaient eus sous leurs ordres."
17. *Ibid.*, pp. 345–46. Original text: "l'une des fins que le Roi se proposait par ces concessions était de fortifier le pays contre les Iroquois; aussi est-il à remarquer que les fiefs nobles qu'il donna à ses officiers furent presque tous situés dans le voisinage de l'île de Montréal, & sur le bord des rivières par où les barbares avaient coutume de descendre, c'est-à-dire sur la rivière appelée de Richelieu, & sur le fleuve Saint-Laurent, à

partir du lac Saint-Pierre." "S'y établissant avec un certain nombre de leurs soldats devenus agriculteurs, ils [les officiers] donnèrent lieu à la formation de divers bourgs qui, avec Villemarie, furent la sûreté & comme le Boulevard du reste de la colonie Française."

18. William Henry Atherton, *Montreal*, 1:212;* Alan Gowans, *Church Architecture in New France*, pp. 99–155.*
19. Alexandre Jodoin, "Le château de Longueuil," *BRH* 6, no. 3 (March 1900):76–78.
20. Richard Colebrook Harris, *The Seigneurial System in Early Canada: A Geographical Study*, pp. 176 ff.
21. Joseph Bouchette, *A Topographical Dictionary of the Province of Lower Canada*, see "Longueuil" and "Chambly."
22. Munro, *Documents, 1598–1854*, p. 110. Original text: "malgré la nécessité qu'il y avoit de le perfectionner afin de pouvoir secourir en peu de tems le fort de Chambly s'il estoit attaqué, au lieu que le secours, à le conduire par eau, doit faire 36 lieues."
23. Bouchette, *A Topographical Dictionary*, see "Chambly."
24. *Ibid.*, "Berthier."
25. Guy Frégault, "Le régime seigneurial et l'expansion de la colonisation dans le bassin du St-Laurent au dix-huitième siècle," *CHAR*, 1944, p. 66.
26. Raoul Blanchard, *L'Ouest du Canada français*, 1, *Montréal et sa région*, pp. 60–73.*
27. Max Derruau, "A l'origine du 'rang' canadien," *CGQ* 1 (1956):39–47.
28. See Harris, *The Seigneurial System*, pp. 179 ff. See also Pierre Deffontaines, "The Rang-Pattern of Rural Settlement in French-Canada," in *French-Canadian Society*, 1, *Sociological Studies*, pp. 3–19.
29. In 1671 three of these noble fiefs had already been granted: one to Lambert Closse; another, near Fort Ville-Marie, to Hautmesnil; and a third one, more to the west, to the Sieur de La Salle. This fief was named at first Saint-Sulpice, then Lachine.
30. H. Beaugrand, ed., and P. L. Morin, illus., *Le Vieux Montréal 1611–1803*, n.p.
31. Olivier Maurault, "Les moulins du séminaire," in *Marges d'histoire*, 3, *Saint-Sulpice*, p. 126. The ruined windmill one can see today at Pointe-aux-Trembles was probably built in 1718, and is the second mill built on this "arrière-fief."
32. Gowans, *Church Architecture*, p. 113.
33. Beaugrand and Morin, *Le Vieux Montréal*, n.p.; Maurault, *Marges d'histoire*, 3:127; Gowans, *Church Architecture*, p. 122.
34. For more details concerning the concession of these noble fiefs, see Faillon, *Histoire de la colonie française*, pp. 337.
35. *Ibid.*, p. 342. Original text: "en érigeant ainsi les fiefs que nous venons d'énumérer & en les donnant en toute propriété à des militaires, les seigneurs de Montréal faisaient ce qui était en leur pouvoir pour protéger les colons & mettre l'île en état de se défendre." For further infor-

mation on the redoubts and the chapel, see Beaugrand and Morin, *Le Vieux Montréal*, n.p., and Gowans, *Church Architecture*, p. 131.

36. Jean de Laplante, "La communauté montréalaise," *CESH* 1 (1952): 57–107.

37. Quebec (Province), "Aveu et dénombrement de Messire Louis Normand, prêtre du séminaire de Saint-Sulpice de Montréal," in *RAPQ, 1941–42*, p. 94. Original text: "qu'au dessus de la terre de l'Eglise et la joignant est un terrain Cent toises de front sur environ quatre-vingt-dix toises de profondeur, sur lequel est construit le fort dud. Lieu de la pointe-aux-trembles, clos de pieux, flanqué et bastionné ct dans lequel est construit en maçonnerie la d[ite] Eglise de l'Enfant Jésus."

38. *Ibid.*, pp. 94, 135. Original text: "en Emplacements distribués par Rues en forme de Bourg." "Est un village commencé d'un arpent en superficie appartenant auxd. seigneurs."

39. Munro, *Documents, 1598–1854*, p. 101.

40. Harris, *The Seigneurial System*, pp. 176 ff.

41. Quebec (Province), "Le recensement des gouvernements de Montréal et des Trois-Rivières" in *RAPQ 1936–37*, p. 119.

42. Munro, *Documents, 1598–1854*, p. 99. Original text: "les habitans y estoient autre fois fort à leur aise par le commerce qu'ils faisoient avec les sauvages, qui y abordoient en descendant à Montréal. Mais depuis la désolation que les Iroquois y portèrent en 1689, qui brûlèrent les maisons et emmenèrent la plus part des habitans captifs, elle a dégénéré en tout."

43. *Ibid.*, p. 101. Original text: "les Iroquois, pour avoir détruit la plus part des habitans, ont causé du retardement à son établissement."

44. Joseph Bouchette, *A Topographical Description of the Province of Lower Canada*, pp. 135, 139–40.

45. See Bouchette, *A Topographical Dictionary*.

46. Beaugrand and Morin, *Le Vieux Montréal*, n.p.

47. Arthur R. M. Lower, *Canadians in the Making: A Social History of Canada*, pp. 41–42.*

48. Harris, *The Seigneurial System*, pp. 186 ff.; Jean-Charles Falardeau, "The Seventeenth Century Parish in French-Canada," in *French-Canadian Society*, 1, *Sociological Studies*, p. 22.

49. Marcel Trudel, *An Atlas of New France*, pp. 172–73.

50. Québec, "Aveu et dénombrement de Messire Normand," p. 145. Original text: "Que dans l'Etendüe de la d[ite] Coste St-Michel partagée en deux Rangs d'habitants par une commune de deux arpens de large au milieu de laquelle il y a un chemin de Roy qui court Nord'est et sud'ouest."

51. Munro, *Documents, 1598–1854*, p. 97. Original text: "est divisée en six paroisses, sçavoir, Montréal, La Chine, Haut de l'Isle, la Pointe au Tremble, la Rivière des Prairies et la Mission du Sault au Récollet."

52. *Ibid.* Original text: "dépendent les habitans le long du fleuve, depuis Verdun jusques à la Longue Pointe; en outre la moitié des Costes St-Pierre et St-Paul, les costes de Nostre Dame des Neiges, de Liesse,

des Vertues, St-Laurent, Ste-Catherine et St-Michel et la Visitation."

53. *Ibid.*, p. 101. Original text: "Paroisse de la Pointe au Tremble d'où dépend la coste St-Lionnard."

54. "Carte de l'Ile de Montréal désignant les chemins publics, les paroisses, les fiefs et les villages qui s'y trouvent, le canal de Lachine, les différentes parties de l'Ile qui ne sont pas encore en état de culture, etc., etc., faite en 1834 par A. Jobin."

55. Québec, "Aveu et dénombrement de Messire Louis Normand," p. 88.

56. See E.-Z. Massicotte, "Notre-Dame-des-Neiges," in *Les cahiers des Dix*, no. 4, pp. 141–66.

57. With the exception of the Côtes Saint-Charles, Saint-Jean, and des Sources, in the western part of the island, where the strips of land ran from the southwest to the northeast in keeping with some features of the natural topography of the region.

58. Jacques Godbout, "La Côte-des-Neiges," *Liberté* 5, no 4 (July–Aug. 1963): 303. Original text: "Côte-des-Neiges est à Montréal un des rares quartiers qui soit une entité vivante, identifiée et facilement cernable."

59. Marcel Bélanger, "De la région naturelle à la région urbaine: problèmes d'habitat," in *Architecture et urbanisme au Québec*, p. 54.

60. Hans Blumenfeld, *The Modern Metropolis: Its Origins, Growth, Characteristics and Planning*, p. 27.*

Chapter 3 SOCIETY DURING THE OLD REGIME

1. Pierre-François-Xavier de Charlevoix, *Histoire et description générale de la Nouvelle-France avec la journal historique d'un voyage fait par ordre du roi dans l'Amérique septentrionale*, 3: 137–38.

2. Ramsay Traquair, *The Old Architecture of Quebec*, p. 93.

3. Canada, Ministry of Agriculture, *Census of Canada, 1870–71*, 4, *1665–1871*, pp. 2–48.

4. The site of this first building of the Hôtel-Dieu, built in 1644, was on the northeast corner of Saint-Paul and Saint-Sulpice streets. The first chapel of Notre-Dame-de-Bonsecours was built in 1657.

5. H. Beaugrand, ed., and P. L. Morin, illus., *Le Vieux Montréal 1611–1803*, n.p.

6. [Etienne-Michel Faillon], *Histoire de la colonie française en Canada*, 3: 375.*

7. *Census of Canada (1665–1871)*, pp. 64–68: an appraisal according to the census of 1765.

8. *Ibid.*

9. Constance McLaughlin Green, *The Rise of Urban America*, p. 11.*

10. *Ibid.*, pp. 30–31.

11. See Georges Langlois, *Histoire de la population canadienne-française*, pp. 33–60, 187–230.*

12. This is, according to Jean Hamelin, *Economie et société en Nouvelle-France*, p. 77, the distribution of French immigrants who settled in New France over a period of 150 years:

1608–1640	296
1640–1660	964
1660–1680	2,542
1680–1700	1,092
1700–1720	659
1720–1740	1,008
1740–1760	3,565
Total	10,126

13. Joseph-Noël Fauteux, *Essai sur l'industrie au Canada sous le régime français,* 1: xii.
14. Arthur R. M. Lower, *Canadians in the Making: A Social History of Canada,* pp. 15–17.*
15. Hamelin, *Economie et société,* p. 77.
16. *Ibid.,* pp. 79–84.
17. Peter Kalm, *Travels into North America,* 3: 59.
18. Alan Gowans, *Building Canada: An Architectural History of Canadian Life,* p. 15.*
19. Gérard Morisset, *L'architecture en Nouvelle-France,* p. 15.* Original text: "l'esprit du style roman qu'on perçoit dans les murailles nues . . . pour peu qu'on examine notre architecture d'autrefois."
20. Richard Colebrook Harris, *The Seigneurial System in Early Canada: A Geographical Study,* p. 172.
21. Fernand Ouellette, *Histoire économique et sociale du Québec, 1760– 1850: Structures et conjoncture,* pp. 559 ff.*
22. W. J. Eccles, "Buade de Frontenac et de Palluau, Louis de" in *DCB,* 1: 133–42.
23. *Ibid.,* p. 134.
24. Pierre-Georges Roy, *La ville de Québec sous le régime français,* 1: 389. Original text: "Je trouve qu'on a fait jusques ici, ce me semble, une très grande faute en laissant bâtir les maisons à la fantaisie des particuliers, et sans aucun ordre." "D'y faire marquer les rues et les places qu'on y pourrait faire, afin que dans la suite lorsque quelque particulier voudra bâtir, il le fasse avec symétrie, et d'une manière que cela puisse augmenter la décoration et l'ornement de la ville."
25. Lower, *Canadians in the Making,* p. 46. As a matter of fact, this title should have been given to Champlain or Dollier de Casson.
26. John William Reps, *The Making of Urban America: A History of City Planning in the United States,* pp. 65–68.*
27. Yves F. Zoltvany, "Rigaud de Vaudreuil, Philippe de," in *DCB,* 2: 565–74.
28. Gustave Lanctôt, *Images et figures de Montréal sous la France,* p. 73.
29. Gowans, *Building Canada,* p. 25.
30. See Marie-Madeleine Azard-Malaurie, "De l'architecture monumentale classique à Québec," *Vie des Arts,* no. 49 (Winter 1967–68), pp. 42–49.
31. Guy Frégault, *Le XVIIIe siècle canadien: études,* p. 87. Original text: "se ressemblent comme des frères. . . . Ils sont réellement frères. Ils se recrutent dans les mêmes couches sociales et, à l'occasion, jusque dans les mêmes familles. Ils ont une conception analogue de la vie publique,

de l'autorité, des préséances et du prestige attachés à leurs fonctions."

32. *Ibid.*, p. 131. Original text: "qu'on en ignore l'origine, comme celle du Nil."

33. Alan Gowans, *Church Architecture in New France*, pp. 52–53.

34. *Ibid.*, pp. 40–47.

35. Olivier Maurault, "Un professeur d'architecture à Québec en 1828," *JRAIC* 3, no. 1 (Jan.–Feb. 1926): 32.

36. Traquair, *The Old Architecture*, p. 2.

37. See E. R. Adair, "The Church of l'Enfant Jésus, Pointe-aux-Trembles," *BRH* 42, no. 7 (July 1936): 411–21.

38. Traquair, "The Church of Ste-Jeanne-de-Chantal on the Ile Perrot, Quebec," *JRAIC* 9, no. 5 (May 1932): 124–31, and no. 6 (June 1932): 147–52.

39. E. R. Adair, "The Church of Saint-Michel de Vaudreuil," *BRH* 49, no. 2 (Feb. 1943): 38–49, and no. 3 (March 1943): 75–89.

40. Traquair and Adair, "The Church of the Visitation—Sault-au-Récollet, Quebec," *JRAIC* 4, no. 12 (Dec. 1927): 437–51.

41. Michel Lessard and Huguette Marquis, "La maison québécoise, une maison qui se souvient," *Forces*, no. 17 (1971), pp. 12 ff.

42. *Census of Canada (1665–1871)*, pp. 2 ff.

43. Gustave Lanctôt, *L'administration de la Nouvelle-France; l'administration générale*, pp. 145 ff. Original text: "règlemente effectivement et complètement." "Dans ce système administratif, quelle est la part du peuple?" "Elle est nulle."

44. Gustave Lanctôt, "Le régime municipal en Nouvelle-France," *Culture* 9, no. 3 (Sept. 1948): 283. Original text: "de cette revue de l'administration municipale du temps de la Nouvelle-France, on peut conclure que les villes étaient régies et règlementées par des autorités indépendantes de toute représentation populaire. . . . En définitive, cette administration, à la fois bienveillante et paternelle, assurait, selon les conceptions et les méthodes de l'époque, un ordre moral et matériel, qui englobait les bonnes moeurs, la sécurité, l'hygiène, la voirie, les incendies, l'alimentation et même le coût de la vie. Mais elle ne réservait aucune place à l'initiative personnelle ni à la coopération collective, qui auraient permis à ces petites villes de progresser et de grandir et à leurs citoyens de développer leurs qualités d'intelligence, de travail et d'ambition, toutes avenues fermées aux citadins du Canada, bien qu'elles fussent ouvertes à ceux de la France métropolitaine."

45. Jean-Charles Falardeau, "The Changing Social Structures," in *Essais sur le Québec contemporain*, pp. 112 ff.

46. Falardeau, "The Role and Importance of the Church in French Canada," in *French-Canadian Society*, 1, *Sociological Studies*, pp. 342–57.

47. Lower, *Canadians in the Making*, p. 56.

48. Maurice Tremblay, "Orientations de la pensée sociale," in *Essais sur le Québec contemporain*, pp. 195 ff.

49. Falardeau, "The Changing Social Structures," p. 120.

50. Kathleen Jenkins, *Montreal: Island City of the St. Lawrence*, p. 397.

Chapter 4 THE FRONTIER TOWN

1. Peter Kalm, *Travels into North America*, 3: 72–73.
2. [Etienne-Michel Faillon], *Histoire de la colonie française en Canada*, 3: 375 ff.*
3. SHM, *Les origines de Montréal*, pp. 119–20.
4. *Ibid.*, pp. 134–35.
5. *Ibid.*, p. 120. Original text: "si les seigneurs avoient besoin de partie de ce terrain pour l'établissement de la ville, ils pourroient le prendre en remplaçant pareille quantité dans la profondeur, et en payant le terrain défriché selon l'estimation qui en serait faitte de sa valeur par des expers."
6. *Ibid.*, p. 168. Original text: "à prendre sur le bord de la commune 3 perches de large sur 31 perches et six pieds."
7. Faillon, *Histoire*, 3: 377. Original text: "à la mémoire de ce brave major, mort pour la défense du pays."
8. See also on this subject the "Plan partiel du Vieux Montréal montrant les premières concessions dressé sur le plan terrier des seigneurs et sur le plan de Montréal en 1729, de Chaussegros de Léry, ingénieur du Roi, par Aristide Beaugrand-Champagne, architecte, avril 1942." Municipal Archives of Montreal.
9. Archives of the Seminary of Ville-Marie, 12 January 1675. Quoted in Faillon, *Histoire*, 3: 378. Original text: "élever leurs bâtiments, destinés à l'ornement & à la décoration de leur ville, & à faciliter le commerce tant avec les habitants qu'avec les étrangers."
10. John Williams Reps, *The Making of Urban America: A History of City Planning in the United States*, pp. 160 ff.*
11. Raoul Blanchard, *L'Ouest du Canada français*, 1, *Montréal et sa région*, p. 222.* Original text: "le plan tout entier de l'immense ville est sorti des cartons du Sulpicien."
12. SHM, *Les origines de Montréal*, attached plans.
13. Gustave Lanctôt, *Images et figures de Montréal sous la France*, p. 53.
14. *Ibid.*
15. Villemarie dans l'isle de Montréal (1684), 13 x 9½, Ministry of the Colonies, Depository of the Fortifications of the Colonies, no. 446. Original text: "envoyé par M. Denonville le 13 novembre 1685."
16. Stephen Leacock, *Lahontan's voyages*, p. 15.
17. *Ibid.*
18. Faillon, *Histoire*, 3: 245. Original text: "la commodité des particuliers, qui avaient à se pourvoir des choses nécessaires à la vie, & aussi pour l'avantage des gens de la campagne, qui désiraient de vendre leurs denrées ou les produits de leur industrie."
19. Lanctôt, *Images et figures*, p. 59.
20. *Census of Canada (1665–1871)*, p. 16.
21. *Plan de la ville de Montréal levé en l'année 1704*, Ministry of the Colonies, Depository of the Fortifications of the Colonies, no. 468. E.-Z. Massicotte attributes this plan to Levasseur de Néré: see his "Inven-

taire des cartes et plans de l'île et de la ville de Montréal," *BRH* 20, no. 2 (Feb. 1914): 35.

22. The census of 1706 mentions 2025 inhabitants for Montreal and its suburbs. See *Census of Canada (1665–1871)*, p. 48.

23. Leacock, *Lahontan's Voyages*, p. 15.

24. Lanctôt, *Images et figures*, pp. 59–60.

25. E.-Z. Massicotte, *Répertoire des arrêts, édits, mandements, ordonnances et règlements conservés dans les archives du Palais de justice de Montréal 1640–1760*, p. 39.

26. SHM, *Annales de l'Hôtel-Dieu de Montréal, rédigées par la soeur Morin*, pp. 25–26. Original text: "il ya a à présent une manière de ville enclosse, de pieux de cèdre de 5 à 6 pieds [français] de haut plantés de terre du bas en haut sont attachés les uns avec les autres avec de gros clous et chevilles de bois et cela depuis dix ans. Voilà les murailles du Canada pour enfermer les villes; il y a plusieurs grandes portes pour entrer et sortir qui sont fermées tous les soirs par des officiers de guerre que le Roy de France y entretient pour nous défandre sy nos ennemis nous voulois inquiéter; ils ouvrent les deux portes le matin à des heures réglées, etc."

27. Massicotte, *Répertoire des arrêts*, p. 58. Original text: "pour la décoration et la commodité publique."

28. Lanctôt, *Images et figures*, p. 60. Original text: "où les jardins, les potagers et les emplacements en culture occupent les deux tiers de son étendue."

29. *Plan de la ville de Montréal en Canada*, from drawings by Mr. de Catalogne, engraving by Moullart Sanson, Paris, 1723.

30. *Plan de la ville de Montréal en Canada Nouvelle France dans l'Amérique Septentrionale*, Fait à Québec ce 20 octobre 1724 par Chaussegros de Léry, Echelle de 400 toises, avec Renvoy.

31. *Plan de la ville de Montréal dans la Nouvelle-France, 1731*, avec Renvoy.

32. Estimate according to the census of 1739 which mentions 4210 inhabitants for Montreal and its suburbs. See *Census of Canada (1665–1871)*, p. 60.

33. Pierre-François-Xavier de Charlevoix, *Journal of a Voyage to North-America*, 1: 213.

34. *Ibid.*, 1, p. 214.

35. Massicotte, *Répertoire des arrêts*, p. 88.

36. E. R. Adair, "The Evolution of Montreal under the French Regime," *CHAR*, 1942, pp. 38–39.

37. *Ibid.*, pp. 35–36.

38. Pierre Lavedan, *Les villes françaises*, p. 99.*

39. Abbé Auguste Gosselin, "Le 'Traité de Fortifications' de Chaussegros de Léry," *BRH* 7, no 5 (May 1901): 157–58. Original text: "tout ce qui regarde la manière de fortifier les places, les attaquer et les défendre."

40. Montreal would surrender to the British without a fight in 1760, and to the American rebels in 1775.

41. Lanctôt, *Images et figures*, pp. 61–62.

42. Charles P. De Volpi and P. S. Winkworth, eds., *Montreal: A Pictorial Record,* 1, plate 5.
43. *Ibid.,* plates 6 and 4.
44. Montreal in 1761, according to Paul Labrosse. Plan published, with additions by E.-Z. Massicotte, in SMH, *Les origines de Montréal.*
45. *Census of Canada (1665–1871),* pp. 64–68.
46.. Robert E. Dickinson, *The West European City: A Geographical Interpretation,* p. 318.
47. Massicotte, *Répertoire des arrêts,* pp. 108–10, 130.
48. Charlevoix, *Journal of a Voyage,* 1: 215.
49. Lewis Mumford, *Sticks and Stones: A Study of American Architecture and Civilization,* p. 1.*
50. See Emrys Jones, *Towns and Cities,* pp. 45–46,* and Arthur E. Smailes, *The Geography of Towns,* pp. 20–23.*
51. Charlevoix, *Journal of a Voyage,* 1: 215.
52. Reps, *The Making of Urban America,* p. 29.
53. Jacques Mathieu, "Dollier de Casson, François," in *DCB,* 2: 190–97; Olivier Maurault, "Un seigneur de Montréal: Dollier de Casson," in *Marges d'histoire,* 2, Montréal, pp. 33–51.
54. Reps, *The Making of Urban America,* pp. 2–4.
55. Lavedan, *Les villes françaises,* pp. 73–88; Dickinson, *The West European City,* pp. 353–59.
56. Reps, *The Making of Urban America,* pp. 71–73.
57. In a residence which was probably located at the northwest corner of the present Saint-Paul and Saint-Sulpice Streets.
58. Lavedan, *Les villes françaises,* pp. 87–88.
59. Reps, *The Making of Urban America,* pp. 29–32.

Chapter 5 ARCHITECTURE AND ENVIRONMENT IN THE FRONTIER TOWN

1. Gérard Morisset, *Coup d'oeil sur les arts en Nouvelle-France,* p. ix.*
2. E.-Z. Massicotte, "Coins historiques du Montréal d'autrefois," in *Les cahiers des Dix,* 2: 152–55.
3. Olivier Maurault, "Notre-Dame de Montréal," *RTC,* 11th year, no. 42 (June 1925), pp. 123 ff.
4. L'histoire de notre château," *CANJ* 1, no. 1–4 (1930): 48. Original text: "maison sera de soixante-six pieds de long de dehors en dehors et de trente-six pieds de large aussy."
5. Old measure of length equivalent to approximately 33 centimetres. The actual Anglo-Saxon measure of length for the foot is equivalent to 30.47 centimetres.
6. "L'histoire de notre château," p. 76. Original text: "le Rétablissement et augmentation de Lhotel de la Comp[agni]e scize En cette Ville Rue Notre-Dame de quatre Vingt douze Pieds de Longs sur quarante huit Pieds de Large."
7. This enlargement of the château is confirmed by Victor Morin: see "Les Ramesay et leur château," in *Les cahiers des Dix,* 3: 12.
8. Ramsay Traquair, *The Old Architecture of Quebec,* p. 51.

9. Pierre-Georges Roy, *Les vieilles églises de la province de Québec, 1647—1800*, pp. 25—31.

10. Traquair, *The Old Architecture*, p. 91.

11. [Etienne-Michel Faillon], *Histoire de la colonie française en Canada*, 3: 378 ff. This church is the third parish church of Montreal. The first one was the chapel of the fort of Ville-Marie in 1642, replaced in 1656 by a second one built on Saint-Paul Street, near the Hôtel-Dieu.

12. Pierre-François-Xavier de Charlevoix, *Journal of a Voyage to North America*, 1: 215.

13. This church of the monastery of the Récollets was pulled down in 1867.

14. Alan Gowans, *Church Architecture in New France*, pp. 63—64, 76—80.*

15. On the east side, the view shows a wing of the new building which was to replace it and to which it is awkwardly attached; the project was later abandoned in favor of a new seminary to be built on Sherbrooke Street.

16. Olivier Maurault, "Notre-Dame de Montréal," pp. 117—41.

17. Alan Gowans, *Building Canada: An Architectural History of Canadian Life*, pp. 25—26.

18. Robert-Lionel Séguin, *La civilisation traditionnelle de l'"habitant" au 17e et 18e siècles; fonds matériel*, p. 308. Original text: "la maison montréalaise prend l'aspect d'une petite forteresse domestique carrée, massive, flanquée de lourdes cheminées, elle est construite de gros cailloux des champs, noyés dans le mortier. Les carreaux qui crèvent les murs se dérobent sous d'épais contrevents bardés de fer. . . . Cette dernière demeure est plutôt d'inspiration bretonne."

19. Traquair, *The Old Architecture*, pp. 38 ff.

20. Michel Lessard and Huguette Marquis, *Encyclopédie de la maison québécoise*, pp. 250—310.*

21. Raymond Tanghe, *Géographie humaine de Montréal*, pp. 234—35.*

22. France. Lois, statuts . . . *Edits, ordonnances royaux, déclarations et arrêts du Conseil d'Etat du roi concernant le Canada*, 2: 292—94. (Hereafter: *Edits, ordonnances royaux*.) Original text: "Ordonnance portant règlement pour la reconstruction des maisons en matériaux incombustibles et pour d'autres fins; du huitième juillet, mil sept cent vingt-un."

23. Peter Kalm, *Travels into North America*, 3: 73. Original text of the ordinance: "portant Règlement pour la construction des Maisons, en matériaux incombustibles, dans les Villes de la Colonie; du 7 juin 1727." "De bâtir aucune maison dans les villes et gros bourgs, où il se trouvera de la pierre commodément, autrement qu'en pierres; défendons de les bâtir en bois, de pièces sur pièces et de colombage." "Quelques maisons dans la ville sont bâties en pierre; la plupart le sont en bois de charpente, mais très élégamment construites."

24. Edward Allen Talbot, *Five Years' Residence in the Canadas*, 1: 65. Original text of the ordinance: "caves et celliers [soient] voûtés le plus qu'il sera possible, pour éviter la pourriture des poutres et planchers qu'on met dessus." "Les escaliers du dehors dans le dedans des maisons, de

façon qu'il n'y ait jamais dehors dans la rue que trois marches au plus en hauteur et en saillie."

25. According to R. H. Hubbard, this was simply a form of cultural heritage: see "The European Backgrounds of Early Canadian Art," *Art Quarterly* 27, no. 3 (1964): 297–323. In his opinion this type of house is frequently found in the rural regions of Northern France. However, it is rather surprising that it was seldom encountered in Brittany, which seems to have been the country of origin of our domestic architecture. Original text of the ordinance: "de mêler dans la construction des murs de face et de pignons extérieurs des maisons aucuns bois apparens." "De couvrir en bardeau aucune des maisons qui se construisent actuellement dans les villes et dans les faubourgs des villes." "Toits brisés, dit à la mansarde . . . qui font sur les bâtiments une forêt de bois." "De poser et d'adosser aucune cheminée ou tuyau de poêles sur des cloisons, pans de bois et colombages." "De faire sur les planchers des greniers et galetas un hourdi ou aire de chaux ct sable, épais au moins de deux pouces, afin que le plancher supérieur des maisons étant ainsi à l'abri du feu, permette plus aisément d'abattre et jeter bas le toît des mêmes maisons, si le cas arrivoit de feu dans la maison, ou d'un incendie dans le voisinage des dites maisons." "Murs de refend qui en excèdent les toits et les coupent en différentes parties, ou qui les séparent d'avec les maisons voisines, à l'effet que le feu se communique moins de l'une à l'autre."

26. Concerning this ordinance of 7 June 1727, see *Edits, ordonnances royaux*, 2: 314–21. original texts: "il ne faut pas moins songer à la bonne disposition et à la décoration de la ville, qu'à la durée de ses édifices." "Il ne sera assis aucun nouveau bâtiment . . . qu'après avoir pris, par le propriétaire de la maison à bâtir ou à rétablir, son alignement sur le terrain même, et par écrit du Sieur de Bécancourt, grand-voyer du Canada." "Sous peine d'amende contre les maîtres maçons et entrepreneurs, et d'encourir, par les propriétaires la démolition de leurs maisons à leurs frais et dépens." "Qu'on ne mette aucune porte à faux sur les rues, qu'on n'anticipe point sur les places publiques, tant par le corps du bâtiment que par les escaliers qui seront réglés en même temps que l'alignement, et qu'on ne construise point de maison, trop près des portes de la ville, des remparts, des batteries, dans les places publiques et autres lieux destinés à la défense et à la décoration des villes, et pour qu'il soit donné aux places et aux rues des largeurs et pentes convenables pour l'écoulement des eaux, la commodité, la sûreté et la salubrité publique." "Nous ordonnons, pour faire sur cela une juste compensation et procurer aux seigneurs un dédommagement convenable, qu'à l'égard de ceux qui, pour se conformer aux alignemens donnés, perdront de leur terrain, ils seront déchargés du payement des cens et rentes dues aux seigneurs, au *prorata* de ce qu'il leur sera ôté du terrain, comme aussi que ceux dont les emplacements seront augmentés par les alignemens qui leur auront été donnés, payeront les cens et rentes seigneuriales à proportion du terrain qu'ils acquerront d'augmentation."

27. Gérard Morisset, *L'architecture en Nouvelle-France*, p. 26.* Original

text: "cheminées formant éperons à chaque bout de l'édifice et con-
tenant autant de gaines que de pièces à chauffer."

28. *Ibid.*, p. 28.

29. E.-Z. Massicotte, "Maçons, entrepreneurs, architectes," *BRH* 35: no. 3 (March 1929): 132. Original text: "qui disait maître maçon indiquait un homme également versé dans la théorie et dans la pratique de l'art de bâtir; la pensée, à cette époque, ne se séparait pas de la main."

30. "L'histoire de notre château," *CANJ* 1, no. 1–4 (1930): 49. Original text: "maître maçon et architecte."

31. *Ibid.*, p. 76.

32. E.-Z. Massicotte, "Mémento historique de Montréal, 1636–1760," *MSRC*, Section I, ser. 3, 27 (May 1933): 128 ff.

33. Born in Paris, date unknown, and died in Montreal in 1743: see Moris-set, *L'architecture en Nouvelle-France*, p. 133.

34. Probably born in Quebec City in 1701, died in that city in 1762. *Ibid.*

35. Massicotte, "Mémento historique," pp. 128 ff. Original text: "auteur de plans de maisons."

36. Victor Morin, *La légende dorée de Montréal*, pp. 86–88.

37. *Edits, ordonnances royaux*, 2: 260. Original texts: "à tous les habitans de quelque qualité et condition qu'ils soient de jeter aucunes immon-dices, terres et fumier dans les dites rues" and "de garder dans leurs maisons aucuns cochons . . . et de laisser vaquer dans les rues aucunes bêtes à corne."

38. E.-Z. Massicotte, *Répertoire des arrêts, édits, mandemants, ordon-nances et règlements conservés dans les archives du Palais de justice de Montréal 1640–1760*, p. 107. Original text: "tous les habitants de Montréal, propriétaires ou locataires, à ramasser au-devant de leurs ter-rains les fumiers, immondices et ordures qui y seront, chaque jour, de les mettre en tas, à côté de la voie publique, pour ne pas nuire aux voitures."

39. *Edits, ordonnances royaux*, 2: 137. Original text: "d'y faire des latrines et privés, afin d'éviter l'infection et la puanteur que ces ordures apport-ent lorsqu'elles se font dans les rues."

40. J. H. Plumb, *England in the Eighteenth Century*, p. 12.

41. *Edits, ordonnances royaux*, 2: 258. Original text: "Ayant connu en ar-rivant en cette ville le désordre qui étoit dans toutes les rues, lesquelles sont quasi impraticables dans toutes les saisons, non seulement aux gens de pied, mais même aux carosses et charrois, et ce à cause des bourbiers qui se trouvent dans les dites rues qui proviennent tant de la mauvaise nature et inégalité du terrain que des immondices que les habitans y jettent journellement."

42. Joseph Hadfield, *An Englishman in America, 1785*, p. 46.

43. Massicotte, *Répertoire des arrêts*, p. 107. Original text: "chaque pro-priétaire de Montréal à tirer ou à faire tirer durant l'hiver toutes les pièces de bois nécessaires pour faire des banquettes devant leurs mai-sons, et ce afin que dans les temps de glace, les gens de pied puissent y marcher en sûreté."

44. Plumb, *England in the Eighteenth Century*, p. 12.
45. M. Dorothy George, *England in Transition: Life and Work in the Eighteenth Century*, p. 71.
46. Kalm, *Travels into North America*, 3: 72–73.
47. *Ibid.*, p. 73.

Chapter 6   YEARS OF TRANSITION

1. Quoted in Henry Stern Churchill, *The City Is the People*, p. 108.*
2. Edouard-Charles-Victurnien Colbert, comte de Maulevrier, *Voyage dans l'intérieur des Etats-Unis et au Canada*, pp. 58–59. Original text: "Trois rues parallèles à la rivière, d'environ un mille, coupées par une dizaine d'autres, à angle droit ou à peu près forment la ville qui est entourée en partie d'un vieux mur."
3. Isaac Weld, *Travels through the States of North America, and the Provinces of Upper and Lower Canada During the Years 1795, 1796, and 1797*, p. 181.
4. Donald Creighton, *The Empire of the St. Lawrence*, p. 24.
5. *Ibid.*
6. Alexander Henry, *Travels and Adventures in Canada and the Indian Territories, between the Years 1760 and 1776*, p. 2.
7. Désiré Girouard, *Lake St. Louis, Old and New*, p. 222.
8. Census of Canada (1665–1871), pp. 86 ff., 118 ff.
9. See Edgar Andrew Collard, *Oldest McGill*.
10. John Summerson, *Georgian London*, p. 133.
11. Alan Gowans, *Building Canada: An Architectural History of Canadian Life*, pp. 72 ff.*
12. Oliver W. Larkin, *Art and Life in America*, pp. 35–36.*
13. Lewis Mumford, *Sticks and Stones: A Study of American Architecture and Civilization*, p. 23.*
14. *Ibid.*, pp. 26 ff.
15. Eric McLean, "The Papineau House," *Habitat* 7, no. 5 (Sept.–Oct. 1964): 2–7.
16. Olivier Maurault, "Un professeur d'architecture à Québec en 1828," *JRAIC* 3, no. 1 (Jan.–Feb. 1926): 32–36.
17. Ramsay Traquair, *The Old Architecture of Quebec*, pp. 287–89; Gowans, *Building Canada*, pp. 59–63.
18. *Journal of the House of Assembly of Lower-Canada, from the 28th of March to the 3rd of June, 1799, in the thirty-ninth year of the Reign of His Majesty George III*, pp. 188–90.
19. *Journal of the House of Assembly of Lower-Canada, from the 8th of January to the 8th of April, 1801, in the forty-first year of the Reign of His Majesty George III*, pp. 322 ff.
20. Albertine Ferland Angers, *La citadelle de Montréal, 1658–1820*, p. 508.
21. N. E. Dionne, "Joseph Bouchette," *BRH* 20, no. 7 (July 1914): 226–30.
22. Joseph Bouchette, *A Topographical Description of the Province of Lower Canada*, p. 154.

23. Comte de Maulevrier, *Voyage*, p. 59. Original text: "derrière les murs de la ville, au Nord, est un ruisseau bourbeux qu'on pourrait aisément changer en un canal, qui ajouterait à la salubrité de l'endroit au lieu d'y nuire comme à présent."
24. Bouchette, *A Topographical Description*, pp. 154 ff.
25. E.-Z. Massicotte, "Quelques rues et faubourgs du vieux Montréal," in *Les cahiers des Dix*, 1: 130 ff.
26. *Ibid.*, pp. 110 ff.; Angers, *La citadelle de Montréal*, pp. 508 ff.
27. John M. Duncan, *Travels through Part of the United States and Canada in 1818 and 1819*, 2: 152–53.
28. Olivier Maurault, *La Paroisse; histoire de l'église Notre-Dame de Montréal*, p. 104.
29. Duncan, *Travels*, p. 153.
30. Raoul Blanchard, *L'Ouest du Canada français*, 1, *Montréal et sa région*, pp. 229–31.
31. Alfred Sandham, *Ville-Marie, or, Sketches of Montreal, Past and Present*, pp. 80–81.*
32. For an inventory of this progress, see William Henry Atherton, *Montreal* 2: 397 ff., 413 ff.*
33. George Heriot, *Travels through the Canadas*, p. 114.
34. John Lambert, *Travels through Lower Canada, and the United States of North America, in the Years 1806, 1807 and 1808*, 2: 64.
35. Sir James Edward Alexander, *Transatlantic Sketches*, 2: 191.
36. Duncan, *Travels*, p. 150.
37. Adam Fergusson, *Practical Notes Made During a Tour in Canada*, p. 64.
38. Weld, *Travels through Canada*, p. 178.
39. Edward Allen Talbot, *Five Years' Residence in the Canada*, 1: 66.
40. Théodore Pavie, *Souvenirs atlantiques: voyage aux Etats-Unis et au Canada*, 1: 157. Original text: "Les maisons sont toutes bâties en pierres grises, qui répandent un aspect sombre sur ces rues longues et resserrées; ce qui frappe surtout les yeux d'un étranger, c'est la blancheur des toits tout couverts en fer blanc, et les contrevents doublés en tôle, pour prévenir les incendies; cette manière de construire cause une grande monotonie."
41. Bouchette, *A Topographical Description*, p. 142.
42. Benjamin Silliman, *Remarks Made on a Short Tour between Hartford and Quebec, in the Autumn of 1819*, p. 358.
43. *Ibid.*, p. 359.
44. Alexander, *Transatlantic Sketches*, 2: 192.
45. [Rev. Newton] Bosworth, ed., *Hochelaga Depicta; the Early History and Present State of the City and Island of Montreal*, p. 91.
46. Bouchette, *A Topographical Description*, p. 143.
47. Lambert, *Travels through Lower Canada*, 2: 68.
48. Pavie, *Souvenirs atlantiques*, 1: 160. Original text: "une des plus délicieuses positions."
49. Joseph Hadfield, *An Englishman in America, 1785*, p. 46.
50. Weld, *Travels through Canada*, p. 178.

51. E.-Z. Massicotte, "Montréal se transforme," in *Les cahiers des Dix*, 5: 207.

52. *Ibid.*, pp. 207–10.

53. Duncan, *Travels*, p. 153.

54. Lambert, *Travels Through Lower Canada*, 2: 70; Bouchette, *A Topographical Description*, p. 150; Silliman, *Remarks*, p. 367; Fergusson, *Practical Notes*, p. 66; Sir Richard Henry Bonnycastle, *The Canadas in 1841*, 1: 75.

55. James Silk Buckingham, *Canada, Nova Scotia, New Brunswick, and the other British Provinces in North America*, p. 129.

56. Talbot, *Five Years' Residence*, 1: 71.

57. Merrill Denison, *Canada's First Bank: A History of the Bank of Montreal*, pp. 115 ff.

58. Gérard Morisset, *L'architecture en Nouvelle-France*, p. 136.* John Bland, "Deux architectes au 19ème siècle—Two 19th Century Architects," *ABC* 8, no. 87 (July 1953): 20. Ariane de Jongh Isler, "L'ancienne Douane de Montréal," *Vie des Arts*, no. 79 (Summer 1975), pp. 39–41.

59. Frank Dawson Adams, *A History of Christ Church Cathedral*, pp. 56ff.

60. Silliman, *Remarks*, p. 369.

61. Talbot, *Five Years' Residence*, 1: 69.

62. Bouchette, *The British Dominions in North America*, 1: 222.

63. Plan of 36.6 metres long by 24.4 metres wide, with extension 3.7 metres deep by 12.2 metres wide.

64. Peter Kidson, Peter Murray, and Paul Thompson, *A History of English Architecture*, p. 193.*

65. Franklin Toker, *The Church of Notre-Dame in Montreal: An Architectural History*, pp. 29 ff., and 38 ff.

66. Pavie, *Souvenirs atlantiques*, 1: 159. Original text: "vaste et beau monument."

67. E. T. Coke, *A Subaltern's Furlough*, pp. 334–35.

68. Hugh Murray, *An Historical and Descriptive Account of British America*, 1: 260–61.

69. Maurault, *La Paroisse*, pp. 99–100.

70. Quoted in *ibid.*, p. 95. Translation by the author.

71. See *ibid.*, passim, and Franklin Toker, "James O'Donnell: An Irish Georgian in America," *JSAH* 29, no. 2 (May 1970): 132–43.

72. Toker, *Church of Notre-Dame*, pp. 83–86.

73. Quoted in Maurault, *La Paroisse*, p. 58. Translation by the author.

74. Toker, *Church of Notre-Dame*, pp. 29 ff.

75. Alexander, *Transatlantic Sketches*, 2: 192.

76. Toker, *Church of Notre-Dame*, p. 84.

77. Quoted in Maurault, *La Paroisse*, p. 72. Original text: "Votre bâtisse devant être gothique et n'ayant étudié que l'architecture grecque et romaine, ce que j'ai cru suffisant pour le pays, je n'ai pris qu'une connaissance superficielle du gothique et je me crois donc de ce côté au-dessous de cette tâche."

78. *Ibid.*, p. 90.

Chapter 7 NEW FORCES

1. H. de Lamothe, *Cinq mois chez les Français d'Amérique*, pp. 78–79.
2. Henry Stern Churchill, *The City Is the People*, p. 6.
3. See Joseph Arthur Lower, *Canada: An Outline History*, pp. 88–89.*
4. John Lambert, *Travels through Lower Canada, and the United States of North America, in the Years 1806, 1807 and 1808*, 2: 64–65.
5. See Raoul Blanchard, *L'Ouest du Canada français*, 1, *Montréal et sa région*, pp. 247–51, 278–80;* Benoît Brouillette, "Le port et les transports," in *Montréal économique*, pp. 115–82.
6. See Blanchard, *L'Ouest du Canada français*, 1: 251–52, 276–78; Brouillette, "Le port et les transports."
7. Blanchard, *L'Ouest du Canada français*, 1: 268–76.
8. Leroy O. Stone, *Urban Development in Canada: An Introduction to Demographic Aspects*, p. 29.
9. Jean de Laplante, "La communauté montréalaise," *CESH* 1 (1952): 95 ff.
10. John Irwin Cooper, *Montreal: A Brief History*, pp. 18–19.*
11. Cooper, "The Social Structure of Montreal in the 1850s," in *CHAR*, 1956, pp. 64–65.
12. *Census of Canada (1665–1871)*, pp. 202–7.
13. Cooper, *Montreal: A Brief History*, pp. 94–95.
14. Blanchard, *L'Ouest du Canada français*, 1: 228–33, 281–88.
15. Cooper, *Montreal: A Brief History*, p. 92.
16. Cooper, "The Social Structure of Montreal," p. 69.
17. See Albert Faucher and Maurice Lamontagne, "History of Industrial Development," in *Essais sur le Québec contemporain*, pp. 23–37.
18. Blanchard, *L'Ouest du Canada français*, 1: 271–76; Jean Delage, "L'industrie manufacturière," in *Montréal économique*, pp. 183–241.
19. Asa Briggs, *Victorian Cities*, p. 64.
20. Gabrielle Roy, *The Tin Flute*, p. 30.
21. *Harper's New Monthly Magazine*, June 1889; article reproduced in part in Edgar Andrew Collard, *Call Back Yesterdays*, pp. 202–8.
22. George Monro Grant, ed., *Picturesque Canada: The Country as It Was and Is*, 1: 112.
23. Canada, *Census 1870–71*, 1: 38–39; Blanchard, *L'Ouest du Canada français*, 1: 275 ff.
24. Canada, *Census 1880–81*, 1: 52–53; *Fourth Census 1901*, 1: 104–5.
25. Robert Furneaux Jordan, *Victorian Architecture*, p. 18.
26. Herbert Brown Ames, *"The City below the Hill": A Sociological Study of a Portion of the City of Montreal, Canada*, pp. 41–47.
27. Roy, *The Tin Flute*, p. 25.
28. Blanchard, *L'Ouest du Canada français*, 1: 292.
29. *Ibid.*, p. 276. A large section of the municipality of Hochelaga was annexed to Montreal in 1883, and the remaining part was named Maisonneuve.
30. *Ibid.*, pp. 288–96. Canada, *Census 1870–71*, 1: 38–39; *Fifth Census*

1911, 1: 110. Paul Gauthier, "Montréal et ses quartiers municipaux," *BRH* 67, no. 4 (1961): 115–35.
31. Cooper, *Montreal: A Brief History*, pp. 104–6.
32. Electric light is first introduced in 1879.
33. Canada, *Fifth Census 1911*, 1: 103–8. The construction in 1886 of the C.P.R. bridge on the St. Lawrence River marked the beginning of the modern Lachine.
34. Laplante, "La communauté montréalaise," pp. 85–86.
35. *Ibid.*, p. 90.
36. Blanchard, *L'Ouest du Canada français*, 1: 294–96.
37. Cooper, "The Social Structure of Montreal," pp. 72–73.
38. Edgar Andrew Collard, *Call Back Yesterdays*, p. 207.*
39. *Ibid.*, p. 176.
40. Arthur R. M. Lower, *Canadians in the Making: A Social History of Canada*, pp. 212–25.
41. Murray Ballantyne, "J'ai grandi au Canada français," in *Le Canada français aujourd'hui et demain*, pp. 56–57. Translation by the author.
42. Lower, *Canadians in the Making*, p. 247.
43. Grant, *Picturesque Canada*, 1: 113–14.

Chapter 8   SOMEWHERE BETWEEN GOOD AND MEDIOCRE: PUBLIC AND
RELIGIOUS ARCHITECTURE

1. Alan Gowans, *Building Canada: An Architectural History of Canadian Life*, p. xix.*
2. Robert Furneaux Jordan, *Victorian Architecture*, p. 19.
3. John Bland, "Effects of Nineteenth Century Manners on Montreal," *JRAIC* 33, no. 11 (Nov. 1956): 417.
4. Following the fire which, in 1849, burnt down the Parliament of the Union on Place d'Youville.
5. Because of the difference in level of its site, the market has two storeys on Saint-Paul Street, three storeys on des Commissaires Street.
6. See Maréchal Nantel, "Le palais de Justice de Montréal et ses abords," in *Les cahiers des Dix*, 12: 197–230.
7. Bland, "Effects of Nineteenth Century Manners," p. 416.
8. *Ibid.*
9. Percy E. Nobbs, "Architecture in the Province of Quebec during the Early Years of the 20th Century," *JRAIC* 33, no. 11 (Nov. 1956): 418.
10. The other buildings attributed to Father Martin, Caughnawaga Church (1842) and the central part of the Jesuits' novitiate at Sault-au-Récollet, show that he was better builder than he was architect. See Paul Desjardins, *Le collège Sainte-Marie de Montréal*, 1: 211 ff. The College Sainte-Marie was demolished in 1976–77.
11. *Ibid.*, pp. 180 ff.
12. "L'architecture en Canada," *La Minerve*, 28 avril 1866. Original text: "aux exigences du culte, mais de plus aux grandes idées qu'elle était appelée a représenter." "Lorsqu'on entre dans l'église, on est frappé de ses

belles proportions nettes et bien dessinées." Concerning Saint Patrick's, refer to Robert Lipscombe, *The Story of Old St. Patrick's*, and R. H. Hubbard, "Canadian Gothic," *Architectural Review* 116, no. 8 (Aug. 1954): 102–8.

13. See Kenneth Clark, *The Gothic Revival: An Essay in the History of Taste*, especially chapter 8, pp. 134–58.

14. Hubbard, "Canadian Gothic," p. 107.

15. Philip J. Turner, "Christ Church Cathedral, Montreal," *Construction* 20, no. 11 (Nov. 1927): 347–54; Franklin Morris, "Christ Church Cathedral, Montreal," *Dalhousie Review* 35 (Summer 1955): 176, 178.

16. Baron Etienne Hulot, *De l'Atlantique au Pacifique à travers le Canada et le Nord des Etats-Unis*, p. 158. Original text: "des 'toits d'argent' qui scintillent se dressent les tours de Notre-Dame, le dôme de Saint-Pierre et les flèches d'une trentaine d'églises, plus ou moins gothiques."

17. As a replacement to the previous church built in 1834 from plans by John Wells.

18. Desjardins, *Le Collège Sainte-Marie*, 2: 127. Original text: "le beau style de St-Louis, celui de la Sainte-Chapelle, de la cathédrale d'Amiens, et, plus particulièrement celui de la cathédrale de Cologne"; "en pur gothique XIIe siècle."

19. *Ibid.*, pp. 136–52.

20. *Ibid.*, p. 127. Original text: "l'évêque seul à fixer le plan et les principales dimensions des églises qui se [bâtissaient] dans son diocèse"; "sans autre contrôle que celui du Souverain Pontife."

21. This palace was destroyed by the great fire of 9 July 1852.

22. Olivier Maurault, *Marges d'histoire*, 2, *Montréal*, pp. 247 ff.* The campanile was built in 1926 by architect J. O. Marchand.

23. *Ibid.*, pp. 269–91. Gowans, *Building Canada*, pp. 109–11.

24. In that sense, other "neo" styles could have been identified: the neo-Romanesque (Grey Nuns' Convent, Dorchester Blvd.), the neo-Byzantine (Notre-Dame-de-Lourdes Chapel, Sainte-Catherine Street), and others. These styles are obviously not so widespread as the ones cited here.

25. Post Office: northeast corner of St. James and Saint-François-Xavier Streets; demolished. Banque des Marchands: northwest corner of St. James and Saint-Pierre Streets; many storeys have been added to it. Molsons Bank: southeast corner of St. James and Saint-Pierre Streets. Dominion Block: northwest corner of McGill and Saint-Paul Streets.

26. Henry-Russell Hitchcock, *Architecture: Nineteenth and Twentieth Centuries*, p. 132.*

27. Bland, "Effects of Nineteenth Century Manners," p. 416.

28. See *The Windsor Hotel Guide to the City of Montreal and for the Dominion of Canada*.

29. What is left today of Windsor Hotel is a later extension of the original building.

30. Hitchcock, *Architecture*, p. 144.

31. Gowans, *Building Canada*, pp. 122–213.

32. Philip J. Turner, "The Development of Architecture in the Province of

Quebec since Confederation," *Construction* 20, no. 6 (June 1927): 193–94.

33. "Bibliothèque Saint-Sulpice, Montréal. Eugène Payette, architecte," Portfolio of current architecture, *The Architectural Record* 41, no. 4 (April 1917): 341–48. Thomas W. Ludlow, "The Montreal Art Gallery: E. & W. S. Maxwell, architects," *The Architectural Record* 37, no. 2 (Feb. 1915): 132–48.
34. Turner, "The Development of Architecture," p. 194.
35. See the fire station of the old municipality of Maisonneuve, on Notre-Dame Street, built by Marius Dufresne in 1915.
36. Hitchcock, *Architecture*, pp. 226–27.
37. Turner, "The Development of Architecture," p. 192.
38. Hitchcock, *Architecture*, p. 206.
39. Turner, "The Development of Architecture," p. 193.
40. The present tower of Château Frontenac was added in 1923 by architects E. & W. S. Maxwell.
41. See Allen Scribner, ed., *Dictionary of American Biography*, 15: 210–11.
42. Erskine and American United Church, Sherbrooke Street at the northeast corner of du Musée Avenue, built in 1893, is another example of architecture inspired by the style of Richardson. The interior of this church was considerably transformed in 1938 by architects Nobbs and Hyde.
43. Edgar Andrew Collard, *Call Back Yesterdays*, p. 200.*

Chapter 9   HOPES AND DISAPPOINTMENTS: COMMERCIAL ARCHITECTURE

1. Sigfried Giedion, *Space, Time and Architecture: The Growth of a New Tradition*, pp. 100–101.
2. Melvin Charney, "The Old Montreal No One Wants to Preserve," *The Montrealer* 38, no. 12 (Dec. 1964): 22.
3. Henry-Russell Hitchcock, *Architecture: Nineteenth and Twentieth Centuries*, p. 234. Winston Weisman, "Philadelphia Functionalism and Sullivan," *JSAH* 20, no. 1 (March 1961): 6.
4. Engravings reproduced in Charles De Volpi and P. S. Winkworth, eds., *Montreal: A Pictorial Record*, 2, plate 228. This building seems to have since been demolished.
5. These warehouses were built on the site of the old Hôtel-Dieu of Jeanne Mance.
6. This architectural texture will develop in the first expression of the curtain wall as one can see in the style of the façade of the commercial building on 47–55 de la Commune Street West.
7. Giedion, *Space, Time and Architecture*, pp. 134–38.
8. Hitchcock, *Architecture*, p. 237.
9. Alan Gowans maintains that, as a rule, the first Canadian buildings of this style were inspired by models in Great Britain whereas the last ones were inspired by models in the United States. See *Building Canada: An Architectural History of Canadian Life*, p. 105.*
10. John Bland, "Effect of Nineteenth Century Manners on Montreal,"

JRAIC 33, no. 11 (Nov. 1956): 416. Philip J. Turner, "The Development of Architecture in the Province of Quebec since Confederation," *Construction* 20, no. 6 (June 1927): 190.

11. Turner, "The Development of Architecture," p. 193. Thomas Ritchie, *Canada Builds 1867–1967*, p. 73.
12. Turner, "The Development of Architecture," p. 195.
13. The Aldred Building is located on the northeast corner of Notre-Dame Street and Place d'Armes.
14. *Montreal, Old (and) New*, p. 351.* This elevator was demolished in 1978.
15. Charney, "The Old Montreal," p. 22; also, "The Grain Elevators Revisited," *Architectural Design* 37 (July 1967): 328–31.
16. Lionel Thomas Caswell Rolt, *Victorian Engineering*, p. 28.
17. Henry-Russell Hitchcock, *Early Victorian Architecture in Britain*, 1: 518–21; 2: 35–38. Rolt, *Victorian Engineering*, pp. 27–31.
18. H. de Lamothe, *Cinq mois chez les Français d'Amérique*, p. 74. Original text: "Disons-le tout de suite, cette merveille de l'art des ingénieurs impressionne plus vivement l'esprit que la vue, car la distance en réduit étrangement les gigantesque proportions. La longue ligne rigide de la galerie, les formes grêles et également rectilignes des arches vues de face lui donnent de loin d'humble apparence d'un pont de chevalets."
19. Lewis Mumford, *The Brown Decades: A Study of the Arts in America, 1865–1895*, pp. 97 ff.*
20. Concerning Victoria Bridge, see Charles Legge, *A Glance at the Victoria Bridge and the Men Who Built It*.

Chapter 10 FROM EXTRAVAGANCE TO INDIGENCE: DOMESTIC ARCHITECTURE

1. Melvin Charney, "Pour une définition de l'architecture au Québec," in *Architecture et urbanisme au Québec*, p. 23.*
2. See Stephen Leacock, *Leacock's Montreal*, pp. 233–35.
3. Today, Allan Memorial of the Royal Victoria Hospital.
4. John Bland, "Domestic Architecture in Montreal," *Culture* 9, no. 4 (Dec. 1948): 403.
5. Edgar Andrew Collard, "Of Many Things . . ." *The Gazette*, Montreal, 30 May 1970, p. 6. Concerning John George Howard, see Marion MacRae and Anthony Adamson, *The Ancestral Roof: Domestic Architecture of Upper Canada, 1783–1867*, pp. 87 ff., 102, 202.
6. J. Russell Harper and Stanley Triggs, eds., *Portrait of a Period: Collection of Notman Photographs, 1856–1915*, photographs 72, 73, and 74.
7. John Bland, "Effect of Nineteenth Century Manners on Montreal," *JRAIC* 33, no. 11 (Nov. 1956): 416; J. Philip Turner, "The Development of Architecture in the Province of Quebec since Confederation," pp. 189–95.
8. See the introduction to Lewis Mumford, *The Brown Decades: A Study of the Arts in America, 1865–1895*.*

9. Edgar Andrew Collard, *Call Back Yesterdays*, p. 201.*
10. Mumford, *The Brown Decades*, p. 110.
11. Hans Blumenfeld, "L'habitation dans les métropoles," *ABC* 21, no. 241 (May 1966): 23. Blake McKelvey, *The Urbanization of America, 1860–1915*, pp. 76–77.
12. John Irwin Cooper, "The Social Structure of Montreal in the 1850s," *CHAR*, 1956, p. 68.
13. Roy Kervin, "Faubourg à la Mélasse . . . Victim of Progress," *The Montrealer* 38, no. 6 (June 1964): pp. 16–19.
14. Raymond Tanghe, *Géographie humaine de Montréal*, pp. 244–45;* Stuart Wilson, "A Part of Le Faubourg," *JRAIC* 43, no. 11 (Nov. 1966): 71–74.
15. R. J. Mitchell and M. D. R. Leys, *A History of London Life*, p. 82.
16. Bland, "Domestic Architecture," pp. 399–407.
17. *Ibid.*, p. 405; Tanghe, *Géographie humaine*, pp. 259 ff.
18. Bland, "Domestic Architecture," p. 405.
19. Marcel Parizeau, "L'urbanisme," in *Montréal économique*, pp. 377–97 passim; Raoul Blanchard, *L'Ouest du Canada-français*, 1, *Montréal et sa région*, pp. 346–49, 359–63.
20. Société des Ecrivains canadiens, ed., *Ville, ô ma ville*, p. 291. Original text: "ces logements-corridors allongés d'une échelle improprement appelée escalier . . . ces escaliers extérieurs dont personne ne nous disputera la paternité devant l'histoire."
21. Canada, *Census 1890–91*, 1: 96–97; *Sixth Census*, 1921, 1: p. 220.
22. Abbé Norbert Lacoste, *Les caractéristiques sociales de la population du grand Montréal*, pp. 89 ff.
23. Blumenfeld, "L'habitation dans les metropoles," p. 23.
24. Note that this flat roof is surmounted by a false roof which slopes gently towards the drain.

Chapter 11 THE VICTORIAN LEGACY

1. Asa Briggs, *Victorian Cities*, pp. 16–17.
2. Lewis Mumford, *The City in History: Its Origins, Its Transformations, and Its Prospects*, especially chapter 15, "Palaeotechnic Paradise: Coketown," pp. 446–81.*
3. Quoted in Briggs, *Victorian Cities*, p. 92.
4. *Ibid.*, pp. 11–58.
5. *Ibid.*, pp. 16–17.
6. William Henry Atherton, *Montreal*, 2: 407 ff., 671.*
7. John William Reps, *The Making of Urban America*, pp. 296–99.*
8. Stuart Wilson, "A Part of Le Faubourg," *JRAIC* 43, no. 11 (Nov. 1966): 74.
9. Stuart Wilson, "Avenue Lartigue—L'Avenue Lartigue," *Habitat* 8, no. 2 (March–April 1965): 2–15. *Idem*, "Avenue Delorme," *JRAIC* 42, no. 3 (March 1965): 78–80.
10. Stephen Leacock, *Leacock's Montreal*, p. 234.*

11. *Montreal, Old (and) New*, p. 68.*
12. William H. Carre, *Art Work on Montreal.*
13. Melvin Charney, "The Old Montreal No One Wants to Preserve," *The Montrealer* 38, no. 12 (Dec. 1964): 22.
14. T. Morris Longstreth, *Quebec, Montreal and Ottawa*, p. 217.
15. Edgar Andrew Collard, *Montreal Yesterdays*, pp. 59 ff.
16. Joseph-Cléophas Lamothe, *Histoire de la corporation de la Cité de Montréal depuis son origine jusqu'à nos jours*, p. 107.
17. *Ibid.*, pp. 105–6.
18. Atherton, *Montreal*, 2: 643–44.
19. Joe McDougall, "Passing Show: Forty Years in Retrospect," *The Montrealer* 40, no. 5 (May 1966): 17.
20. Steen Eiler Rasmussen, *London the Unique City*, pp. 135–51.
21. Lewis Mumford, *The Brown Decades: A Study of the Arts in America 1865–1895*, pp. 82–96.
22. Reps, *The Making of Urban America*, pp. 325–39.
23. Christopher Tunnard and Henry Hope Reed, *American Skyline: The Growth and the Form of our Cities and Towns*, pp. 108 ff.*
24. Robert Furneaux Jordan, *Victorian Architecture*, p. 168.
25. Atherton, *Montreal*, 2: 646–47.
26. Julius G. Fabos, Gordon T. Milde, and V. Michael Weinmayr, *Frederick Law Olmsted, Sr.: Founder of Landscape Architecture in America.* Concerning Mount Royal Park, see A. L. Murray, "Frederick Law Olmsted and the Design of Mount Royal Park, Montreal," *JSAH* 26, no. 3 (Oct. 1967): 163–71.
27. Frederick Law Olmsted, *Mount Royal, Montreal*, p. 26.
28. Longstreth, *Quebec, Montreal and Ottawa*, p. 218.
29. Olmsted, *Mount Royal, Montreal*, p. 2.
30. Jacques Simard, "Il était une fois une très jolie montagne," *ABC* 15, no. 168 (April 1960): 67.
31. Olmsted, *Mount Royal, Montreal*, p. 26.
32. Atherton, *Montreal*, 2: 644.
33. Jules Bazin, "L'île Ste-Hélène et son histoire," *Vie des Arts*, no. 48 (Autumn 1967), pp. 18–23.
34. John Irwin Cooper, "The Social Structure of Montreal in the 1850s," *CHAR*, 1956, p. 73.

Chapter 12 THE METROPOLIS

1. Michel Régnier, *Génération: poèmes*, p. 94.
2. Montreal, Quebec, City Planning Department, *Urbanisation: A Study of Urban Expansion in the Montreal Region*, p. 3.
3. Leroy O. Stone, *Urban Development in Canada: An Introduction to Demographic Aspects*, p. 29; Statistics Canada, Census 1971.
4. Montreal, Quebec, City Planning Department, *Métropole*, les Cahiers d'urbanisme, no. 1, pp. 5–9. Refer also to the Census of 1971. This Montreal region as defined by the City Planning Department includes Mon-

treal, Laval, Perrot, and Bizard islands, and the counties of Soulanges, Vaudreuil, Deux-Montagnes, Terrebonne (in part), Assomption, Verchères, Saint-Hyacinthe, Chambly, Rouville, Laprairie, Saint-Jean and Iberville, Napierville, Châteauguay, and Beauharnois.

5. *Ibid.*, pp. 17–23.
6. *Urbanisation*, pp. 4–6.
7. Hans Blumenfeld, *The Modern Metropolis: Its Origins, Growth, Characteristics and Planning*, pp. 61–76.*
8. *Métropole*, les Cahiers d'urbanisme, no. 1, p. 15.
9. "L'exode rural; Montréal attire 100 personnes par jour," *Le Devoir*, Monday, 5 April 1971, p. 3.
10. Benoît Brouillette, "Le port de Montréal, hier et aujourd'hui," *RGM* 21, no. 2 (1967): 195–233. Montreal harbour is no longer the second largest in America, but is now surpassed by about ten ports in the United States.
11. Claude Manzagol, "Manufacturing Industry in Montreal," in *Montreal: Field Guide*, pp. 125–35.
12. Peter Foggin, "Urban Land Use Patterns: The Montreal Case," in *Montreal: Field Guide*, pp. 36–37.
13. Montreal, Quebec, City Planning Department, *Downtown Montreal*, pp. 5–6.
14. Montreal, Quebec, City Planning Department, *Métropole*, les Cahiers d'urbanisme, no. 2, pp. 6–13.
15. *Downtown Montreal*, p. 55.
16. Paul-Yves Denis, "Conditions géographiques et postulats démographiques d'une rénovation urbaine à Montréal," *RGM* 21, no. 1 (1967): 154.
17. Hans Blumenfeld, "L'habitation dans les métropoles," *ABC* 21, no. 241 (May 1966): 24.
18. Montréal, Québec, Service d'urbanisme, *Familles et ménages 1951–1961*, pp. 5–13.
19. Especially considering that the demand for small units is urgent in this sector because of the presence of educational institutions (McGill University, etc.) and the lure of this sector for the tourists.
20. Blumenfeld, "L'habitation dans les métropoles," p. 24.
21. *Métropole*, les Cahiers d'urbanisme, no. 2, pp. 20–23.
22. *Ibid.*, p. 22.
23. *Urbanisation*, p. 78.
24. *Métropole*, les Cahiers d'urbanisme, no. 1, p. 26.
25. *Familles et ménages 1951–1961*, pp. 10–13.
26. *Ibid.*, p. 2.
27. The construction of Habitations Jeanne-Mance, near the city's centre, and the renovation of Little Burgundy, in a traditional industrial ward, are the result of the following reasoning: to give adequate dwellings and a satisfactory environment to poor families unable to follow the definite settlement pattern of richer families.
28. Christopher Tunnard and Henry Hope Reed, *American Skyline: The Growth and Form of our Cities and Towns*, p. 178.*

29. John Irwin Cooper, *Montreal: A Brief History*, pp. 129–30.*
30. Paul Ritter, *Planning for Man and Motor*, pp. 271–72; development located on the southeast corner of Rosemont Boulevard and Viau Street.
31. Cyril Paumier, "New Town at Montreal's Front Door," *Landscape Architecture* 57, no. 1 (Oct. 1966): 67.
32. Aimé Cousineau, "City Planning Activities in Montreal," *JRAIC* 20, no. 4 (April 1943): 51–53.
33. See *JRAIC* 22, no. 5 (May 1945): 89–107.
34. See Alain Coucharrière, "Montréal, horizon 2000," *Commerce* 71 (April 1969): 62–66; (May 1969): 26–31; "Horizon 2000, Montréal," *ABC* 23, no. 263 (April 1968): 32–38.
35. Harvey Cox, *The Secular City: Secularisation and Urbanisation in Theological Perspective*, pp. 31 ff.
36. André Saumier, "La ville humaine," *Habitat* 10, no. 1 (Jan.–Feb. 1967): 15. Original text: "d'autant mieux structuré et plus grandiose qu'il était plus coupé du monde réel des révolutions urbaines et industrielles."
37. See *Urbanisation*, p. 68.

Chapter 13 THE NEW CORE OF THE CITY

1. Peter Blake, "Downtown in 3-D," *The Architectural Forum* 125, no. 2 (Sept. 1966): 31.
2. Alan Gowans, *Building Canada: An Architectural History of Canadian Life*, Illustration 205.*
3. Blake, "Downtown in 3-D," p. 34. Guy Desbarats, "Montreal—laboratoire urbain," *Habitat* 10, no. 1 (Jan.–Feb. 1967): 26–32.
4. Blake, "Downtown in 3-D," p. 47.
5. These lots are roughly bounded by Cathcart Street to the north, Mansfield and de l'Inspecteur Streets to the west, Saint-Antoine Street to the south, and University Street to the east.
6. Commission industrielle de Montréal, "Les Termini de Montréal du Canadien National," *Montréal, la Métropole du Canada*, pp. 61–64.
7. "A Modern Station for Montreal," *Architectural Record* 94, no. 12 (Dec. 1943): 91–101.
8. "Place Ville-Marie," *The Architectural Forum* 118, no. 2 (Feb. 1963): 74–89.
9. For a historical account of the development of these lots belonging to the C.N., see Jan C. Rowan, "The Story of Place Ville-Marie," *Progressive Architecture* 41, no. 2 (Feb. 1960): 123–35.
10. Jean Pelletier and Ludger Beauregard, "Le centre-ville de Montréal," *RGM* 21, no. 1 (1967): 31.
11. Henri N. Cobb, "Some Notes on the Design of Place Marie," *JRAIC* 40, no. 2 (Feb. 1963): 54–57.
12. "Place Ville-Marie," *The Architectural Forum*, p. 83.
13. Arthur Boyd, "The Skyscraper," *The Canadian Architect* 7, no. 6 (June 1962): 46.
14. "C.I.L. House, Montreal," *The Canadian Architect* 7, no. 6 (June 1962): 53–63.

15. Pelletier and Beauregard, "Le centre-ville de Montréal," pp. 26–27.
16. "Downtown Bank Tower," *Progressive Architecture*, 44, no. 9 (Sept. 1963): 140–45.
17. Boyd, "The Skyscraper," pp. 45–46.
18. Stuart Wilson, "Place Victoria," *JRAIC* 42, no. 10 (Oct. 1965): 64.
19. Melvin Charney, "Place Victoria," *The Canadian Architect* 10, no. 7 (July 1965): 37–54.
20. Steen Eiler Rasmussen, *Experiencing Architecture*, pp. 56–82.*
21. Ray T. Affleck, lecture at the School of Architecture of the University of Montreal, 9 October 1969.
22. Ray T. Affleck, "Place Bonaventure: The Architect's View," *Architecture Canada* 44, no. 7 (July 1967): 32.
23. *Ibid.*, p. 37. The exterior style of this building has been greatly influenced by the Yale Art and Architecture Building (New Haven) built by Paul Rudolph. This building was inaugurated in 1963.
24. Paul-Yves Denis, "Conditions géographiques et postulats démographiques d'une rénovation urbaine à Montréal," *RGM* 21, no. 1 (1967): 164.
25. Desbarats, "Montréal—laboratoire urbain," pp. 26–32.
26. Percy Johnson-Marshall, *Rebuilding Cities*, pp. 126–29.
27. Blake, "Downtown in 3-D," p. 47.
28. Pelletier and Beauregard, "Le centre-ville de Montréal," pp. 19–20. Original text: "des plus remarquables phénomènes d'adaptation géographique."
29. Affleck, "Place Bonaventure," p. 36.
30. For criticism on this new pole of attraction in the city centre, see Norbert Schoenauer, "Critique One," *The Canadian Architect* 8, no. 2 (Feb. 1963): 55–57. J. Lehrman, "Critique Two," *The Canadian Architect* 8, no. 2 (Feb. 1963): 63–64.
31. Robert Gretton and Norman Slater, "Metro," *The Canadian Architect* 12, no. 2 (Feb. 1967): 27.
32. See Ludger Beauregard, "Public Transport in Montreal," in *Montreal: Field Guide*, pp. 179–88.
33. Hans Blumenfeld, *The Modern Metropolis: Its Origins, Growth, Characteristics and Planning*, p. 152. The population is particularly well served in the city centre where the eight metro stations are located in alternate positions on two parallel lines which are at a distance of about 610 metres from one another. Thus, in this area of 243 hectares, one has to walk fewer than three minutes to reach a metro station. Outside the city centre, the distance between each station is about 610 metres, instead of 488 metres as in the city centre.
34. These sites may be useful for commercial purposes as a great number of passengers go through each station daily.
35. Blumenfeld, *The Modern Metropolis*, p. 149.
36. Under the direction of chief architect Gerard Masson and the architect in charge of the metro, Mr. Pierre Bourgeau, the Public Works Department designed ten stations. Private architects planned the other sixteen stations. Since then this first metro network has been enlarged by the eastern extension of line no. 1 (nine stations) and by the western exten-

sion of the same line no. 1 (eight stations). Many of these new stops, particularly Radisson, LaSalle, and Angrignon, are of great architectural quality.

37. Gretton and Slater, "Metro," p. 33.
38. Victor Prus, "Reflections on the Subterranean Architecture of Subway Systems," *The Canadian Architect* 12, no. 2 (Feb. 1967): 35–36. "Bonaventure Subway Station, Montreal," *The Canadian Architect* 12, no. 8 (Aug. 1967): 45–48.
39. Guy R. Legault, "Le Métro de Montréal," *Architecture Canada* 43, no. 8 (Aug. 1966): 44–48. Blumenfeld, *The Modern Metropolis*, pp. 147–54.
40. Henry-Russell Hitchcock, *Architecture: Nineteenth and Twentieth Centuries*, pp. 230–31.*
41. John William Reps, *The Making of Urban America*, pp. 497–525.
42. St. Helen's Island, originally covering 55 hectares, was joined to Green Island upstream and to Rond Island downstream, adding 20 and 59 hectares respectively to the site. A part of Expo, an area of 61 hectares, was also built in Pointe Saint-Charles, on Mackay pier. Finally, Notre-Dame Island, reclaimed from the river, added another 125 hectares to the site.
43. S. M. Staples, "Tranportation Network at Expo 67," *Architecture Canada* 43, no. 8 (Aug. 1966): 33–34; also, "Expo 67: Is It a Success?" *Architecture Canada* 44, no. 8 (Aug. 1967): 39–42.
44. Staples, "Expo 67: Is It a Success?" p. 40.
45. Edouard Fiset, "Introduction d'un concept urbain dans la planification de l'exposition," *JRAIC* 42, no. 5 (May 1965): 55–62. Jerry Miller, "Expo 67: A Search for Order," *The Canadian Architect* 12, no. 5 (May 1967): 44–54. Laurent Lamy, "Le design, roi et maître de l'Exposition universelle," *Vie des Arts*, no. 48 (Autumn 1967): 52–55.
46. Guy Desbarats, "Montréal—laboratoire urbain"; Guntis Plesums, "Architecture and Structure as a System: Man the Producer Pavilion," *Architecture Canada* 46, no. 4 (April 1969): 23–33.
47. Peter Blake, "Quebec's Shimmering Vitrine," *The Architectural Forum* 126, no. 5 (June 1967): 29–37.
48. *Ibid.*, p. 36.

Epilogue

1. Statistics Canada, five-year census, 1976.
2. Ronald Abler and John S. Adams, *A Comparative Atlas of America's Great Cities: Twenty Metropolitan Regions*, p. 447.
3. Hans Blumenfeld, "Au-delà de la métropole," *Critère*, no. 19 (Autumn 1977), p. 46.
4. Eva H. Vecsei, "La Cité de la Métropole," *Architecture Concept* 33 (May–June 1977): 10–17. The consulting urbanists were Roger Montgomery, Vincent Ponte, and Cossuta & Ponte.
5. Donna Gabeline, Dane Lanken, and Gordon Pape, *Montreal at the Crossroads*, pp. 67–68.
6. See Jean-Claude Marsan, "Le complexe Desjardins: le syndrome de la

Place Ville-Marie," *Le Devoir*, 13 March 1976, p. 15; also "Le complexe Desjardins: la première véritable place en dépit d'une expression spatiale conservatrice," *Le Devoir*, 20 March 1976, p. 13.

7. See Jean-Claude Marsan et al., *Le village olympique*, passim; J.-C. Marsan, "La question du village olympique," *Architecture Concept* 28, no. 139 (November 1973): 26–29.
8. Roger Taillibert, *Construire l'avenir*, legend of one of the illustrations.
9. *Ibid.*, p. 21.
10. *Ibid.*
11. See Jean-Claude Marsan et al., *Le parc olympique*, passim; and also J.-C. Marsan, "Construire l'avenir mais comment?" *Le Devoir*, 7 January 1978, pp. 30, 40.
12. Québec, Office de planification et de développement du Québec, *Esquisse de la région de Montréal: évolution et orientation du développement et de l'aménagement*, pp. 98–105.

Selective
BIBLIOGRAPHY

This selective bibliography refers only to printed sources; other references are indicated in the introduction and in the notes to the chapters. This bibliography is divided into seventeen sections. The first three refer to bibliographical, cartographical, and pictorial sources, and also to general sources. The following fourteen sections refer to each chapter of the study and to the epilogue.

Bibliographical Sources

The Art Index. New York: H. W. Wilson, 1933.

Brown, George W. et al., eds. *Dictionary of Canadian Biography.* 5 vols. (to date). Toronto: University of Toronto Press, 1966–.

Canadian Library Association. *Canadian Periodical Index—Index des Périodiques canadiens.* Ottawa: 1938–.

Dionne, Narcisse-Eutrope. *Inventaire chronologique des livres, brochures, journaux et revues publiés . . . depuis l'établissement de l'imprimerie au Canada jusqu'à nos jours.* 4 vols. Québec: n.p., 1905–12.

Dumont, Fernand, and Martin, Yves, dirs. *Situation de la recherche sur le Canada français; Premier colloque de la revue Recherches Sociographiques du département de Sociologie et d'Anthropologie de l'Université Laval.* Québec: Presses de l'Université Laval, 1962.

Garigue, Philippe. *A Bibliographical Introduction to the Study of French Canada.* Montreal: Department of Sociology and Anthropology, McGill University, 1956.

———. *Bibliographie du Québec, 1955–1965.* Montréal: Presses de l'Université de Montréal, 1967.

Lacoste, Norbert. "Bibliographie sommaire des études sur Montréal." *Recherches sociographiques* 6, no. 3 (Sept.–Dec. 1965):277–81.

Lanctôt, Gustave. *L'oeuvre de la France en Amérique du Nord. Bibliographie sélective et critique.* Ouvrage publ. par la section française de la Société Royale du Canada. Montréal: Fides, 1951.

Scribner, Allen, ed. *Dictionary of American Biography*. Under the auspices of the American Council of Learned Societies. 22 vols. New York: Charles Scribner's Sons, 1928–1958.

Cartographical and Pictorial Sources

Beaugrand, H., ed., and Morin, P. L., illus. *Le Vieux Montréal 1611–1803*. Montréal: n.p., 1884.

Carre, William H. *Art Work on Montreal*. 12 vols. N.p.: 1898.

De Volpi, Charles P., and Winkworth, P. S., eds. *Montréal: Recueil iconographique—A Pictorial Record*. 2 vols. Montréal: Dev-Sco Publications, 1963.

Greenhill, Ralph. *Early Photography in Canada*. Toronto: Oxford University Press, 1965.

Harper, J. Russell, and Triggs, Stanley, eds. *Portrait of a Period: A Collection of Notman Photographs, 1856–1915*. Montreal: McGill University Press, 1967.

Hopkins, Henry Whitmer, ed. *Atlas of the City and Island of Montreal, Including the Counties of Jacques Cartier and Hochelaga. From Actual Surveys, Based upon the Cadastral Plans Deposited in the Office of the Department of Crown Lands*. N.p.: Provincial Surveying and Pub. Co., 1879.

Lanctôt, Gustave. *Images et figures de Montréal sous la France*. Toronto: La Société Royale du Canada, 1943.

Massicotte, E.-Z. "Inventaire des cartes et plans de l'île et de la ville de Montréal." *BRH* 20, no. 2 (Feb. 1914): 33–41, no. 3 (March 1914): 65–73.

McLean, Eric, and Wilson, R. D. *Le passé vivant de Montréal—The Living Past of Montreal*. Rev. ed. Montreal: McGill-Queen's University Press, 1976.

Miller, Emile. "Inventaire chronologique des cartes et des plans de Montréal 1611–1915, avec annotations." *Rapport annuel du département des archives municipales pour l'année 1915*. Appendix 3, pp. 39–80. Montréal: Perrault, 1916.

Québec (Province), Ministère des Affaires Culturelles et Service d'urbanisme de Montréal. *Relevé et études des ensembles historiques de la ville de Montréal*. Exécuté par la section de recherche des Monuments historiques de l'école d'Architecture de l'Université de Montréal. Dir. L. Demeter; coll. étudiants de l'école d'Architecture de l'Univ. de Montréal et de l'Univ. McGill.

Roy, Pierre-Georges. *Les vieilles églises de la province de Québec, 1647–1800*. Commission des monuments historiques de la province de Québec. Québec: Proulx, 1925.

———. *Vieux manoirs, vieilles maisons*. Commission des monuments historiques de la province de Québec. Québec: Proulx, 1927.

Spendlove, F. St. George. *The Face of Early Canada: Pictures of Canada Which Have Helped to Make History*. Toronto: Ryerson Press, 1958.

Trudel, Marcel. *Atlas de la Nouvelle-France—An Atlas of New France*. Québec: Presses de l'Université Laval, 1968.

General Sources

Adamson, Anthony; Alison, Alice; Arthur, Eric; and Goulding, William. *Historic Architecture of Canada—Architecture historique du Canada.* Ottawa: Royal Architectural Institute of Canada, 1967.

Argan, Giulio Carlo. *The Renaissance City.* New York: G. Braziller, 1970.

Arthur, Eric R. *Toronto: No Mean City.* Toronto: University of Toronto Press, 1964.

Atherton, William Henry. *Montreal (1535–1914).* 3 vols. Montreal: S. J. Clarke, 1914.

Bacon, Edmund M. *Design of Cities.* New York: Viking Press, 1967.

Beauregard, Ludger. *Toponymie de la région métropolitaine.* Québec: Ministère des terres et forêts du Québec, 1968.

———, ed. *Montréal: Guide d'excursions—Field Guide.* 22e Congrès international de géographie. Montréal: Presses de l'Université de Montréal, 1972.

Bertrand, Camille. *Histoire de Montréal.* 2 vols. Montréal: Beauchemin, 1935–42.

Blanchard, Raoul. *L'Ouest du Canada français,* vol. 1, *Montréal et sa région.* Montréal: Beauchemin, 1953.

———. *Le Canada français—Province de Québec: Etude géographique.* Paris: Fayard, 1960.

Blumenfeld, Hans. *The Modern Metropolis: Its Origins, Growth, Characteristics and Planning.* Selected essays, ed. by Paul D. Spreiregen. Montreal: Harvest House, 1967.

Charney, Melvin. "Pour une définition de l'architecture au Québec." In *Architecture et Urbanisme au Québec,* pp. 11–42. Conférences J.-A. De-Sève, 13 14. Montréal: Presses de l'Université de Montréal, 1971.

Choisy, Auguste. *Histoire de l'Architecture.* 2 vols. Paris: Vincent, Fréal, 1954.

Churchill, Henry Stern. *The City Is the People.* New York: Norton, 1962.

Colgate, William. *Canadian Art: Its Origin and Development.* Toronto: Ryerson, 1943.

Collard, Edgar Andrew. *Montreal Yesterdays.* Toronto: Longmans, 1962.

———. *Call Back Yesterdays.* Don Mills, Ont.: Longmans, 1965.

Condit, Carl W. *American Building Art: The Nineteenth Century.* New York: Oxford University Press, 1960.

———. *American Building: Materials and Techniques from the First Colonial Settlements to the Present.* Chicago: University of Chicago Press, 1968.

Cooper, John Irwin. *Montreal: The Story of Three Hundred Years.* Montreal: n.p., 1942.

———. *Montreal: A Brief History.* Montreal: McGill-Queen's University Press, 1969.

Creighton, Donald. *Dominion of the North: A History of Canada.* New ed. Toronto: Macmillan, 1957.

Easterbrook, W. T., and Watkins, M. H., eds. *Approaches to Canadian Economic History.* Toronto: McClelland and Stewart, 1967.

[Faillon, Etienne-Michel.] *Histoire de la colonie française en Canada.* 4 vols. Villemarie: Bibliothèque paroissiale, 1865–1866.

Falardeau, Jean-Charles, ed. *Essais sur le Québec contemporain—Essays on Contemporary Quebec.* Symposium du centenaire de l'Université Laval. Québec: Presses de l'Université Laval, 1953.

Fletcher, Sir Banister. *A History of Architecture on the Comparative Method.* 17th rev. ed. London: Athlone Press, University of London, 1967.

Geddes, Patrick. *Cities in Evolution.* Ed. by the Outlook Tower Ass., Edinburgh, and the Ass. for Planning and Regional Reconstruction, London. New rev. ed. London: Williams & Norgate, 1949.

Gowans, Alan. *Church Architecture in New France.* Toronto: University of Toronto Press, 1955.

———. *Looking at Architecture in Canada.* Toronto: Oxford University Press, 1958.

———. *Building Canada: An Architectural History of Canadian Life.* Toronto: Oxford University Press, 1966.

Groulx, Chanoine Lionel. *Histoire du Canada français depuis la découverte.* 2 vols. Montréal: L'Action nationale, 1950–52.

Hitchcock, Henry-Russell. *Architecture: Nineteenth and Twentieth Centuries.* 2nd ed. Baltimore: Penguin, 1963.

Hubbard, Robert Hamilton. *The Development of Canadian Art.* Ottawa: Queen's Printer, 1963.

Jacobs, Jane. *The Death and Life of Great American Cities.* New York: Random House, 1961.

Jenkins, Kathleen. *Montreal: Island City of the St. Lawrence.* Garden City, New York: Doubleday, 1966.

Johns, Ewart. *British Townscapes, with Drawings by the Author.* London: E. Arnold, 1965.

Johnson-Marshall, Percy. *Rebuilding Cities.* Edinburgh: Edinburgh University Press, 1966.

Jones, Emrys. *Towns and Cities.* London: Oxford University Press, 1966.

Kidson, Peter; Murray, Peter; and Thompson, Paul. *A History of English Architecture.* Harmondsworth: Penguin, 1965.

Korn, Arthur. *History Builds the Town.* London: Lund Humphries, 1955.

Lacour-Gayet, Robert. *Histoire du Canada.* Paris: Fayard, 1966.

Lacoursière, Jacques, and Vaugeois, Denis. *Canada-Québec: Synthèse historique.* Montréal: Ed. du Renouveau pédagogique, 1969.

Langlois, Georges. *Histoire de la population canadienne-française.* Montréal: Lévesque, 1934.

Larkin, Oliver W. *Art and Life in America.* New York: Rinehart, 1949.

Latreille, André; Dumont, Fernand; Rocher, Guy, et al. *Le Canada français aujourd'hui et demain.* Paris: Arthème Fayard, 1961.

Lavedan, Pierre. *L'architecture française.* Paris: Larousse, 1947.

———. *Les villes françaises.* Paris: Éditions Vincent, Fréal, 1960.

Leacock, Stephen. *Leacock's Montreal.* Ed. by John Culliton. Toronto: McClelland and Stewart, 1963.

Lessard, Michel, and Marquis, Huguette. *Encyclopédie de la maison québé-*

coise. Encyclopédie de l'Homme, no. 4. Montréal: Les Éditions de l'Homme, 1972.

Lower, Arthur R. M. *Canadians in the Making: A Social History of Canada.* Toronto: Longmans, Green, 1958.

Lower, Joseph Arthur. *Canada: An Outline History.* Toronto: Ryerson Press, 1966.

Lynch, Kevin. *The Image of the City.* Cambridge: M.I.T. Press, 1960.

———. *Site Planning.* Cambridge: M.I.T. Press, 1962.

Maurault, Olivier. *Marges d'histoire.* 3 vols. Montréal: Librairie d'Action canadienne-française, 1929.

Mayrand, Pierre, and Bland, John. *Trois siècles d'architecture au Canada— Three Centuries of Architecture in Canada.* Montréal: Federal Publications Service/George Le Pape, 1971.

McLaughlin Green, Constance. *The Rise of Urban America.* London: Hutchinson, 1966.

Montreal, Old (and) New. Montreal: International Press, n.d.

"Montréal." Special issue of *Liberté* 5, no. 4 (July–Aug. 1963).

Morisset, Gérard. *Coup d'oeil sur les arts en Nouvelle-France.* Québec: n.p., 1941.

Mumford, Lewis. *The Culture of Cities.* New York: Harcourt, Brace, 1938.

———. *Sticks and Stones: A Study of American Architecture and Civilization.* 2nd rev. ed. New York: Dover Publications, 1955.

———. *The Brown Decades: A Study of the Arts in America, 1865–1895.* 2nd rev. ed. New York: Dover Publications, 1955.

———. *The City in History: Its Origins, Its Transformations, and Its Prospects.* New York: Harcourt, Brace and World, 1961.

———. *Technics and Civilization.* New York: Harcourt, Brace and World, 1963.

Nobbs, Percy E. "Architecture in Canada." *Journal of the Royal Institute of British Architects,* ser. 3, 31 (1924): 199–211, 238–50.

Ouellet, Fernand. *Histoire économique et sociale du Québec, 1760–1850. Structures et conjoncture.* Montréal: Fides, 1966.

Pevsner, Nikolaus. *An Outline of European Architecture.* 7th rev. ed. Harmondsworth: Penguin, 1963.

Rasmussen, Steen Eiler. *Experiencing Architecture.* New rev. ed. London: Chapman and Hall, 1964.

———. *Towns and Buildings Described in Drawings and Words.* Cambridge: M.I.T. Press, 1969.

Reps, John William. *The Making of Urban America: A History of City Planning in the United States.* Princeton, N.J.: Princeton University Press, 1955.

Richards, James Maude. *An Introduction to Modern Architecture.* London: Cassell, 1961.

Rioux, Marcel, and Martin, Yves, eds. *French-Canadian Society,* vol. 1, *Sociological Studies.* Carleton Library no. 18. Toronto: McClelland and Stewart, 1964.

Rumilly, Robert. *Histoire de Montréal.* 5 vols. Montréal: Fides, 1970–74.

Sandham, Alfred. *Ville Marie, or, Sketches of Montreal, Past and Present.* Montreal: Bishop, 1870.

Séguin, George-F. *Toponymie.* Bulletin d'information no. 7. Montréal: City Planning Department, 1971.

Smailes, Arthur E. *The Geography of Towns.* 5th rev. ed. London: Hutchinson, 1966.

SHM. *Mémoires et documents relatifs à l'histoire du Canada.* 8 vols. Montreal: Duvernay, 1859–1921.

Tanghe, Raymond. *Géographie humaine de Montréal.* Montréal: Librarie d'Action canadienne-française, 1928.

Tunnard, Christopher. *The Modern American City.* Princeton, N.J.: Van Nostrand, 1968.

——, and Reed, Henry Hope. *American Skyline: The Growth and Form of Our Cities and Towns.* Drawings by John Cohen. New York: New American Library, 1956.

Wade, Mason. *The French-Canadians, 1760–1967.* Rev. ed., 2 vols. Toronto: Macmillan, 1968.

Chapter 1   The Key to the West

Biggar, H.P., ed. *The Works of Samuel de Champlain.* Reprinted, translated and annotated by six Canadian scholars under the general editorship of H. P. Biggar. 6 vols. Toronto: Champlain Society Publications, 1922–36.

——, trans. *The Voyages of Jacques Cartier.* Published from the originals with translation, notes, and appendices. Ottawa: Acland, 1924.

Bouchette, Joseph. *A Topographical Dictionary of the Province of Lower Canada.* London: Colburn, 1831.

Brunet, Michel; Frégault, Guy; and Trudel, Marcel, comps. *Histoire du Canada par les textes.* Montréal: Fides, 1952.

Daveluy, Marie-Claire. *La Société de Notre-Dame de Montréal, 1639–1663. Son histoire, ses membres, son manifeste.* Montréal: Fides, 1965.

Lanctôt, Gustave. *Montréal sous Maisonneuve, 1642–1665.* Montréal: Librarie Beauchemin, 1966.

Laverdière, Abbé Charles Honoré, ed. *Oeuvres de Champlain.* Publ. sous le patronage de l'Université Laval. 2nd ed. 2 vols. Québec: Desbarats, 1870.

Leacock, Stephen, ed. *Lahontan's Voyages.* Ottawa: Graphic Publishers, 1932.

Longley, Richmond Wilberforce. *Le climat de Montréal.* Ministère des Transports, Division de la météorologie. Ottawa: Impr. de la Reine, 1954.

Montreal, Quebec, City Planning Department. *Superficies des municipalités—Areas of Municipalities.* Bulletin d'information no. 2. Montreal: 1964.

——, City Planning Department. *Caractéristiques physiques de la région—Physical Characteristics of the Region.* Bulletin technique no. 4. Montreal: 1966.

Munro, William Bennett, ed. *Documents Relating to the Seigniorial Tenure in Canada, 1598–1854.* Toronto: Champlain Society, 1908.

Powe, Norman N. *The Climate of Montreal: Climatological Studies*

Number 15. Department of Transport, meteorological branch. Ottawa: Queen's Printer, 1969.

Roy, Gabrielle. *The Tin Flute.* Trans. by Hannah Josephson. New York: Reynal & Hitchcock, 1947.

SHM. *Mémoires. Les véritables motifs de Messieurs et Dames de la Société de Notre-Dame de Montréal.* 9th instalment. Montréal: Berthiaume & Sabourin, 1880.

Stanfield, J. *The Pleistocene and Recent Deposits of the Island of Montreal, Canada.* Department of Mines, Geological Survey. Ottawa: Government Printing Bureau, 1915.

Thwaites, Reuben Gold, ed. *The Jesuit Relations and Allied Documents: Travels and Explorations of the Jesuit Missionaries in New France, 1610–1791.* 73 vols. Cleveland: Burrows Brothers, 1896–1901.

Trudel, Marcel. "Cartier, Jacques." In *DCB*, 1: 165–72.

———. "Champlain, Samuel de." In *DCB*, 1: 186–99.

Chapter 2   The Island Colony

Bélanger, Marcel. "De la région naturelle à la région urbaine: problèmes d'habitat." In *Architecture et urbanisme au Québec*, pp. 45–63. Conférences J.-A. DeSève, 13–14. Montréal: Presses de l'Université de Montréal, 1971.

Bouchette, Joseph. *A Topographical Description of the Province of Lower Canada, with Remarks upon Upper Canada and on the Relative Connexion of Both Provinces with the United States of America.* London: Faden, 1815.

Deffontaines, Pierre. "The Rang-Pattern of Rural Settlement in French-Canada." In *French-Canadian Society*, vol. 1, *Sociological Studies*, ed. by Marcel Rioux and Yves Martin, pp. 3–19. Carleton Library no. 18. Toronto: McClelland and Stewart, 1964.

Derruau, Max. "A l'origine du rang canadien." *CGQ* 1 (1956): 39–47.

Falardeau, Jean-Charles. "The Seventeenth Century Parish in French-Canada." In *French-Canadian Society*, vol. 1, *Sociological Studies*, ed. by Marcel Rioux and Yves Martin, pp. 19–32. Carleton Library no. 18. Toronto: McClelland and Stewart, 1964.

Frégault, Guy. "Le régime seigneurial et l'expansion de la colonisation dans le bassin du St-Laurent au dix-huitième siècle." *CHAR*, 1944, pp. 61–73.

Godbout, Jacques. "La Côte-des-Neiges." *Liberté* 5, no. 4 (July–Aug. 1963): 300–303.

Harris, Richard Colebrook. *The Seigneurial System in Early Canada: A Geographical Study.* Madison: University of Wisconsin Press, 1966.

Heneker, Dorothy A. *The Seigniorial Regime in Canada.* Montreal: n.p., 1926.

Jodoin, Alexandre. "Le château de Longueuil." *BRH* 6, no. 3 (March 1900): 76–78.

———, and Vincent, J.-L. *Histoire de Longueuil et de la famille de Longueuil.* Montréal: Impr. Grebhart-Berthiaume, 1889.

Laplante, Jean de. "La communauté montréalaise." *CESH* 1 (1952): 57–107.

Massicotte, E.-Z. "Notre-Dame-des-Neiges." In *Les cahiers des Dix*, no. 4, pp. 141–66. Montréal: 1939.

Maurault, Olivier. "Les moulins du séminaire." In *Marges d'histoire*, vol. 3, *Saint-Sulpice*, pp. 113–54. Montréal: Librarie d'Action canadienne-française, 1930.

Québec (Province). "Le recensement des gouvernements de Montréal et des Trois-Rivières." In *RAPQ, 1936–37*, pp. 1–121. Québec: R. Paradis, imp. de sa Majesté le Roi, 1937.

———. "Aveu et dénombrement de Messire Louis Normand, prêtre du séminaire de Saint-Sulpice de Montréal, au nom et comme fondé de procuration de Messire Charles-Maurice Le Pelletier, Supérieur du séminaire de Saint-Sulpice de Paris, pour la seigneurie de l'île de Montréal (1731)." In *RAPQ, 1941–42*, pp. 3–163. Québec: R. Paradis, imp. de sa Majesté le Roi, 1942.

Rasmussen, Steen Eiler. *London the Unique City*. Harmondworth: Penguin, 1960.

Rich, Edwin Ernest. *Montreal and the Fur Trade*. Montreal: McGill University Press, 1966.

Salone, Emile. *La colonisation de la Nouvelle-France, étude sur les origines de la nation canadienne-française*. 3rd ed. Paris: Guilmoto, 1906.

Sulte, Benjamin. "Verdun." *BRH* 20, no. 2 (Feb. 1914): 42–45.

Summerson, John. *Georgian London*. Rev. ed. Harmondsworth: Penguin, 1962.

Trudel, Marcel. *Le Régime seigneurial*. Canadian Historical Association Special Publications, Brochure no. 6. Ottawa: 1956.

Chapter 3   Society during the Old Regime

Adair, E. R. "The Church of l'Enfant Jésus, Pointe-aux-Trembles." *BRH* 42, no. 7 (July 1936): 411–21.

———. "The Church of Saint-Michel de Vaudreuil." *BRH* 49, no. 2 (Feb. 1943): 38–49; no. 3 (March 1943): 75–89.

Azard-Malaurie, Marie-Madeleine. "De l'architecture monumentale classique à Québec." *Vie des Arts*, no. 49 (Winter 1967–68): pp. 42–49.

Bruemmer, Fred. "Les vieux moulins du Québec." *La Revue Impérial Oil* 50, no. 3 (June 1966): 14–19.

Canada, Ministry of Agriculture. *Census of Canada, 1870–71—Recensements du Canada, 1870–71*. 5 vols. Ottawa: Taylor, 1873–78.

Carless, William. "The Architecture of French Canada." *JRAIC* 2, no. 4 (July–Aug. 1925): 141–45. Reprinted in *McGill University Publications*, series 13 (Art and Architecture), no. 3. Montreal: 1925.

Charlevoix, Pierre-François-Xavier de. *Histoire et description générale de la Nouvelle France avec le journal historique d'un voyage fait par ordre du roi dans l'Amérique septentrionale*. 3 vols. Paris: Nyon, 1744.

Dollier de Casson, Abbé François. *Histoire de Montréal, 1640–1672*. Montréal: Sénécal, 1871.

Eccles, W. J. "Buade de Frontehac et de Palluau, Louis de." In *DCB*, 2: 133–42.

Falardeau, Jean-Charles. "The Changing Social Structures." In *Essais sur le Québec contemporain—Essays on Contemporary Quebec*, ed. by Jean-C. Falardeau, Symposium du centenaire de l'Université Laval. Québec: Presses de l'Université Laval, 1953.

———. "The Role and Importance of the Church in French Canada." In *French-Canadian Society*, vol. 1, *Sociological Studies*, ed. by Marcel Rioux and Yves Martin, pp. 342–57. Carleton Library no. 18. Toronto: McClelland and Stewart, 1964.

Fauteux, Joseph-Noël. *Essai sur l'industrie au Canada sous le régime français*. 2 vols. Québec: Proulx, 1927.

Frégault, Guy. *La Société canadienne sous le régime français*. Canadian Historical Association Special Publications, Brochure no. 3. Ottawa: 1954.

———. *Le XVIIIe siècle canadien; études*. Collection Constantes, vol. 16. Montréal: Editions HMH, 1968.

Gardiner, J. Rawson. "The Early Architecture of Quebec." *JRAIC* 2, no. 6 (Nov.–Dec. 1925): 228–34.

Gowans, Alan. "The Earliest Church Architecture of New France from the Foundation to 1665." *JRAIC* 26, no. 9 (Sept. 1949): 291–98.

Hamelin, Jean. *Economie et société en Nouvelle-France*. Les Cahiers de l'Institut d'histoire, Université Laval, no. 3. Québec: Presses de l'Université Laval, 1960.

Kalm, Peter. *Travels into North America; Containing its Natural History, and a Circumstantial Account of its Plantations and Agriculture in General, with the Civil, Ecclesiastical And Commercial State of the Country, the Manners of the Inhabitants, and Several Curious and Important Remarks on Various Subjects*. Trans. by John Reinhold Forster. 3 vols. London: 1770–71.

Lanctôt, Gustave. *L'administration de la Nouvelle-France; l'administration générale*. Paris: Champion, 1929.

———. "La participation du peuple dans le gouvernement de la Nouvelle-France." *RTC* 59 (Sept. 1929): 225–39.

———. "Le régime municipal en Nouvelle-France." *Culture* 9, no. 3 (Sept. 1948): 255–83.

Lessard, Michel, and Marquis, Huguette. "La maison québécoise, une maison qui se souvient." *Forces*, no. 17 (1971), pp. 4–22.

Maurault, Olivier. "Un professeur d'architecture à Québec en 1828." *JRAIC* 3, no. 1 (Jan.–Feb. 1926): 32–36.

Roy, Antoine. *Les lettres, les sciences et les arts au Canada sous le régime français*. Paris: n.p., 1930.

Roy, Pierre-Georges. *La ville de Québec sous le régime français*. 2 vols. Service des archives du gouvernement de la province de Québec. Québec: R. Paradis, imp. de sa Majesté le Roi, 1930.

Traquair, Ramsay. "The Old Architecture of the Province of Quebec." *JRAIC* 2, no. 1 (Jan.–Feb. 1925): 25–30.

———. "The Cottages of Quebec." *McGill University Publications*, series 13 (Art and Architecture), no. 5. Montreal: 1926.

————. "The Church of Ste Jeanne de Chantal on the Ile Perrot, Quebec." *JRAIC* 9, no. 5 (May 1932): 124–31, no. 6 (June 1932): 147–52. Reprinted in *McGill University Publications*, series 13 (Art and Architecture), no. 35. Montreal: 1932.

————. *The Old Architecture of Quebec.* Toronto: Macmillan, 1947.

————, and Adair, E. R. "The Church of the Visitation—Sault-au-Recollet, Quebec." *JRAIC* 4, no. 12 (Dec. 1927): 437–51. Reprinted in *McGill University Publications*, series 13 (Art and Architecture), no. 18. Montreal: 1927.

Tremblay, Maurice. "Orientations de la pensée sociale." In *Essais sur le Québec contemporain—Essays on Contemporary Quebec*, ed. by Jean-Charles Falardeau, pp. 193–208. Symposium du centenaire de l'Université Laval. Québec: Presses de l'Université Laval, 1953.

Zoltvany, Yves F. "Rigaud de Vaudreuil, Philippe de." In *DCB*, 2: 565–74.

Chapter 4 The Frontier Town

Adair, E. R. "The Evolution of Montreal under the French Regime." *CHAR*, 1942, pp. 20–41.

Azard-Malaurie, Marie-Madeleine. "La Nouvelle-France dans la cartographie française ancienne." *Vie des Arts*, no. 46 (Spring 1967), pp. 20–28, 60.

Berry, Maurice; Mayrand, Pierre; and Palardy, Jean. "Louisbourg." *Vie des Arts*, no. 46 (Spring 1967), pp. 29–39, 60.

Charlevoix, Pierre-François-Xavier de. *Journal of a Voyage to North America. Undertaken by Order of the French King. Containing the Geographical Description and Natural History of that Country, Particularly Canada. Together with an Account of the Customs, Characters, Religion, Manners and Traditions of the Original Inhabitants. In a Series of Letters to the Duchess of Lesdiguieres.* Trans. from the French. 2 vols. London: R. and J. Dodsley, 1761.

Dickinson, Robert E. *The West European City: A Geographical Interpretation.* 2nd rev. ed. London: Routledge & Kegan Paul, 1961.

Gosselin, Abbé Auguste. "Le 'Traité de Fortifications' de Chaussegros de Léry." *BRH* 7, no. 5 (May 1901): 157–58.

Gottmann, Jean. "Plans de villes des deux côtés de l'Atlantique." In *Mélanges géographiques canadiens offerts à Raoul Blanchard*, pp. 237–42. Publiés sous les auspices de l'Institut de Géographie de l'Université Laval. Québec: Presses de l'Université Laval, 1959.

Massicotte, E.-Z. *Répertoire des arrêts, édits, mandements, ordonnances et règlements conservés dans les archives du Palais de justice de Montréal 1640–1760.* Montréal: G. Ducharme, 1919.

Mathieu, Jacques. "Dollier de Casson, François." In *DCB*, 2: 190–97.

Maurault, Olivier. "Un seigneur de Montréal: Dollier de Casson." In *Marges d'histoire*, vol. 2, *Montréal*, pp. 33–51. Montréal: Librarie d'Action canadienne-française, 1929.

Saalman, Howard. *Medieval Cities.* New York: G. Braziller, 1968.

SHM. *Mémoires. Les origines de Montréal.* 11th instalment. Montréal: Ménard, 1917.

————. *Annales de l'Hôtel-Dieu de Montréal, rédigées par la Soeur Morin.* 12th instalment. Coll. et ann. par A. Fauteux, E.-Z. Massicotte, et C. Bertrand; Intr. par V. Morin. Montréal: Imprimerie des Éditeurs, 1921.

Chapter 5   Architecture and Environment in the Frontier Town

Anburey, Thomas. *Travels through the Interior Parts of America.* 2 vols. Boston: Houghton Mifflin, 1923.

France. Lois, statuts . . . *Edits, ordonnances royaux, déclarations et arrêts du Conseil d'Etat du roi concernant le Canada.* Rev. et corr. d'après les pièces originales déposées aux archives provinciales. 3 vols. Québec: Fréchette, 1854–56.

Gauthier, Paul. "La 'maison du patriote,' rue St-Paul, à Montréal." *BRH* 67, no. 1 (Jan.–March 1961): 17–19.

Gauthier-Larouche, Georges. *L'évolution de la maison rurale laurentienne.* Québec: Presses de l'Université Laval, 1967.

George, M. Dorothy. *England in Transition: Life and Work in the Eighteenth Century.* Harmondsworth: Penguin, 1953.

Hadfield, Joseph. *An Englishman in America, 1785, Being the Diary of Joseph Hadfield.* Ed. and ann. by Douglas S. Robertson. Toronto: 1933.

"L'histoire de notre château." *CANJ* 1, nos. 1–4 (1930): 31–120.

Hubbard, Robert Hamilton. "The European Backgrounds of Early Canadian Art." *Art Quarterly* 27, no. 3 (1964): 297–323.

Massicotte, E.-Z. "Maçons, entrepreneurs, architects." *BRH* 35, no. 3 (March 1929): 132–42.

————. "Mémento historique de Montréal, 1636–1760." *MSRC*, Sect. 1, sér. 3, 27 (May 1933): 111–31.

————. "Coins historiques du Montréal d'autrefois." In *Les cahiers des Dix,* no. 2, pp. 115–55. Montréal: 1937.

Maurault, Olivier. "Notre-Dame de Montréal." *RTC,* 11th year, no. 42 (June 1925): 117–41.

————. *La Paroisse; histoire de l'église Notre-Dame de Montréal.* Montréal: Louis Carrière, 1929.

McLean, Eric. "Papineau House." *Habitat* 7, no. 5 (Sept.–Oct. 1964): 2–7.

Morin, Victor. "Les Ramezay et leur château." In *Les cahiers des Dix,* no. 3, pp. 9–72. Montréal: 1938.

————. *La légende dorée de Montréal.* Montréal: Les Editions des Dix, 1949.

Plumb, J. H. *England in the Eighteenth Century.* Harmondsworth: Penguin, 1950.

Robitaille, André. "Evolution de l'habitat au Canada français." *ABC* 21, no. 240 (April 1966): 32–38.

Roy, Antoine. "L'architecture du Canada autrefois." *ABC* 2, no. 11 (Feb. 1947): 23–29, 40.

Roy, Pierre-Georges, ed. *Inventaire des ordonnances des intendants de la Nouvelle-France conservés aux archives provinciales de Québec.* 4 vols. Beauceville: "L'Eclaireur," 1919.

Séguin, Robert-Lionel. *La civilisation traditionnelle de l'"habitant" aux 17e et 18e siècles; fonds matériel.* Montréal: Fides, 1967.

———. *La maison canadienne*. Musée National du Canada, Bulletin no. 226. Ottawa: l'imprimeur de la Reine, 1968.

Talbot, Edward Allen. *Five Years' Residence in the Canadas, Including a Tour Through Part of the United States of America, in the Year 1823.* 2 vols. London: Longman . . . , 1824.

Traquair, Ramsay, and Neilson, G. A. "The House of Simon McTavish no. 27 St. Jean Baptiste Street, Montreal." *JRAIC* 10, no. 11 (Nov. 1933): 188–92. Reprinted in *McGill University Publications*, series 13 (Art and Architecture), no. 37. Montreal: 1933.

Chapter 6 Years of Transition

Adams, Frank Dawson. *A History of Christ Church Cathedral, Montreal*. Montreal: Burton, 1941.

Alexander, Sir James Edward. *Transatlantic Sketches, Comprising Visits to the Most Interesting Scenes in North and South America, and the West Indies. With Notes on Negro Slavery and Canadian Emigration.* 2 vols. London: Bentley, 1833.

Angers, Albertine Ferland. *La citadelle de Montréal, 1658–1820*. Montreal: Ducharme, 1950.

Bland, John. "Deux architectes au 19e siècle—Two 19th Century Architects." *ABC* 8, no. 87 (July 1953): 20.

Bonnycastle, Sir Richard Henry. *The Canadas in 1841*. 2 vols. London: Colburn, 1841.

Bosworth [Rev. Newton], ed. *Hochelaga Depicta; the Early History and Present State of the City and Island of Montreal*. Montreal: Greig, 1839.

Bouchette, Joseph. *The British Dominions in North America; or, A Topographical and Statistical Description of the Provinces of Lower and Upper Canada, New Brunswick, Nova Scotia.* 2 vols. London: Colburn and Bentley, 1831.

Bourguignon, J.-C. "Montréal, ville portuaire, 1535–1867. Du XVIe au XVIIIe siècle en Amérique du Nord, les colons-pionniers se font citadins." *Revue canadienne d'urbanisme* 12, no. 3 (Autumn 1963): 18–25.

———. "Montréal au bord du St-Laurent." *Vie des Arts*, no. 33 (Winter 1963–64), pp. 20–25.

Buckingham, James Silk. *Canada, Nova Scotia, New Brunswick, and the other British Provinces in North America with a Plan of National Colonization*. London: Fisher, 1843.

Coke, E. T. A. *A Subaltern's Furlough: Descriptive of Scenes in Various Parts of the United States, Upper and Lower Canada, New Brunswick, and Nova Scotia, During the Summer and Autumn of 1832*. London: Saunders, 1833.

Colbert, Edouard-Charles-Victurnien, comte de Maulevrier. *Voyage dans l'intérieur des Etats-Unis et au Canada*. Introduction and notes by Gilbert Chinard. Baltimore: Hopkins, 1935.

Collard, Edgar Andrew. *Oldest McGill*. Toronto: Macmillan, 1946.

Creighton, Donald. *The Empire of the St. Lawrence*. Toronto: Macmillan, 1956.

Denison, Merrill. *Canada's First Bank: A History of the Bank of Montreal.* Montreal: McClelland and Stewart, 1966.

Dionne, N.-E. "Joseph Bouchette." *BRH* 20, no. 7 (July 1914): 226–30.

Duncan, John M. *Travels through Part of the United States and Canada in 1818 and 1819.* 2 vols. Glasgow: University Press, 1823.

Fergusson, Adam. *Practical Notes Made During a Tour in Canada, and a Portion of the United States in MDCCCXXXI.* 2nd ed., *to Which Are Now Added Notes Made During a Second Visit to Canada in MDCCCX-XXIII.* Edinburgh: W. Blackwood, 1834.

Gauthier, Paul. "Montréal et ses quartiers municipaux." *BRH* 67, no. 4 (Oct.–Dec. 1961): 115–35.

Girouard, Désiré. *Lake St. Louis, Old and New.* 2 vols. Montreal: Poirier, 1893.

Gowans, Alan. "Notre-Dame de Montréal." *JSAH* 11, no. 1 (March 1952): 20–26.

———. "Thomas Baillargé and the Québécois Tradition of Church Architecture." *Art Bulletin* 34 (1952): 117–37.

Henry, Alexander. *Travels and Adventures in Canada and in the Indian Territories Between the Years 1760 and 1776.* New York: Riley, 1809.

Heriot, George. *Travels through the Canadas, Containing a Description of the Picturesque Scenery on Some of the Rivers and Lakes; with an Account of the Productions, Commerce, and Inhabitants of Those Provinces. To Which is Subjoined a Comparative View of the Manners and Customs of Several of the Indian Nations of North and South America.* London: Phillips, 1807.

Lambert, John. *Travels through Lower Canada and the United States of North America, in the Years 1806, 1807, and 1808.* 3 vols. London: Richards Phillips, 1810.

Lower Canada. *Journal of the House of Assembly of Lower Canada—Journal de la Chambre d'Assemblée du Bas-Canada.* Quebec: n.p., 1799, 1801.

Massicotte, E.-Z. "Quelques rues et faubourgs du vieux Montréal." In *Les cahiers des Dix,* no. 1, pp. 105–56. Montréal: 1936.

———. "Evocation du vieux Montréal." In *Les cahiers des Dix,* no. 3, pp. 131–64. Montréal: 1938.

———. "Montréal se transforme." In *Les cahiers des Dix,* no. 5, pp. 177–215. Montréal: 1940.

Maurault, Olivier. "Un professeur d'architecture à Québec en 1828." *JRAIC* 3, no. 1 (Jan.–Feb. 1926): 32–36.

McLean, Eric. "The Papineau House." *Habitat* 7, no. 5 (Sept.–Oct. 1964): 2–7.

Murray, Hugh. *An Historical and Descriptive Account of British America . . . to Which is Added a Full Detail of the Principles and Best Modes of Emigration.* 2nd ed. 3 vols. Edinburgh: Oliver and Boyd, 1839.

Pavie, Théodore. *Souvenirs atlantiques: voyage aux Etats-Unis et au Canada.* 2 vols. Paris: Roret, 1833.

Sandham, Alfred. *Montreal and Its Fortifications.* Montreal: Daniel Rose, 1874.

Silliman, Benjamin. *Remarks Made on a Short Tour Between Hartford and Quebec, in the Autumn of 1819.* 2nd ed. New Haven: S. Converse, 1824.

Toker, Franklin. *The Church of Notre-Dame in Montreal: An Architectural History.* Montreal: McGill-Queen's University Press, 1970.

———. "James O'Donnell: An Irish Georgian in America." *JSAH* 29, no. 2 (May 1970): 132–43.

Warburton, George D. *Hochelaga or, England in the New World.* 2 vols. 2nd rev. ed. London: Colburn, 1846.

Weld, Isaac. *Travels Through the States of North America, and the Provinces of Upper and Lower Canada During the Years 1795, 1796, and 1797.* London: John Stockdale, 1799.

Chapter 7   New Forces

Ames, Herbert Brown. *"The City below the Hill": A Sociological Study of a Portion of the City of Montreal, Canada.* Montreal: Bishop Engraving and Printing Co., 1897; rpt. Toronto: University of Toronto Press, 1972.

Auclair, Abbé Elie-J. "Saint-Henri des Tanneries à Montréal." *MSRC*, Sect. 1, sér. 3, 37 (May 1943): 1–16.

Ballantyne, Murray. "J'ai grandi au Canada français." In *Le Canada français aujourd'hui et demain*, pp. 53–67. Paris: Arthème Fayard, 1961.

Beauregard, Ludger. "Géographie manufacturière de Montréal." *CGQ*, 3rd year, no. 6 (April–Sept. 1959), pp. 275–94.

Blumenfeld, Hans. "The Modern Metropolis." In *Cities*, pp. 49–66. A Scientific American Book. Harmondsworth: Penguin, 1967.

Briggs, Asa. *Victorian Cities.* Harmondsworth: Penguin, 1968.

Brouillette, Benoît. "Le développement industriel du port de Montréal." *L'Actualité Economique*, 14th year, 1, nos. 3 and 4 (June–July 1938): 201–21.

———. "Le port et les transports." In *Montréal économique*, pp. 115–82. Etudes sur notre milieu, Esdras Minville, dir. Montréal: Fides, 1943.

Canada. Ministry of Agriculture. *Census of Canada 1880–81—Recensement du Canada.* 4 vols. Ottawa: Maclean, Roger, 1882–85.

———. *Census of Canada 1890–91—Recensement du Canada.* 4 vols. Ottawa: S. E. Dawson, 1893–97.

———. *Fourth Census of Canada 1901.* 4 vols. Ottawa: S. E. Dawson, 1902–06.

———. *Fifth Census of Canada 1911.* 6 vols. Ottawa: C. H. Parmelee, 1912–15.

———. *Sixth Census of Canada 1921.* 4 vols. Ottawa: F. A. Acland, 1924–29.

Cooper, John Irwin. "The Social Structure of Montreal in the 1850s." *CHAR*, 1956, pp. 63–73.

Delage, Jean. "L'industrie manufacturière." In *Montréal économique*, pp. 183–241. Etudes sur notre milieu, Esdras Minville, dir. Montréal: Fides, 1943.

Faucher, Albert, and Lamontagne, Maurice. "History of Industrial Development." In *Essais sur le Québec contemporain—Essays on Contemporary*

Quebec, ed. by Jean C. Falardeau, pp. 23–27. Symposium du centenaire de l'Université Laval. Québec: Presses de l'Université Laval, 1953.

Germain, Claude. "Evolution démographique et polarisation de la région de Montréal." *L'Actualité Economique* 38, no. 2 (1962): 245–76.

Grant, George Monro, ed. *Picturesque Canada: The Country as It Was and Is.* 2 vols. Toronto: Belden, 1882.

Jordan, Robert Furneaux. *Victorian Architecture.* Harmondsworth: Penguin, 1966.

Lamothe, H. de. *Cinq mois chez les Français d'Amérique. Voyage au Canada et à la rivière Rouge du Nord.* Paris: Hachette, 1879.

Massicotte, E.-Z. *La cité de Sainte-Cunégonde de Montréal. Notes et souvenirs.* Montréal: Houle, 1893.

Minville, Esdras, dir. *Montréal économique.* Etudes sur notre milieu. Montréal: Fides, 1943.

Stone, Leroy O. *Urban Development in Canada: An Introduction to the Demographic Aspects.* Dominion Bureau of Statistics. Ottawa: Queen's Printer, 1967.

Chapter 8   Somewhere Between Good and Mediocre: Public and Religious Architecture

"L'architecture en Canada." *La Minerve*, 28 April 1866.

"Bibliothèque Saint-Sulpice, Montréal. Eugène Payette, architecte." Portfolio of current architecture, *The Architectural Record* 41, no. 4 (April 1917): 341–48.

Bland, John. "Effect of Nineteenth Century Manners on Montreal." *JRAIC* 33, no. 11 (Nov. 1956): 414–17.

Clark, Kenneth. *The Gothic Revival: An Essay in the History of Taste.* Harmondsworth: Penguin, 1964.

Desjardins, R. P. Paul. *Le collège Sainte-Marie de Montréal.* 2 vols. Montréal: Collège Sainte-Marie, 1940–45.

Gowans, Alan. "The Baroque Revival in Quebec." *JSAH* 14, no. 3 (Oct. 1955): 8–14.

Hubbard, Robert Hamilton. "Canadian Gothic." *Architectural Review* 116, no. 8 (Aug. 1954): 102–8.

Hulot, Baron Etienne. *De l'Atlantique au Pacifique à travers le Canada et le Nord des Etats-Unis.* Paris: Plon, 1888.

Lipscombe, Robert. *The Story of Old St. Patrick's.* Montreal: n.p., 1967.

Ludlow, Thomas W. "The Montreal Art Gallery: E. & W. S. Maxwell, architects." *The Architectural Record* 37, no. 2 (Feb. 1915): 132–48.

Maurault, Olivier. "The University of Montreal." *JRAIC* 3, no. 1 (Jan.–Feb. 1926): 5–12.

Morris, Franklin. "Christ Church Cathedral, Montreal." *Dalhousie Review* 35 (Summer 1955): 176, 178.

Nantel, Maréchal. "Le palais de Justice de Montréal et ses abords." In *Les cahiers des Dix*, no. 12, pp. 197–230. Montréal: 1947.

Nobbs, Percy E. "Architecture in the Province of Quebec During the Early Years of the 20th Century." *JRAIC* 33, no. 11 (Nov. 1956): 418–19.

Ritchie, Thomas. "The Architecture of William Thomas." *Architecture Canada* 44, no. 5 (May 1967): 41–45.

Summerson, John. *Victorian Architecture: Four Studies in Evaluation.* New York: Columbia University Press, 1970.

Traquair, Ramsay. "The Buildings of McGill University." *JRAIC* 2, no. 2 (March–April 1925): 45–63.

Turner, Philip J. "Christ Church Cathedral, Montreal." *Construction* 20, no. 11 (Nov. 1927): 347–54.

———. "The Development of Architecture in the Province of Quebec since Confederation." *Construction* 20, no. 6 (June 1927): 189–95. Reprinted in *McGill University Publications*, series 13 (Art and Architecture), no. 16. Montreal: 1927.

The Windsor Hotel Guide to the City of Montreal and for the Dominion of Canada. Montreal: Lovell, 1890.

Chapter 9   Hopes and Disappointments: Commercial Architecture

Charney, Melvin. "The Old Montreal No One Wants to Preserve." *The Montrealer* 38, no. 12 (Dec. 1964): 20–23.

———. "The Grain Elevators Revisited." *Architectural Design* 37 (July 1967): 328–31.

Condit, Carl W. *The Rise of the Skyscraper.* Chicago: University of Chicago Press, 1952.

———. *The Chicago School of Architecture: A History of Commercial and Public Buildings in the Chicago Area, 1875–1925.* Chicago: University of Chicago Press, 1964.

Giedion, Sigfried. *Space, Time and Architecture: The Growth of a New Tradition.* Cambridge, Mass.: Harvard University Press, 1949.

Hitchcock, Henry-Russell. *Early Victorian Architecture in Britain.* 2 vols. New Haven: Yale University Press, 1954.

Legge, Charles. *A Glance at the Victoria Bridge and the Men Who Built It.* Montreal: J. Lovell, 1860.

Ritchie, Thomas. *Canada Builds 1867–1967.* Toronto: University of Toronto Press, 1967.

Rolt, Lionel Thomas Caswell. *Victorian Engineering.* London: Lane, 1970.

Rowe, Colin. "Chicago Frame." *Architectural Design* 40 (Dec. 1970): 641–47.

Siegel, Arthur, ed. *Chicago's Famous Buildings: A Photographic Guide to the City's Architectural Landmarks and Other Notable Buildings.* Chicago: University of Chicago Press, 1965.

Weisman, Winston. "Philadelphia Functionalism and Sullivan." *JSAH* 20, no. 1 (March 1961): 3–19.

Chapter 10   From Extravagance to Indigence: Domestic Architecture

Barcelo, Michel. "Montreal Planned and Unplanned." *Architectural Design* 37 (July 1967): 307–10.

Bland, John. "Domestic Architecture in Montreal." *Culture* 9, no. 4 (Dec. 1948): 399–407.

Blumenfeld, Hans. "L'habitation dans les métropoles." *ABC* 21, no. 241 (May 1966): 23–29.

Bolton, Sybil. "The Golden Square Mile." *The Montrealer* 40, no. 5 (May 1961): 35–39.

Kervin, Roy. "Faubourg à la Melasse . . . Victim of Progress." *The Montrealer* 38, no. 6 (June 1964): 16–19.

Lacoste, Norbert. *Les caractéristiques sociales de la population du grand Montréal; étude de sociologie urbaine.* Faculté des sciences sociales, économiques et politiques. Montréal: Presses de l'Université de Montréal, 1958.

MacRae, Marion, and Adamson, Anthony. *The Ancestral Roof: Domestic Architecture of Upper Canada, 1783–1867.* Toronto: Clarke, Irwin, 1963.

McKelvey, Blake. *The Urbanization of America, 1860–1915.* New Brunswick, N.J.: Rutgers University Press, 1963.

Mitchell, R. J., and Leys, M. D. R. *A History of London Life.* Harmondsworth: Penguin, 1963.

Parizeau, Marcel. "L'urbanisme." In *Montréal économique*, pp. 377–97. Etudes sur notre milieu, Esdras Minville, dir. Montréal: Fides, 1943.

Société des Ecrivains Canadiens, ed. *Ville, ô ma Ville.* Montréal: 1941.

Wilson, Stuart. "A Part of le Faubourg." *JRAIC* 43, no. 11 (Nov. 1966): 71–74.

Chapter 11   The Victorian Legacy

Bazin, Jules. "L'île Sainte-Hélène et son histoire." *Vie des Arts*, no. 48 (Autumn 1967), pp. 18–23.

Collard, Edgar Andrew. *The Story of Dominion Square, Place du Canada.* Don Mills: Longmans, 1971.

Fabos, Julius G.; Milde, Gordon T.; and Weinmayr, V. Michael. *Frederick Law Olmsted, Sr.: Founder of Landscape Architecture in America.* Amherst: University of Massachusetts Press, 1968.

Lamothe, Joseph-Cléophas. *Histoire de la corporation de la Cité de Montréal depuis son origine jusqu'à nos jours.* Ed. by LaViolette et Massé. Montréal: Montreal Print and Publ., 1903.

Longstreth, T. Morris. *Quebec: Montreal and Ottawa.* New York: Century, 1933.

McDougall, Joe. "Passing Show: Forty Years in Retrospect." *The Montrealer* 40, no. 5 (May 1966): 16–19.

Murray, A. L. "Frederick Law Olmsted and the Design of Mount Royal Park, Montreal." *JSAH* 26, no. 3 (Oct. 1967): 163–71.

Olmsted, Frederick Law. *Mount Royal, Montreal.* New York: Putnam's Sons, 1881.

Simard, Jacques. "Il était une fois une très jolie montagne . . ." *ABC* 15, no. 168 (April 1960): 66–68.

Wilson, Stuart. "In Memoriam." *JRAIC* 41, no. 8 (Aug. 1964): 67–71.

———. "Les rues Savignac et Christin à Montréal." *Habitat* 7, no. 6 (Nov.–Dec. 1964): 11–13.

———. "Avenue Delorme." *JRAIC* 42, no. 3 (March 1965): 78–80.

———. "Avenue Lartigue—L'Avenue Lartigue." *Habitat* 8, no. 2 (March–April 1965): 2–15.

Chapter 12   The Metropolis
Brouillette, Benoît. "Le port de Montréal, hier et aujourd'hui." *RGM* 21, no. 2 (1967): 195–233.
Cousineau, Aimé. "City Planning Activities in Montreal." *JRAIC* 20, no. 4 (April 1943): 51–53.
Cox, Harvey. *The Secular City: Secularisation and Urbanisation in Theological Perspective.* Harmondsworth: Penguin, 1968.
Denis, Paul-Yves. "Conditions géographiques et postulats démographiques d'une rénovation urbaine à Montréal." *RGM* 21, no. 1 (1967): 149–64.
Foggin, Peter. "Les formes de l'utilisation du sol à Montréal—Urban Land Use Patterns: The Montreal Case." In *Montreal: Guide d'excursions—Field Guide*, ed. by Ludger Beauregard, pp. 32–45. 22e Congrès international de géographie. Montréal: Presses de l'Université de Montréal, 1972.
Manzagol, Claude. "L'industrie manufacturière à Montréal—Manufacturing Industry in Montreal." In *Montréal: Guide d'excursions—Field Guide*, ed. by Ludger Beauregard, pp. 125–35. 22e Congrès international de géographie. Montréal: Presses de l'Université de Montréal, 1972.
Montreal, Quebec, City Planning Department. *Métropole.* Les Cahiers d'urbanisme, nos. 1, 2, 3. Montréal, 1963, 1964, 1965.
———. *Centre ville de Montréal—Downtown Montreal.* Bulletin technique no. 3. Montreal: 1964.
———. *Familles et ménages 1951–1961.* Bulletin technique no. 2. Montréal: 1964.
———. *Urbanisation. Etude de l'expansion urbaine dans la région de Montréal. A Study of Urban Expansion in the Montreal Region.* 2nd ed. Bulletin technique no. 5. Montreal: 1968.
Paumier, Cyril. "New Town at Montreal's Front Door." *Landscape Architecture* 57, no. 1 (Oct. 1966): 67.
"Planning for Montreal: A Summary of the Montreal Master Plan Preliminary Report 1944." *JRAIC* 22, no. 5 (May 1945): 89–107.
Régnier, Michel. *Génération; poèmes.* Quebec: Editions de l'Arc, 1964.
Ritter, Paul. *Planning for Man and Motor.* Oxford and New York: Pergamon Press, 1964.
Saumier, André. "La ville humaine." *Habitat* 10, no. 1 (Jan.–Feb. 1967): 14–15.

Chapter 13   The New Core of the City
Affleck, Ray T. "Place Bonaventure: The Architect's View." *Architecture Canada* 44, no. 7 (July 1967): 32–39.
Beauregard, Ludger. "Les transports en commun à Montréal—Public Transport in Montreal." In *Montréal: Guide d'excursions—Field Guide*, ed. by Ludger Beauregard, pp. 179–88. 22e Congrès international de géographie. Montréal: Presses de l'Université de Montréal, 1972.

Blake, Peter. "Downtown in 3-D." *The Architectural Forum* 125, no. 2 (Sept. 1966): 31–49.

———. "Quebec's Shimmering Vitrine." *The Architectural Forum* 126, no. 5 (June 1967): 29–37.

"Bonaventure Subway Station, Montreal." *The Canadian Architect* 12, no. 8 (Aug. 1967): 45–48.

Boyd, Arthur. "The Skyscraper." *The Canadian Architect* 7, no. 6 (June 1962): 44–51.

Charney, Melvin. "Place Victoria." *The Canadian Architect* 10, no. 7 (July 1965): 37–54.

"C-I-L House, Montreal." *The Canadian Architect* 7, no. 6 (June 1962): 53–63.

Cobb, Henri N. "Some Notes on the Design of Place Ville Marie." *JRAIC* 40, no. 2 (Feb. 1963): 54–60.

Commission industrielle de Montréal, éd. *Montréal, la métropole du Canada*. Montréal: n.p., 1931.

Desbarats, Guy. "Montréal—laboratoire urbain." *Habitat* 10, no. 1 (Jan.–Feb. 1967): 26–32.

"Downtown Bank Tower." *Progressive Architecture* 44, no. 9 (Sept. 1963): 140–45.

Fiset, Edouard. "Introduction d'un concept urbain dans la planification de l'exposition—Introduction of an Urban Concept in the Planning of the Exposition." *JRAIC* 42, no. 5 (May 1965): 55–62.

Gretton, Robert, and Slater, Normand. "Metro." *The Canadian Architect* 12, no. 2 (Feb. 1967): 27–34.

Lamy, Laurent. "Le design, roi et maître de l'Exposition universelle." *Vie des Arts*, no. 48 (Autumn 1967), pp. 52–55.

Legault, Guy-R. "Le Métro de Montréal." *Architecture Canada* 43, no. 8 (Aug. 1966): 44–48.

Lehrman, Jones. "Critiques Two." *The Canadian Architect* 8, no. 2 (Feb. 1963): 63–64.

Miller, Jerry. "Expo 67: A Search for Order." *The Canadian Architect* 12, no. 5 (May 1967): 44–54.

"A Modern Station for Montreal." *Architectural Record* 94, no. 12 (Dec. 1943): 91–101.

Pelletier, Jean, and Beauregard, Ludger. "Le centre-ville de Montréal." *RGM* 21, no. 1 (1967): 5–40.

"Place Ville Marie." *The Architectural Forum* 118, no. 2 (Feb. 1963): 74–89.

Plesums, Guntis. "Architecture and Structure as a System: Man the Producer Pavilion." *Architecture Canada* 46, no. 4 (April 1969): 23–33.

Prus, Victor. "Reflections on the Subterranean Architecture of the Subway Systems." *The Canadian Architect* 12, no. 2 (Feb. 1967): 35–36.

———. "Metro Architecture." *Architectural Design* 37 (July 1967): 325–27.

Rowan, Jan C. "The Story of Place Ville Marie." *Progressive Architecture* 41, no. 2 (Feb. 1960): 123–35.

Schoenauer, Norbert. "Critique One." *The Canadian Architect* 8, no. 2 (Feb. 1963): 55–57.

———. "The New City Centre." *Architectural Design* 37 (July 1967): 311–24.

Staples, S. M. "Transportation Network at Expo 67." *Architecture Canada* 43, no. 8 (Aug. 1966): 33–34.

———. "Expo 67: Is It a Success?" *Architecture Canada* 44, no. 8 (Aug. 1967): 39–42.

Wilson, Stuart. "Place Victoria." *JRAIC* 42, no. 10 (Oct. 1965): 60–69.

Epilogue

Abler, Ronald, ed., and Adams, John S., texts. *A Comparative Atlas of America's Great Cities: Twenty Metropolitan Regions.* Minneapolis: University of Minnesota Press, 1976.

Aubin, Henry. *Les vrais propriétaires de Montréal.* Trans. by Denyse Demers-Beaudry. Montréal: Editions l'Etincelle, 1977.

Blumenfeld, Hans. "Au-delà de la métropole." *Critère*, no. 19 (Autumn 1977), pp. 41–50.

Gabeline, Donna; Lanken, Dane; and Pape, Gordon. *Montreal at the Crossroads.* Montreal: Harvest House, 1975.

Marsan, Jean-Claude. "La question du village olympique." *Architecture Concept* 28, no. 139 (Nov. 1973): 26–29.

———. "Le complexe Desjardins: le syndrome de la Place Ville-Marie." *Le Devoir*, 13 March 1976, p. 15.

———. "Le complexe Desjardins: la première véritable place en dépit d'une expression spatiale conservatrice." *Le Devoir*, 20 March 1976, p. 13.

———. "Construire l'avenir mais comment?" *Le Devoir*, 7 Jan. 1978, pp. 30, 40.

——— et al. *Le village olympique.* Rapport du Comité consultatif chargé d'étudier l'avenir des installations olympiques. Montréal, Feb. 1977.

——— et al. *Le parc olympique.* Rapport du Comité consultatif chargé d'étudier l'avenir des installations olympiques. Montréal, Sept. 1977.

Québec, Ministère des Affaires municipales, Direction générale de l'urbanisme et de l'aménagement du territoire. *L'urbanisation dans la conurbation montréalaise; tendances actuelles et propositions d'orientation.* Québec: April 1977.

Québec, Office de planification et de développement du Québec. *Esquisse de la région de Montréal: évolution et orientation du développement et de l'aménagement.* Collection: Les schémas régionaux. Québec: l'Editeur officiel du Québec, 1978.

Taillibert, Roger. *Construire l'avenir.* Préface de Jean Drapeau, maire de Montréal; postface de René Huyghe de l'Academie française. Paris: Presses de la Cité, 1977.

Vecsei, Eva H. "La Cité de la métropole." *Architecture Concept* 33 (May–June 1977): 10–17.

INDEX